PITTSYLVANIA
County, Virginia

DEED BOOKS
1, 2 and 3

Abstracted and Compiled

by

Lucille C. Payne

Neil G. Payne

Please direct all correspondence and orders to:

www.southernhistoricalpress.com
or
SOUTHERN HISTORICAL PRESS, Inc.
PO BOX 1267
375 West Broad Street
Greenville, SC   29601
southernhistoricalpress@gmail.com

ISBN #0-89308-466-2

Printed in the United States of America

PITTSYLVANIA COUNTY, VIRGINIA

PITTSYLVANIA COUNTY was formed in 1767 from Halifax County. Some documents created in 1765 were not recorded until the county's books opened some two years later. The county was named for William Pitt, noted British statesman and staunch friend of the colony of Virginia.

Justices of the peace for the new county immediately called for a list of tithables and found that there were 938 white persons and 316 slaves in the area, which then included the present counties of Henry and Patrick and part of Franklin.

It is noteworthy that William Tunstall, clerk of the court, served in that capacity from the organization of the county until his son, William Tunstall, Jr., took over the responsibilities of the office in 1791. In turn, William Jr. surrendered the office to William H. Tunstall, grandson of the original clerk. The three clerks served the county for a total of 83 years!

When the county was organized George III of England was on the throne. His reign lasted until 1820.

Governors of the colony at the time the deeds in this publication were recorded were Major General Sir Jeffrey Amherst, who held office from 1759 to 1768. He never visited Virginia. Then Norborne Berkeley, Baron de Botetourt, held the office from 1768 to 1770. Third governor during this period was John Murray, Earl of Dunmore, who presided from Sept., 1771 until Jun., 1775.

This book includes abstracts of deeds, sales and other data for the years 1765 to 1774. The names of sellers, buyers and witnesses are included, along with names of adjoining property owners. Roads and many watercourses are named, aiding in the location of tracts of land.

As conditions changed, so did the names of localities. Peytonsburg, once the county seat of Halifax and beehive of activity around 1781, now is open country. In fact, the exact location of the vanished court buildings is open to discussion.

Hours have been spent in proofreading these pages. Even so, the reader is referred to original documents to avoid the possibility of error.

HOMEPLACE BOOKS
Rt. 2, Box 419,
Axton   VA   24054

February, 1991

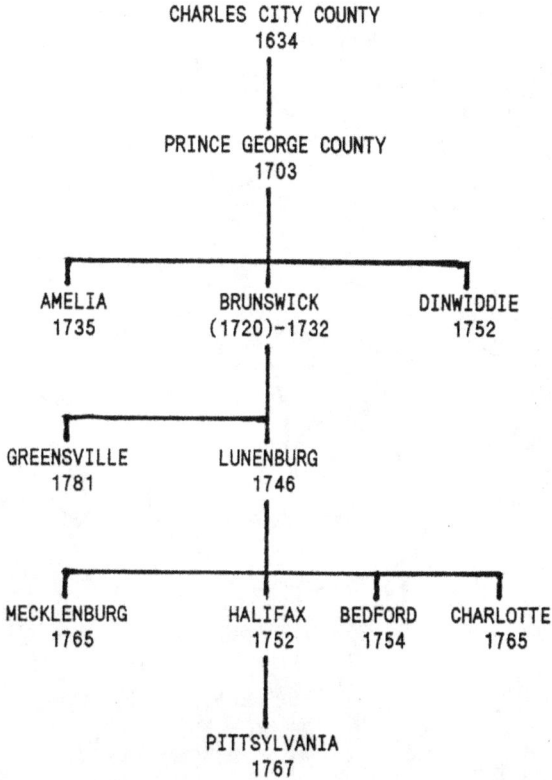

HOW PITTSYLVANIA WAS FORMED

CHARLES CITY COUNTY
1634

PRINCE GEORGE COUNTY
1703

AMELIA   BRUNSWICK   DINWIDDIE
1735   (1720)-1732   1752

GREENSVILLE   LUNENBURG
1781   1746

MECKLENBURG   HALIFAX   BEDFORD   CHARLOTTE
1765   1752   1754   1765

PITTSYLVANIA
1767

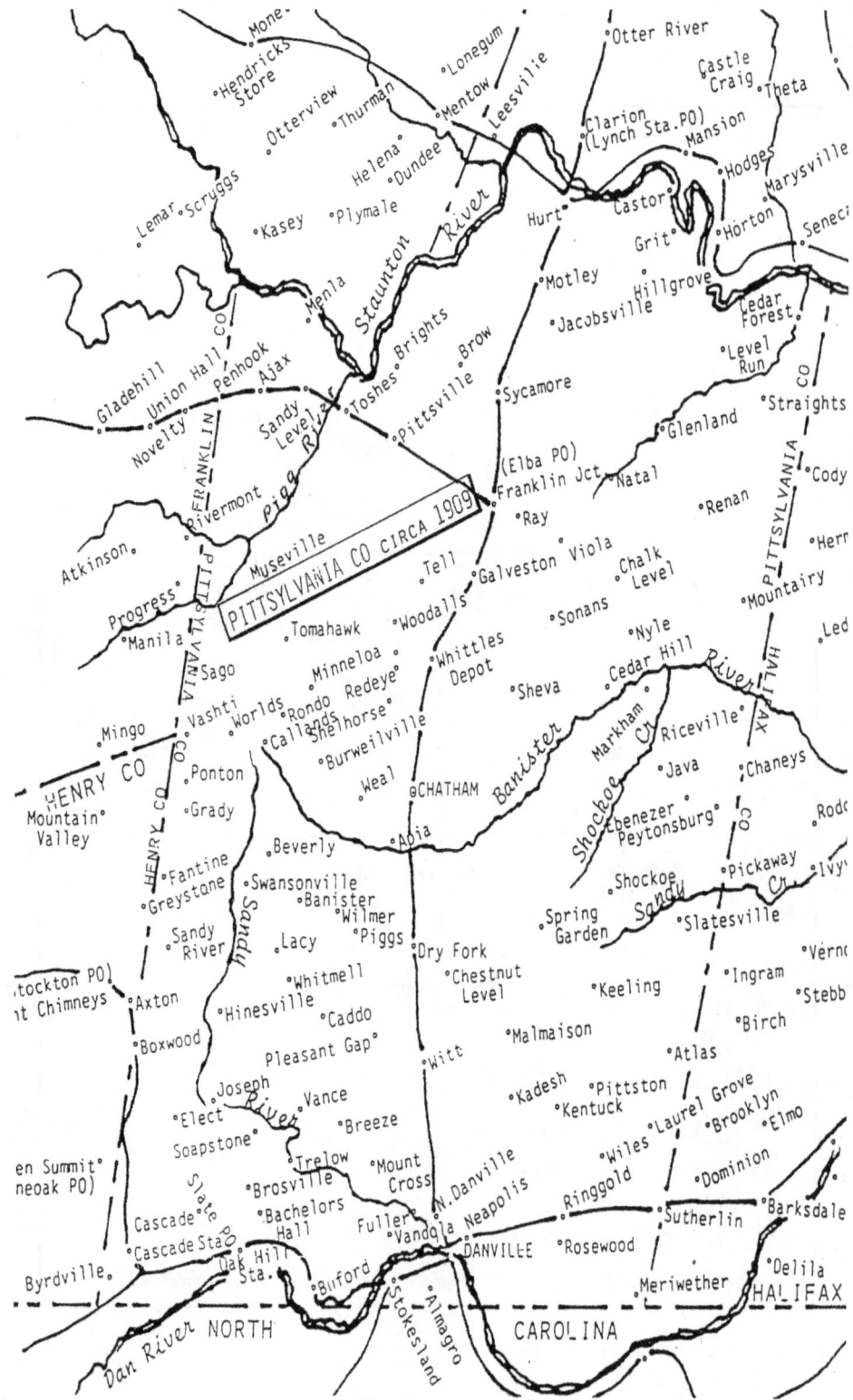

PITTSYLVANIA CO CIRCA 1909

PITTSYLVANIA COUNTY, VIRGINIA
DEED BOOK 1, 1767 - 1770

DB 1, p.1 - COOPER from COPLAND   DEED, 30 Apr 1765
Peter COPLAND of Province of North Carolina of one part and Thomas COOPER of
Virginia of other part...for £106 Current Money of Virginia...177 acres in
Halifax County and Dominion of Virginia, on waters of Beaver Creek.
Wit: Richard COPLAND, Charles COPLAND   Peter COPLAND (Seal)
Rec: 26 Jun 1767

DB 1, p.2 - COOPER from COPLAND   DEED, 30 Apr 1765
Peter COPLAND of Province of North Carolina of one part and Thomas COPER of
Virginia of other part..for £120 Current Money of Virginia paid by said Tho-
mas COOPER...190 acres in Halifax County and Dominion of Virginia...land on
Beaver Creek and the Branches.
Wit: Rich^d. COPLAND, Charles COPLAND   Peter COPLAND (Seal)
Rec: 26 Jun 1767

DB 1, p.4 - COOPER from COPLAND   DEED, 30 Apr 1765
Peter COPLAND of Province of North Carolina of one part and Thomas COOPER,Jr.
of Virginia of other part...for £180 Current Money of Virginia...300 acres
in Halifax County and Dominion of Virginia...on Beaver Creek and its Branches.
Wit: Richard COPLAND, Charles COPLAND   Peter COPLAND (Seal)
Rec: 26 Jun 1767

DB 1, p.6 - ROBERTS from COPLAND   DEED, 30 Apr 1765
Peter COPLAND of Province of North Carolina of one part and James ROBERTS
of Virginia of other part..for £100 Current Money...165 acres in Halifax Co..
land on Reedy Creek and its branches.
Wit: Richard COPLAND, Charles COPLAND   Peter COPLAND (Seal)
Rec: 26 Jun 1767

DB 1, p.7 - HAILS from COPLAND   DEED, 30 Apr 1765
Peter COPLAND of Province of North Carolina of one part and John HAILS of
Virginia of other part..for £90 Current money of Virginia...154 acres in Hal-
ifax County...on Reedy Creek and branches...beginning at white oak in Ran-
dolph's line.
Wit: Richard COPLAND, Charles COPLAND   Peter COPLAND, L.S.
Rec: 26 Jun 1767

DB 1, p.9 - MORRIS from COPLAND   DEED, 30 Apr 1765
Peter COPLAND of Province of North Carolina of one part and Thomas MORRIS of
Virginia of other part..for £70 Current money of Virginia...120 acres in Hal-
ifax County...on Beaver Creek and branches...on Beaver Creek & running south.
Wit: Richard COPLAND, Chas. COPLAND   Peter COPLAND, L.S.
Rec: 26 Jun 1767

DB 1, p.11 - DUNN from COPLAND   DEED, 30 Apr 1765
Peter COPLAND of Province of North Carolina of one part and Waters DUNN of
Halifax County Virginia of other part..for £240 Current money of Virginia...
405 acres in Halifax County on Irvin River and Beaver Creek...Beginning at
tree on north side of Irvin River...Randolph's Corner...crossing both forks
of Beaver Creek...to Irvin River, down the river as it meanders.

Wit: Richard COPLAND, Charles COPLAND   Peter COPLAND L.S.
Rec: 26 Jun 1767

DB 1,p.12 - TORIAN from JUNIL   DEED, 18 Jun 1767

Silvester JUNIL/JUNIEL/JUINL of Halifax County and Parish of Antrim of one part and Peter TORIAN/TORIANN of same county and parish of other part...for £55 Current money of Virginia...300 acres in county formerly call'd Halifax but now Patensburg, on both sides Stewart's Creek...beginning at a chestnut in Drury STITH's line...crossing a Branch and said creek...crossing two branches.
Wit: Jno. DONELSON, Hugh INNES,   Silvester JUINL (Seal)
Abra. SHELTON, Thos. TUNSTALL   Rec: 26 Jun 1767

DB 1, p.14 - POLLEY from BUCKNALL   DEED, 26 Jun 1767

Francis BUCKNALL, Planter of one part and David POLLEY, planter of other part...150 acres on both sides Reedies Creek...beginning at pointers in the Patent line, part of Larger Tract granted by patent to said Francis BUCKNALL.
No witnesses.   Francis BUCKNALL L.S.
Received of David POLLEY the sum of £10 Current money.   Rec: 26 Jun 1767

DB 1, p.16 - PAYNE from WADE   DEED, 26 Jun 1767

Edward WADE and Mary his wife of one part and Philemon PAYNE of other part... for £10 Current money of Virginia...100 acres on Buck Branch, it being part of a tract of land containing 1,180 acres which was granted to Timothy DOLTON by Patent bearing date 4 Jul 1759 and from said Timothy DALTON, part of said Tract containing 700 acres convey^d. to said Edward WADE by Deed.
Wit: James DILLARD,   Edward WADE (Seal)
William BOBIT, John GOAD, Junr.   her
                            Mary + WAID
Rec: 26 Jun 1767   Mark

DB 1,, p.17 - VANBEBBER from GORDON   DEED, 24 Jun 1767

Archibald GORDON of one part and John VANBEBBER of other part...for £120 Current money of Virginia...400 acres on Stony Creek, land granted to said Archibald GORDON by Letters Patent bearing date 26 Jul 1765 as by said Patent of Record in the Secretarys office of this colony...crossing the creek...crossing Jumping Run...crossing Fox Run...south side of said Creek.
No witnesses.   Arch^d. GORDON L.S.
Rec: 26 Jun 1767

DB 1, p.19 - LANKFORD   BOND FOR SHERIFF

Benjamin LANKFORD, Thomas DILLARD, j^r., John DONELSON, John WARD and John DIX are bound to Sovereign Lord King George in sum of £500 Current money... the Condition of above obligation is such that if above bound Benjamin LANKFORD...collect all Quitrents, fines, forfeitures...pay same to Officers... on or before second Tuesday in June Annually...faithfully execute said Office of Sheriff.
Rec: 26 Jun 1767   Ben. LANKFORD, Tho. DILLARD, j^r.,
                    Jno. DONELSON, John WARD, John DIX

DB 1, p.20 - LANKFORD   BOND FOR SHERIFF

Benjamin LANKFORD, Thomas DILLARD, j^r., John DONELSON, John WARD and John DIX are bound in sum of £1000...condition of above obligation is such that above bound Benjamin LANKFORD do collect and receive of and for each Tithable

person and from every owner or Proprietor of Lands in Pittsylvania County
such sum or sums of money and tobacco that is now laid and which shall or
may be hereafter laid.
Rec: 26 Jun 1767   Ben. LANKFORD, Tho. DILLARD, j^r.,
                                           Jno. DONELSON, John WARD, John.DIX

DB 1, p.21 - LANKFORD   BOND FOR SHERIFF
Benjamin LANKFORD, Thomas DILLARD, jun^r., John DONELSON, John WARD, John DIX
are firmly bound in sum of £1000 current money...Condition of obligation is
that above bound Benjamin LANKFORD is constituted and appointed sheriff of
Pittsylv^a. County...from his Honour the Governor under the Seal of the Colony
dated 1st Day of June last past...collect all officers fees and dues put
into his hands, pay same to officers to whom such fees are due.
Rec: 26 Jun 1767   Ben. LANKFORD, Tho. DILLARD, jr.,
                                           Jno. DONELSON, John WARD, John DIX

DB 1, p.21 - WILSON from CARGILL   DEED, 24 Jul 1767
James CARGALL and Susannah his Wife of one part and John WILSON of other
part...for £200 Current money...400 acres, being part of 400 acres granted
to James CARGILL and Susannah his Wife by Letters Patent bearing date 16 Aug
1756...crossing the forks of the Fall Creek...crossing the Creek below fork.
No witnesses.   James CARGILL   L.S.
Rec: 24 Jul 1767

DB 1, p.23 - DODSON from LITTLE   DEED, 17 Jul 1767
Charles LITTLE and Hester his Wife to Isaac DODSON...for £50 Current money...
400 acres on both sides Sandy Creek...north said Sandy Creek.
 No witnesses   his
Rec: 24 Jul 1767   Charles (LITTLE
                                                        mark

DB 1, p.25 - BARTON from JONES   DEED, 21 Jul 1767
Robert JONES of one part and Benjamin BARTON of other part...for £20 Lawfull
Money of Virginia...50 acres on both sides Pigg River...north side Island
Run...down Pigg River as it meanders to walnut on north side the River.
                                        his
Wit: Wm. MURPHY, Sarah MURPHY, Jeremiah ⌐ POOR
                                        Mark
Rec: 24 Jul 1767   Robert JONES   L.S.

DB 1, p.27 - JONES j^r. from JONES S^r.   DEED, 21 Jul 1767
Robert JONES Senior of Halifax County in Colony of Virginia of one part and
Robert JONES Junior of same county and colony...for £90 Lawful Money of Vir-
ginia...150 acres more or less in Pittsylvania County of both sides Pigg
River.
Wit: Wm. MURPHY, John MURPHY, Sarah MURPHY   Robert JONES L.S.
Rec: 24 Jul 1767

DB 1. p.28 - GWINN from BOSTICK   DEED, 23 Jul 1767
Nathan BOSTICK of one part and George Homs/Homes GWIN/GWINN of other part...
for £90 Current money...90 acres on both sides Sandy River in Pittsylvania
County.
Wit: Jno. WILSON, John DIX,   Nathan BOSTICK L.S.

                  his
 James CARGILL, Charles (LITTLE
                  mark
Rec: 24 Jul 1767

4.

DB 1, p.30 - CUNNINGHAM from SHIELDS & wife   DEED, 24 Jul 1767
James SHIELDS and Eliz^a. his Wife of one part and Thomas Cunningham of other
part, all of Pittsylvania County...for £10 Current money of Virginia...?114
acres on south side south Fork of Sandy River, being part of a larger quantity granted by Letters Patent to??...pointers in Joseph CUNNINGHAM's line...
along Patent line...to John SHIELDS' corner...along Samuel SHIELDS' lines...
to north fork of Sandy River.
No witnesses.   James SHIELDS L.S.
Rec: 24 Jul 1767

DB 1, p.31 - TOUNSEND from LOVING   DEED, 14 Jul 1767
John LOVING of Amherse County of one part and Thomas TOWNSAND of other part...
for £10 Current money of Virginia...150 acres, it being part of greater quantity on both sides Cherrystone Creek, being the land said TOUNSAND lives on...
joining land of John WATSON to the Little Branch below the Plantation, runing
up said branch as far as the said TOWNSEND shall think convenient.
                    his   his
Wit: Jeremiah ✝ WORSHAM, Joseph ✚ GORMLEY,   Jno.   LOVING L.S.
                   mark   mark
John WATSON, Junr., John WATSON Senr., Shadrack TURNER   Rec: 24 Jul 1767

DB 1, p.33 - WORSHAM from LOVING   DEED, 14 Jul 1767
John LOVING of Amherse County of one part and Jeremiah WORSHAM of Pittsylvania
County of other part...for £10 Current money of Virginia...150 acres, being
part of a greater quantity...being land said WORSHAM lives on and joining
George CURRIE's order and the lands of Thomas WATSON and John WATSON...to little
Branch and up said Branch as far as said WORSHAM think convenient.

Wit: Thomas ⊤ TOWNSEND, Joseph I GORMAN,
                                                       Jno. LOVING L.S.
John WATSON, jun^r., John WATSON, Shadrack TURNER   Rec: 24 Jul 1767

DB 1, p.34 - CROWLEY from YOUNG   DEED, 24 Jul 1767
George YOUNG and Susanna his Wife of one part and Samuel CROLEY of other
part, all of Pittsylvania County...for £25 Current Money...210 acres on both
sides south fork Sandy River...beginning at LANSFORD's corner...in GREYS line.
No witnesses.   his
Rec: 24 Jul 1767   George ℓ YOUNG L.S.
Susannah, wife of said George, being privily   mark
Examined as Law directs Relinquished her
right of Dower to the Land.   Susannah X YOUNG L.S.
                                                      mark

DB 1, p.36 - WATSON from WATSON   DEED, 23 Jul 1767
John WATSON, Senr. of one part and John WATSON, jun^r. of other part...both
of Pittsylvania County..for £10 Current money...220 acres on both sides great
Cherrystone Creek, it being the land said John WATSON, jun^r. lives on and
bounded as the Pattent Mentions.
                    his   his
Wit: Shadrack TURNER, Edmond ✝ HOGES, Stephen Q BELLOW
                       Mark   Mark
Rec: 24 Jul 1767   John WATSON L.S.

DB 1, p.38 - TITTEL/TITLE from VANBEBBER   DEED, 22 Jul 1767
Isaac VANBEBBER of one part and Anthony TITTLE of other part; all of Pittsylvania County...for £40 ...all that piece of land lying and being on Mill Run and both sides said Run, being a branch of Black Water River...containing 170 acres more or less.

Wit: William HUNGATE, Peter VANBEBBER,   Isaac ⌒ VANBEBBER L.S.
James RENTFRO, Mark FOSTER   Mark

                                        Sarah ○ VANBEBBER L.S.
Rec: 24 Jul 1767   Mark

DB 1, p.39 - BIRD from BIRD   DEED, 23 Jul 1767
Joseph BIRD of one part and Francis BIRD of other part; all of Pittsylvania County...for £40...250 acres on both sides south Branch of Black Water Run... in Daniel DONOHO's line.

Wit: William HUNGATE, Vachel DILLINGHAM,   Joseph ✝ BIRD L.S.
James RENTFRO   Mark
Rec: 24 Jul 1767   Hannah BIRD L.S.

DB 1, p.40 - STEPHENS from BELLEW   DEED, 24 Jul 1767
Stephen BELLEW and Ann his Wife of one part and Joshua STEPHENS of other part, all of Pittsylvania County...60 acres on south side Banister River... for £5 Current money...beginning at James LOGANS line...mouth of Allen's Creek...along MURPHYS line.

                                       Stephen BELLEW L.S.
Wit: Elisha DYER, James ✗ HODGES, Willcom William HODGES   Ann BELLEW L.S.
                 Mark
Memorandum signed by: Elisha DYER, Edmond ✝ HODGES, Welcom W. HODGES
Rec: 24 Jul 1767   Mark

DB 1,p.42 - ROSS from WALTON   DEED, 2 Mar 1767
John WALTON and Robert WALTON and Fanny the said Robert's Wife of Charlotte of one part and David ROSS of Goochland of other part...for £460 Current money...665 acres in Halifax County on south side Saunton River...down Pigg River as it meanders to the mouth, up Stanton River as it meanders to include a small Island...it being same land that Robert WALTON dec'd. purchased from Richard RANDOLPH the Elder and by Richard STITH Attorney for said RANDOLPH"s Estate conveyed to said John WALTON by Deed Recorded in Halifax Court.
Wit: Jn. READ, John WILLIAMS, Paul   John WALTON L.S.
CARRINGTON, Henry MARTIN   Robert WALTON L.S.
Rec: 24 Jul 1767   Fanny WALTON L.S.

DB 1, p.44 - WIMBISH from WALLER   DEED TRUST, 24 Aug 1767
Zachariah WALLER of one part and John WIMBISH of other part; both of Pittsylvania County...for £17·14·1 Lawfull Money of Virginia which said Zachariah WALLER is justly indebted to sᵈ. John WIMBISH and honestly desires to secure and pay said WIMBISH and in consideration of 5s like Money to said Zachariah WALLER is paid by sd. John WIMBISH before sealing...WALLER acknowledges and exonerates sd. WIMBISH...284 acres on Double Creek...lines of Thomas WALTERS, John WILLSON, John MADDIN and on south side of piece of land formerly surveyed for William WEATHERFORD, it being the Land Zachariah WALLER purchased of Thomas WALTERS and by him conveyed to said WALLER by Deed recorded in Halifax Court in 1766...being land Zachariah WALLER Now lives upon.
Wit: Abraham SHELTON, John MADDING, junʳ.,   his
John WATKINS, John WALTERS   Zachariah   WALLER L.S.
Rec: 28 Aug 1767   (mark illegible)   Mark

DB 1, p.46 - FULLER from AUSTON   DEED, 26 Aug 1767
Jo^s. AUSTON of one part and Arthor FULLER of other part; both of Pittsylvania
County in Virginia...370 acres more or less, on Buflow Fork of Sanday River...
in Elisha WALLING's line.
No witnesses.   Joseph AUSTIN L.S.
Rec: 28 Aug 1767

DB 1, p.47 - WARRING from FULLER   DEED, 26 Aug 1767
Arthur FULLER of one part and John WARRING of other part; both of Pittsylvania
County...100 acres on a Ridge west...on a Branch...on the Boflow Fork of
Sandy River.   his
No Witnesses.   Arthor FULLER l.s.
Rec: 28 Aug 1767   Mark

DB 1, p.48 - ADDOMS from ADDOMS   DEED, 28 Sep 1767
John ADDOMS and his wife Elizabeth of one part and Allen ADDOMS of other
part...for £5 Current money...200 acres on Branches of Middle Creek...upper
part of Track of 600 acres granted to said John ADDOMS by Jeremiah HATCHER
by Deed dated January 1766, it being part of tract by Letters Patant to said
Jeremiah HATCHER dated 5 Jun 1765...on BAKER's line on the Miery Branch thence
across a Rig to John HIXES line...across the same Rig to BAKER's line.
No witnesses.   John ADDOMS L.S.
Rec: 28 Aug 1767   Elizabeth ADDOMS L.S.
(n.b. A Rig is a ridge of land; a strip of land between two furrows,
chiefly Scot.)

DB 1, p.50 - HEARD from STITH   DEED, 29 Jul 1767
Richard STITH on behalf of the executors of Richard RANDOLPH Gent. of Hen-
rico County, dec'd. of one part and William HEARD of other part...for
£11·1·6 Current Money of Virginia...200 acres on North Branch of Snow Creek...
corner of the Patent line of which above 200 acres is a part...being part of
land conveyed by the executors of said Richard RANDOLPH Gent. deceased to sd.
Richard STITH by a Power of attorney 7 Nov 1761 and recorded in General
Court and also recorded in Bedford Court.   d
Wit: Isaac READ, Isham TALBOTT, John WILLIAMS, Edm . WINSTON
Rec: 28 Aug 1767   Richard STITH L.S.

DB 1, p.51 - HEARD from LEVINS   DEED, 25 Jul 1767
Nicholas Perkins LEVINS and Mary his Wife of one part and John HEARD of other
part; both of Pittsylvania County...for £25 Current Money of Virginia...150
acres on both sides Crablow fork of Snow Creek, it being part of 400 acres
granted Obediah WOODSON.
Wit: Hugh INNES, William T. MILLS, W. YOUNG   Nicholas Perkins LEVINS L.S.
                                                         her
                                                   Mary LEVINS L.S.
Rec: 28 Aug 1767   Mark

DB 1, p.52 - DILLARD from MIDLETON   BILL SALE, 7 Apr 1767
John MIDLETON of Cambden Parish in Pittsylvania, Planter...for £30 Current
Money of Virginia paid by Thomas DILLARD, j^r. of same, Gent...one Milk and
Cyder Roan Mare branded on near Shoulder, Chesnut Sorrel Mare branded D, 7
head of Cowkind, 15 head Hoggs, 1 foot Wheel, 1 Feather Bed and Furniture, 2
Iron potts, 2 Pewter Dishes, 6 plates, 1 Iron gray Mare Colt, 7 Barrells of
Corn.

Wit: Abraham SHELTON, W^m.+ RAGSDALE
his
Mark

Rec: 28 Aug 1767   John MIDLETON L.S.

DB 1, p.53 - ARMSTRONG from COX .   MORT , 23 Feb 1767
Francis COX of Orange County and Province of North Carolina and John
ARMSTRONG of Halifax County in Virginia...for £160 Current Money...Three
Negroes: Negro man named Bobb, one Winch named Siner and her Child named
graw together with all and every their increase.
Wit: John WILLSON, John ARMSTRONG, jun^r.
Rec: 28 Aug 1767   Francis COX, L.S.

DB 1,p.54 - CLEMENTS from LANKFORD   DEED, 22 Sep 1767
Benjamin LANKFORD and Winefred his Wife of one part and James CLEMENTS of
other part; all of Pittsylvania County in Virginia...for £30 Current Money
of Virginia...136 acres on Potter's Creek...in BEARDING's line.

Wit: Benjamin CLEMENT, Thomas ∫ ROBERSON, Benjamin CLEMENT, jun^r.
his
Mark

Rec: 25 Sep 1767   Ben LANKFORD L.S.
                                                   Winefred LANKFORD L.S.

DB 1, p.55 - HODGES from DYER   DEED, 23 Jul 1767
Elisha DYER and Amey his Wife of Halifax County of one part and Welcome
William HODGES of Pittsylvania County of other part...100 acres south side
Banister River...for £5 Current Money...beginning at Stephen BELLEWS upper
corner in MURPHY's line on the River Hill.

Wit: Stephen BELLEW, Edmond X HODGES, Joshua ∮ STEPHENS
his   his
Mark   Mark

                                                    Elisha DYER L.S.
Rec: 25 Sep 1767   Amey DYER L.S.

DB 1, p.57 - MC DANIEL from COPLAND   DEED, 13 Apr 1765
Peter COPLAND of Province of North Carolina of one part and Terrence MC DANIEL
of Virginia of other part...for £115 Current Money of Virginia...192 acres
in Halifax County and Dominion of Virginia on Beaver Creek.
No witnesses.
Rec: 25 Sep 1767   Peter COPLAND L.S.

DB 1, p.58 - COPLAND to NELSON   MORT., 25 Sep 1767
Peter COPLAND of Pittsylvania County of one part and William NELSON Esq. of
County of York of other part...for £360·03·11 Current Money...three Tracts
of Land: one Tract of 177 acres...one other tract of 190 acres and one other
tract containing 192 acres...to Beaver Creek thence down the Creek...two
tracts being conveyed by Thomas COOPER to said Peter COPLAND by a Deed dated
24 day of this Current and the last mentioned tract being that conveyed by
Terrance MC DANIEL to said Peter COPLAND by Deed dated 24 day of this Currt.
No witnesses.
Rec: 25 Sep 1767   Peter COPLAND L.S.

DB 1, p.60 - NELSON from HAILS   MORT., 27 Jul 1767
John HAILS of County of Pittsylvania of one part and William NELSON of County
of York Esq. of other part...for £93·11·08 Current Money of Virginia...154

acres on Reedy Creek, is the Land including the Plantation whereon said John
HAILS now lives and is the land conveyed by Peter COPLAND to said John HAILS
by deed dated 30 Apr 1765 and recorded in Pittsylvania Court.
Wit:_d Peter COPLAND, Waters DUNN, Thomas COOPER, j^r., Paul CARRINGTON,
Rich^d. COPLAND
Rec: 25 Sep 1767

John   HAILS   L.S.
his   +
Mark

DB 1, p.62 - WADE from WADE   DEED, 25 Sep 1767
Edward WADE and Mary his Wife of County of Pittsylvania and Parish of Camden
of one part and James WADE of County and Parish aforesaid of other part...
for £20 Current Money...174 acres on both sides Frying Pann Creek it being
part of larger Tract granted to Timothy DALTON by Pattent bearing date 4 Jul
1759...crossing Frying Pann Creek...crossing Buck Branch.
No witnesses.
Rec: 25 Sep 1767   Edward WADE   L.S.
Mary, Wife of said Edward, being Privily Examined as Law directs relinquished
her right of Dower.

DB 1, p.63 - DYER from CHISUM   DEED, 1 Jun 1767
John CHISUM and Ellen his Wife of County of Pittsylvania of one part and
John DYER, Senr. of Halifax County and Parish of Antrim of other part... 50
acres south side Stanton River in the fork of the River and Straitstone...
for £40 Current Money...beginning at Mouth of the Creek Straitstone then up
the Creek as it Meanders to CALLOWAY line.

Wit: Thos. WATKINS, Thomas TINSLEY, James COLLINS, Joshua   STEVENS,
his   ∅
Ja^s.   DYER, jr., Elisha DYER, James CHISUM   Mark
his |
Mark   John CHISUM   L.S.
Rec: 25 Sep 1767   Eleanor CHISUM   L.S.

DB 1, p.65 - INNES from CHOICE   DEED TRUST, 25 Sep 1767
Tully CHOICE of County of Pittsylvania of one part and Hugh INNES of other
part...for £69·11·07 Lawful Money of Virginia which said Tully CHOICE is
justly indebted to Hugh INNES and honestly desires to pay INNES...604 acres
on Goard Creek...as by Patent granted to Joseph WILLIAMS and conveyed by him
to Amos RICHARDSON and by said RICHARDSON to Tully CHOICE...after 1 Aug 1768
land may be sold for best price...discharge above sum with interest from
25 Sep 1767 until same be fully discharged.
No witnesses.
Rec: 25 Sep 1767   Tully CHOICE   L.S.

DB 1, p.66 - EVERSON from LYLES   BILL SALE, 1 Jun 1767
David LYLES of County of Pitslvan^a. and Colony of Virg^a. to Mathias EAVERSON
of same Colony and County...for £12 Current Money of the Colony...18 head of
Cattle, 2 horses, 1 Roan Horse about 14 hands high Branded L on near Shoulder
and R on thy, 1 Bay horse about 14 hands high branded IK , 17 head of Hoggs,
2 feather beds and Furniture, 1 Rifle Gun.
Wit: Grigman ?? , Charles SKAGGS, Edward YOUNG   his
Rec: 25 Sep 1767   Defead   P   LYLES   L.S.
                                         mark

DB 1, p.67 - ANTRIM PARISH from CARTER   DEED, 20 Oct 1767
Richard CARTER of Halifax County of one part and the Vestry of Antrim Parish
of other part...one acre whereon the Vestry hath Established and built a

Church at the head of one of the South Branches of Toby's Creek...for Sum of
£00·10...Land is to ly Square round said Church whereon it now stands.
Wit: Champ. TERRY, John MADDING, Christopher SNEAD
Rec: 27 Nov 1767   Rich^d. CARTER L.S.

DB 1, p.68 - CADLE from MILLER   DEED, 27 Nov 1767
Henery MILLER and Elener his Wife of County of Pittsylvania of one part and
Benjamin CADLE of same county of other part...for £20 Current Money...100
acres on John ABSTON's south line...crossing Straitstone Creek...on a Hill
side at head of the faul Branch.
No witnesses.   Hen^r. MILLER L.S.
Rec: 27 Nov 1767   Elener MILLER L.S.
Elenor, Wife of Henry MILLER, privily Examined and relinquishes her right
of Dower.

DB 1, p.70 - EVANS from PERRIN   DEED, 27 Nov 1767
William PERRIN of Charlotte County of one part and George EVANS of Halifax
County of other part...for £31 Current Money of Virginia...land in Halifax
County on bouth sides Greatstraitstone Creek granted to said William PERRIN
by Pattent baring date 10 Aug 1759...south side said Creek corner white oak
of Francis POLLARD...in James HUNT's line...crossing the creek.
Wit: Tho. DILLARD j^r., Dav. WALKER, W^m. WARD, Epa. WHITE
Rec: 27 Nov 1767   W^m. PERRIN L.S.

DB 1, p.71 - BELL from TERRY   DEED, 16 Aug 1767
Nathaniel TERRY of Halifax County in Virginia of one part and David BELL of
Buckingham County in Virginia of other part...for £75 Current Money of Vir-
ginia paid by said David BELL for use of James TERRY...772 acres in Pittsyl-
vania County, being part of greater quantity granted John Robinson SPEAKES
and by him transfer'd by Deed of Sail to said Nath. TERRY...oak of Clement
READ's...to CHISWELL's line...along WADE's line...to Stephen TERRY's...in
Tucker WOODSON's line.
No witnesses.
Rec: 27 Nov 1767   Na TERRY L.S.

DB 1, p.73 - TERRY from TERRY   DEED, 16 Aug 1767
Nathaniel TERRY of Halifax County in Virginia of one part and James TERRY in
Orange County in North Carolina Province of other part...for £20 Current
Money of Virginia...200 acres, part of greater quantity granted to John Rober-
son SPEAKES/SPEAKER and by him transferred to said Nathaniel TERRY by Deed
of Sail...land in Halifax County...corner of William MAC DANIEL's...James
ALLEN's corner.
No witnesses.
Rec: 27 Nov 1767   Na TERRY L.S.

DB 1, p.75 - TERRY from TERRY   DEED, 16 Aug 1767
Nath^1. TERRY of Halifax County in Virginia of one part and Stephen TERRY of
same County of other part...for £40 Current Money of Virginia...400 acres in
Pittsylvania County and part of greater Quantity granted to John Robinson
SPEAKES/SPEAKER and by him transferred to said Nath^1. TERRY by Deed of Sale
in General Court as by said Pattent...beginning at David BELL's...crossing
Shocko Creek.
No witnesses.
Rec: 25 Nov 1767   Na TERRY L.S.

DB 1, p.76 - LOGAN from WATKINS   BILL SALE, 3 Apr 1767
John WATKINS of Halafax County for and in Consideration of £09·08 Current
Money of Virginia which be due to James LOGIN of ye same County...1 white
horse, 1 Mans Sadle, 1 feather Bed and firniture and Bed stid, 1 Chist and
Trunk, 7 Stools, 2 Pots and hooks, 2 Dishes, 3 Basons and 8 Plates, a Coten
Wheale, a Linin Wheale, a Scilit, a Looking Glas, a Pair of Scales, a Churn,
2 Barels, a Table, 2 Irons, a ?hackle, a frein pan, 1 Black Cow and hefer
Calf Marked with a Crop and 2 Slits a Crop and a hole, 1 pide Cow with a Crop...
if said WATKINS pays before 3 Apr 1770 obligation to be void.

Wit: John ROBERSON, James *his* ⌒ CALDWELL   John WATKINS L.S.
                            Mark   Rec: 27 Nov 1767

DB 1, p.77 - PIGGS WILL
Paul PIGG of Parish of Antram and County of Halifax being Very Sick and Weeke
in Body but of Parfect mind and Memary...to be Buried in a Christian Like and
Desent Manner...to Well beloved Wif Sarah PIGG one negro Woman named Phillis...
to son James PIGG 200 acres of land on south side Banister River...100 acres
to Robert ADDAMS it being the place whereon he now lives...to son William PIGG
200 acres on upper part of my Land on great Cherrystone Creek, also 1 negro
Woman named Darkis, 1 negro garle named Judy...to son Richard PIGG the remainder part of my Land with Plantation whereon I live after the death of his
Mother...if creditors will not Weight till negros can clear the Estate By
Crops that my Negro Man named James be sold to discharge my Just Depts...rest
of negroes with all Muveable Estate be kept together on the Plantation where
on I now live during my Wifes Sarah PIGGS life...be Suficently mantained
During her Life out of estate...after her death all negros and Muveable Estate
be Equally Divided among my Last Wifes children namely James PIGG, William
PIGG, Richard PIGG, Pattea PIGG, Sarah PIGG, Ann PIGG and Mary PIGG...1 cut
off my son John PIGG and my son Paul PIGG with one shilling Starling apease.
also my Daughter Elizabeth OSTON with one shilling Starling. 16 Sep 1766.

                                              Mark
                                        Pall ⌒ PIGG L.S.
                                              his

(Added item) To my three Daughters Pattea PIGG, Sarah PIGG, Ann PIGG, Mary
PIGG remainder of my Land on South side Banister River be sold and Money be
Equily Devided them fore garles above mentioned. Reuben PAIN, Henery MC
DANIEL, John ADDOMS are executors.
                            his   his
Wit: William GRIFFITH, Robert R ADDOMS, George X PARSON
                             Mark   Mark
Presented: 27 Nov 1767 by Henry MC DANIEL and Certificate granted him for
administration of estate. John DONELSON Gent. his Security.

DB 1, p.79 - OWEN from PREWIT   DEED, 10 Aug 1767
Samuel PREWIT of Parish of Cambden in county of Pittsylvania of one part and
William OWEN of same of other part...for £25 Current Money of Virginia...100
acres, part of tract of 335 acres granted by pattent to said Samuel PREWIT...
on Sandy Creek, including the Plantation whereon said William OWEN now lives.
Wit: John DIX, John OWEN, Daniel AYRES, James Smallwood OWEN
Rec; 22 Jan 1768   his
                                   Sam^1. ⌒ PREWITT L.S.
                                          Mark

DB 1, p.80 - MULLINS from DOSS   DEED, 18 Jan 1768
James DOSS, Senr. Gent. of County of Pittsylvania of one part and Henery
MULLINGS of same Parish and county of other part...for £20 Current Money...
150 acres on East and West side of a creek commonly known by name of
Vollingtines Creek.   his
Rec: 22 Jan 1768   James ☩ DOSS L.S.
                                                        Mark

DB 1, p.81 - CHISUM from CHISUM   DEED, 1 Jun 1767
John CHISUM of Pittsylvania County of one part and James CHISUM of same
county of other part...for £50...150 acres on south side Stanton River, being
the Upper part of 330 acres granted to Zachariah GREEN by patent dated at
Williamsburgh 10 Aug 1759 and by him conveyed to said John CHISHAM.
                                                        his
Wit: Thos. WATKINS, James COLLINS, Thomas TINSLEY, Joshua ⨍ STEPHENS,
John DYER   Mark
Rec: 22 Jan 1768   John CHISUM L.S.

DB 1, p.83 - HATCHER from BOSTICK   DEED, 26 Feb 1768
Absalom BOSTICK of Pittsylvania County of one part and Valentine HATCHER of
same County of other part...for £100 Current money...77 acres on North side
Dan River, the upper end of a Tract of Land Pattend for Abraham LITTLE and
containing 154 acres.
No witnesses   Absalom BOSTICK L.S.
Rec: 26 Feb 1768
Bethenia, Wife of said Absalom BOSTICK, privily Examined as Law directs and
Relinquished her right of Dower.

DB 1, p.85 - HATCHER from BOSTICK   DEED, 28 Jul 1767
Nathan BOSTICK of Pittsylvania County of one part and Valentine HATCHER of
said County of other part...for £100 Current Money of Virginia...120 acres
on north side Dan River, the Lower end of a Tract of land pattented for
Nathaniel TERRY containing 254 acres.
Wit: Peter PERKINS, Thos. GAINES, Isaac ROBERTS, Absalom BOSTICK
Rec: 26 Feb 1768   Nathan BOSTICK L.S.

DB 1, p.86 - HUGHS & WIMBISH from LANKFORD   DEED, 26 Feb 1768
Nicholas LANKFORD of County of Pittsylvania of one part and Arch^s. HUGHS and
John WIMBISH of County aforesaid of other part...for £20 Current Money of
Virginia...150 acres on both sides Mill Creek of Mayo River.
Wit: Charles PERKINS, Elipaz SHELTON, Peter PERKINS
                                                        his
Rec: 26 Feb 1768   Nich^s. ⟦ LANGFORD L.S.
                                                        Mark

DB 1, p.87 - KING from COLLINS   DEED, 26 Feb 1767
William COLLINS and Mary his Wife of County of Pittsylvania of one part and
Edmund KING of same County of other part...for £20 Current Money of Virginia..
150 acres on great Straitstone Creek...on Isaac ALLEN's...on Robert HANDCOK's.
Wit: Robin BOWMEN/BOWMER, Francis LUCK
Rec: 26 Feb 1768   William COLLINS L.S.
                                               Mary COLLINS L.S.

DB 1, p.88 - SNEED from THOMAS　　　　　　　　　　　　　　　DEED, 26 Feb 1768
William THOMAS and Joice his Wife of Pittsylvania County of one part and
Zechariah SNEED of said County of other part...for £20 Current Money...160
acres on both sides Sugar Tree Creek...to COX's corner...near mouth of Branch.
Wit: Hugh INNES, Crispen SHELTON, John PIGG
Rec: 26 Feb 1768　　　　　　　　　　　　　　　　　　　　W^m. THOMAS L.S.

DB 1, p.90 - COX from THOMAS　　　　　　　　　　　　　　　　DEED, 26 Feb 1768
William THOMAS and Joice his Wife of Pittsylvania County of one part and John
COX of said County of other part...for £20 Current Money...240 acres on both
sides Sugar Tree Creek...fork of Sugar Tree Creek...to Zachariah SNEEDS line,
on branch near to the Mouth, across the Creek.
Wit: Hugh INNES, John PIGG　　　　　　　　　　　　　　　W^m. THOMAS L.S.
Rec: 26 Feb 1768

DB 1, p.91 - CROWLEY from EDWARDS　　　　　　　　　　　　DEED, 26 Feb 1768
Thomas EDWARDS and Lucy his Wife of Parish of Cambden in County of Pittsyl-
vania of one part and Benjamin CROWLEY of same place of other part...for £20...
Land on both sides south fork of Sandy River, granted by pattent to said
Thomas EDWARDS..to Henry LANSFORD's corner...containing 48 acres.
No witnesses
Rec: 26 Feb 1768　　　　　　　　　　　　　　　Thomas EDWARDS L.S.
Lucy, Wife of said Thomas, privily　　　　　　　　　　her
Examined and relinquished her Dower right.　　　Lucy X EDWARDS L.S.
　　　　　　　　　　　　　　　　　　　　　　　　　Mark

DB 1, p.93 - HUBBARD from GRESHAM　　　　　　　　　　　DEED, 28 Aug 1767
Thomas GRESHAM of Parish of Camden and Pittsylvania County of one part and
Benjamin HUBBARD of County and Parish aforesaid of other part...for £25
Current Money of Virginia...124 acres, it being a tract of Land granted to
said Thomas GRESHAM by Letter Pattent dated at Williamsburgh...on South side
Irwin River.
No witnesses　　　　　　　　　　　　　　　　Thomas GRESHAM L.S.
Rec: 26 Feb 1768　　　　　　　　　　　　　　　her
Elizabeth, Wife of said Thomas,Examined　　Elisibeth X GRESHAM L.S.
and Relinquished her right of Dower　　　　　Mark

DB 1, p.94 - COLLINS from COLLINS　　　　　　　　　　　DEED, 12 Sep 1767
James COLLINS of County of Halifax of one part and William COLLINS of Pittsyl-
vania of other part...for £20 Current Money of Virginia...400 acres on both
sides Camping Branch of great Straitstone Creek.
Wit: Ben LANKFORD, John GEORGE, Tho. DILLARD, j^r., Joseph COLLINS
Prv: 25 Sep 1767, further prv. 26 Feb 1768 & rec.　　　James COLLINS L.S.

DB 1, p.96 - SPRADLINGS WILL　　　　　　　　　　　　　　28 Mar 1766
Memorandum Halifax County 28th of March 1766, I Joseph SPRADLING being Weak of
Body but of Perfect Mind and Memory...lend to beloved Wife Susanah SPRADLING
all Household furniture During her Widowhood...land I now Live on be Equally
Devided between my Two Sons Jessey and Obediah after Obediah shall arrive to
age of 21 years...if my wife is alive and a widow, she to have use of it during
her widowhood...if my Wife should die before my Children be rased to a age
Capable of ?geting their Living that my Friends David and Champness TERRY should
take the children and bring them up...if Wife should Intermarry with any Person
that should misuse my Children then friends aforesaid should take the Children
and if so teach them to read and write and my Daughters to Read.

Wit: Theop^s. LACY, Joseph TERRY, John X SNEED

Wit: Theop^s. LACY, Joseph TERRY, John ✗ SNEED

No date presented   Joseph SPRADLING L.S.

DB 1, p.97 - PAUL PIGGS INVENTORY
A True and Perfect Inventory of the Estate of Paul PIGG, deceased:
Negroes: James, Peter, Wench named Darkis, Lucy, Lad named Harry, Boy
named Phill, Girl named Hannah, Boy named Abram, Wench named Phillis; small
Bay Mare, Gray Horse, 28 head Black Cattle, grind stone, pair Cart Wheels,
Stack Wheat, 2 Hh^ds., 4 fatt Hoggs, 1 Craus Cutsaw, 1 old Broad Ax, 6 old
hoes, 1 Fodder Stack, 2 Plow hoes, 2 Iron Wedges, Parcel old Iron, Weavers
Slay, parcel potts panns, Cotton Wheel, Walnut Table, Chest and Trunk, Two
Beds and furniture, pair Cotton Cards, Sheep shears, a Smoth Bourd Gun,
parcel Pewter, parcell Wooden Ware, 2 Casks, grubing hoe, old Ax, old Sadle,
3 Sows and 3 Piggs, Black Mare, Pewter, frow, 2 Juggs, Negro Girl named
Judith, pair Cards, foot Wheel, 2 pair Traces, ?Juory comb (?Curry Comb).
Total: £518·13.
In Obedience to order of Worshipfull Court of Nov 1767 the Estate of Paul
PIGG Dece'd given under our hands 6 Jan 1768.

Hugh HENRY, WIlliam GRIFFITH, Robt. R ADDAMS
                                    Mark
Returned 26 Feb 1768 by Henry MC DANIEL Executor and recorded.

DB 1, p.98 - CANTERBERRY from JENKINS   DEED, 24 Mar 1768
Benjamin JENKINS of County of Pittsylvania of one part and Samuel CANTBERY
of said County of Pittsylvania of other part...for £8 Current Money of Vir-
ginia...250 acres on Island Creek...to GRAYS old order line.
Wit: W. YOUNG, Lewis GENKINS, Abner COCKERHAM
Rec: 25 Mar 1768   Benjamin GENKINS L.S.

DB 1, p.100 - JEFFERSON from READ   DEED, 14 Aug 1767
Clement READ of Charlotte County of one part and George JEFFERSON of Mecklen-
burgh County of other part...for £7600 Current Money of Virginia...8,000
acres on both sides Turkey Cock Creek...Mouth of a Branch...said tract of
Land granted to said Clement READ BY Patent dated 15 Aug 1764.
Wit: P. CARRINGTON, John BALLARD, j^r., David CALDWELL, Jno. WILLIAMS,
Jno. WILLIAMS, j^r.
Proved 28 Aug 1767, 25 Sep 1767 and further proved and recorded 25 Mar 1768
                                              Clement READ L.S.

DB 1, p.102 - JEFFERSON from READ   DEED
To Josiah MORTON, Henry ISBELL and James VENABLE Gent. or any two his Majestys
Justices of County of Charlotte...Clement READ by his Indenture of Feoffment
dated 14 Aug hath conveyed to George JEFFERSON of County of Pittsylvania...
8,000 acres...Mary, wife of said Clement, cannot conveniently travel to said
County Court of Pittsylvania...apart from said Husband Relinquishes her
right of Dower...30 Aug in 7th Year of our Reign.
Signed 19 Sep 1767   Josiah MORTON, L.S.
Rec: 28 Mar 1768   Henry ISBELL, L.S.

DB 1, p.103 - QUARLES froM TERRY   DEED, 19 Apr 1768
Nathaniel TERRY of Antrim Parish in Halifax County of one part and John
QUARLES of King William County of other part...for £100 Current Money of Vir-

ginia...Land in Parish of Camden in County of Pittsylvania on both sides
Echoles Fork...east side Echoles fork...pointers in patent line...in old line
run for John DONELSON...to Theophilus LACY Gent...1,007 acres it being part
of greater Quantity granted to said Nathaniel TERRY by Letters Pat. 31 Oct
1759.
Wit: John DIX, Champ. TERRY, Jo. TERRY
Rec: 27 May 1768   Nath. TERRY L.S.

DB 1, p.104 - DUNKING from HEARD   DEED, 27 May 1768
Stephen HEARD of County of Pittsylvania of one part and Benjamin DUNCKING of
said County of Pittsylvania of other part..for £30 Current Money of Virginia...
229 acres on Black Water River...MEAD's corner...pointers on Stephen HEARD's
line.   his
No witnesses   Stephen 𝒪 HEARD L.S.
Rec: 27 May 1768   Mark
Mary, Wife of said Stephen, privately Examined
and Relinquishes her right of Dower

DB 1, p.106 - SHELTON from COX   DEED, 1768
John COX of County of Pittsylvania and Frances his Wife of one part and James
SHELTON of same County of other part...for £10 Current Money of Virginia and
Negro Boy...400 acres...on a Branch of Leatherwood Creek...crossing Bever
Creek.   John COX L.S.
No witnesses
Rec: 27 May 1768   Frances X COX L.S.

DB 1, p.107 - PERRYMAN from STREET &c   DEED 12 Dec 1767
Anthony STREET and William HAWKINS of Halifax County of one part and Rich^d.
PERRYMAN of Pittsylvania County of other part...for £50 Current Money of Vir-
ginia...125 acres on both sides Mill Creek being part of land that STREET &
HAWKINS Rec^d. of Jno. ADAMS adjoining lines of Christopher GORMAN and John
GORMAN.
          his   his   his
Wit: Jno. I ADAMS, Robert R ADAMS, John I A ADAMS, Junr.
         Mark   Mark   Mark
Rec: 27 May 1768   Anthony STREET L.S.
                                                   William HAWKINS L.S.

DB 1, p.109 - PAULLEY from STREET &c   DEED, 10 Dec 1767
Anthony STREET and William HAWKINS of County of one part and Edward PAWLEY of
County of Pittsylvania of other part...for £20 Current Money of Virginia...
125 acres on both sides Mill Creek, which was granted to said Anthony STREET
and William HAWKINS this day of 1767 by Patent of Record in Secretarys Office
in this Colony...land lying on Lower end of said Tract.
        his   his   his
Wit: John I ADAMS, Robert R ADAMS, John I A ADAMS, Junr.
        Mark   Mark   Mark
Rec: 27 May 1768   Anthony STREET L.S.
                                                   William HAWKINS L.S.

DB 1, p.110 - ROGERS from DYE   DEED, 12 Mar 1768
Jacob DYE of Halifax County of one part and Peter ROGERS of same County of
other part...for £18·08·01 Current Money of Virginia...150 acres on both sides
Mill Creek a Branch running into south side of north Fork of Mayo River adjoining John THOMAS Land in Pittsylvania County.

Wit: William STOKES, Micajah $\curvearrowright$ SNEAD, Jacob H‑H DYE, jun^{r}.,
 his   Mark   Mark
William \\/ DYE
 Mark   his
Rec: 27 May 1768   Jacob $\dagger$ DYE L.S.
                                                        Mark

DB 1, p.111 - PATTEY from GILBERT   5 Dec 1767
Jesey PATTEY of Pittsylvania County of one part and Aquilla GILBERT and Eliz-
abeth his Wife of Bedford County of other part...77 acres in Pittsylvania
County opposite to Mush Island...Between lands of Thomas DILLARD, j^{r}. and
James DOSS, being land once conveyed by said Jesey PATTEY to said Aquilla
GILBERT...Sum of £50.

 his   her   his
Wit: Wil^{m}. HOWARD, Elizabeth $\times$ GILBERT, Robert R SEXTON, Dan GILBERT
 mark   mark   mark
                                                  Acquila GILBERT L.S.
Rec: 27 May 1768   her
Elizabeth, Wife of said Acquila Privately   Elizabeth GILBERT L.S.
Examined and Relinquishes her Dower right   Mark

DB 1, p.112 - SIMPSON from GRAYHAM   DEED, 27 May 1768
Archable GRAHAM of Parish of Camden and County of Pittsylvania of one part
and William SIMPSON of Augusta County of other part...for £50 Current Money
of Virginia...168 acres...in Isaac CLOUD's...crossing two Branches and the
Creek...same land granted to Col^{o}. John CHISWELL by letters patent dated
10 Sep 1755.
Rec: 27 May 1768   No witnesses   Archable GRAHAM L.S.

DB 1, p.113 - TERRY from TERRY   DEED, 26 Nov 1767
Joseph TERRY of Parish of Camden and County of Pittsylvania of one part and
Champ. TERRY of same County and Parish of other part...for £50 Current Mon-
ey of Virginia...400 acres on both sides Burches Creek between the Land
whereon said Joseph now lives and Thomas DODSONS Mill which is on said
Creek...East side Lower Mill Branch marked on north side t C, down the
Branch to the mouth, down Birtches Creek to first Branch that comes in on
South side of said Creek.   his
Wit: Richd. CARTER, John MADING, Thomas $\top$ PAYNE
                                        Mark
Rec: 27 May 1768   Joseph TERRY L.S.

DB 1, p.115
A True and Perfect Inventory of the Estate of Joseph SPRADLING Deceased:
One Iron Pott and Hooks, 1 Pewter Porrenger, 1 Rugg, Dutch Blankett, old
Bead, Porkitt Book, Dish, 2 Plates, Bason, 3 Spoons, Hair Sive, old Bagg,
Bible, pale, Table, 4 forks, grubbing Hoes, flat Iron, hatchet, Bottle,
Gimblet. Total £03·12·05.
Appraised by: David TERRY, Lazarous DODSON, Elijah KING
Certified 5 Mar 1768   Rec: 27 May 1768

DB 1, p.115 - LANKFORD from HAMILTON   DEED, 18 Apr 1768
John HAMILTON of County of Pittsylvania and Parish of Camden of one part
and Benjamin LANKFORD of County and Parish aforesaid...for £48·11·10 Current
Money of Virginia...200 acres on bouth sides bouth forks Allens Creek it
being the Lower end of 400 acres granted said John HAMILTON by patent dated
15 Aug 1764...beginning at Joseph FARRIS line where it Crosses the Cool
Spring Branch, down Cool Spring branch to south Fork of Allens Creek.

Wit: John PEMBERTON, John FARRIS, John GEORGE, Joseph <u>his</u> I FARRIS,
    <u>his</u>   Mark
William ✪ EAST
    mark
Rec: 27 May 1768, further proved 24 Jun 1768   John HAMILTON L.S.

DB 1, p.117 - FARRIS from HAMILTON   DEED, 18 Apr 1768

John HAMILTON of County of Pittsylvania of one part and Joseph FARRIS of
County aforesaid of other part...for £50 Current Money...200 acres on South
Fork of Allens Creek on bouth sides, Beginning at Joseph FARRIS's old line
where it Crosses the Cool Spring Branch and keeping down said Branch for a
Dividing line between said John HAMILTON and Joseph FARRIS...on BAKERS line.

Wit: Ben LANKFORD, John GEORGE, John FARRIS, William <u>his</u> ✪ EAST,
John PEMBERTON   Mark
Proved 27 May 1768 and Rec: 24 Jun 1768   Jno. HAMILTON L.S.

DB 1, p.119 - HUDSON from GORMAN   DEED, 9 Oct 1767

Christopher GORMAN of Pittsylvania County of one part and John HUDSON of
Prince Edward County of other part...for £60 Current Money of Virginia...194
acres on branches of Panther Creek and part of Tract of Land granted to said
Christopher GORMAN 25 Sep 1762...at John SLOANS Corner in a Branch...on John
ADAMS line...crossing said GORMANS Spring branch to a small branch... to
Joseph HICKS Line.
Wit: Edm^d. BOOKER, Nicholas HUDSON, Thomas HUDSON   his
Rec: 24 Jun 1769   Christopher ✝ GORMAN L.S.
Susannah, Wife of said Christopher,   Mark
privily Examined and relinquishes her Dower right

DB 1, p.120 - JENKINS from POTTER   DEED, 1 Apr 1768

Thomas POTTER of one part and Lewis JENKINS of other part, both of County of
Pitselviny...for £60 Current Money of Virginia...land on both sides Pigg
River...along order line...to Benj^a. JENKINSES line and on his line to the
River...100 acres all Exceptin one Acre for a burying yard that were my
Wife is now Buryed.
Wit: Samuel CANTERBERRY, John LAW, Thos. POTTER, jun^r.
Rec: 24 Jun 1768   Thomas POTTER L.S.

DB 1, p.121 - STEWART from CHOICE   23 Jun 1768

Tully CHOICE of County of Pittsylvania of one part and James STEWART of said
County of other part...for £30 Current Money of Virginia...sell to said James
STEWART in his actual possession, 220 acres on both sides Chesnut Creek...in
Robert HODGES line.
No witnesses
Rec: 24 Jun 1768   Tully CHOICE L.S.

DB 1, p.123 - DIX from CARGILL   DEED, 17 Feb 1768

John CARGILL of County of Barkley in Province of South Carolinia of one part
and John DIX of Pittsylvania County of other part...for £100 Current Money
of Virginia...210 acres on north side Dan River...beginning at James HOGANS
uper corner...which said land was granted said John CARGILL by Letters Patent
12 Jan 1746.
Wit: Theop^s. LACY, William WYNNE, Joseph TERRY   John CARGILL L.S.
Proved 27 May 1768 and Rec: 24 Jun 1768

DB 1, p.125 - HOGAN from HENDRICK   DEED, 17 Feb 1768
Hance HENDRICK and Margaret his Wife of Province of South Carolina of one
part and James HOGAN of Pittsylvania County of other part...for £100 Current
Money of Virginia...100 acres North side Dann River...beginning at Mouth of
Spring Branch...to CARGILLS lower line.
Wit: Theop^s. LACY, W^m. WYNNE, J. TERRY   Hans HENDRICK L.S.
Proved: 27 May 1768   her
Rec: 24 Jun 1768   Margaret -+- HENDRICK L.S.
                                                        Mark

DB 1, p.127 - DICKSON from CORNELIUS   DEED, 24 Jun 1768
William CORNELIUS of County of Pittsylvania of one part and Henry DIXON of
said County of other part...for £40 Current Money of Virginia...60 acres on
north side Dann River...Edmond FLOYDS corner...in William HOGAN's line...
except 3 or 4 acres Bounded by a Branch at the Lower end of said Tract and
joyning said CORNELIUS line.
No witnesses
Rec: 24 Jun 1768   W^m. CORNELIUS L.S.

DB 1,p.128 - COOK from INNES   DEED, 23 Jun 1768
Hugh INNES of County of Pittsylvania of one part and John COOK of said county
of other part...for £60 Current Money of Virginia...290 acres, now in his
actual Possession, on both sides Crabtree Fork of Snow Creek...corner of said
John COOKS line...in Samuel PATTERSONS line...on John HERDS line.
No witnesses
Rec: 24 Jun 1768   Hugh INNES L.S.

DB 1, p.130 - MURPHY from CALDWELL
James CALDWELL for sum of £16 paid by James MURPHY make over to said MURPHY
one still and Worm and three Cows now in the Possession of said CALDWELL...
if said Debt shall be paid before June 1768 then this Sale will be Void.
Rec: 24 Jun 1768   James 7) CALDWELL L.S.

DB 1, p.130 - HENDERSON from MC CLEAN   DEED, 4 Mar 1768
William MACCLAIN of County of Rowan in Province of North Carolina of one part
and Thos. HENDERSON of County of Pitselvaney Virginia of other part...for £25
Current Money...800 acres on both sides Midle fork of Steabery Creek.
Wit: Richard PILSON, John HENDERSON,
          his   William M^{c}CLEAN L.S.
Humphry -+- POSEY   Rec: 26 Aug 1768
        Mark

DB 1, p.132 - LEAKEY from HENDERSON   DEED, 26 Aug 1768
Thomas HENDERSON, Senr. of County of Pittsylvania of one part and Adam LEAKEY
of County of Orange North Carolinia of other part...for £46 Current Money...
252 acres granted by patent 10 Sep 1767 to said Thomas HENDERSON...on Midle
fork of Strawbery on both sides...in HARGETTES line...crossing three small
Branches of Strawbery.
No witnesses
Rec: 26 Aug 1768   Thomas HENDERSON L.S.

DB 1, p.134 - PILSON from HENDERSON   DEED, 26 Aug 1768
Thomas HENDERSON of County of Pittsylvania of one part and Richard PILSON of
other part and County aforesaid...for £16...400 acres on both sides South
fork of Strawberry Creek...beginning at John MORTONS.

No witnesses
Rec: 26 Aug 1768   Thomas HENDERSON L.S.

DB 1, p.135 - BLACKLY from HENDERSON   26 Aug 1768
Thomas HENDERSON, Senr. of County of Pittsylvania of one part and James
BLACKLY of said County of other part...for £20 Current Money of Virginia...
400 acres on Middle Fork of Strawberry on both sides...at MORTON's line...
along ROBERTS line.
No witnesses
Rec: 26 Aug 1768   Thomas HENDERSON L.S.

DB 1, p.137 - ARMSTRONG from ARMSTRONG   DEED, 7 Mar 1768
John ARMSTRONG, Junr. of County of Orange in Province of North Carolina of
one part and William ARMSTRONG of same Province and County of other part...
for £100...65 acres on South side Dan River beginning at GREENS corner on the
Country line.
Wit: Jno. HAMILTON, Hugh ARMSTRONG, Ja^s. ARMSTRONG, Danl. OBARR,Matthew GREGG
Rec: 26 Aug 1768   John ARMSTRONG, Junr. L.S.

DB 1, p.139 - WARD from MULLINS   DEED, 11 Jul 1768
William MULLINGS and Elizabeth his wife of County of Pittsylvania of one part
and Jeremiah WARD of County of Bedford of other part...for £60 Lawful Money
of Virginia...100 acres on north side Pigg River...along John KIERBYS line.
Wit: J. CHALLES, Isham DALTON/DUTTON, Ann CHALLES, Willm. BOBIT
Rec: 26 Aug 1768   his
Elizabeth, wife of said William, privily   William |\ MULLINS L.S.
Examined as Law directs Relinquished her   mark
Right of Dower   Eliz^a. MULLINS L.S.

DB 1, p.141 - ARMSTRONG from ARMSTRONG   DEED, 7 Mar 1768
John ARMSTRONG, Junr. of Pittsylvania County and Colony of Virginia of one
part and William ARMSTRONG of Orange County North Carolinia of other part...
135 acres on South side Dan River...for £80 Current Money of Virginia.
Wit: Jno. HAMILTON, Hugh ARMSTRONG, Ja^s. ARMSTRONG, Danl. OBARR,Matthew GREGG
Rec: 26 Aug 1768   John ARMSTRONG L.S.

DB 1, p.143 - PATTERSON from MEAD   DEED, 25 Aug 1765
William MEAD of Bedford County of one part and Samuel PATTERSON of Hallefax
County of other part...for £50 Current Money...470 acres in Hallefax County
on Pig River...south side Pig River on a branch of Camp Creek...Mouth of the
Branch.
No witnesses
Rec: 26 Aug 1768   WMEAD L.S.

DB 1, p.145 - WITCHER from ADKINSON   DEED, 26 Aug 1768
William AKINSON of Pittsylvania County of one part and William WITCHER of
same County of other part...for £25 Current Money of Virginia...50 acres on
Pig River...North side of River...on harping Creek.
Wit: James MITCHELL, David POLLEY, Jno. WITCHER   his
Rec: 26 Aug 1768   Wm. y ATKINSON
                                                        Mark

DB 1, p.147 - VAUGHAN from VAUGHAN   DEED, 25 Aug 1768
John VAUGHAN of County of Pittsylvania of one part and Thomas VAUGHAN of
Charlotte County of other part...for £30 Current money of Virginia...200 acres

on North west side of great Strait Stone Creek...beginning at a great Rock on Great Strait Stone Creek and Included within the following Lines, John VAUGHAN, Shadrick TREBLES, William GREGORYS and Edward HUBBARDS lines...the said Creek being the line betwixt the said John VAUGHANS Land and the above 200 acres.
Wit: James SMITH, Robin BOWMER, Jo^s. LUCK
Rec: 26 Aug 1768   John VAUGHAN L.S.

DB 1, p.149 - HARBOUR from SHELTON   DEED, 25 Aug 1768
Palatiah SHELTON and Mary his wife of Colony and Dominion of Virginia of one part and Adonijah HARBOUR of County of Pittsylvania within said Colony of other part...for £100 Current money...200 acres on both sides Falling Creek of Mayo River...end of a division line between David WITT and said Palatiah SHELTON, said Strait devision line Equally Devides a Tract containing 400 acres between said David WITT and Palatiah SHELTON.
No witnesses
Rec: 26 Aug 1768   Palatiah SHELTON L.S.

DB 1, p.151 - SHELTON from HARBOUR   DEED, 25 Aug 1768
Thomas HARBOUR and Sary his wife of the Colony and dominion of Virginia of one part and Palatiah SHELTON of County of Pittsylvania and said Colony of other part...for £100 Current money of Virginia...land on both sides Irvin River...beginning at a Mouth of Peeping Creek...130 acres.
Wit: Abner A.⋀^his HARBOUR, Sam DALTON, j^r., Adonijah HARBOUR
          mark   Thomas HARBOUR L.S.
   Rec: 26 Aug 1768
DB 1, p.153 - TERRY from PREWETT   DEED, 26 Aug 1768
Samuel PREWETT of County of Pittsylvania of one part and Champness TERRY of same County of other part...for £50 Current Money of Virginia...350 acres on both sides Birtches Creek...crossing two branches.
No witnesses
Rec: 26 Aug 1768   Samuel PREWIT L.S.

DB 1, p.155 - WARD from DILLARD   DEED, 26 Aug 1768
James DILLARD of County of Pittsylvania of one part and John WARD of County of Bedford of other part...for £70·11 Current Money of Virginia...land on Pigg River Comenly known by name of the frying pan including the Land and plantation whereon said James DILLARD now lives...235 acres granted by Patent to W^m. RODGERS...James DILLARD is justly indebted to said John WARD...to pay on or before 26 Aug 1771 with leagual Interest.
Wit: Isaac READ, Hugh INNES, H. PENDLETON
Rec: 26 Aug 1768   James DILLARD L.S.

DB 1, p.157 - ATKINSON from WITCHER   DEED, 26 Aug 1768
William WITCHER of Pittsylvania County of one part and William ATKINSON of same County of other part...for £25 Current Money of Virginia...50 acres on Pigg River...to Small Branch Called Buffeloe Branch, down the branch to Pigg River.
Wit: James MITCHELL, DAVID POLLEY, John WITCHER
Rec: 26 Aug 1768   William WITCHER L.S.

DB 1, p.159 - WALDROPE from DILLARD   DEED, 22 Aug 1768
James DILLARD of County of Pittsylvania of one part and James WALDROPE and John WALDROPE of aforesaid County of other part...for £30 Current Money of

Virginia...Land on South side of Pigg River and Runing a Straight line from
the kings Cassil on said River to Mouth of the frying Pan Creek including all
the lands up said Creek belonging to said James DILLARD and what Lands Belongs
to him on Pig River Below the king Cassel [a high rock].

Wit: James MITCHELL, W^m. WITCHER, William ⊬ ATKINSON
                                        mark

Rec: 26 Aug 1768   James DILLARD L.S.

DB 1, p.160 - WALKER from BEAN   DEED, 26 Aug 1768
William BEAN of County of Pittsylvania in Colony of Virginia of one part and
Jeremiah WALKER of County aforesaid of other part...for £20 Current money of
Virginia...150 acres being part of the Tract whereon said William BEAN now
lives...in CHILLS line.
No witnesses
Rec: 26 Aug 1768   William BEAN L.S.
Lydia, wife of said William, Privily Examined,
Relinquished her Right of Dower

DB 1, p.162 - BIRD from CHILES   DEED, 25 Aug 1768
Henry CHILES of Pittsylvania County and Colony of Virginia of one part and
Joseph BIRD of the County and Colony aforesaid of other part...for £60 Lawfull
Money of Virginia...184 acres on Butterm Town Creek and Bounded as directed
in the Pattent of said Land dated 10 Aug 1759.
                                        his
Wit: Shadrick TURNER, John TURNER, David A ADKISON
                                       mark
Rec: 26 Aug 1768   Henry CHILES L.S.

DB 1, p.164 - SHORT from COX   DEED, 26 Aug 1768
Samuel COX of Roan County in North Carolinia of one part and William SHORT of
parish of Cambden in County of Pittsylvania of other part...for £65 Current
Money of Virginia...Land on Both sides Stinking River...in Patent line...in
William LEIGHTFOOT Esq^rs. line...200 acres it being part of a Larger Tract
Granted by patent to Joseph MAYES.   his
No witnesses   Samuel X COX L.S.
Rec: 26 Aug 1768   mark

DB 1, p.167 - DUGGER from DUGGER   BILL SALE, 20 Mar 1768
I William DUGGER do Bargain, Sell and deliver unto Benjamin DUGGER; Read and
white Cow Markt two Crops, Brindle and white Cow with two Crops, Red &
white Cow marked a Crop & a Slit in the Rite Eare & a Slite in Left Eare, Red
heafer marked 2 Smoth Crops & under Ceel in Rite Eare, 1 Stear Read & white
Marked 2 Smoth Crops & Nick in Each Eare, Sorrel Mare with Blase in her face
Branded on Sholder thus ⏤ , Colt Branded on Near Sholder C , Young mare
Colt with Blase in her face, Gray horse Branded on near Sholder with a three
Bard Stirrup Iron with a Bold face, old Sow Marked with a Crop & a Slite in
Reight Eare & a Slite in Left, all rest Marked with a Crop & a Nick in each
Eare.   his   William DUGGER L.S.
Wit: Samuel ⏌ HALL   Rec: 26 Aug 1768
            Mark
DB 1, p.168 - BOWMAN from ABSTON   DEED, 26 Aug 1768
Joshua ABSTON of parish of Cambden in County of Pittsylvania of one part and
John BOWMAN of same place of other part...for £30...Land on uper side of
frying Pan Creek...400 acres Granted by Patent to Charles BOSTICK.

No witnesses
Rec: 26 Aug 1768   Joshua ABSTON L.S.

DB 1, p.171 - PAYNE from BEAN   DEED, 25 Aug 1768
William BEAN of County of Pittsylvania of one part and John PAYNE of County
of Goochland of other part...for £480 Current Money of Virginia...Two Tracts
of Land joyning on North side Dan River...one Tract of 354 acres on the
River below the Doubles Creeks...as by Patent dated 1 Oct 1747. The other
Tract of 179 acres Joyning on the first Tract Beginning in said BEANS old
line...Crossing a fork five times...as by Patent dated 12 Jul 1762 Granted
to said William BEAN...containing in the whole 433 acres after deducting
100 acres at uper end of first tract already laid off for John HARDIMAN and
the remaining part now conveyed is the Lands and Plantations whereon Godian
MARR now lives.
Wit: G. MARR, Robt. PAYNE, Hugh ARMSTRONG
                                                    William BEAN L.S.
Rec: 26 Aug 1768
Lydia, Wife of said William, Privily Examined as Law directs Relinquished
her Right of Dower

DB 1, p.175 - TUNSTALL from COX   DEED OF TRUST, 26 Feb 1768
Samuel COX of County of Halifax of one part and Thomas TUNSTALL of same County
of other part...for £10 and whatsoever other sum said Thomas TUNSTALL may ad-
vance and pay...200 acres on Stinking River, according to known Ancient and
Reputed Bounds, also one Bay horse, 1 white Horse, 8 head of Cattle, about
40 Head of Hoggs and all Household and Kitchen Furniture of him said Samuel
COX...with Lawfull Interest at or upon 1 Apr next ensuing.
Wit: Jean PHELPS, Mary TUNSTALL, William TODD, Ju^r., John CARLTON
                                                        his
Rec: 23 Sep 1768   Samuel X COX L.S.
                                                       Mark

DB 1, p.177 - PREWITT from WATKINS   DEED, 23 Sep 1768
Thomas WATKINS of Bedford County of one part and Richard PREWET of Pittsylvania County of other part...for £30 of good and Lawfull Money of Virginia...
150 acres on both sides Strawberry Creek...a new line Devicing the Survey...
which said Land was granted to said Thomas WATKINS by patent dated at Williamsburg 10 Aug 1759 and now in possession of said Richard PREWET and now
living on same.
No witnesses
Rec: 23 Sep 1768   Thomas WATKINS L.S.

DB 1, p.178 - ABSTON from CALLAWAY   DEED, 25 Oct 1768
William CALLAWAY of County of Bedford of one part and Joshua ABSTON of Pittsyl-
vania County of other part...for £35 Current Money of Virginia...250 acres
Survaid formily for William MOBBERLY on both sides Sycamore Creek...in
CLEMENTS line.
Wit: Benjamin CLEMENT, Thomas ROBERTSON, Richard HOLLAWAY
Rec: 25 Nov 1768   William CALLAWAY L.S.

DB 1, p.180 - ROBERTSON from CALLAWAY   DEED, 25 Oct 1768
William CALLAWAY of County of Bedford of one part and Thomas ROBERTSON of
County of Pittsylvania of other part...for £20 Current Money of Virginia...
200 acres on both sides Sycamore Creek...Beginning at CLEMENTS corner.
Wit: Joshua ABSTONE, Richard HOLLAWAY, Benjamin CLEMENT
Rec: 25 Nov 1768   William CALLAWAY L.S.

DB 1, p.182 - CLEMENT from CLEMENT   DEED, 3 Nov 1768
Benjamin CLEMENT Senior and Susannah his Wife of County of Pittsylvania of
one part and Benjamin CLEMENT Junior of same County of other part...for £60
Current Money of Virginia...229 acres...beginning in Benjmain CLEMENTS line.
Wit: Thomas ROBERTS,Joshua ABSTONE, Richard HOLLAWAY
Memorandum wit: Thomas ROBERTSON   Benjamin CLEMENT L.S.
Rec: 25 Nov 1768   Susanah CLEMENT   L.S.

DB 1, p.184 - BENNETT from WADE   DEED, 20 Oct 1768
Edward WADE of County of Pittsylvania of one part and Stephen BANNETT of
aforesaid County...for £10 Current Money of Virginia...226 acres on both sides
frying pan Creek Joyining James WADES line and Running Down Both sides of
said Creek to Christopher SUTTONS line.
Wit: Joshua ABSTONE, Thomas ROBERTSON, Benjamin CLEMENT
Rec: 25 Nov 1768   Edward WADE L.S.

DB 1, p.186 - SHELTON from CHANDLER   DEED, 22 Nov 1768
Thomas CHANDLER and Catherine his wife of Dinwiddie County of one part and
Beverley SHELTON of Pittsylvania County of other part..for £66·03·09½ Current
Money of Virginia...400 acres, land granted to said Thomas CHANDLER by Patent
dated 3 Mar 1760 and on both sides panther Creek...where Ambrose HALEY cor-
ners on Edward HALEY.
Wit: Crispin SHELTON, Jn°. GRIGGARY, Will. TUNSTALL, William PAYNE,
Abraham SHELTON, Abraham MOTTLEY
Rec: 25 Nov 1768   Thomas CHANDLER L.S.

DB 1, p.189 - HILL from HAYNES   DEED, 21 Nov 1768
William HAYNES of County of Bedford of one part and William HILL of County
of Pittsylvania of other part...for £26 Current Money of Virginia...120 acres
being part of Tract of Land containing 243 acres the pattern bearing date
22 Sep 1766 and on both sides Bull Run...Running towards Black Water and
crossing Bull Run.
No witnesses
Rec: 25 Nov 1768   William HAYNES L.S.

DB 1, p.191 - DILLARD from WARD   DEED, 25 Nov 1768
Jeremiah WARD of County of Bedford planter of one part and James DILLARD of
County of Pittsylvania Planter of other...100 acres on North side pigg River...
being same land said Jeremiah WARD purchased of William MULLINS and was by
said William MULLINS and Elizabeth his wife by Indenture dated 11 Jul in year
aforesaid conveyed to said Jeremiah WARD.
Rec: 25 Nov 1768
Ann, wife of Said Jeremiah WARD, Relinquished   Jeremiah ✝ WARD L.S.
her Right of Dower

DB 1, p.193 - WARD from DILLARD   DEED, 23 Sep 1768
John WARD of County of Bedford and James DILLARD of County of Pittsylvania
and Priseylla his wife of one part and Jeremiah WARD of County of Bedford of
other part..for £281 Current Money of Virginia...100 acres Land Called or
known by name of the frying Pan...on lower side Pigg River...Beginning at
Mouth of frying pan Creek thence down pigg River to a high Rock known by
name of kings Castle.
Rec: 25 Nov 1768   No witnesses   James DILLARD L.S.
Presilla, wife of said James, Relinquished her right of Dower.

DB 1, p.196 - SWANSON from SASBEARY   DEED, 25 Nov 1768
Jeremiah SOSBEARY of County of Pittsylvania of one part and William SWANSON
of County of Bedford of other part..for £130 Current Money of Virginia...
400 acres on both sides Bull Run...near a Small Branch...Crossing said Run.
No witnesses
Rec: 25 Nov 1768   Jeremiah SOSBEARY L.S.

DB 1, p.197 - WATKINS from HALL   DEED, 24 Oct 1766
Robert HALL of Johnson County in North Carolinia of one part and Thomas
WATKINS of County of Bedford in Virginia of other part...for £30 Current
Money of Virginia...Land in Halifax County on Both Sides Wetsleave Creek...
on South side said Creek.
                    his
Wit: Miles   /\ BARROT, John EPPERSON, Cornelius MACMEHAUNE,
              Mark
      her \/   Robert HALL L.S.
Sarah   /\ MACMEHAUNE
      Mark   Rec: 25 Nov 1768

DB 1, p.199 - JONES from JONES   DEED, 23 Nov 1768
Robert JONES of County of Pittsylvnia of one part and Isaace JONES of county
aforesaid of other part...186 acres...for £20 Current Money...both sides
North fork Pigg River.
Wit: John DONELSON, Thos. DILLARD, Junr., John PERSONS
Rec: 25 Nov 1768   Robert JONES L.S.

DB 1, p.201 - POOR from JONES   DEED, 23 Nov 1768
Robert JONES of County of Pittsylvania of one part and Jerimiah POOR of other
part...for £50 Current Money of Virginia...214 acres Both sides North fork
Pig River...pointers in Patent Line, along patent lines.
Wit: John DONELSON, Thomas DILLARD, John PERSONS
Rec: 25 Nov 1768   Robert JONES L.S.

DB 1, p.204 - SOSBEARY from STANDEFER   DEED, 25 Nov 1768
James STANDEFER of County of Bedford of one part and Jeremiah SOSBEARY of
Pittsylvania County of other part...for £57 Current money of Virginia...
166 acres being part of Tract of 303 acres which is Called the ?mind oald
feild Surveay the Pattern Bearing date 30 Aug 1763...on Black Water River.
No witnesses   his
Rec: 25 Nov 1768   James /\ STANDEFORD
                                                 mark

DB 1, p.206 - SHIELDS from SHIELDS   DEED, 25 Nov 1768
Patrick SHIELDS of County of Pittsylvania of one part and Joseph SHIELDS of
said county of other part...for £25 Current Money of Virginia paid by said
Joseph SHEILDS the Lawfull heir of said Patrick SHIELDS...51 acres on Both
sides South fork Sandy River being a Tract Granted to said Patrick SHIELDS
by Patent dated 16Sep 1765...beginning at Thomas GRISAM corner...in SHIELDS
old line...crossing Sandy River...crossing a Branch.
No witnesses
Rec: 25 Nov 1768   Patrick SHIELDS L.S.

DB 1, p.208 - CHALLES from MC DANIEL   DEED, 23 Jun 1769
Henry MC DANIEL and Mary Ann his wife of County of Pittsylvania of one part
and Hugh CHALLES of Bedford County of other part...for £150 Current Money of

Virginia...400 acres on South side Banister River and Granted to said Henry
MC DANIEL by Patent dated 7 Jul 1763.
Wit: Hugh INNES, Will. TUNSTALL, John COX, Theop. LACEY
Rec: 23 Jun 1769   Henry MC DANIEL L.S.
Mary Ann, wife of said Henry, privily   her
Examined and relinquishes her right   Mary Ann X MC DANIEL L.S.
of Dower.   Mark

DB 1, p.211 - EASTES from INNES   DEED, 27 Jan 1769
Hugh INNES of County of Pittsylvania of one part and Elisha EASTES of said
county of other part...for £200 Current Money of Virginia...604 acres on
Goard Creek and in his actual Possession now being...crossing Goard Creek...
as by Patent granted to Joseph WILLIAMS and conveyed by him to Amos RICHARDSON
and by said RICHARDSON to Tully CHOICE and by said Tully CHOICE to said Hugh
INNES by Deed of Trust.
No witnesses
Rec: 23 Jun 1769   Hugh INNES L.S.

DB 1, p.214 - LAYNE from DENTON   DEED, 30 Dec 1768
James DENTON of County of Pittsylvania in Colony of Virginia of one part and
Dutton LANE of County aforesaid of other part...for £50 Current Money of
Virginia...83 acres on South Side Dan River.
Wit: Peter PERKINS, Thos. HARGETT, Nicholas PERKINS
Rec: 23 Jun 1769   James DENTON L.S.

DB 1, p.215 - ROBERTS BOND FOR SHERIFALTY   23 Jun 1769
We James ROBERTS, John DONELSON, William TUNSTALL, John COOK, Abraham SHELTON
and Robert CHANDLER are firmly Bound to our Sovereign Lord king George the
third...Sum of £1000 Current Money...Above bound James ROBERTS is Constituted
and appointed Sherriff of County of Pittsylvania...said ROBERTS shall truly
collect all Quitrents fines Forfeitures...due to his Majesty...pay to officers
of his Majestys, Revinue on or before Second Tuesday in June Annually...Faith-
fully Execute said office of Sheriff.
Rec: 23 Jun 1769   James ROBERTS L.S.   Jno. DONELSON L.S.
                        Will. TUNSTALL L.S.   Jno. COOK L.S.
                        Abraham SHELTON L.S.   Robert CHANDLER L.S.

DB 1, p.217 - ROBERTS BOND FOR SHERIFALTY   23 Jun 1769
We James ROBERTS, William TUNSTALL, John DONELSON, John COOK, Abraham SHELTON,
and Robert CHANDLER are bound to Sovereign Lord king George the third in sum
of £1000 Current Money...Condition of above obligation...above bound James
ROBERTS constituted and appointed Sherrif of County of Pittsylvania...under
Seal of Colony dated 26 May last Past...shall Collect all offices Fees and
Dues put in his hands...pay same to officers to whom such Fees are Due...
Perform Office of Sherrif During Term of his Continuance.
Rec: 23 Jun 1769
                        James ROBERTS L.S.   Jno. DONELSON L.S.
                        Will TUNSTALL L.S.   John COOK L.S.
                        Abraham SHELTON L.S.   Robert CHANDLER L.S.

DB 1, p.218 - CARR from GLASS   BILL SALE, 15 Jun 1769
John GLASS of County of Pittsylvania and John CARR of County of Halifax...for
£22 Current Money of Virginia...2 fether Beds and furniture, 5 head Cattle,
2 horses and 1 mare, 6 pewter plates, 2 Dishes, 2 Basons, Chest, Table, 6

Knives and forks, 2 Spinning wheals, 1 Saddle.
Rec: 23 Jun 1769   John GLASS L.S.

DB 1, p.219 - COOK from EASTIS   DEED, 4 Apr 1769
Elisha EASTIS of County of Pittsylvania of one part and Harmon COOK of other
part...for £80 Current Money of Virginia...260 acres on both sides Turkey
Cock Creek, now being in his actual possession...East side said Creek near
READE and Companys line...crossing three Branches...in OWINSES line...cross-
ing Little Turkey Cock Creek.
Wit: Hugh INNES, Constan RIKENS, Fred^k. RIVES
Rec: 23 Jun 1769   his
Frances, wife of said Elisha, Privily Examined   Elisha ╪ EASTIS L.S.
and relinquished her right of Dower   Mark

DB 1, p.222 - HARGETT from COX   DEED, 26 May 1769
John COX of County of Pittsylvania of one part and Thomas HARGETT of same
County of other part...for £60 Current Money of Virginia...400 acres on
Branches of North fork of Sandy River it being one Moiety of 800 acres con-
veyed by Richard SWEPSTON to said John COX by Indenture Recorded in County
Court of Halifax and dated 1 Sep 1761...bounded by Dividing Line Agreed upon
by said John COX and Joseph AUSTIN to whom said COX Conveyed the Remainder
Part of said 800 acres by Indenture Recorded in said County Court and dated
26 May 1769.
No witnesses
Rec: 23 Jun 1769   John COX L.S.

DB 1, p.225 - HUBBARD from LARGE   DEED, 1768
Robert LARGE of County of Pittsylvania of one part and Jacob HUBBARD of said
County of other part...for £30 Current money of Virginia...200 acres on Pigg
River...on Jeremiah WARD line...to Robert BALLEW line.

Wit: John KEARBY, Josiah ╪ KEARBY, Jesse KEARBY
                                                     Robert ✗ LARGE L.S.
Rec: 23 Jun 1769

DB 1, p.226 - BARNETT from COX   DEED, 20 Jun 1769
John COX of Pittsylvania County of one part and James BARNETT of said County
of other part...for £20 Current Money of Virginia...36 1/2 acres on both
sides South fork Shugar Tree Creek...to large fork in said Creek...down
Creek to the Mouth, Cross the main Creek.   his
Wit: Peter PURKINS, Nicholas PURKINS   John ╪ COX L.S.
Rec: 23 Jun 1769   Mark

DB 1, p.229 - SMITH & CO. from SIMMON   TRUST DEED, 7 Feb 1769
John SIMMONS of Pittsylvania County of one part and James SMITH & Copy. of
other part...for £06·01·06 Current Money of Virginia which said John SIMMONS
is justly Indebted to them and Honestly desires to Secure and pay to them
and for further Consideration of Sum of 5s like Money to said John SIMMONS
paid by said James SMITH & Co...one Negroe Winch named Caroline, 2 feather
Beds and furniture, 2 Iron Potts, 15 Pewter Plates, 2 dishes, 3 Basons, 8
head of Cattle and all household furniture...after 1 Mar 1770 sell for best
price after 10 days publick Notice...out of Money arising from Sale Discharge
said sum with Interest.   his
Wit: John SALMON, Gregory DURHAM, Hezekiah ✗ SALMON
                                                  Mark

Rec: 23 Jun 1769   John SIMMONS L.S.

DB 1, p.232 - BOWMER from BOWMER   DEED, 10 Mar 1769
John BOWMER of Pittsylvania County of one part and Robin BOWMER of same
County of other part...for £15 Current Money of Virginia 200 acres part
of patent of 400 acres granted first to Charles BOSTICK dated 10 Aug 1759 and
on frying pan Creek being the Lower part of said Tract.

Wit: James KING, Jn°. ⟍⟋ DOLTON, Charles BENNETE
                      his
                      Mark

Rec: 23 Jun 1769   John BOWMER L.S.

DB 1, p.234 - ELLES from HALL   DEED, 10 Dec 1768
Isam HALL of Pittsylvania County of one part and John ELLES of same County of
other part...for £6 Current Money of Virginia...100 acres on South side Pig
River...head of a Branch.
                   his   his
Wit: Robert BOULTON, Wᵐ. ⟋⟋ MULLINS, James X BOULTON   his
                      Mark   Mark   Isam X HALL L.S.
Rec: 23 Jun 1769   Mark

DB 1, p.235 - POTTER, Junʳ. from JINKINS   DEED, 15 Oct 1768
Lewis GENKINS of County of Pittsylvania of one part and Thomas POTTER, Junʳ.
of said County of other part...for £6 Current Money of Virginia...100 acres
on South side Pig River being the Land said Thomas POTTER now lives.
                                   his
Wit: Hugh INNES, Jn°. LAW, Junʳ., William ⟋⟋ DILLINGHAM, Junʳ.
                                   Mark   his
Rec: 23 Jun 1769   Lewis V GENKINS L.S.
                                                Mark

DB 1, p.238 - WEBB from JENKINS   DEED, 16 Oct 1768
Lewis GINKINS of County of Pittsylvania of one part and William WEBB of said
County of other part...for £07 Current Money of Virginia...100 acres on North
side of Pig River being the Land said William WEBB now lives on and in his
Actual Possession.
                                   his
Wit: Hugh INNES, John LAW, Junʳ., William ⟋⟋ DILLINGHAM, Junʳ.
                                   Mark   his
Rec: 23 Jun 1769   Lewis ⟍ GINKINS L.S.
                                                Mark

DB 1, p.241 - PERKINS from MC BEE   DEED, 17 Sep 1768
Vardry MC BEE of County of MᶜLingburg of North Carolinia of one part and
Charles PERKINS of County of Rowann of other part...for £40 Current Money of
Virginia...200 acres on both sides Russells Creek...in Thomas JONES Corner
at dividing Line of apeace of Land taken out of same Patent.
Wit: Peter PERKINS, Dutton LANE, John WILLIAMS, Nicholas PURKINS
Rec: 23 Jun 1769   Vardry MC BEE L.S.

DB 1, p.244 - BUCKINGHAM from LACY   DEED, 23 Jun 1769
Theophilus LACEY of Pittsylvania County of one part and Thomas BUCKINGHAM of
County of Maclingbaurg of other part...for £165 Current Money of Virginia...
400 acres on Sandy Creek and is same Land said Theopˢ. LACEY purchased of
Champness TERRY...North side Sandy Creek...an old Line Formerly James TERRYS...
corner pine Formerly CULDWELLS...by side of small Branch.
No witnesses
Rec: 23 Jun 1769   Theopˢ. LACY L.S.

DB 1, p.247 - ROBERTS Junr. from DUNLAP   BILL SALE, 11 Jun 1768
Henry DUNLOP for consideration of £30 Current Money hath sold unto James
ROBERTS, Junr.: Bay Mare Branded thus ᛏᚹ four years old, Black Horse a
natural pacer and Brand unknown 6 years old, 2 Sows and piggs the Sows Mark^d.
in Abraham PASLEYS Marke, 3 Shoats marked with Crop in Left Ear and Swallow
fork in Right, 2 Blanketts, Bed Tyche, Iron Pott and Hooks, Frying Pan, Water
pail Piggen and Cann, Case Knives and forks, Chest, Saddle and Bridle, Meal
sifter.   his
Wit: Jno. SALMON, Samuel STREET   Henry   DUNLOP L.S.
Rec: 24 Jun 1769   Mark

DB 1, p.248 - APPRAISEMENT OF DOBSON EAST.   Taken 21 Mar 1769
Inventory of estate of Isaace DODSON Dec'd.: 14 head hogs, Bay mare and
Colt, Black Mare, Roan Mare, Bell, Brown horse, Dark Bay horse, Bell, 33 head
Cattle, 7 head Sheep, Wolf Trap, 2 Bells and Collars, 3 Axes, 3 hoes, Mattock,
Cracked pott, Pott & hooks, old Frying pann, Rifle Gunn and Brass Molds, Smooth
Gun, Mans Saddle, Plow Cleveses & Geers, Bell & 2 Bridles, 3 Collars, Washing
Tub, 2 piggins, 2 Pails, 5 Basons, 3 Dishes, 6 plats, 11 Spoons, 5 Knives &
6 forks, Saddle, flesh fork, Candle Stick, Linen Whell, Wooling ditto, Pair
Cotton Cards, Feather bed & furniture, 3 Bed steed & Cord, 3 Bed furniture,
Syth, 4 Slays, 2 wheat Seves, Powdering Tub, Bushell Measure, 2 old Hhd^s.,
Chest, Box Iron & Heaters, old Religes Book, p^r. Shears, churn, Jug, Cart
Whells, Yearling. Total £129·11·01 ½.
By: Absalom BOSTICK, John FULTON, John WILSON   Rec: 23 Jun 1769

DB 1, p.249 - JOHN SLONES LAST WILL AND TESTAMENT
I John SLOANE of Pittsylvania County in Perfect health and Memory...to Loving
wife Elenar SLONE all whole Estate of Moveables and my Lands for her life and
after her Decease I leave my Lands to my son Jno. SLONE and the Moveables as
she thinks Proper...to son William SLONE one Shilling sterling...to son James
SLONE one Shilling Sterling...to son Thomas SLONE one Shilling Sterling...to
daughter Mary JUSTICE one shilling Sterling...to daughter Elenar JOHNSON one
Shilling Starling...appoint my well beloved wife Elenar SLONE my hole and
Sole Executor...11 Nov 1768.   his
                                              John   SLONE L.S.
Wit: Rich^d. HAMMACK, Daniel Χ WITCHER, Mary HAMMACK   Mark

Rec: 23 Jun 1769 and Executrix, Eleanar SLOAN, granted Certificate with
James SLOAN and Daniel WITCHER her securities.

DB 1, p.250 - PAYNE from CHRISWELL   DEED, 10 Dec 1768
Lewis Green CHRISWELL and Ann his wife of County of Pittsylvania of one part
and Robert PAYNE of said County of other part...for £165 Current Money of
Virginia...100 acres on South side Dan River...beginning at the county line
where it crosseth said River...to PARISHES corner.
Wit: Benjamin MOSBY, Jno. WINSTON, George LUMKIN, Junr., Jno. DIX,
Thomas DUDLEY   his
Rec: 28 Jul 1769   Lewis green   CHRISWELL
                                                           Mark

                                              her
                                              Anne   CHRISWELL L.S.
                                              Mark

DB 1, p.253 - DILLARD, Junr. from DILLARD, Senr.   DEED, 12 Nov 1768
Thomas DILLARD Senior of County of Pittsylvania of one part and Thomas

DILLARD Junior of other part...for £30 Current Money of Virginia...202 acres on north fork Straitstone Creek...a Branch in Edward DILLARDS old Plantation in James HUNTS, now said Thos. DILLARD Junior lyne...Crossing the creek... into Last line mentioned in patent of 404 acres of which this deed is for part.
Wit: Benj. LANKFORD, Jno. GEORGE, Joseph COLLINS, Jeremiah WARD
Rec: 28 Jul 1769

Thomas DILLARD L.S.

DB 1, p.256 - FRANCE from WALTON   DEED, 26 Mar 1769
George WALTON of County of Prince Edward of one part and Henry FRANCE of County of Pittsylvania of other part...for 5s Current Money of Virginia... 100 acres on South side Mayo River...against claim and Demand of all other Persons...or the Heirs of his Brother Robert WALTON deceased.
Wit: Isaac READ, Robert WILLIAMS, Edmond WINSTON
Rec: 28 Jul 1769

George WALTON L.S.

DB 1, p.257 - THOMPSON from BEARD   DEED, 24 Mar 1769
Adam BEARD Gen^t. for and in behalf of Catherine, daughter and Heir at Law of Joseph MILLER Dece^d. of County of Bedford of one part and William THOMSON, son and Legatee of William THOMPSON Dec^d. of said County of other part... William THOMPSON having purchased of said Joseph MILLER a cartain Tract of Land in Hallefax County, now Pittsylvania, on South side Blackwater River containing 200 acres and having directed Title of said Land be made to said son William THOMPSON by his Last Will and Testament Departed this Life and afterward said Joseph MILLER Departed this life Intestate leaving said Catherine heirs at Law and said Catharine being an infant under age of 21 years, came into County Court of Bedford and made choice of said Adam BEARD her Guardean to convey said Land...in RANDOLPHS Line.
Wit: G. JEFFERSON, Jno. WILSON, Champ. TERRY, David WALKER, Absalom BOSTICK, Jno. COX
Rec: 28 Jul 1769

Adam BEARD L.S.

DB 1, p.260 - FARRELL from SHORT   DEED, 28 Jul 1769
Francis SHORT of parish of Cambden in County of Pittsylvaia Virginia of one part and John FARRELL of same place of other part...for £20 Current money of Virginia...100 acres on Both sides of a fork of Allins Creek, it being part of Tract granted to said Francis SHORT by Patent dated 20 Jul 1768...beginning at corner of Patent line...on Waggon Road...crossing the Creek and Branch.
No witnesses
Rec: 28 Jul 1769

Francis / SHORT L.S.
his
Mark

DB 1, p.262 - SALMON from HARRIS   DEED, 6 Aug 1768
Charles HARRIS of County of Granvile North Carolinia of one part and John SALMON of Pittsylvania County Virginia of other part...for £10...116 acres granted by patent to said Charles HARRIS...Edmond GRAYS & Companys on Smiths River...to RANDOLPHS & Companys corner.
Wit: James ROBERTS Junior, Thomas HARGETT, Jo^s. MORTON, Hugh ARMSTRONG
Rec: 28 Jul 1769

Charles HARRIS L.S.

DB 1, p.265 - FARGUSON from VANBEBBER   DEED, 6 Apr 1769
Peter VANBEBER Senior of County of Pittsylvania and Colony of Virginia of one part and John FARGUSON of other part of County and Colony aforesaid...for £80 Lawfull Money of Virginia...130 acres on Pig River...Crossing the River... crossing a Branch.
Wit: Hugh INNES, Wm. TREDWAY, Robert HILL, James STANDEFER, William / DAVIS,
his
Mark

Peter *his* D HENLEY
Mark
Rec: 28 Jul 1769   Peter VANBEBBER L.S.

DB 1, p.267 - BLEVINS from WYNNE   BILL SALE, 28 Jul 1769
Thomas WYNNE of County of Pittsylvania for Sum of £17 Current Money of Virginia Sell to John BLEAVINS of said County: 5 head Grown Cattle Marked with
a Crop and under Keel in Right and a half upper Crop in Left Ears, 3 Cows
and Calves of same Mark, white Horse Branded on near Buttock thus *H* .
Wit: George LUMKIN, W. WRIGHT   his
                                              Thomas Z WYNNE
Rec: 28 Jul 1769   Mark
                                              John BLEVINS

DB 1, p.268 - WHITE from BILLINGS   DEED, 1769
Jasper BILLINS of County of Pittsylvania and Colony of Virginia of one part
and Benjamin WHITE of said County of other part...for £15 Current Money of
Virginia...at Waggon Ford of Sandy River...in Isaace DOBSONS line...contain-
ing 50 acres...south side Sandy River...part of large tract granted Billens.
Wit: Edward *his* F SMITH, Isaace F GROSE, Genuet X DOBSON
            Mark
Rec: 28 Jul 1769   Jasper BILLINGS L.S.

DB 1, p.271 - HAILE from MEAD   DEED, 15 Mar 1769
William MEAD of Bedford County Attorney for Nicholas HAILE of Baltimore Coun-
ty in Maryland of one part and Stephen HEARD of Pittsylvania County in Vir-
ginia of other part...for £07·10...52 acres on Meads Branch...pointers in
Patents line.
Wit: Jesse HERD, John HERD, Francis FARLEN
Rec: 28 Jul 1769   Nicholas HAILE L.S.

DB 1, p.273 - PAYNE from ARMSTRONG   DEED, 22 Jul 1769
William ARMSTRONG of County of Orrange and Province of North Carolinia of
one part and Robert PAYNE of County of Pittsylvania in Virginia of other
part...for £55 Current Money of Virginia...65 acres on South Side Dan River...
Beginning at Lewis green CHRISWELLS corner...on the Contry Line.
Wit: Jno. DIX, Thomas DUDLEY, John HAMILTON, Dudley GATWOOD, Benj. MOSBY,
Robt. BURTON
Rec: 28 Jul 1769   William ARMSTRONG L.S.

DB 1, p.275 - CERTAIN from KENNE   DEED, 24 Feb 1769
William KENNE now or Late of Pittsylvania County and Parish of Cambden and
Elizabeth his wife of one part and Josiah CARTAIN of County and parish
aforesaid of other part...for £40 Current Money of Virginia...190 acres on
frying pann Creek, land purchased by William KENNE of Jno. GOADE.
Wit: John GLASS, Jno. JUSTICE, Ezra JUSTICE, Simeon JUSTICE
                                                   his
Rec: 28 Jul 1769   William X KENNE L.S.
                                                   Mark

DB 1, p.278 - FRANCE from COX   DEED, 28 Jul 1769
Jacob COX of Parish of Cambden in County of Pittsylvania of one part and
Henry FRANCE of other part and County and parish aforesaid...for £80 Current
money of Virginia...161 acres on N^o. side South fork of Mayo River

and being part of a large Tract Taken up by Robert WALTON Deceased...beginning
at Mouth of a Small north Branch of said River...up said Branch, it being
Alexander VANDEGRIFFS Creek.
No witnesses
Rec: 28 Jul 1769   Jacob COX L.S.

DB 1, p.280 - ELLES from JONES   DEED, 20 Mar 1769
Robert JONES of Pittsylvania County in Virginia of one part and Joseph ELLES
of County and Colony aforesaid...for £60 Lawfull Money...164 acres on Both
sides the North fork Pig River, it Being part of a Survey of 320 acres the
Patent dated 6 Sep 1760.
Wit: William MURPHY, Francis BIRD
Rec: 28 Jul 1769   Robert JONES L.S.

DB 1, p.283 - STEWART Junr. from STEWART   DEED, 20 Apr 1769
James STEWART of County of Pittsylvania of one part and James STEWART Junior
of said County of other part...for £1 Current Money of Virginia...land now
being in his actual possession...100 acres being part of Tract of Land said
James STEWART now lives on...on Chesnut Creek and laid off of upper end of
said Tract...South side said Tract.
Wit: Samuel PATTERSON, John X RAMSEY, Robert R GRIMET
                          his mark   his mark
Rec: 28 Jul 1769   James STEWART L.S.

DB 1, p.286 - PATTEY from PATTEY   POWER OF ATTORNEY, 7 Dec 1768
James PATTEY of Barkly County in South Carrolina planter appoint my Trusty
and well beloved Friend Jessey PATTEY of County of Pittsylvania in Virginia
Black Smith my True and Lawfull Attorney to receive all Sums of Money or
Tobacco due to me within Colloney of Virginia...to Sell a Tract of Land left
me by Will of James PATTEY deceased...land on Nixes Creek.
Wit: James TALBOTT, John DOSS, Elizabeth DOSS, (other wit. illegible)
Rec: Illegible   James PATTY L.S.

DB 1, p.287 - PERKINS from BEAN   DEED, 25 Jul 1769
William BEAN of Pittsylvania County of one part and Nicholas PERKINS of said
County of other part...for £100 Current Money...650 acres on Both sides Mount-
ain Creek...on Jeremiah WALKERS line...crossing 2 Branches and the Creek.

Rec: 28 Jul 1769   William BEAN L.S.

DB 1, p.289 - HAIRSTONE from CLEMENT   DEED, 28 Jul 1769
Adam CLEMENT and Agness his wife of one part of County of Bedford and Robert
HAIRSTONE of same County of other part...for £100 Lawfull Money of Virginia...
200 acres at the fork of Runnetbag Creek a north branch of Irvin River...
crossing Otter Creek one of Forks of said Runnet Bag and Four branches.
No witnesses
Rec: 28 Jul 1769   Adam CLEMENT L.S.

DB 1, p.291 - RENTFROW from JONES   DEED, 20 Jul 1769
Thomas JONES of Pittsylvania County and Colony of Virginia of one part and
William RENTFROW Planter of County and Colony above said...for £80 Lawfull
Money of Virginia...140 acres on Runnett Bagg Creek...South side of Creek
aforesaid.

No witnesses   Thomas JONES L.S.
Rec: 28 Jul 1769
Mary, the wife, being privily Examined as Law Directs Relinquished her
right of Dower.

DB 1, p.293 - RICE from PERKINS   DEED, 20 Jul 1769
Peter PERKINS of Pittsylvania County of one part and John RICE of said County
of other...for £12·10 Current Money of Virginia...land on Both sides South
fork of Cascade Creek...125 acres taken out of a Survey of Land pattened for
said Peter PERKINS and containing 1,200 acres.
No witnesses
Rec: 28 Jul 1769   Peter PERKINS L.S.

DB 1, p.296 - HEARD from ATKINSON   BILL SALE, 8 May 1769
David ATKINS of County of Pittsylvania and Colony of Virginia do sell & make
over in open market to Jesse HIRD of County and Colony aforesaid...for £02·10:
Red and white Cow Name Silk and mark in Rite Ear a Crop and 2 Slits and in
Left Ear a Crop and under and over Keel.
                                his
Wit: Swinfel HILL, William /\/\ MOLLANS, Stephen HEARDY, John GRAHAMES
                                Mark

Rec: 28 Jul 1769   David ATKINS

DB 1, p.296 - KERBY from HILL   DEED, 14 Apr 1769
William HILL of Pittsylvania County Planter of one part and Francis KERBY of
other part...for £50 Current Money of Virginia...300 acres on Both sides of
Jonekin Creek...head of Little Jonakin...on Main Creek.
            his   his
Wit: W^m. JUSTICE, Jno. + HALL, John + KERBY
            Mark   Mark
Rec: 28 Jul 1769   William HILL L.S.

DB 1, p.298 - MORTON from PEAK   DEED, 20 Mar 1769
Robert PEAK of Parish of St. Patrick and County of Prince Edward of one part
and John MORTON of Parish Cambden and County of Pittsylvania of other part...
for £90 Current Money of Virginia...677 acres on both sides Sandy River...
along LUMKINS line...400 acres purchased by said PEAK from Richard WARMACK
by deed Recorded in Halifax Court and the Remainder granted to said PEAK by
Letters patent dated 24 Mar 1767.   her
Wit: P. CARRINGTEN, Jehu MORTON, George ROWLAND, Anne ──── TEN
                                              Mark   his
Proved 24 Jun 1769 and rec: 28 Jul 1769   Robert /R\ PEAK L.S.
                                                      marke

DB 1, p.301 - KEYSEE from COX   DEED, 26 May 1769
Samuel COX of County of Rowan in province of North Carolinia of one part
and Arther KEYSEE of County of Pittsylvania of other part...for £06·11
Current Money...12 1/2 acres.
Wit: William TUNSTALL, James STEVENSON, Thomas TUNSTALL, Crispin SHELTON
Prov: 28 Jul 1769 and further   his
proved and rec: 25 Aug 1769   Samuel + COX L.S.
                                                    mark

DB 1, p.303 - TUNSTALL from COX   DEED, 26 May 1769

Samuel COX of Rowan County in province of North Carolina of one part and

32.

Thomas TUNSTALL of Halifax County in Colony of Virginia of other part...for
£50 Current Money of Virginia...187 1/2 acres on Stinking River...part of
the Land purchased by said Samuel COX of James MC KINDREE deceased and ad-
joins Lands of Arther KEYSEE, Thomas FARRIS, William SHORT and Joseph LEWIS.

Wit: James STEVENSON, Will. TUNSTALL, Arthur / KESEE, Crispin SHELTON
                                            mark

Prv: 28 Jul 1769   his
Rec: 25 Aug 1769   Samuel X COX L.S.
                                                   Mark

DB 1, p.305 - VARDEMAN from COOK & wife   DEED, 24 Aug 1769
William COOK and Margaret his wife of Pittsylvania County and Colony of Virginia of one part and Peter VARDEMAN of County and Colony aforesaid...for
£35 Current Money of Virginia...50 acres on Both sides Pig River.
                                                    his
Wit: James RENTFROW, Joshua BARTON, Peter SAUNDERS, W^m. / TURPIN
                                                       mark

                                           William COOK L.S.
Rec: 25 Aug 1769   Margaret COOK L.S.

DB 1, p.307 - DALTON, Junr. from DALTON   DEED, 24 Aug 1769
John DALTON of County of Pittsylvania of one part and Robert DALTON Junior of
same County of other part...for £25 Current Money of Virginia...45 acres on
Both Sides Pig River...in William ATKINSONS Line...in Lewis POTTERS line.
                       his   his
Wit: James MITCHELL, James X BOBIT, David X DALTON
                            mark   mark
Rec: 25 Aug 1769   John DALTON L.S.

DB 1, p.310 - SMITH & Co. from BISWELL   TRUST DEED, 12 Aug 1769
John BISWELL of Pittsylvania County of one part and James SMITH & Company
of other part...Jno. BISWELL is Justly Indebted for sum £65,Honestly desires
to pay...Two Tracts of Land...first of 150 acres on Wet Sleave Creek where
said BISWELL now Lives, the other the Lower part of that Tract of 303 acres
whereon Richard PRUET Lives containing 153 acres., Both Tracts was Bought of
Thomas WATKINS of Bedford County. Also three Entrys or Surveys of Land, the
first a Joning the first mentioned Tract on Wet Sleave bought of William
ROBERTS, the other a Joning the other mentioned Tracks Bought of Robert
WOODING Containing 409 acres the Last a Jonining the uper part of first Men-
tioned Track Bought of Abraham PERSLEY...after 1 Sep 1772...Sell for Best
Price after Ten Days Publick Notice...out of Money arising from Sale dis-
charge themselves the above sum of £65 with Interest.
Wit: Jno. MORTON, James BREWER, _____ DURHAM
Rec: 25 Aug 1769   John BISWELL L.S.

DB 1, p.313 - LAYNE from TERRELL   DEED, 31 Mar 1769
David TERRELL of County of Louisa of one part and Dutton LANE of County of
Pittsylvania of other part...for £15 Current money of Virginia...275 acres
on Both sides Mountain Creek...Beginning at John CARGILS and Samuel HARRISONS
Line on said Creek...David TERRELL and Sarah his Wife Sett their hands and
Seals...   his   his
Wit: William WILLIAMS, Joseph P POLLEY, Peter X POLLEY
                        Mark   Mark
Rec: 25 Aug 1769   David TERRELL L.S.

DB 1, p.316 - BOULTON from JINKINS   DEED, 25 Aug 1769
Lewis JINKES Of Pittsylvania County of one part and Robert BOULTON of same
County of other part...for £250 Current Money of Virginia...1,200 acres on
Both sides Pig River...on Jacob HUBBARDS Line...on the patent Line to Pig
River, up River to order Line, on their order Line to ?dinner Creek, down the
Creek to Pig River, up River and Cross to Captain ANNESES Line, on his Line
to James DANIELS line, on his to Benjamin POTTERS line...crossing William
WEBB line...crossing James DANIELS line on his line to Isham HALLS Line.
No witnesses   his
                                          Lewis   JENKINS L.S.
Rec: 25 Aug 1769   Mark

DB 1, p.318 - TALBOT from KERBY   DEED, 22 Jun 1769
Francis KERBY of Pittsylvania County Planter of one part and Charles TALBOT
of Bedford County...for £80 Current Money of Virginia...100 acres on Pig
River...Beginning on North side of Pigg River...in John KERBYS Line.
No witnesses
Rec: 25 Aug 1769
Elizabeth, wife of Francis, Privily Examined
and Relinquished her right of Dower   Francis KERBY L.S.

DB 1, p.320 - SAUNDERS from ANDERSON   DEED, 6 Mar 1769
Thomas ANDERSON of County of Pittsylvania of one part and Peter SAUNDERS of
same County of other part...for £35 Current Money of Virginia...130 acres on
Little Otter Branch of Arvin River...crossing said Creek...South fork of
Otter Creek.
Wit: Robert HAIRSTON, Robert JONES, William STROTHER, Peter HAIRSTONE
                                               his
Proved: 28 Jul 1769 and further proved and   Thomas A. ANDERSON L.S.
Rec: 25 Aug 1769   Mark

DB 1, p.323 - CHILTON from CREEL   DEED, 22 Aug 1769
John CREEL and Rhody his wife of Pittsylvania County of the one and Thomas
CHILTON of same County of other Part...for £20 Current Money of Virginia...
198 acres on Branches of Burches Creek...Branch in PRISLAYS line...in CAMSES
line...at the Road.
                      his
Wit: Champ TERRY, Charles X CHILTON, William LYNCH, Abner SMITH
                      mark

                                          John CREEL L.S.
                                               her
                                     Rhody R CREEL L.S.
Rec: 25 Aug 1769   Mark

DB 1, p.326 - BISWELL from WATKINS   DEED, 25 Aug 1769
Thomas WATKINS of County of Bedford of one Part and John BISWELL of County
of Pittsylvania of other Part...for £35 Current Money of Virginia...Two Tracts
of Land one Lying on Both sides Wet Sleave Creek...150 acres...other Tract
Lying on Both sides aforesaid Wet Sleave Creek and Strawberry Creek and contains 153 acres...Beginning at Ashford HUGHES's Corner...to Richard PRUITS
corner.
Wit: James SMITH, William SMITH, Frances KERBY
Rec: 25 Aug 1769   Thomas WATKINS L. S.

DB 1, p.328 - MEDKIFF from MEDKIFF   DEED, 23 Aug 1769
Joseph MEDKIFF of Halifax County in Colony of Virginia of one part and James
MEDKIFF of Cambden Parish in County of Pittsylvania of other part...for £20
Current Money of Virginia...land on Both sides Elkhorn Creek it being part
of Two Tracts granted said Joseph MEDKIFF by Patents, Beginning at John
MEDKIFFS corner...to Joseph MIDKIFFS, Junr. Corner...crossing Elkhorn Creek...
321 acres.
Wit: Archelius HUGHES, John WIMBUSH, John MEDKIFF   his
                                                   Joseph + MIDKIFF L.S.
Rec: 25 Aug 1769   Mark

DB 1, p.331 - DYER from HODGES   DEED, 14 Feb 1769
Welcom William HODGES and Mary his wife of Pittsylvania County of one part
and Elisha DYER of said County of other part...100 acres on South Side Bann-
ister River...in MURPHEYS line on south side Bannister River...for £30
Current Money.
                                        his   her
Wit: William SHORT, William ADDAMS, Edm^d. X HODGES, Sarah X HODGES
                                        mark   Mark
Rec: 25 Aug 1769   Welcom W^m. HODGES L.S.
                                                     Mary HODGES L.S.

DB 1, p.334 - MEDKIFF from MEDKIFF   DEED, 23 Aug 1769
Joseph MEDKIFF of County of Halifax in Colony of one part and John MEDKIFF
of parish of Cambden in County of Pittsylvania and Colony of Virginia of
other part...for £20 Current money of Virginia...land on both sides Elkhorn
Creek and being part of Two Tracts granted to said Joseph MEDKIFF by patents...
100 acres of Land.
                                         his
Wit: John WIMBUSH, Archelius HUGHES, James + MEDKIFF
                                         mark
                                                    his
                                            Joseph + MEDKIFF L.S.
Rec: 25 Aug 1769   Mark

DB 1, p.337 - SHORT from HODGES   DEED, 14 Feb 1769
Welcom William HODGES and Mary his wife of Pittsylvania County of one part
and William SHORT of aforesaid county of other part...100 acres on north side
Banister River...for £35 Current Money...beginning at Mouth of said HODGES
Spring Branch, up said Branch to MURPHYS line, along MURPHEYS line to Edmond
HODGES corner in MURPHEYS line, along HODGES line to the River.
                                   her
Wit: Elisha DYER, William ADDAME, Amy X DYER
                                   mark
                                              Welcom W. HODGES L.S.
Rec; 25 Aug 1769   Mary HODGES L.S.

DB 1, p.341 - CREEL from WALTON   DEED, 15 Jun 1769
Sherwood WALTON of Charlotte County of one part and John CREEL of Pittsylvania
of other part...for £60 Current Money of Virginia...300 acres on both sides
Ivain/Irain River...on an Ivey Hill...crossing flat Creek.
Wit: Thos. DILLARD, Junr., Champ. TERRY, William LYNCH, David TERRY
Prv.: 28 Jul 1769 and further prv.and
                                                           d
Rec: 25 Aug 1769   Sher^d. WALTON L.S.

DB 1, p.344 - YUILLE, MURDOCK & Co. from SMITH   TRUST DEED, 22 Nov 1768

William SMITH of Pittsylvania County of one part and Thomas YUILLE, James
MURDOCK & Company of other part...for £80 Current Money of Virginia which
said William SMITH is Justly indebted to them and honestly desires to Secure
and pay to them...further sum of 5s like Money to said William SMITH paid
by said Thomas YUILLE, James MURDOCK & Co...sell to said YUILLE, MURDOCK &
Co.: negroe Winch named Judith, negroe Girl named Feanny and said Judiths
child named Philes; 2 feather beds and furniture, 2 chests, 4 Iron potts,
womans and mans Saddle, all household furniture...YUILLE, MURDOCK & Co.
after 1 Sep 1771 to sell for best price after 10 days publick Notice...with
Interest from 1 Dec 1769.

Wit: Joseph ECHOLS, James SMITH, Obediah his / mark   COLLINS

Rec: 25 Aug 1769   William SMITH L.S.

DB 1, p.347 - SMITH from KERBY   DEED, 25 Aug 1769

Francis KERBY and Elizabeth his wife of Pittsylvania County of one part and
Peyton SMITH of same County of other part...for £97 Current money...100 acres
on South side Pig River...Beginning East side Snow Creek...mouth of Snow
Creek, then up said Creek.
Wit: Bryan Ward NOWLIN, Steven BINNITT
Rec: 25 Aug 1769
Elizabeth, wife of KERBY, privily Examined and   Francis KERBY L.S.
Relinquished her right of Dower   Elizabeth KERBY L.S.

DB 1, p.349 - REAVES from STEGALL   DEED, 30 Mar 1769

George STEAGELL and his wife Agness STEAGALL of County of Brumswick of one
part and Fredrick REAVES of other part in County of Pittsylvania...for £150
Current Money of Virginia...5,400 acres it being all the Land that we Fredrick
REAVES and George STEGALL bought of Robert WEAKLY lying on both sides Pigg
River.

Wit: Abner COCKERHAM, Jn°. his ‡ mark   LAW, Senr., Jn°. LAW, Junr.
Prv.: 28 Jul 1769 & further prv. and   George his X Mark   STEAGALL L.S.
Rec: 25 Aug 1769

DB 1,p.350 - MUTER from WALLER   TRUST DEED, 21 Jul 1769

Zachariah WALLER of County of Pittsylvania of one part and George MUTER of
County of Halifax of other part...for £32·07·08 Current Money of Virginia in
which said Zackariah WALLER stands Justly indebted to said George MUTER and
desires to Honestly pay him and for further Consideration of 5s Current Money
paid by MUTER ...sell to George MUTER negro man named Bristol living at said
WALLERS plantation in Pittsylvania County...after 1 Nov 1769 sell by Publick
Auction said negroe man to Satisfy Debt with interest at 5% per annum from
1 Nov next ensuing...give WALLER 10 days notice of such sale and pay said
WALLER over plus money from such Sale.

Wit: William DOUGLASS, Joseph BROWN, Samuel his Mark   LEWIS

                   Zachariah his / Mark   WALLER L.S.

Rec: 25 Aug 1769

DB 1, p.352 - BEAMS from DUNKIN   DEED, 23 Aug 1769
Benjamin DUNKIN of county of Pittsylvania of one part and William BEAMS of
said county of other part...for £40 Current Money of Virginia...229 acres in
his actual possession now being, on Blackwater River...Beginning at MEADS
Corner...along MEADS line...in Stephen HERD line. Being land said Benjamin
DUNKIN Bought of Stephen HERD and granted to said HERD by Patent dated
31 Oct 1765.
Wit: John FORD, Junr., John COOK, Joseph COOK   his
                                                    Benjamin $\int$ DUNKIN L.S.
Rec: 25 Aug 1769   Mark

DB 1, p.355 - CHELTON from CREEL   DEED, 22 Aug 1769
John CREEL and Rhody his wife of Pittsylvania County of one part and Charles
CHELTON of other part...for £20 Current Money of Virginia...202 acres on
branches of Burches and Sandy Creek...to CAMPS corner.

                                                                his
Wit: Champ. TERRY, William LYNCH, Abner SMITH, Thos. $\int$ $\int$ CHILTON
                                                                mark

                                                    John CREEL   L.S.

                                                      her
                                              Rhody $\bigwedge$ CREEL L.S.
Rec: 25 Aug 1769   mark

DB 1, p.358
D^r. the Estate of Paul PIGG Dec^d. - from Dec 1767 to Jan 1769 - in Acc^t. with
Henry MC DANIEL. Paid: Jno. WIMBISHE; Richard PIGG; Jno. PIGG for 5 Bushells
wheat for Estates use; Richard FARTHING per Mr. ROBERTS order for carage of
ahhd. of Estates Tob^a..; Henry PREWET for covering a corn house and Seting up
6 Tob^a. Hh^{ds}.; Thomas HARDY Junr. for Wheat; Peter GREENSTREET for Building
2 Tob^a. houses; Allen ADAMS for fodder and Making 3 pair Shoes; William
GRIFFITH for making a plow; Agness NICHOLDS for Sundrys; Capt. Benj. LANKFORD
per A. SHELTON; Mr. TUNSTALL Clk. for Recording the will of Mr. Paul PIGGS
Decd.; James PIGG for Corn for Estates use; Jno. ADAMS overseer boarding himself,
William WRIGHT for Smiths work done for Plantation use; William PIGG for Rye;
expenses in Roling down hhd. Tob^a.; Edmond PENDELTON for defending a Suit
Brought against the Estate by Jno. PIGG; Cow bell, Bacon, Rye, Shoe Leather;
Col^o. Thomas TABBS order; Joseph PREWET for Making Shoes. Total: £108·16·01/2.
C^r. the Estate of Paul PIGG from 18 Feb 1769 to 22 May 1769 - Tob^a. at War-
wick; William PIGG; Tob^a. at Blandford in name of Jno. ADAMS; Inspecters at
OSBORNS; Hugh HENRY; Henry PREWET; Agness NICHOLDS; Richard PIGG; William
TUNSTALL; Jno. FLOYD; Jno. ADAMS; William PIGG, Jno. JONES. Total: £95·18·112
Rec: 25 Aug 1769   By Ballance due......£12·15·1

DB 1, p.361 - HALL from HALL   DEED, 25 Oct 1769
Icam HALL of Pittsylvania County of one part and John HALL of other part...
for £15 Current Money of Virginia...100 acres on South side Pig River.
No witnesses
Rec: 27 Oct 1769   Icam HALL L.S.

DB 1, p.363 - COPLAND from RICHARDSON   DEED, 30 Aug 1769
Landey RICHARDSON and Sarah his wife of one part and Peter COPLAND of County
of Pittsylvania of other part...for £60 Current Money of Virginia...450
acres...crossing main Branch of Daniels Mill Creek...on same old line.
Wit: John WELLS, Jo^s. SHELTON, Thomas COOPER, j^r., William COPLAND
Rec: 27 Oct 1769   Landie RICHARDSON L.S.
                                              Sarah RICHARDSON   L.S.

DB 1. p.365 - ECKHOLS from MURPHEY   DEED, 16 Apr 1769
William MURPHEY of Augusta County in Virginia of one part and Jacob ECKHOLS
of County of Bedford and Colony of Virginia of other part...for £15 lawfull
money...113 acres on both sides north fork of Gobbintown Creek...land being
first Conveyed from Isham BARNET the patent dated 10 Sep 1755.

Wit: Jeremiah ⟋ MORROW, Dorrity 𝒟 MURROW, Tully CHOICE
             his mark   her mark
Rec: 27 Oct 1769   William MURPHEY L.S.

DB 1, p.367 - CROWLEY from COX   DEED, 26 Jan 1770
John COX, Son and heir at Law of William COX deceased, of one part and Benjamin CROWLEY of County of Pittsylvania of one part...for £15 Current Money
of Virginia...300 acres on both sides South fork of Sandy River...Beginning
at Thomas GRISHAMS...crossing two branches...in GRAYS line.
No witnesses
Rec: 26 Jan 1770   John COX L.S.

DB 1, p.369 - HARDY from HARDY   DEED, 23 Jan 1770
John HARDEY of County of Pittsylvania within Colony of Virginia to Thomas
HARDEY of county aforesaid...for £50 good and Lawfull money of Virginia...
330 acres on Drafts of Banister River...Beginning on HARDEYS corner...in
FINNES line...paying unto John HARDEY the rent of one ear of Indain Corn
at the feast of the nativity of Blessed Lord and Saveow Jesus Christ next
ensuing if same be Lawfully Demanded.
No witnesses   his
Rec: 26 Jan 1770   John ⟋ HARDY L.S.
Martha, wife of said John, Relinquished   Mark
her right of Dower

DB 1, p.371 - CANESTER from CANTEBERRY   DEED, 12 Sep 1769
Samuel CANTERBRUARY and wife Elizabeth of County of Pittsylvania of one part
and Mathius CANESTER of said county of other part...for £40 Current Money of
Virginia...200 acres on Irland Creek...Beginning upon the Rode and new div-
iding line...Deed that I got of Benjamin JINKINS out of the old order joining
Federeck REAVES.
                             his   Samuel CANTERBUARY L.S.
Wit: Abner CORKERHAM, Jnᵒ. ⟋ LAW,   her
?Harman COOK   mark   Elizabeth ✗ CANTERBUARY L.S.
Rec: 26 Jan 1770 and Elizabeth wife of   mark
Samᵗ. CANTERBERY, Relinquished her right of Dower

DB 1, p.373 - INNES BOND FOR COLECTING TOBᵒ.   27 Jan 1770
Know all men by these presents that we Hugh INNES and ISaace READ, Gent. are
bound to Justices of Pittsylvania County in sum of 32,540 pounds of Nett Tobacco...above bound Hugh INNES hath this day been appointed by said Justices
to Receave all the Tobacco levied in the publick proportion for said County
in the year 1769 for use of same...after deducting 5% for his Trouble in
Collecting same.
Wit: Will. TUNSTALL   Hugh INNES L.S.
Rec: 27 Jan 1770   Isaace READ L.S.

DB 1, p.374 - HUGHES from HARRIS   DEED, 26 Sep 1769
Samuel HARRIS of County of Pittsylvania of one part and John WIMBUSH and
Archelius HUGHES of said County of other part...for £20 Current Money of Vir-

ginia...160 acres on Both sides Spoon Creek it being the Land granted said
Samuel HARRIS by Patent dated 22 Sep 1766...in MILLERS line...crossing two
branches.
Wit: Theop^s. LACEY, James CANAWAY, Joseph TERRY, Abraham SHELTON
Rec: 23 Feb 1770   Samuel HARRIS L.S.

DB 1, p.376 - HARDY from ADAMS   DEED,?4 Feb 1770
John ADAMS of Pittsylvania County and John HARDEY of County of Pittsylvania...
for £27 good and Lawfull Money of Virginia...314 acres on both sides Pollas
Branch of Banister River...Beginning at Francis LUCKS corner.
No witnesses   his
Rec: 23 Feb 1770   John X ADAMS L.S.
Elizabeth, wife of said John, privily   Mark
Examined and Relinquished her right   her
of Dower   Eliz^a. X ADAMS L.S.
                                                     Mark

DB 1,p.378 - HANLEY from BEAMS   DEED, 30 Jan 1770
William BEAMS of County of Pittsylvania of one part and Peter HANLEY of same
County of other part...for £43 Current Money of Virginia...229 acres now in
his actual possession, on black water River...Beginning at MEADS Corner...in
Stephen HERDS line.   his
Wit: Hugh INNES, Shem COOK, Ja^S. COOK   William X BEAMS L.S.
Rec: 23 Feb 1770 & Elizabeth relinquishes dower   mark

DB 1, p.381 - EASTIS from MORROW   DEED, 29 Jan 1770
Jeremiah MORROW and Darraty his wife of County of Pittsylvania and Colony of
Virginia of one part and William ESTES of County and Colony aforesaid...for
£150 Current Money of Virginia...266 acres part of 800 acres granted to David
COLWELL 10 Apr 1751...along Patent lines...crossing Snow Creek...to Tulley
CHOICES...crossing Snow Creek Dividing above Land from said CHOICES.
                                                     his
Wit: Hugh INNES, Tulley CHOICE, W^m. HALL, Elisha F EASTES
                                                     Mark
Rec: 23 Feb 1770   his
Dorothy, wife of said Jeremiah, privily   Jeremiah F MURROW L.S.
Examined and Relinquished her right   Mark
of Dower   her
                                              Darraty D MURROW L.S.
                                                     Mark

DB 1, p.383 - TARRANT from TARRANT   DEED, 28 Oct 1769
Leonard TARRANT of County of Amherst of one part and Benjamin TARRANT of
County of Pittsylvania of other part...for and in Consideration of paternal
Love and affection which he bears to said Benjamin TARRANT but more expec-
ially for sum of 5s Current money of Virginia...685 acres on both sides
Lynches Creek and South Side Stanton River...at RANDOLPHS Corner...crossing
a Branch.
Wit: James MITCHELL, W^m. WITCHER, Robert DALTON   his
                                              Leonard Z TARRANT L.S.
Rec: 23 Feb 1770   mark

DB 1, p.386 - HALL from CHOICE   DEED, 23 Feb 1770
Tully CHOICE of County of Pittsylvania of one part and William HALL of said
County and Elizabeth his wife of other part...in consideration of natural

Love and affection which he hath and Beareth to said William HALL and Elizabeth his wife as also for better mantinance livelyhood and Preferment of
them...land on both sides Snow creek in Pittsylvania County, being part of
400 acres granted said Turlley CHOICE by Letters Patent dated 15 Sep 1765...
pointers in old Line...Crossing a Branch...crossing pickings Creek...200 acres.
No witnesses
Rec: 23 Feb 1770   Tulley CHOICE L.S.
Elizabeth, wife of Tully CHOICE, privily
Examined as Law directs and Relinquished her right of Dower

DB 1, p.388 - CRIST from MURROW   DEED, 16 Feb 1770
Jeremiah MURROW of County of Pittsylvania of one part and Henry CRIST of said
County of other part...for £35 Current Money of Virginia...260 acres now in
his actual possession by Virtue of a Bargain and Sale...on KEATONS Creek of
Snow Creek...Beginning where RANDOLPHS Line corners at pointers in KEATONS
Line...to HERDS line...in COLWELLS Line...along Joseph KEATONS line.
Wit: Hugh INNES
Rec: 23 Feb 1770   his
Dorothy, wife of said Jeremiah, Relinquished   Jeremiah ⟋ MURROW L.S.
her right of Dower   Mark

DB 1, p.391 - CREEL from CORNWELL   DEED, 12 Aug 1769
Peter CORNWELL and Sarah Ann his wife of County of Fauquier in Colony of Virginia of one part and Jn°. CREEL of County of Pittsylvania and Colony of Virginia of other part...for £20 Current Money of Virginia...Land on both sides
Mine   Branch and was Granted to said Peter CORNWELL by Letters Patent dated
2 Sep 1766...300 acres.

            his   his   his   her
Wit: Jn°. ⟋ BENNETT, Alex ᴿ. ⟋ LEE, William ⟋ BENNETT, Agathey ⟋ CREEL
           mark   mark   mark   mark
                                            Peter CORNWELL L.S.

                                                  her
                                       Sarah Ann ⟋ CORNWELL L.S.
Rec: 23 Feb 1770   mark

DB 1, p.394 - ROWLAND from RICHARDSON   DEED, 30 Aug 1769
Landey RICHARDSON of County of Louisa and Sarah his wife of one part and
John ROWLAND of County of Pittsylvania of other part...for £90 Current money
of Virginia...450 acres...upper end of an Island in Irvin River...nigh the
Creek called Daniels Mill Creek in old Line; along old Line...crossing said
Daniels Mill Creek at mouth of it.
Wit: William STEGER, Daniel BAILEY, Joseph AKIN, Peter COPLAND, William
COPLAND, Jn°. WELLS, Jaˢ. SHELTON, Thomas COOPER, Junior
                                        Landie RICHARDSON L.S.
Rec: 23 Feb 1770   Sarah RICHARDSON L.S.

DB 1, p.396 - PARR from PERKINS   DEED, 21 Mar 1770
Charles PERKINS of County of Roann of one part and John PARR, Junʳ. of County
of Pittsylvania of other part...for £40 Current money of Virginia...Land on
Russels Creek...South side creek...200 acres.
Wit: Archˢ. HUGHES, Fredrick FULKERSON, John PARR
Rec: 23 Mar 1770   Charles PURKINS L.S.

DB 1, p.399 - BOSTICK from COX   DEED, 23 Mar 1769
John COX of County of Pittsylvania of one part and Nathan BOSTICK of County

aforesaid of other part...for £10 Current Money of Virginia...250 acres on
both Sides Sandey River, which was granted to said John COX by patent dated
1760...beginning at Abraham ARDENS corner.
No witnesses
Rec: 23 Mar 1770   John COX L.S.

DB 1, p.401 - GIDIANE from CHADWELL   DEED, 23 Mar 1770
David CHADWELL of Pittsylvania County of one part and Richard GIDIANE of other
part...for £55...237 acres on both sides Beens Creek...crossing a Branch...
crossing said creek three times.   his
Wit: ISaace READ, Jnº. WIMBUSH   David X CHADWELL L.S.
Rec: 24 Mar 1770   mark

DB 1, p.403 - COX from FULKERSON   DEED, 29 Jan 1770
Fulker FULKERSON of County of Halifax of one part and Jacob COX of County of
Pittsylvania of other part...for £22 Current Money of Virginia...land on
Green Creek Beginning at Fredrick FULKERSONS upper corner upon South Mao Riv-
er...crossing the Creek to James ROBERTS Lower line...119 1/2 acres.

                                                 his   s
Wit: Jesse WOODSON, Fredrick FULKERSON, Samuel X COX, Arch . HUGHES,
                                                 mark

George GRAY
Rec: 23 Mar 1770   Fulker FULKERSON L.S.

DB 1, p.405 - COLLINSWORTH from ROBERTS   DEED, 1769
James ROBERTS of Cambden Parish in Pittsylvania County of one part and James
COLLINSWORTH Late of same County and Parrish of other part...for £35 Current
Money of Virginia...250 acres on North fork of Chesnutt Creek...Crossing a
Branch...crossing the Creek.
Wit: Jnº. SALMON, Andrew GIBSON; Abraham ERN
Rec: 23 Mar 1770
Elizabeth, wife of James ROBERTS, Relinquished   James ROBERTS L.S.
her right of Dower   Elizabeth ROBERTS L.S.

DB 1, p.408 - YUILLE, MURDOCK & CO. from FARRIS   TRUST DEED, 19 Aug 1769
Joseph FARRIS of Pittsylvania County of one part and Thomas YUILLE, James
MURDOCK & Company of other part...for £62·01·01 1/2 Current Money of Virginia
which said Joseph FARRIS is Justly indebted to said YUILLE & MURDOCK & Co.
and honestly desires to pay them...for further sum of 5s Like money to said
Joseph FARRIS paid by YUILLE, MURDOCK & Co...Sells to them: 2 horses, 3 mares,
Colt, 15 head of Cattle, 8 head Sheap, about 20 hoggs, the cattle, Sheap and
hoggs are Marked with a Smooth Crop in Left ear and a Swallow fork in Right;
4 feather beds and furniture and every other Article of household furniture
or personal Estate...YUILLE, MURDOCK & Co. after 1 Aug 1772 sell for best
price after 10 day publick notice and out of money arising from Sale discharge
pay and Satisfy themselves above sum with Lawfull interest from date of these
presents til fully discharged...pay overplus to said Joseph FARRIS.
Wit: John SMITH, Joseph ECHOLS, Charles COBBS   his
                                                 Joseph F FARRIS L.S.
Rec: 23 Mar 1770   mark

DB 1, p.410 - DONALD & Co. from MANKIN   TRUST DEED, 27 Feb 1770
I, James MANKIN of Bedford County having this day came to a Settlement of
Accounts with Jnº. HOOK for dealings heretofore with him on Account of

William DONALD Junior & Company Merchants in north Brittain and such Settlement failing in arear...just sum of £88·09·02 Current Money of Virginia and
being truly desireous to do said DONALD & Co. justice and secure them said
sum with lawfull interest...further sum of 5s paid by said John HOOK...do
sell to said John HOOK for said William DONALD & Co. 400 acres on both sides
Straight Stone Creek, 200 acres of which I lately purchased of Richard
DICKENS and other 200 acres of James YOUNG Senr., Like wise two negroe fell-
ows both named Tom...DONALD & Co. after 27 Feb 1771 dispose of after giving
10 days notice and pay over plus from sale.
Wit: Edmond WINSTON, RWILLIAMS, John AYLETT

Rec: 23 Mar 1770   James MANKIN L.S.

DB 1,p.412 - CHALLES from COX   DEED, 23 Mar 1770
John COX of County of Pittsylvania and Mary his wife of one part and Hugh
CHALLES of said County of other part...for £100 Current Money of Virginia...
680 acres now in Tenure and Occupation of said CHALLES...north side Wolfden
Branch...crossing three branches.
No witnesses   John COX L.S.
Prv: 23 Mar 1770 and Rec: 27 Aug 1772
Mary, wife of John COX, came into Court and relinquished her right of Dower.

DB 1, p.414 - DIX from WYNNE   DEED TRUST, 30 Oct 1769
Thomas WYNNE, Senr. of County of Pittsylvania of one part and John DIX Merchant of other part...Thomas WYNNE justly indebted to said John DIX in Sum
of £5 Current Money of Virginia and is willing and Deserose to Secure said
sum to DIX...further consideration of £70 Current Money..Sells to DIX 165
acres as p^r. deed...DIX shall at end of 6 months after date of these presence
sell land for most that can be got...pay and Satisfy himself aforesaid sum
with Lawfull Interest...overplus to be paid to said WYNNE.
Wit: Thomas DUNCAN, Ambrose JONES, James   his
SHELTON, Joseph SMITH   Thomas __ WYNNE L.S.
Rec: 23 Feb 1770, further prv: 23 Mar 1770   mark

DB 1, p.416 - CALLAWAY from CALLAWAY, Junr.   DEED, 22 Sep 1769
William CALLAWAY of County of Bedford of one part and William CALLAWAY Junior
of said County of other part...William CALLAWAY Senr. for £500 Current Money
of Virginia...450 acres on Both sides Pigg River...crossing two branches...
Top of a Hill.
Wit: Edmond WINSTON, John COX, Jno. AYLETT, Hugh INNES
Rec: 23 Mar 1770   William CALLAWAY L.S.

DB 1, p.419 - COX from COX   DEED, 9 Oct 1769
James COX of Pittsylvania County of one part and William COX of said County
of other part...for £50 Current Money...100 acres on both sides South fork
Sandey River...corner of John STRONGS...crossing a branch...crossing south
fork of Sandey River.
Wit: Richard FARRAR, James WADE, John STRONG, John COX
Rec: 23 Mar 1770   James COX L.S.

DB 1, p.421 - ROSS from BOBBIT   DEED, 1 Sep 1769
William BOBBIT and Nancey his wife of one part of Pittsylvania County and
David ROSS of County of Goochland of other part...for £15 Current Money of
Virginia...land on both sides Frying Pan Creek being the place commonly known

by name of BOBBITS Mill Seat...and on James WALDROPS line, up a branch,
along said WALDROPS line as far as said BOBBITS Land and so along old line
to SUTTONS as far as it extends to old line...12 acres...ROSS may cut timber
(board Stuff) excepted from said BOBBITS Land for use of said Mill.

Wit: Jonathan JENNINGS, Dav^d. WALKER, John BOBBIT, Joseph ┼ LAW
                                                      his
                                                     mark

Rec: 23 Mar 1770   William BOBBIT L.S.
Nancy, wife of said William, privily   her
Examined as Law directs Relinquished   Nancey ─┼─ BOBBIT L.S.
her right of Dower   mark

DB 1, p.423 - ROBERTS BOND FOR COLLECTING TOB^o.   24 Mar 1770
James ROBERTS, John DONELSON, Abraham SHELTON and William TUNSTALL are bound
unto our Sovereign Lord the king his heirs and Successors in Penalty of
31,600 Pounds of Tobacco...Condition of above obligation is such that if
above James ROBERTS G^t. will and Truly Collect from each Tithable Person in
this county sum of 9 Pounds of Tobacco per Poll...account with Court.
                                             James ROBERTS   L.S.
                                             John DONELSON   L.S.
                                             Abraham SHELTON L.S.
Rec: 24 Mar 1770   William TUNSTALL L.S.

DB 1, p.424 - DODSON from BENNETT   DEED, 21 Sep 1768
Peter BENNETT and Frances his wife of one part and Hannah DODSON of Pittsylvania County of other part...for £40 Current Money of Virginia...150 acres
on South side Pigg River it being part of tract of 300 acres granted to William ROYSDON by patent dated 30 Aug 1763 and since sold to Peter BENNET by
William ROYSDON...have set our hands and Seals this 21 Sep 1769.

                      r   his
Wit: John GOAD, Sen . , Robert ℛ GOAD, Abraham GOAD
                                mark
                                               Peter BENNET L.S.
Rec: 23 Feb 1770 and further prv.   her
23 Mar 1770   Frances ─┴─ BENNET L.S.
                                             mark

DB 1, p.426 - STONE from CHADWELL   DEED, 22 Mar 1770
John CHADWELL, Bethunia CHADWELL of Pittsylvania County of one part and Henry
STONE of said county of other part...for £45 Current Money of Virginia...John
CHADWELL and Bethunia his wife...190 acres on South side Dan River...at
PERKINS Lower corner...crossing two Branches...in KESTERSONS line.
No witnesses   John CHADWELL   L.S.
Rec: 23 Mar 1770   Bethunia CHADWELL L.S.
Bethenia, wife of John CHADWELL, Relinquished her right of Dower

DB 1, p.429 - HENDERSON Senr. from HARBOUR   DEED, 22 Sep 1769
Elisha HARBOUR of County of Pittsylvania of one part and Thomas HENDERSON
Senior of County aforesaid of other part...for £35 Virginia Money...150 acres
on both sides Irvin River...beginning at Charles WHITS.
Wit: Edmond WINSTON, Jno. COX, Hugh INNES
No rec. date   Elisha HARBOUR L.S.

DB 1, p.432 - STINNET from CREEL   DEED, 29 Nov 1769
Jno. CREEL of County of Pittsylvania in Colony of Virginia of one part and
Benjamin STINNET of County and Colony aforesaid of other part...Land on both

sides Irvin River containing by Letters patent 150 acres...against Mouth of
flat Creek...received £40 Current Money of Virginia.
Wit: Timothy STAMPS, Jn°. STAMPS, Thomas STAMPS
Rec: 23 Mar 1770   John CREEL L.S.
Rosana, wife of John, privily Examined and Relinquished her right of Dower

DB 1, p.433 - FIELD & CALL from MARR   TRUST DEED, 17 Oct 1769

Gidian MARR of County of Pittsylvania of one part and FIELD & CALL of Prince
George County Merchants of other part...for £79·16·01 Current Money of Virginia...400 acres being Tract whereon said MARR now lives lying on main
markett Road and on Lower fork of beens Creek; Also five Negroe slaves Named
Tom, Dinah and her Children Pleasant, Step and Daniel with their future Increase. Shall pay with interest on or before Last day of February next Ensuing 1770...to Sell for best price and pay to MARR the Residue of Money
arising from sale after paying Theophilus FIELD and William CALL.
Wit: Edward WADE, George BOYD, Junr., Daniel CALL, Junr., Jn°. FOWLER
Rec: 23 Mar 1770   G. MARR L.S.

DB 1, p.437 - ADAMS from PREWETT   DEED, 22 Mar 1770

Henry PREWET and his wife Rebaca of County and Parrish of Pittsylvania of
one part and Allen ADAMS of County aforesaid of other part...for £38 Current
Money of Virginia...100 acres on Bannester River it being part of Tract of
354 acres granted to said PREWET by patent dated 7 Jul 1763.
No witnesses   his
                                             Henry ⚬   PREWETT L.S.
                                                  mark
Rec: 23 Mar 1770   her
Rebacca, wife of said PREWETT, being Privily
Examined, Relinquished her right of Dower   Rebacca / PREWETT L.S.
                                                  mark

DB 1, p.439

Order of Court of County of Pittsylvania William EDWARDS, James EDWARDS and
Julius SCRUGGS appointed to Appraise the Estate of Elijah HARBOUR Dec^d. and
after being Sworn have appraised the following Articles: Stock of Hogs,
Sundrey Cattle, 3 horses, pair Shears, Shoe Makers Tools, Carpenters Tools,
Reap Hook, pair Wedges, hackle, 3 axes, 2 Razors, Lumber, parcel pewter,
Earthen ware, pair wool cards, box Iron and 3 heaters, Sugar Box, 2 potts
and hooks, 2 pails, Churn, frying pann, plow hoe, hilling hoe, 2 Spinning
wheles, parcel books, 2 Sack bags, Bed and furniture, Side Saddle. Total:
£57·18·06. Given under our hands 11 Dec 1769.

                                                         Julius SCRUGGS
                                                              his
                                                      James —/— EDWARDS
                                                             mark
Rec: 23 Mar 1770   William EDWARDS

DB 1, p.440   29 Apr 1770

We the Subscribers have met and Appraised the Estate of Samuel NOWLING Decd.
as follows: Roan horse, Suit Cloaths, old great coat and hatt, pair Stock-
ings, pair old bretches Shirts and Jackett, Coopers adds and Center Bitt,
pair Shoe Buckles, Mans Saddle and Bridle, pair Shoes. Total: £16.
                                                         Benjamin TURRANT
                                                         Jeremiah WARD
Rec: 25 May 1770   Edward WADE

44.

DB 1, p.440 - INNES & JEFFERSON from DURHAM &c   BOND FOR REPAIR TO PRISON
Gregary DURHAM, John BISWELL and James ROBERTS bound to Hugh INNES and George
JEFFERSON two of his Majesties Justices of peace for Pittsylvania County in
sum of £03·15 Current Money...5 Aug 1769...condition of above obligation is
such that Gregary DURHAM has this Day undertaken to Repair the prison of said .
County let by said H. INNES & G. JEFFERSON to be compleated and done by next
Court.
Wit: James SMITH, John COOK   Gregary DURHAM L.S.
                                                     John BISWELL L.S.
                                                    James ROBERTS L.S.
The plank that is off is all to be pin'd on a ?geun and all other plank to
have more pins in them the Petition to be put up Strong by being pin'd at
Bottom and Top the Chimney to be mended a Stool made to each necessary hole
for sum of £01·17·06.

DB 1, p.442 - JONES from JONES   DEED, 22 Sep 1769
Jonathan JONES of Pittsylvania County in Colony of Virginia planter of one
part and James JONES of County and Colony aforesaid of other part...for £15
Current Money of Virginia...a line of Jonathan JONESES...uper side north fork
of Stinking River...to Beginning of old Survey...crossing a fork of said
north fork...85 acres...the Right of Dower of Anne, wife of Said Jonathan
JONES, excepted.
Wit: Edmond WINSTON, Hugh INNES, John COX   Jonathan JONES L.S.
                                                          her
Rec: 25 May 1770   Anne Ⱥ JONES
                                                         mark

DB 1, p.444 - SMITH from TORIAN   DEED, 5 Dec 1769
Peter TORIAN of Halifax County of one part and John SMITH of County of Pitt-
sylvania of other part...for £60 Current Money of Va...Land in Halifax County
now Pittsylvania, on both sides Stewarts Creek...in John SMITH's line...cross-
ing a branch...crossing two Brances...on said SMITHS line...300 acres.
                                         his
Wit: John FULTON, Charles PERKINS, George Ɏ YOUNG
                                         mark
Prv. 23 Feb 1770, Further proved and
Rec: 27 Jul 1770   Peter TORIAN L.S.

DB 1, p.446 - LUMKIN from POLSON   TRUST DEED, 6 Jun 1770
George LUMKIN of County of Pittsylvania of one part and Andry/Andrew PAULSON
of same County...hath this day purchased a valuable Tract of Land...on Marrowbone Creek containing 200 Aikers for which said POALSON now Stands Justly
indebted to said George LUMKINS in Sum of £46 with Interest Current Money of
Virginia...PAULSON shall make said det Surcure to him...POALSON hath Sould to
said LUMPKIN all personal aState that he now perses: awaging and team, 7 head
Cattle, 2 feather beds and fernity, 3 pewter dishes, 2 pewter Basons, 20 head
hoggs, Iron pott, Great Plow, 2 narrow axes, rest of my household Goods.
PAULSON shall pay sum before 25 Dec 1770 that then befour mentioned Deed is
to come void.
Wit: Daniel OBARR, Jacob LEWIS, Geo. LUMPKIN Junr.
Rec: 27 Jul 1770   Andrew POLSON L.S.

DB 1, p.447 - VAUGHAN from FARRIS   DEED, 26 Jul 1770
John FARRIS of County of Pittsylvania of one part and William VAUGHAN Junior
of county aforesaid of other part...for £30 Current money of Virginia...100

acres on Allens Creek...beginning at Lower Corner line between Joseph FARRIES
and James FARRIES...keeping James FARRIES old line.

Wit: William $\overset{his}{\times}_{mark}$ CHILDRESS, Thomas CHILDRESS, Sarah $\overset{her}{\times}_{mark}$ VAUGHAN

Rec: 27 Jul 1770   John FARRIS L.S.

DB 1, p.449 - REAVES from JINKINS   DEED, Jul 1770
Lewis JINKINS of Pittsylvania County of Virginia of one part and Frederick
REAVES of said County and Coloney of other part...for £70 Current money of
Virginia...400 acres on Both sides pigg River...beginning at mouth of Jacks
Creek on Pigg River, up the River to Thomas POTTERS line on south side of
River...on the devideing line of the order that was formerly George WALTENS.
No witnesses $\overset{his}{}$
Rec: 27 Jul 1770   Lewis $\overset{}{\underset{mark}{\times}}$ JINKINS L.S.

DB 1, p.451 - DIX from WYNNE   DEED, 28 Mar 1770
Thomas WYNNE, Senr. and Mary his wife of County of Pittsylvania and Coloney
of Virginia of one part and John DIX of said County of other part...for £150
Current Money of Virginia...south side Dan River...John BOYDS on south side
dan River...crossing three Branches down the river...which was granted by
Letters patent to William IRBY Junior 10 Sep 1755 and since conveyed to Will-
iam ARMSTRONG and from ARMSTRONG to William WYNNE and from WYNNE to said
Thomas WYNNE reference seen in Halifax office...165 acres.
Wit: William WYNNE, Thomas DUNCAN, Hugh ARMSTRONG, Larkin DIX
                                                      $\overset{his}{}$
Rec: 27 Jul 1770   Thomas $\underset{mark}{\times}$ WYNNE, Senr. L.S.

DB 1, p.453 - STANDEFER Senr. from VANBEBBER   DEED, 25 Jul 1770
John VANBEBBER of Botetourt County and Colony of Virginia of one part and
James STANDEFER Senior of Bedford County and Coloney of other part...for £100
Current Money of Virginia...on Story Creek...Crossing the Creek...crossing
Jumping Run...crossing fox Run...south side of Creek...crossing south fork.
Wit: James STANDEFER Junior, Jesse HEARD, Stephen HEARD
Rec: 27 Jul 1770   John VANBEBBER L.S.

DB 1, p.455 - CALLAWAY from CALLAWAY   DEED, 25 Apr 1770
John CALLAWAY of Pittsylvania County of one part and Charles CALLAWAY of
Bedford County of other...for £100 Current money of Virginia...land on both
sides Widows Creek...crossing the Little fork of said Creek...Crossing a
branch...95 acres.
Wit: Isaace READ, Edmond WINSTON, RWILLIAMS, John AYLETT
Rec: 27 Jul 1770   John CALLAWAY L.S.

DB 1, p.457 - LANKFORD from GEORGE   TRUST DEED, 28 Jan 1769
James GEORGE of County of Pittsylvania of one part and Benjamin LANKFORD of
other part...for £23·17·01 Lawfull Money of Virginia which said James GEORGE
is Justly Indebted to said Benjamin LANKFORD and honestly desires to Secure
and pay to said LANKFORD...further consideration of sum of 5s paid said
GEORGE...Two negro Boys (Slaves) named Goliah, Euclid...after 16 Jan 1770 to
sell for best price after 10 days publick notice...out of money ariseing
from such Sail pay with lawfull Interest from 16 Oct 1769 til fully paid...

with expenses...to pay said GEORGE overplus if any Remain.

Wit: Edmond KING, Joseph ⟍ FARRIS, Abraham SHELTON
                              his
                             mark

Rec: 28 Jul 1770

James GEORGE L.S.

DB 1, p.459 - MC CONACHY from PERKINS   DEED, 27 Jul 1770
Peter PERKINS of County of Pittsylvania of one part and Robert MC CONACHY of
said County of other part...for £20 Current Money of Virginia...350 acres on
Rocky branch of Leatherwood Creek...beginning at Nathaniel ELKINES's...in
LOMAX & Co. Line...to BOLDINS corner...crossing the Rocky Branch.
No witnesses
Rec: 27 Jul 1770

Peter PERKINS L.S.

DB 1, p.461 - CALLAWAY from CALLAWAY   DEED, 27 Mar 1770
William CALLAWAY of Bedford County of one part and John CALLAWAY of Pittsyl-
vania County of other part...for £300 Current Money of Virginia...80 acres
on Stanton River...possession made by William CALLAWAY Senior to John CALLAWAY.
Wit: Isaace READ, RWILLIAMS, Jn°. AYLETT, Edmond WINSTON, Ja^s. CALLAWAY
Rec: 27 Jul 1770

William CALLAWAY L.S.

DB 1, p.462 - SMITH from SAUNDERS   DEED, 9 Jun 1770
Peter SAUNDERS of County of Pittsylvania of one part and Daniel SMITH of the
County of other part...for £40 Current Money of Virginia...130 acres on Little
Otter a branch of Irvin River...north side said Creek...on South side said
Creek...Crossing a Branch...crossing south fork of Otter Creek.
Wit: Robert HAIRSTON, Geo. HAIRSTON, Peter HAIRSTON
Rec: 27 Jul 1770   Peter SAUNDERS L.S.
Mary, wife of said Peter, privily Examined as Law directs and Relinquished
her right of Dower

DB 1, p.465 - FRANCE from ROGERS   DEED, 16 Jun 1770
Peter ROGERS of Halifax County of one part and John FRANCE of Pittsylvania
County of other part...for £30 Current Money of Virginia...150 acres on Mill
fork of Mayo River.
Wit: H. PENDLETON, Isaace READ, Champ. TERREY, John PARR, Jn°. Fredrick
MILLER, Theop^s. LACEY
Memorandum: Possession of within Land was granted, confirmed and Delivered
by ROGERS to said FRANCE 16 Jun 1768.
Rec: 27 Jul 1770

Peter ROGERS L.S.

DB 1, p.467 - DYSON from REAVES   DEED, 27 Jul 1770
Fredrick RIVES of Pittsylvania County of one part and William DYSON of Brunswick County of other part...for £100 Current Money of Virginia...1,000 acres
on South side Pigg River...in devideing order line...on William STEGALLS
line...on a branch.
No witnesses
Rec: 27 Jul 1770

Fredrick RIVES L.S.

DB 1, p.469 - TAYLOR from BUCKNALL   DEED, 26 Jul 1770
Francis BUCKNALL of County of Pittsylvania of one part and James TAYLOR of
county aforesaid of other part...for £30...238 acres on South fork of Cherri
Stone...on both sides same Creek...in PARSON line on a Branch...Crossing said
Creek...crossing two Branches...crossing a fork of said Creek.
No witnesses
Rec: 27 Jul 1770   Francis BUCKNALL L.S.
Blanch, wife of said Francis, Relinquished her right of Dower.

DB 1, p.470 - FULTON from SMITH   DEED, 27 Jul 1770
John SMITH and Marthey his wife of Parish of Camden and County of Pittsylvania of one part and Jno. FULTON of other part of County and parish aforesaid...for £50 Current Money of Virginia...126 acres being part of Tract
whereon said SMITH now Dwells...Cross a branch to Stewards C^r....crossing
a branch and aforesaid Creek.
Wit: John SHELOR, Thomas HUTCHINGS, Absalom BOSTICK
Rec: 27 Jul 1770   John SMITH L.S.

DB 1, p.473 - SMITH, Junr. from WARD   DEED, 27 Apr 1770
Jeremiah WARD and Anna his wife of County of Pittsylvania of one part and
John SMITH, Junior of same county of other part...for £170 Current Money of
Virginia...190 acres on Stanton River Bank...said Land is part of an order
of Council granted to Richard RANDOLPH Esqr. decd. and by him conveyed to
Timothy DALTON and by said DALTON Conveyed to said Jeremiah WARD by Deed
Recorded in Halifax County Court.
No witnesses   Jeremiah WARD L.S.
Rec: 27 Jul 1770   Anna WARD L.S.
Ann, Wife of said Jeremiah, privily Examined and Relinquished right of
Dower in said Land and Premises

DB 1, p.477 - SENTER from DALTON   DEED, 1770
James DALTON of county of Pittsylvania of one part and Stephen SUNTER of
County of Bedford of other part...for £70 Current Money of Virginia...50 acres
on South side Pigg River.
No witnesses   James DALTON L.S.
Rec: 27 Jul 1770
Elizabeth, wife of James DALTON, Relinquished her Right of dower

DB 1, p.479 - VAUGHAN from LANKFORD   DEED, 6 Jul 1770
William VAUGHAN Junr. of County of Halifax of one part and Benjamin LANKFORD
of County of Pittsylvania of other part...for £50 Current Money of Virginia...
200 acres on Both sides bouth forks Allens Creek...beginning where the line
crosses the Cool Spring branch, down said branch to the Creek, to back line,
keeping Round the old Line.
                        her   her
Wit: John VAUGHAN, Prisilla T HANDCOCK, Isbell X DYERR
                        Mark   Mark
Rec: 27 Jul 1770   Benjamin LANKFORD L.S.

DB 1, p.481 - PATTERSON from HODGES   DEED, 10 May 1770
Isam HODGES of County of Pittsylvania of one part and Samuel PATERSON of
said County of other part...for £20 Current Money of Virginia...100 acres now
in his actual Possession...on Chesnut Creek being part of a Tract said Sam-
uel PATERSON now lives and Bounded by said Isam HODGES Line and said Samuel
PATERSONS own line.   his
No witnesses   Isham /+/ HODGES L.S.
Rec: 27 Jul 1770   mark

DB 1, p.483 - STOTT from HUBBARD   DEED, 12 Feb 1770
Edward HUBBARD of County of Pittsylvania of one part and Solaman STOTT of
County of Halifax of other part...Edward HUBBARD and Elesabeth his wife for
sum of £30 current money...240 acres...the Second corner mentioned in the
Patten...neare Little Strait Stone Creek, down said Creek to Isaace ESKHELS

line...pointers in his own line...to the Mill Branch so Called.
Wit: Thomas DILLARD, Junr., Jno. VAUGHAN, Edmund KING, William COLLINS
Rec: 25 May 1770
Prv.: 28 Jul 1770   his
                                        Edward (HUBBARD L.S.
                                               Mark

DB 1, p.485 - SHOATE from TALBOTT   DEED, 27 Jul 1770
Matthew TALBOT of County of Bedford and Edward SHOATE of County of Pittsyl-
vania of other part...for £40 Current Money of Virginia...275 acres on Both
sides Camp Creek...down the creek.
No witnesses
Rec: 27 Jul 1770   Matthew TALBOT L.S.

DB 1, p.487 - COX from STOKES   DEED, 29 Nov 1769
William STOKES Acting Executor of the Estate of Robert WADE Junior Deceased
of one part and John COX of County of Pittsylvania of other part...for £150
Current Money of Virginia...1,200 acres on Branches of Elkhorn Creek...oak
standing in the Line expressed in the patent (obtained by John ROBINSON Esqr.
for a Larger Quantity of Land)...to CHISWELLS...in Robert WEAKLEYS line...
corner of MEDSELFS...corner of CHANEYS along his line north.
No witnesses
Rec: 27 Jul 1770   William STOKES L.S.

DB 1, p.489 - COPLAND from DUNN   DEED, 3 Mar 1770
Waters DUNN of one part and Peter COPLAND of County of Pittsylvania of other
part...for £300 Current Money of Virginia...405 acres on Smiths River and
beaver Creek...North side Smiths River or Irvin River...RANDOLPHS corner...
crossing both forks of Beaver Creek.   his
Wit: Richard COPLAND, Thos. COOPER, Jno. COOPER, Danl. ⌠ MC BRIDE,
                                               mark

Ambrose JONES, Paul POALSON, William COPLAND, Charles COPLAND
Rec: 27 Jul 1770   Waters DUNN L.S.

DB 1, p.492 - HAMMACK from ADKINSON   DEED, 26 Jul 1770
Richard ADKINSON of Pittsylvania County of one part and Richard HAMMACK of
above said County of other part...for £25 Current Money of Virginia...50
acres on South side Pigg River...cross a Branch.
Wit: William WITCHER, W^m. ADKINSON, Levi SHOCKLE   his
Rec; 27 Jul 1770   Richard R ADKINSON L.S.
                                               mark

DB 1, p.494 - PERKINS from STRONG   POWER OF ATTORNEY, 25 Jul 1770
I, John STRONG of Pittsylvania County appoint Peter PERKINS of said County
my Lawfull attorney to Collect, Contract for or Dispose of all the Estate of
William STRONG or any part that Shall appear to by my Right...proceed by Action
he shall think fit...as I mite or Could do were I present.
No witnesses
Rec: 27 Jul 1770   John STRONG L.S.

DB 1, p.495 - GRISHAM from REAVES   DEED, 27 Jul 1770
Fredrick RIVES of Pittsylvania County of Virginia of one part and Ralph
GRISHAM of Brunswick County of Virginia of other part...for £200...1,600 acres
on North side Pigg River...beginning on South side Jacks Mountain on the order
line...on dividing order line.
No witnesses
Rec: 27 Jul 1770   Fredrick RIVES L.S.

DB 1, p.497 - KERBY from ANDERSON   DEED, 19 Mar 1769
Francis ANDERSON of Amelia County and John KERBY of Pittsylvania County
planter of other part...for £75 Current Money of Virginia...400 acres on
both sides Owens Creek.
Wit: John Fredrick MILLER, Jn°. LAWSON, John MOORE, Jn°. WILSON,
Theo. CARTER
Rec: 27 Jul 1770   Francis ANDERSON L.S.

DB 1, p.499 - KERBY from REAVES   DEED, 13 Jul 1770
Fredrick RIVES of Pittsylvania County and Colony of Virginia of one part and
David KERBY of County and Colony afores^d. of other part...for £250 Current
Money of Virginia...1,500 acres on Both sides Pigg River...beginning below
the great Bend of Pigg River at the mouth of a Branch on North side of the
River, up said branch to the head...on the deviding Ridge between the Glade
Creek and the River...west side Black Water path...on Lewis MORGANS line
about the mouth of Cheknot...mouth of the Rockey Creek, to devinding line
above William STEEGALLS...to mouth of Mountain Creek.
Wit: Lewis MORGAN, Jesse KEARBY, Jn°. THOMPSON
Rec: 27 Jul 1770   Fredrick RIVES L.S.

DB 1, p.502 - ECHOLS from SNEAD   DEED, 27 Aug 1770
Christopher SNEAD of County of Pittsylvania of one part and William ECHOLS
of County of Halifax of other part...for £70 Current Money of Virginia...
400 acres on the Lick Branches of Sandy Creek of Banister River...beginning
at FITZGERALDS corner pine on the Creek...crossing three Branches...on Lick
Branch.
Wit: Jn°. WIMBISH, Ja^s. CONAWAY, John WHITE, John OWEN
Rec: 30 Aug 1770   Christopher SNEAD L.S.

DB 1, p.504 - NEALEY from NEALEY   DEED, 5 Sep 1769
John NEALLY of County of Augusta in Colony of Virginia of one part and Robert
NEALLY of County of Pittsylvania in aforesaid Colony of other part...for
£100...189 acres on South side Tomehawk Creek...corner of William NEALLYS
Land, up said Creek by Lands of William NEALLYS...is part of a Tract the said
John NEALLY purchased of Col°. Jn°. CHISWELL.
Wit: William MC CLENEEHAN, William NEELLEY, William NEULLEY
Rec: 23 Mar 1770 and further
Prv.: 30 Aug 1770   John NEILLEY L.S.

DB 1, p.506 - BUTLER from MAYS   30 Aug 1770
Joseph MAYS in parish of Camden and County of Pittsylvania of one part and
John BUTLER of County and parish aforesaid of other part...said Joseph MAYS
and Margret his wife for sum of £50 Current Money of Virginia...150 acres
being the Tract whereon said BUTLER Dwells...on the River Bank...to HAWKINSES
line.   his
No witnesses   Joseph /M\ MAYS L.S.
Rec: 30 Aug 1770   mark
Margaret, wife of said Joseph, being   her
privily Examined as Law directs Relinquished   Margret/VYV/MAYS L.S.
her right of Dower   mark

DB 1, p.508 - COWAN from TALBOT   DEED, 7 Apr 1770
Isham TALBOT OF County of Bedford of one part and Robert COWAN of above said
County of other part...for £70...100 acres on South side Stanton River Join-

50.

ing upper side of SMITHS Mountain and known by Name of the Round about.
Wit: Edmund WINSTON, John AYLETT, RWILLIAMS
Rec: 30 Aug 1770   Isham TALBOT L.S.

DB 1, p.510 - THOMPSON from KERBY   DEED, 30 Aug 1770
John THOMSON of County of Pittsylvania of one part and John KERBY of same
county of other part...for £80 Current Money...100 acres on South side Owenses
Creek...to Mouth of Josiah KERBY Spring branch, up said Spring branch to the
head...Line to ANDERSONS back line...Near the Poolecat fork.
Wit: Ja^s. DILLARD, Ja^s. TALBOT, John DAVIS   his
Rec: 30 Aug 1770   John ✗ KIRBY L.S.
Joanah, wife of said Jno., privily Exam^d. and   mark
Relinquished her right of Dower

DB 1, p.512 - NEALEY from NEALEY   DEED, 5 Sep 1769
John NEALLEY of County of Augusta of one part and William NEALLEY of County
of Pittsylvania of other part...for £100...on South side Tomehawk Creek the
corner of Robt. NEALLEYS land...Crossing a branch...crossing two branches...
189 acres which Land is part of a Tract said John NEALLEY Purchased of Col^o.
John CHISWELL.
Wit: Robert NEALLEY, Willm. NEALLEY, William MC CLENEEHAN
Rec: 23 Mar 1770 and further
Prv.: 30 Aug 1770   John NEALLEY L.S.

DB 1, p.514 - MUSTAIN from PATEY   DEED, 4 Apr 1770
Jessey PATEY and Delilah his wife of parish of Cambden and County of Pittsylv^a.
of one part and Thomas MUSTAIN of County aforesaid of other part...for £20
Current Money of Virginia...170 acres on both sides Nix's Creek...Beginning
on James DOSSES Line...up both sides said Nix's Creek.
                             his
Wit: Crispin SHELTON, Thos. ✗ HARDY, Abra. SHELTON, Simeon JUSTICE
                            mark
Rec: 30 Aug 1770   Jessey PATEY L.S.

DB 1, p.515 - DALTON from DALTON   DEED, 27 Jul 1770
Robert DAULTON Junior of County of Pittsylvania of one part and James DAULTON
of said County of other part...for £17 Current Money of Virginia...40 acres
on North Side Pigg River...in William ATKINSONS line...in Lewis POTTERS line.
Rec: 30 Aug 1770   No witnesses   Robert DALTON, Junr. L.S.

DB 1, p.517 - BOULTON from BOULTON   DEED, 1 Jun 1770
Robert BOULTON of Pittsylvania County of one part and Benjamin BOULTON of
same county of other part...for £5 Current Money of Virginia...150 acres on
North Branches pigg River...on Jacob HUBBARD line...on Lewis JINKINS pattent
line on that Line to Jacob HUBBARDS corner.
No witnesses
Rec: 30 Aug 1770   Robert BOULTON L.S.

DB 1, p.518 - DILLARD from DEVIN   BILL SALE, 30 Aug 1770
James DILLARD of County of Pittsylvania Gen^t. stands bound with me for Payment of Twenty odd pounds Current Money of Virginia which hath been some Time
going on upon Interest...James is in Danger of being Subjected to the Payment
of said debt to one Israel CHRISTIAN to whom said bond is payable...for Securing said James against any Damages that he may Sustain on Account of said

bond I have deliver and give up to said James in his Actual Possession: Bay
Gelding, Roan Mare, 2 Feather beds and furniture, 2 Iron potts, all house-
hold Stuff, 2 Plows, all plow Irons and Geers, 2 Cows and Calves with all
Rest of my Horned Cattle, all my Corn and that is now Growing and every
other personal Estate to Me belonging...if said James fully Discharges it
himself and obtains an Acquittance, shall make a Redelivery of the Articles.
Wit: Robt. PAYNE, James TALBOT, G. MARR
Rec: 30 Aug 1770   William DEVIN L.S.

DB 1, p.519 - INNES from JINKINS   DEED, "fifteeth" Aug 1768
Benjamin JINKINS of County of Pittsylvania of one part and Hugh INNES of said
County of other part...for £80 Current Money of Virginia...Land in said Hugh
INNES Actual possession Now being...on South side Pigg River being part of
550 acres the said JINKINS bought of Lewis JINKINS...below the fish Trap...
to old Line, to Line that Devides Saml. CANTERBERYS part of said 550 acres...
along CANTERBURYS Line to his corner in William STEGALS Line...down the River
as it Meanders Including the River, a Small Island and the fish trap...con-
taining 300 acres.

                                                   his
Wit: James STEWART, Francis KERBY, John HEARD, Lewis X JINKINS
Prv. 26 Aug 1768 and further   mark
Prv. & Rec: 30 Aug 1770
Tabitha, wife of said Benj., being Privily Examined
Relinquished her right of Dower   Benjamin GINKINS L.S.

DB 1, p.521 - ROSS from CHRISTAIN   BILL SALE, 29 Aug 1770
Know all men by the Presents that I Nathaniel CHRISTAIN of Pittsylvania County
for sum of £65 Currencey paid by David ROSS...have sold to said David ROSS
one Negroe man Named dick; Track of Land Containing 130 acres; also another
Track Joining the above Containing 150 acres; both Tracks Lying on Stanton
and Joining Black Water.
Wit: Edmund WINSTON, John AYLETT, Geo. DIVERS
Rec: 30 Aug 1770   Nathaniel CHRISTAIN L.S.

DB 1, p.522 - KERBY from KERBY   DEED, 12 Apr 1770
John KERBY of Pittsylvania County and Henry KERBY of same County planter of
other part...for £75 Current Money of Virginia...135 acres on North side Pigg
River and bounded with these mentioned Lynes M^r. Charles TALBUTS and William
MULINGS Lines and James DILLARDS...to the river and Down.
          his   his
Wit: Jesse C KEARBY, Jno. THOMPSON, Josiah I KEARBY
          mark   mark   his
Rec: 30 Aug 1770   John I KEARBY L.S.

DB 1, p.524 - SWANSON from HAYNES   DEED, 25 Nov 1768
William HAYNES of County of Bedford of one Part and William SWANSON of above
said County of other Part...for £30 Current Money of Virginia...100 acres
being part of a Tract of Land Containing 243 acres the Patent dated 22 Sep
1766 and on both sides Bull run...on WALTONS Line...along the Deviding line
crossing bull Runn.
Wit: James SMITH, James MITCHELL, David WALKER, Hugh INNES
Rec: 30 Aug 1770   William HAYNES L.S.

DB 1, p.525 - JONES from POOR   DEED, 29 Aug 1770

Jeremiah POOR of Pittsylvania County and Colony of Virginia of one part and Isaace JONES of County and Colony aforesaid of other part...for £24 Current Money of Virginia...214 acres as in Patent of said Land on north fork Pigg River...crossing a bold Branch...Crossing two branches and the Creek...the Patent of which Land dated 20 Jul 1768.

Wit: Robert JONES, Thomas JONES, Thomas JONES Junr.

Rec: 30 Aug 1770   his

                                  Jeremiah X POOR L.S.

                                   mark

DB 1, p.527 - CRUMP from ROBERTS   DEED, 28 Aug 1770

James ROBERTS of County of Pittsylvania of one part and Robt. CRUMP of same county of other part...for £10 Current money of Virginia...109 acres on a Small Creek known by Name of green Creek.

No witnesses

Rec: 30 Aug 1770   James ROBERTS L.S.

DB 1, p.529 - WYNNE from SOUTHERLAND   MORTGAGE, 7 Apr 1770

Know all men by these presents that I Saunders SOUTHERLAND of County of Pittsylvania and Province of Virginia for Sum of £20 Current Money of Virginia do sell to William WYNNE j^r. 8 head of Cattle Viz. aread Cow marked with a Calf by her side, One black and white Cow marked two Smooth Crops and also a Calf with her, one red & white hefer marked two Crops & two Slits and a Calf with her, two yearlings one black the other black & white marked two Crops and two Slits. Also 8 Head of hogs, two Beds with all rest of my Household furniture. If SOUTHERLAND shall pay full sum before 25 Dec 1770 then present Bill of Sale to be Void.

Wit: John SUTTON, Samuel BYNUM, Arthur BYNUM   his

Rec: 25 May 1770   Sanders X SUTHERLAND L.S.

                                      mark

CALLANDS COURTHOUSE AND GAOL

1768	Who Surveyed for	N^o. Acres		Water courses
?2	John WILLES Gen^t. & Co.	30030		on Read Island waters Greasy C^r. & Indian C^r. & burks fork
Nov^r.5	Joseph CLOUED Senr.	134		on Peters C^r. of Dan River
7	Ezekiah SHELTON	228		on the n^o. fork of Mayo River
8	Jno. & Ralph SHELTON Jur.	251		on Spoon C^r. of Mayo River
8	Ralph SHELTON Senr. & Com.	145		on Spoon Creek of Mayo River
9	Jonathan HAMBY & Copy.	297		on the waters of Peters Creek
10	George CARTER	53		on the North fork of Mayo River
10	Ralph SHELTON Junr.	351		on the waters of Mayo River
11	Thomas GAZAWAY	162		on the head of Little Sycamore Creek
11	Thomas HUFF	198		on the waters of the aforesaid Creek
12	John KINDRICK	393		on Buffellow Creek of Smiths River
13	D^o.	250		on the aforesaid Creek and River
14	Christopher BOLLING	187		on Jacks Creek of the aforesaid Creek
16	John NEAVILL	110		on the Head waters of Little Sycamore C^r.
18	Luke FOLEY	173		on the waters of the aforesaid Creek
18	James ELKINS	149		on the North fork of Black castle Creek
18	John NEAVILL	35		on the head of Gills Creek
21	Timothy STAMPS	164		on Flat Creek
21	Timothy STAMPS	348		on Smiths River
22	Bartley FOLEY	171		on Sycamore Creek
22	George DAVIS	139		on Sycamore Creek
23	Luke FOLEY	346		on the waters of Gobling Town Creek
23	Luke FOLEY	176		on the waters of Gobling Town Creek
23	Bartley FOWLEY	219		on the Waters of Smiths River
24	D^o.	64		on Joinerack Creek
24	D^o.	78		on Joinerack Creek
25	Jeremiah CLINCH	251		on the waters of Smiths River
26	Jeremiah CLINCH	59		on the Waters of Gobling Town Creek
26	Bartley FOWLEY	50		on Gobling Town Creek
26	D^o.	59		on the aforesaid D^o.
28	John WARD Gen^t.	236		on the South fork of Wegion C^r.
29	D^o.	100		on the Waters of Rock Castle C^r.
30	D^o.	215		on the waters of Wegion Creek
$Decem^r$.2.	D^o.	128		on the waters of Rock Castle C^r.
5	D^o.	100		on the waters of Wegion and Joinrack Creek

	Who Surveyed for	Nº. Acres	Water courses
6	CHILES's orphans	146	on Wegion Creek
8	John WARD Gen^t.	278	on the head of the middle fork of Jacks C^r.
Decem^r.			
10	Paletiah SHELTON	165	on Sycamore Creek
10	Daniel CAMPBELL	150	on Smiths River
13	Luke FOWLEY	146	on Gobling town Creek
14	Daniel CAMPBELL	383	on Smiths River & Waters of gobling T.C.
Jan^y.			
19	Henry HARDEN	400	on Sandy Creek
24	George JEFFERSON Gen^t.	234	on Snow C^r. and Turkey Cock C^r.
26	Robert CHANDLER Gen^t.	45	on the Waters of Marrowbone Creek
27	William SMITH	354	on Mattreymoney Creek
28	William JAMES	161	on toe Clouet Creek
30	William EDWARDS	174	on Toe Clout Creek
30	James STRONG	271	on turkey pen C^r. of Mettremoney C^r.
31	John MAY	315	on the Draughs of Toe Clout C^r.
31	John SAMMS	368	on the waters of Toe Clout Creek
Feb^y.			
1	William SAMMS Senr.	185	on the Smiths River
1	William SAMMS Junr.	164	on the draughs of Turkey Cock C^r.
2	James WILSON	176	on Smiths River
2	Thomas WILSON	20	on Leatherwood Creek
3	Moses WILSON	232	on Home Creek
5	James SHELTON	177	on the Waters of Beaver Creek
6	Ambrose JONES	95	on the Waters of the aforesaid C^r.
6	Thomas COOPER	159	on the aforesaid Creek
8	Peter COPLAND Gen^t.	246	on the draughs of the aforesaid C
1769			
Feb^y.8	Peter COPLAND gen^t.	252	on the Waters aforesaid
8	Peter COPLAND	323	on the Waters aforesaid
9	Peter COPLAND	50	on Daniels Mill Creek Waters
9	Waters DUNN	212	on Smiths River
11	Peter COPLAND	625	on Wens Creek of Read Creek
11	James ROBERTS	269	On Beaver Creek
12	Cornelious ROBERTS	198	on the Glady fork of Read Creek
13	Daniel MC BRIDE	147	on the waters of Beaver Creek
13	John ISOM dec^d.	200	on the North fork of Beaver C^r.
13	David WALKER	269	on Beaver Creek

	Who Surveyed for	N°. Acres	Water courses
14	George WALKER Gen^t.	236	on Beaver Creek
15	D°.	44	on the South fork of the Crab Tree fork of Snow C^r.
15	William BRADSHAW	172	on the Waters of Snow Creek
16	Hugh INNES Gen^t.	358	on Bennetts Creek of Snow C^r.
16	Edward RICHARDS	250	on Chesnutt C^r.
17	Thomas RAMSEY	320	on Chesnutt Creek
17	John HICKEY & Comp^y.	410	on Chesnutt D°.
18	Robert HODGES	210	on the Muddy fork of Chesnut Creek
18	Robert FRAYSIER	108	on the afforesaid Waters
20	William GRAHAM	279	on the first fork of Snow Creek
20	D°.	250	on tissle Creek of Pigg River
21	D°.	299	on the Waters of Sandy River
23	William HAIL	200	on the waters of Dillaes Creek
Mar.15	John LAVERY Senr.	400	on the waters of Py. Creek
16	George JEFFERSON gen^t.	99	on the Waters of Turkey cock Creek
17	John DAVIS	167	on the Piney fork of Owens Creek
17	William YOUNG	330	on the Waters of Snow Creek
18	W^m. PEAQUE	195	on the Waters of Pig River
18	Levy SHOCKLEY	235	on Little Turkey Cock C^r.
21	James STEWART	400	on Chesnutt Creek
25	Isaace RENTFROW	108	on Runnet bag Creek
27	Peter SANDERS	53	on the waters of the afforesaid Creek
27	John HANDEY	157	on the aforesaid waters
28	Thomas JONES	310	on the Draughs of Pigg River
28	Joshua BARTON	129	on Pig River
29	Elener TURPIN	118	on hatchet Run of pig River
29	Benjamin BARTON	54	on the waters of Pig River
30	Benjamin GUDGER	96	on the waters of Pig River
30	Richard HUFF	232	on the afforesaid waters
31	William COOK	67	on Hatchet run of Pig River
31	D°.	74	on the waters pf pigg River
31	Peter VERDIMAN	30	on Pigg River
31	Henson MC DUEL	50	on Pigg River
Apr^1. 3	Richard DOGETT Gen^t.	154	on the waters of Black water River

	Who Surveyed for	N°. Acres	Water courses
3	Thomas MILLER	123	on the afforesaid Waters
5	James RENTFROW Senior	390	On the afforesaid Waters
5	Thomas MILLER	377	on the afforesaid ditto
6	William MURPHEY	250	on Coles Creek of Black Water River
8	Robert HILL	212	on Pigg River
8	Richard CHOATE	58	on the Waters afforesaid
8	Saberet CHOATE	30	on pig River
10	John LAVERY Junior	233	on Black water River
11	James STANDEFORD Senr.	196	on the afforesaid River
11	Israel STANDEFORD	171	on the waters of the aforesaid River
12	D^o.	126	on the affs^d. Waters
12	Augusten CHOATE	129	on Doe Creek of Pigg River
1769 Apr^1. 17	John ANDERSON	20	on Black water River
17	Joseph BIRD	240	on Pigg River
17	John MEDLEY	109	on Mullins fork of Town Creek
18	James STANDEFORD Junr.	224	on Storrey Creek
18	Ditto	127	on Nicholas's Creek
19	William MULLINS	290	on the East fork of Town Creek
20	John RAMSEY	113	on Chesnutt Creek
22	James PARBERRY	238	on the waters of Frying Pan Creek

P Thomas HUTCHINGS Ass^t. Surv^r.

At a Court held for Pittsylvania County June the 23^d 1769
This List of Surveys was returned by Thomas HUTCHINGS assistant
Surveyor to John DONELSON Surveyor of this County, Ordered that the
same be Recorded -

Teste   Will TUNSTALL CC.

END OF DEED BOOK I

PITTSYLVANIA COUNTY, VIRGINIA
DEED BOOK 2, 1770 - 1772

DB 2, p.1 - MC DANIEL from CHALLES   27 Sep 1770
Hugh CHALLES of County of Pittsylvania and Martha his Wife of one part and
Henry MC DANIEL of same County of other part...for £150 Current Money of Vir-
ginia...400 acres on South Side Banister River being same Tract of Land which
Hugh CHALLES purchased of said Henry MC DANIEL and conveyed by MC DANIEL to
CHALLES by deed 23 Jun 1769.
Rec: 27 Sep 1770   No witnesses   Hugh CHALLES L.S.
Martha, wife of CHALLES privily Examined   Martha CHALLES L.S.
and Relinquished her right of Dower

DB 2, p.2 - DIX from DIX   DEED, 2 Mar 1770
John DIX of County of Pittsylvania of one part and James DIX of said County
of other part...for £120 Current Money of Virginia...Land on North side of
Dan River beginning at Mouth of Long Branch on the River Bank Running up the
River to Edmund FLOYDS Corner, thence along FLOYDS Line to CARGILLS patten,
down said Line along FLOYDS and DANDY Entray Lines to the Extent of them,
then down DENDYS Line to where it Crosseth the Long Branch, down said Branch
as it Meanders ...part of Land John DIX bought of John CARGILS and part of
that John DIX bought of Thomas DENDY, it being all the Land John DIX holds
on west side of Long Branch.
Wit: Thomas DUNCAN, Larkin DIX, Jno. BYNUM
Rec: 27 Sep 1770   John DIX L.S.

DB 2, p.3 - ROWLAND from DUNN   DEED TRUST, 11 Dec 1769
I, Waters DUNN of County of Pittsylvania am this day Indebted to John ROWLAND
of County aforesd. Parrish and County the Just Sum of £150 Current Money of
Virginia being Truly Desirous to do said John ROWLAND Due Justice & Secure to
him paymt. & Lawfull Interest and for Consideration of 5s Currency paid by
said John ROWLAND...said Waters DUNN have sold to said John ROWLAND my Crop
Tob^a. and Corn Growing...with three Negroes (Viz) Tom, Jacob and Lewis with
other Estate Consisting whatsoever belonging to said Waters DUNN...after 2
Nov 1771 dispose of for best price...discharge sum of £150.
                             her
Wit: Joseph AKIN, Eliz^a. \/ BAUGHAN
                            Mark
Rec: 28 Sep 1770   Waters DUNN L.S.

DB 2, p.5 - PAYNE from JONES   DEED, 27 Sep 1770
James JONES and Ellaner his wife of County of Pittsylvania of one part and
Abraham PAYNE of same County of other part...for £35 Current Money of Vir-
ginia...85 acres more or less...beginning in Jonathan JONES line...on upper
side North fork Stinking River...to beginning of old Survey...crossing a
fork of said North fork.
Wit: Crispin SHELTON, Moss ARMISTEAD, Reubin PAIN   James JONES L.S.
Rec: 27 Sep 1770   her
Elener, wife of said James, privily Examined   Ellenar ⫟ JONES L.S.
and Relinquished her right of Dower   mark

DB 2, p.7 - WYNES from WYNNE   DEED GIFT, 26 Mar 1770
William WYNNE Senior of County of Pittsylvania of one part and Mary WYNNE,
John WYNNE, Pattey WYNNE and Frances WYNNE of said County my Grandsons and
Daughters and the sons and Daughter of Thomas WYNNE Senior and Mary his wife...

I give to my Grand Daughter Mary WYNNE one Negroe Girel Named Cloey and her
Issue...I give to my grand Son John WYNNE one negroe Boy Named George...I
give and grant unto my grand daughter Patty one Negro girel Named Nanney and
her Issue...to my grand Son Francis one Negro Woman Named Lucey and her
Issue...said Negroes are now in the Possession of me the said William WYNNE
to be delivered within one year from the date of these presents to them the
said Mary WYNNE, John WYNNE, Patty WYNNE and Francis WYNNE Sones and daughter
of said Thomas WYNNE and Mary his wife.
Wit: Thomas DUNCAN, Hugh ARMSTRONG, Robt. WYNNE
Rec: 27 Sep 1770   William WYNNE L.S.

DB 2, p.8 - TALBOTT from RENTFROW   DEED, 20 Aug 1770
James RENTFROW of County of Pittsylvania of one part and Matthew TALBOTT of
County of Pittsylvania of other part...Sum of £273...all that Meassuage or
Tenement Situate in Pittsylvania County...Beginning where RENTFROS line on
N. Fork of Black Water River and new lines W. of the Creek...on fox Creek.
No witnesses
Rec: 27 Sep 1770
Easter, wife of said James, prively Examined as   James RENTFRO L.S.
Law Directs Relinquishes her Right of Dower   Esther RENTFRO L.S.

DB 2, p.9 - WILSON from BILLING   DEED, 27 Sep 1770
Jasper BILLING of County of Pittsylvania of one part and John WILSON of same
County of other part...for £50 Current Money of Virginia...295 acres more or
less on both sides Sandy River...Crossing a branch...Crossing a branch and
the river to pine on a hill...in Drury STITHS line.
No witnesses
Rec: 27 Sep 1770   Jasper BILLING L.S.

DB 2, p.10 - HAILEY from GILLIAM   DEED, 2 Sep 1770
James GILLIAM of County of Cumberland of one part and David HAILEY of County
of Pittsylvania of other part...for £15 Current Money...94 acres beginning
on North side Smiths River opposite to mouth of Bowings Creek, down said River as it meanders...North side the River...Crossing a Branch.
                                            his
Wit: Michael ROWLAND, Annan BATES, Thomas X SMITH
                                            Mark   James GILLIAM L.S.
Received 2 Sep 1770, wit: John BATES   Rec: 28 Sep 1770

DB 2, p.12 - HENRY from PATEY   DEED, 7 Sep 1770
Charles PATEY of the province of South Carolina in the County of Bartley of
one part and John HENRY of County of Pittsylvania in Virginia of other part...
for £26 Current money of Virginia...130 acres on both sides Nixes Creek...
beginning at upper Line of a Survey of Land formerly patented in name of James
PATEY Deceased, running down both sides Creek as the lines extends...part of
said patent of Land given to said Charles PATEY by his said Fathers Last
will and Testament.
Wit: Crispin SHELTON, Abra. SHELTON, Jesse PATTY, Gabriel SHELTON,
Lewis SHELTON, Beaverly SHELTON, Thomas MUSTAIN
Rec: 27 Sep 1770   Charles PATTY L.S.

DB 2, p.14 - HARRISON from PAYNE   DEED, 18 Jun 1770
John PAYNE the Elder of Goochland County of one part and William HARRISON of
said County of Goochland of other part...for £700 Current Money of Virginia...

Land in Pittsylvania County and Joining on North Side Dann River containing by Estimation 433 acres more or less and being the same Land and plantation which said John PAYNE the Elder purchased of Gideon MAIRE and was conveyed to said John PAYNE the Elder by Cartain Deed of Conveyance made to him by William BEANE and Recorded in County Court of Pittsylvania and bounded as in said Deed.

Wit: Josias PAYNE, Thos. HARRISON, Jno. WARE, John $-\!\!\!\times$ HENSON
his
mark

Rec: 27 Sep 1770   John PAYNE L.S.

DB 2, p.16 - CHANDLER from MADING   DEED, 26 Sep 1770
John MADING of Pittsylvania of one part and William CHANDLER of Halifax County of other part... ___ Current Money...200 acres more or less According to Bounds Bearing date...Beginning in John MADINGS old East Line where Zachariah WALLERS corners...running on WALLERS line...on a Stoney Ridge...crossing two Branches...in Thomas WALTERS old Line...in MADINGS Spring Branch, up Several Meanders of said branch.
Wit: John DUPUIS, George CARTER
Rec: 27 Sep 1770   John MADING L.S.

DB 2, p.18 - ELGIN from JEFFERSON   DEED, 29 Nov 1770
George JEFFERSON of Pittsylvania County in Colony of Virginia of one part and John ELGIN of Charles County in province of Maryland of other part...for £5 Current Money of Virginia...5 acres in Pittylvania County being part of Tract purchased by said George JEFFERSON of Clement READ...Beginning in old line near the Courthouse.
No witnesses
Rec: 29 Nov 1770   G — JEFFERSON L.S.

DB 2, p.20 - ELGIN from JEFFERSON   DEED, 29 Nov 1770
George JEFFERSON of Pittsylvania County in Colony of Virginia of one part and John ELGIN of Charles County in province of Maryland of other part...for £49 Current Money of Virginia...land on Waters of Turkey Cock Creek being part of Windsor Forest which JEFFERSON purchased of Clement READ as by Deed bearing date 14 Aug 1767 and recorded in County of Pittsylvania and Contains 495 acres...near a branch of Tomahack Creek and Running along the old line.
No witnesses
Rec: 29 Nov 1770   George JEFFERSON L.S.

DB 2, p.21 - CROWLEY from SHELTON   DEED, 29 Nov 1770
Palatiah SHELTON of Pittsylvania County and Mary his Wife of same part and Samuel CROWLEY of same County of other part...for £70 Current Money of Virginia...130 acres on Smiths River, a place known by Name of the Mouth of Rock Castle...up peeping Creek...down Smiths River formerly Irwin River.
Wit: Richard WHITE   Palatiah SHELTON L.S.
Rec: 29 Nov 1770   her
Mary, wife of said Paletiah, privily Examined   Mary $\bigcirc$ SHELTON L.S.
as Law directs Relinquished her right of Dower   mark

DB 2, p.23 - JEFFERSON to HOBERT   DEED, 29 Nov 1770
George JEFFERSON of Pittsylvania County in Colony of Virginia of one part and Harrison HOBART of Charles County in province of Maryland of other part... for £108 Current Money...by Estimation 500 acres on Waters of Turkey Cock Creek being part of Windsee Forrest which said JEFFERSON purchased of Clement

READ as by Deed dated 14 Aug 1767 and recorded in County Court of Pittsyl-
vania...oak in a Little Round Mountain in old line.
No witnesses
Rec: 29 Sep 1770   George JEFFERSON L.S.

DB 2, p.24 - SCALES from PERKINS   DEED, 28 Nov 1770
Peter PERKINS of Virginia in Pittsylvania County of one part and Joseph
SCALES of North Carrolina in Rowan County of other part...for £200 Current
Money of Virginia...1075 acres more or less on both sides of a large Branch
of Cascade Creek...Beginning in the Countries line..to RICES corner...west
along country line.
Wit: Ch^s. GALLAWAY, Jno. PARISH, Jo^s. SCALES, Junr.
Rec: 29 Nov 1770   Peter PERKINS L.S.

DB 2, p.26 - WHITE from SHELTON   DEED, 16 Jul 1770
Palatiah SHELTON of County of Pittsylvania and Mary his wife of same part and
Richard WHITE of same County of other part...for £50 Current Money of Vir-
ginia...144 acres on Syckamore a South Branch Smiths River...on South side
said Syckamore...Crossing a branch in Sykamore...crossing two branches.
                his   his   his
Wit: Sam^1. _/_ CROWLEY, James _/_ ELKINGS, Benj. _/_ JOHNSON
               mark   mark   mark
Rec: 29 Nov 1770   Palatiah SHELTON L.S.
Mary, wife of said Palatiah, being privily   her
Examined as law directs Relinquished her   Mary _/_ SHELTON L.S.
right of Dower   mark

DB 2, p.28 - GRAHAM from HANKINS   DEED, 22 Oct 1770
Daniel HANKINS of County of Pittsylvania in Colony of Virginia of one part
and Archebald GRAHAM of said County and Colony of other part...for £80 Current Money of Virginia...all that Tract of Land in County of Pittsylvania formerly Halifax containing by Estimation 380 acres on north fork of Chesnut...
on the breiry Mountain...Crossing a branch and a small mountain...crossing
the Creek to tree on top of a mountain.
               his   his
Wit: Benj. _X_ WHEAT, James _&_ DEAR, William GRAHAM
            mark   mark
Rec: 28 Nov 1770   Daniel HANKINS L.S.

DB 2, p.31 - CLAY from CLAY   DEED, 28 Nov 1770
Charles CLAY of Cumberland County of one part and Charles CLAY of Amelia
County of other part...for £100 Current Money of Virginia...Land in Pittsyl-
vania on Branches of Dann River containing by Estimation 1000 acres being
part of said Charles CLAYS order of Counsel for 9600.
No witnesses
Rec: 28 Nov 1770   Charles CLAY L.S.

DB 2, p.32 - WILSON from TORIAN   DEED, 22 Nov 1770
Andrew TORIAN of parrish of Antrum and County of Halifax planter of one part
and Jno. WILSON of parrish of Camden and County of Pittsylvania of other
part...for £285 Current Money of Virginia...Land in parrish of Camden and
County of Pittsylvania on north side Dan River Beginning at mouth of White
Walnutt Creek, up said Creek as it meanders...Andrew TORIAN Relinquishes all
manner of Right and property to said John WILSON the presunt purchaser of

300 acres on Lower part of said Land.
Wit: Josiah WATKINS, Jn°. OWEN, Thos. SMITH, Mumford SMITH, Hezekiah PIGG
Rec: 29 Nov 1770   Andrew TORIAN L.S.

DB 2, p.34 - CLAY from CLAY   DEED, 26 Nov 1770
Charles CLAY of Cumberland County of one part and Henry CLAY of said County
of other part...for £5 Current Money of Virginia...Tract of Land in County of
Pittsylv^a. on branches of dann river by compalation 800 more or less it being
part of the tract of 9600 in said county...on little Sandy Creek above Val.
Falling...by the road...on DODSON line down Sandy Creek.
Rec: 29 Nov 1770   No witnesses   Charles CLAY L.S.

DB 2, p.36 - HARRISON from CHADWELL   DEED, 24 Nov 1770
George CHADWELL of County of Pittsylvania of one part and William HARRISON
of County of Goochland of other part...for £100 Current money of Virginia...
Land in Pittsylvania County and joining on north side of Dann River containing 125 acres according to a patent granted to said George CHADWELL under the
Seal of the Colony bearing date 10 Jun 1760 in the thirty third year of the
reign of his majectys george the second Francis Fauquier Govenor and is the
land and plantation whereon said George now Dwelleth...walnut of Henry GREENS
standing on bank of the River...in William BEANS line, down said river as it
meanders.
Wit: John WARE, James DIX, Thos. OWEN, William WADLOW, Jn°. STONE
                                                    his
Rec: 29 Nov 1770   George X CHADWELL L.S.
                                                   mark

DB 2, p.38 - WARE from GREEN   DEED, 23 Nov 1770
Henry GREEN of county of Amelia of one part and John WARE of County of Goochland of other part...for £300 Current Money of Virginia...350 acres joining
on north side Dan River and bounded according to two patents granted to said
Henry GREEN under Seal of the Colony and bearing date 5 Jul MDCcLI (1751) in
the twenty fifth year of the Reign of his Majistys george the second Lewis
BURWELL president...Beginning at County Line where it crosses Dan River...
the other patent Bearing date the 11 July 1761 in the first year of the
Reign of his Majestys George the third Francis Fauquier Governor...170 acres...
at Henry GREENS corner in the Country line crossing two Branches.
Wit: Andrew HARRISON, Robt. PAYNE, William HARRISON, Jn°. HAMILTON, John
DIX, Moss ARMISTEAD, James DIX, Thomas OWEN   his
                                            Henry B GREEN L.S.
Rec: 29 Nov 1770   mark

DB 2, p.41 - ROASE from TOMBLINS   DEED, 28 Nov 1770
John TOMLIN of County of Pittsylvania on one part and Frances ROASE of County
aforesd. of other part...for £15 Current money of Virginia...all that Devided
tract of Land on east side of the tract that said TOMBLIN obtained from Thomas
BILLING in County of Pittsylvania...100 acres beginning on Thomas BILLINGS
line and runing boath sides of the Creek.
Rec: 29 Nov 1770   No witnesses   John TOMBLINS L.S.
Mary, wife of said John, privily Examined as Law directs Relinquished
her right of Dower

DB 2, p.42 - OAKES from PERKINS   DEED, 29 Nov 1770
Peter PERKINS of Pittsylvania County of one part and Charles OAKES of said
county of other part...for £20 Current Money of Virginia...Land in fork of

the Mountain Creek containing 50 acres more or less...Beginning at fork of
the Creek thence up the west fork to the crossing line...to the other fork
of the Creek, down said Creek.
No witnesses
Rec: 29 Nov 1770   Peter PERKINS L.S.

DB 2, p.44 - PAYNE Senr. from PERKINS   DEED, 22 Nov 1770
Peter PERKINS of Pittsylvania County of one part and John PAYNE Senr. of said
County of other part...for £40 Current Money...Land on both Sides Mounty
Creek...by estimation 200 acres...on south side said Creek...down said Creek
as it meanders to the fork, up west fork to Charles OAKES line...north side
said Mountain Creek, up said creek.
No witnesses
Rec: 29 Nov 1770   Peter PERKINS L.S.

DB 2, p.46 - HALL from HALL   DEED, 29 Nov 1770
John HALL of County of Pittsylvania of one part and Isham HALL of other part
for £25 Current Money of Virginia...100 acres more or less on south side Pigg
River...fork of a Branch, down said branch on pig River, up said River.
No witnesses   his
Rec: 29 Nov 1770   John ⅃ HALL L.S.
                                                         mark

DB 2, p.47 - RAGSDALE from MURPHEY   DEED, 17 Aug 1770
Richard MURPHY of County of Rowan in north Carolinia of one part and William
RAGSDALE of County of Pittsylvania in Colony of Virginia of other part...for
£40 Current Money of Virginia...all that Tract of Land on Elkhorn Creek containing by Estimation 200 acres being the same land said Richard MURPHY purchased of Nathaniel TERRY Gen^t. and was by said Nathaniel TERRY by deed Recorded in Court of County of Halifax conveyed to said Richard MURPHY.
Wit: RWILLIAMS, Jno. WIMBUSH, Theo^s. LACEY
Rec: 29 Nov 1770   Richard MURPHY L.S.

DB 2, p.48 - LEWIS BYRD from RANEY   DEED, 21 Nov 1770
John RANEY of north Carolinia Orrange County of one part and John Lewis BYRD
of Pittsylvania County Virginia of other part...for £10 Current Money of Vir-
ginia...218 acres on the Contry line...pointers on the Country line...on
THOMAS's line.
Wit: Jno. LEWIS Junr., Robt. MERIWETHER, William MERIWETHER, Moss ARMISTEAD,
John DIX, Charles BOULTON, William THOMAS
Rec: 29 Nov 1770   John RAINEY L.S.

DB 2, p.50 - BOLTON from TERRY   DEED, 29 Nov 1770
Champness TERRY and Sarah TERRY his wife of County of Pittsylvania in Colony
of Virginia of first part and Charles BOLTON of Orange County in province of
north Carolina of second part...for £80 Current money of Virginia...Land formerly the property of Captain Joseph TERRY and Lawfully Conveyed by said
Captain Joseph TERRY to said Champness TERRY...Mouth of a Branch Running in
the South side of Birches Creek and running up several Meanders of said branch
to MOORES old line...to Thomas DODSONS...160 acres.
No witnesses   Champ. TERRY L.S.
Rec: 29 Nov 1770 & Sarah relinquishes dower right   Sarah TERRY L.S.

DB 2, p.52 - HEARD Senr. from HENLY   DEED, 27 Nov 1770
Peter HENLY of parish of Camden in County of Pittsylvania of one part and

Stephen HEARD Senr. of Parish and County aforesd. planter of other part...
for £43 Current money of Virginia...Land in County of Pittsylvania on black
water River...at MEADS corner...along MEADS line...in Stephen HEARDS line...
229 acres.

Wit: Jesse HERD, Lewis ✗ JINKINS, Abraham ARDIN
his
mark

Peter PH HENLY   L.S.
his
mark

Rec: 29 Nov 1770

DB 2, p.54 - ERVINE from ANTHONY   DEED, 30 Nov 1770

William IRVINE Eldest Son and heir at Law of William IRVINE Deceased of one
part and John ANTHONY of Bedford County of other part...150 acres on south
Side Stanton River and County of Pittsylvania...South side said River...
bounded by Smiths Mountain as high as the Waggon Ford thence down the River
Including a Small Island opposite to Cruddocks Creek...for £100.
No witnesses
Rec: 30 Nov 1770   John ANTHONY   L.S.

DB 2, p.55 - CLAY from CLAY   DEED, 25 Nov 1770

Charles CLAY of Cumberland of one part and Eleazer CLAY of Chesterfield of
other part...for £5 Current Money of Virginia...Land in Pittsylvania Co. on
Branches of Dan River by Compalation 800 acres more or less it being part of
his order of 9600 in said County...beginning on Dan River on GWINS corner...
north side Dan River...on WALTONS line...to WORSHAMS line...up Dan River.
No witnesses
Rec: 29 Nov 1770   Charles CLAY   L.S.

DB 2, p.56 - DIX from ASTIN   DEED, 29 Nov 1770

William ASTIN of County of Pittsylvania Virginia of one part and John DIX
Gentlemen of said County of other part...for £04·06 Current Money of Virginia..
one acre of Land on south side Dan River beginning on the River Bank at Lewis
GREENS corner, runing off from the River to said ASTINS back line...being
part of a Larger Tract belonging to ASTIN.
Wit: Robt. PAYNE, Robt. ADAMS, Waters DUNN, Charles BOULTON
Rec: 29 Nov 1770   William ASTIN   L.S.

DB 2, p.58 - HENRY FROM TERRY   DEED, 20 Oct 1770

Champness TERRY of Pittsylvania County in Colony of Virginia Gent. and Sarah
his wife of one part and James HENRY of Accomack County of other part...for
and in consideration of carrying into complete Execution a Contract for sale
of 11,000 acres of Land in County of Halifax and Pittsylvania made with Thomas
GLASCOK of Richmund County Gentleman for sale of said Lands, which said contract GLASCOK has assigned unto said James HENRY and also for further consideration of £200 Current Money of Virginia...all that part of said Tract of
Land in Counties of Halifax and Pittsylvania which a certain John LEWIS Gentleman as attorney in fact for said TERRY conveyed to said GLASCOK by deed in
Halifax County Court and also 9,000 acres more Land adjoining the former also
in Counties of Halifax and Pittsylvania and were granted to TERRY by Patent
bearing date 31 Oct 1765 containing in the whole 20,000 acres being all the
lands included in the Bounds of same patent.
Rec: 29 Nov 1770   No witnesses   Champ. TERRY   L.S.
Sarah, wife of said Champness, being privily Examined as Law directs
Relinquished her right of Dower

DB 2, p.60 - MORTON from GLASS   BILL SALE, 14 May 1770

I John GLASS in consideration of £18 Current Money of Virginia paid Down by
Jehu MORTON...have granted Bargained and Sold 2 fether Beds and furniture,
one bay mare which I had of John RICHEY, one horse, 6 Pewter plats, 2 Dishes,
2 Basons, 1 paringer, 2 Iron potts, 5 Cheers, 2 Tables, 1 chest, 1 Trunk, 1
frying pann, 1 Ax, 2 pails, two Sows and piggs, 1 Spinning wheal, 3 stone
Juggs, 1 Stone Butter pott, 1 Gun, 1 weeding hoe, 2 Meel Sifters, 120 Gallons
Rum.   her

Test   Wealthy   PREWETT
                    mark

Rec: 29 Nov 1770   John GLASS L.S.

DB 2, p.61 - DIX from HOGAN   DEED, 26 Oct 1770

James HOGAN and Silence his wife of County of Pittsylvania of one part and
John DIX of same County of other part...for £130 Current Money of Virginia...
Land on north side Dann River...Begining at mouth of said DIX's Spring Branch
near the Ferry Landing Runing up said Branch to back line of a patent granted
to James HOGAN...to CARGHELLS lower line, along CARGHELLS line to dann River,
down the River. Also one other Tract granted to said James HOGAN by patent
bearing date 6 Apr 1769 beginning on east side of Hogans Creek...crossing the
creek...the first Tract being the Land and Plantation whereon said HOGAN now
lives.

Wit: Hezekiah SMITH, John OWEN, Ja^s. DENTON, Jno. WILSON, Abraham ARDIN,
Robt. PAYNE, James DIX, Drury BURCHETT   his
Wit. to Memorandum: Hezekiah SMITH, Thomas DUNCAN, Jo^s.   DUNCAN, Jno.
                                    his   mark
BYNUM, Joseph SMITH, Junr., Samuel   PREWET, Jno. OWEN, Jno. WILSON,
                                    mark
Robt. PAYNE, James DENTON Ja^s. DIX, Abraham ARDIN, Drury BURCHETT

                                                    James HOGAN L.S.
                                                    Silence HOGAN L.S.

DB 2, p.63 - DIX from HOGAN   DED^s., 25 Oct 1770

To John WILSON, John OWEN and Robert PAYNE Gent....we command you or any two
of you whereas James HOGAN and Silence his wife by their certain Indenture of
Bargain and Sale bearing date 26 Oct 1770 have conveyed to John DIX Gent. of
County of Pittsylvania a certain Tract of Land containing 430 acres...whereas
Silence, the wife of James, cannot conveniently travel to said Court is exam-
ined apart from her husband whether she doth freely Relinquish her Right of
Dower...did freely relinquish her right to said land 26 Oct 1770.

                                            John OWEN L.S.
Rec: 29 Nov 1770   Robt. PAYNE L.S.

DB 2, p.64 - CLAY from CLAY   DEED, 26 Nov 1770

Charles CLAY of Cumberland of one part and the Reverend Charles CLAY of
Albermar County of other part...for £5 Current Money of Virginia...800 acres
on Branches of dan River, being part of the tract of 9,600 in his order.
No witnesses
Rec: 29 Nov 1770   Charles CLAY L.S.

DB 2, p.65 - SHIELDS WILL   22 Sep 1770

I Patrick SHIELDS of Pittsylvania County Planter being sick and Low in body
but in Perfect mind and Memory do make this my last will and Testement...To
Jeane SHIELD my beloved wife her full thirds of all Goods and Chattles and

mouvable Effects as also her Living on the plantation where we now live upon
while she Continuce Single and one Rone mare. To son Thomas SHIELDS the
whole and sole Right of my plantation which I now possess to him his Heirs
and assigns as also a colt belonging to the Rone mare. To Robt. SHIELDS my
son one negroe Winch Named filles as also fiftey pounds to be Raised of my
Mouveble Esteat. I bequeth to Patrick SHIELDS my grandson and son of Samuel
SHIELDS £10 to be Reased and Levied of my Mouveble eastet. To Joseph SHIELDS
my son Two Heffers. If there is eaney Remander after Each of the Legacys is
payed that it be Devided Eaquily Betwixt Thomas and Robert. At Robert's
Disesse the negro wench to be sold and that and his other Estate be devided
Equily Betwixt Samuel SHIELDS, James SHIELDS, John SHIELDS, William SHIELDS,
Joseph SHIELDS and Thos. SHIELDS. Samuel SHIELDS, James SHIELDS and John
SHIELDS to be my Executors.   his
Wit: Joseph CUNINGHAM, Thos. CUNINGHAM   Patrick _Ø_ SHIELDS L.S.
                                                          mark

At Court held for Pittsylvania County 29 Nov 1770 the within last will and
Testament of Patrick SHIELDS Dec^d. was Exhibited in Court by Samuel SHIELDS
and James SHIELDS two of the Executors and Certificate granted for obtaining
a probate of said will, ordered recorded.   John FULTON and John SMITH their
securities entered into Bond.

DB 2, p.67 - INVENTORY OF G. THOMAS ESTATE   23 Oct 1770
Inventory of the Estate of George THOMAS Deceased appraised by Benjamin
LANKFORD, William COLLINS and William CHECK; negro man Isham, negro woman
Patt, negro girl Amey, negro boy James, negro boy Isaac, mares colts, cattle,
sheep, bed, rug, Bolster and sheet, parcell pewter, small iron pott and hooks,
frying pann, axes, parcell old Iron, Drawing knife, claw hammer, meal Sifter,
Water pail and Piggian, mans saddle, Womans Saddle and Bridle, Rifle Gunn,
chest, small Juggs, 2 old spinning wheels, hoggs, tobacco, 2 old Chizwells,
shott bag, powder horn, Bullett mould, flatt Irons, Looking Glass, stone
plates. Valued at £256·09·04.
Rec: 29 Nov 1770

DB 2, p.68 - ROSS from JINNING   DEED, 29 Mar 1771
Jonathan JINNINGS of County of Botetourt of one part and David ROSS of County
of Goochland of other part...for £135 Current Money of Virginia...all that
Tract of Land on north side Pigg River...beginning at mouth of frying pan
Creek, up said Creek as it meanders to OWENS line...on Lewis POTTERS Creek...
161 acres more or less which Land was Conveyed by John BOBBIT to said Jona-
than JINNINGS by Deed Recorded in County Court of Halifax.
No witnesses
Rec: 29 Mar 1771   Jonathan JINNINGS L.S.

DB 2, p.70 - ROBERTS from AUSTIN   DEED, 9 Mar 1771
Hannah AUSTIN of Amelia County of one part and James ROBERTS of Pittsylv^a.
County of other part...for £45 Current money...Land on Head of Sandy River
and containing by Estimation 303 acres, bounded by lands of George JEFFERSON
and James SMITH.   his   his
Wit: Joseph AUSTIN, Adam _A_ SHIELDS, Joseph _X_ MORTON
                          mark   mark
                                       her
                                Hannah _×_ AUSTIN L.S.
Rec: 29 Mar 1771   mark

DB 2, p.72 - RANDOLPH &c from GREEN &c   28 Mar 1771
John GREEN, Aquilla GREEN and Joseph GREEN all of County of Bedford planters

and Richard RANDOLPH, Tho[S]. WHYLING, David JAMESON, Jerman BAKER, George
BOOTH, Thomas LIVESAY and John HOLDAYS...for £300 Current Money of Virginia...
all that Tract of Land on the Grassey hill containing 50 acres by patent bearing date 15 Dec 1757...in David GRIFFITHS line.

No witnesses   John GREEN L.S.

Rec: 28 Mar 1771   Aquilla GREEN L.S.

Ann, wife of Joseph GREEN, and Elizabeth, wife   his
of Aquilla GREEN Privily Examined as Law directs   Joseph ✗ GREEN L.S.
and Relinquish their rights of Dower   mark

DB 2, p.74 - OWEN from MC DANIEL   **DEED, 29 Aug 1771**

William MC DANIEL of parish of Antrim in County of Halifax on one part and
Thomas OWEN of County of Pittsylvania of other part...for £160 Current Money
of Virginia...all that Tract of Land containing by Estimation 240 acres being
the Land which said MC DANIEL purchased of Robert WADE, Jun[r]. and was by said
Robert WADE by Indenture bearing date 22 Feb 1760 which said Land was purchased by said Robert WADE of Joseph PARISH and by said Joseph PARISH by Indenture
bearing date 18 Jan in year aforesaid Conveyed to said Robert WADE by Indenture of Record on Court of County of Halifax.

Wit: Jn[o]. WIMBISH, John WHITE, Thomas BALDWIN, Johnson MC DANIEL
Rec: 29 Aug 1771 & Ann, wife of Wm., Relinq.   William MC DANIEL L.S.
her dower right

DB 2, p.77 - TODD from SHORT   **DEED, 28 Mar 1771**

John SHORT and Elizabeth his wife of County of Pittsylvania of one part and
William TODD of County of Halifix of other part...for £250 Current Money of
Virginia...Land in County of Pittsylvania on the head Branches of Flayblow
Creek Containing 400 acres more or less...Granted to said Elizabeth SHORT by
Patent bearing date 14 Feb 1761.   his

No witnesses   John ⌐ SHORT L.S.
                                        mark
                                      her
                    Elizabeth ✗ SHORT L.S.

Rec: None   mark

DB 2, p.79 - TODD from SHORT   **DED[s]., 3 April "in 11th year of our Reign**

To Thomas DILLARD, John DONELSON and Crispin SHELTON Gen[t]. or any Two of his
Majestys Justices of County of Pittsylvania...John SHORT by his Certain Indenture of Feoffment hath Conveyed to William TODD of County of Pittsylvania
400 acres and Elizabeth the wife of said John cannot conveniantly Travel to
Court...Examine Elizabeth apart from her Husband whether she does freely Relinquish her Right of Dower to said Land.

Signed: 24 Apr 1771   John DONELSON L.S.
Rec: 30 May 1771   Crispin SHELTON L.S.

DB 2, p.80 - WIMBISH from TERRY   **BILL SALE, 29 Jan 1771**

I Champness TERRY of Pittsylvania County for sum of £100 Current Money of
Virginia paid by John WIMBISH of said County have sold to said John WIMBISH
one negro Man Slave Named Cato.   her

Wit: John DONELSON, Elizabeth ✗ YATES
                    mark   Champness TERRY L.S.

I David TERRY of Pittsylvania County do agree and oblige myself to keep John
WIMBISH indemnified and do along with Champness TERRY Bind myself in sum of
£200 Currency to maintain and Support to said John WIMBISH a good and Lawfull
Right to a negro fellow named Cato which Champ[n]. TERRY hath this day Sold to

said John WIMBISH. 29 Jan 1771
Wit: John DONELSON, Elizabeth _I_ YATES

Rec: 29 Mar 1771   David TERRY L.S.

DB 2, p.81 - DENHAM from BURKS   BILL SALE, 7 Mar 1771
I John BURKS of Pittsylvania County for sum of £13·06·04 Current Money by me
justly owing to Hugh DENHAM have this day sold one Bay horse about 13 hands
high no Brand Perceivable a snip on his nose Trots and Gallops, one Bay mare
Branded _MW_ about four feet Two or three Inches, one Cow Marked with two
swallow forks and Two over Keels in both Ears, one Cow marked with two Smooth
Crops two Slits & two underkeels, one Cow with a swallow fork in the Right
ear a Crop and Slit in the left ear, two yearling Cattle.
Wit: Edmund LYNE, Julius SCRUGGS   his
                                                   John _+++_ BURKS L.S.
Rec: 28 Mar 1771   Mark

DB 2, p.82 - SCOTT from PAYNE   DEED, 19 Nov 1770
William PAYNE of Halifax County of one part and Lurana SCOTT of Pittsylvania
County of other part...for £02·19 Current Money of Virginia...all that Tract
of Land on Both sides upper Dubble Creek containing 161 acres more or less...
at John LEWES Road to Paytonsburgh...crossing a branch...in WALTERS line...to
SMITHS corner...crossing said Creek along said road as it now Runs.
                                  his
Wit: John BLAIR, Robert _X_ SCOTT, Allen CALDWILL, John WALTERS, Robert WALTERS
                                mark
Rec: 28 Mar 1771   William PAYNE L.S.

DB 2, p.85 - EAST from THOMAS   DEED, 29 Mar 1770
William THOMAS of Pittsylvania County of one part and John EAST of said County
of other part...for £105 Current Money of Virginia...all that Tract of Land
on Stractstone Creek containing by Estimation 400 acres...Beginning at
COLLIN's corner...crossing a bold Branch...crossing said creek.
Wit: Peter PERKINS, Isaiah WATKINS, John STAMPS
Rec: 28 Mar 1771   William THOMAS L.S.

DB 2, p.87 - BALLINGER from HUBBARD   DEED, 26 Mar 1771
Edward HUBBARD of County of Pittsylvania of one part and John BALLENGER of
same County of other part...for £50 Current Money of Virginia...Edward
HUBBARD and Elizabeth his wife sell all that Tract of Land Containing by Estimation 100 acres on Both sides Straitstone Creek. Beginning where my Line
crosses John BALLENGERS Spring Branch...crossing a Branch and a Creek below
the fork...untill you come oppersett to the mouth of the Branch that Runs
into the South fork of Straitstone Creek below the Scaley bark low grownd...
a strait course to the mouth of said branch, down south fork to the fork of
Straitstone, up North fork to Mouth of aforesd. Spring Branch.
Wit: Thomas DILLARD Junr., John VAUGHAN, William COLLINS

                                                   his
                                          Edward _Q_ HUBBARD L.S.
Rec: 28 Mar 1771   mark

DB 2, p.89 - ROBERTS from WALTON   DEED, 23 Dec 1770
George WALTON of County of Prince Edward of one part and James ROBERTS of
County of Pittsylvania of other part...for £10 Current Money of Virginia...
200 acres on south side south fork of Mayo River...Beginning at the most South

part of the Next south bent of said River above the place where SHORT lived,
south to FONTAINS line, west as far as to run due north to said River. Above
Deed is in Lien of a Deed passed many year ago and this deed is only intended
to pass the said George WALTONS Interest as Titil in the Land.
Wit: Andrew GIBSON,Joseph COOK, John SALMON, Rich^d. MARR
Rec: 28 Mar 1771   George WALTON L.S.

DB 2, p.91 - WYNNE from BUTLER   DEED, 16 Jan 1771
John BUTLER of County of Prince George of one part and Thomas WYNNE of County
of Pittsylvania of other part...for £167 Current Money of Virginia...Two
Tracts of Land containing 835 acres both ajoyning Together being on both
sides of Sandy Creek of Dan River and said Two Tracts of Land was Granted to
said John BUTLER both bearing date 15 Aug 1764...one Tract contains 400 acres
and other contains 435 acres and both bounded by said pattents.
Wit: John Richard TALIAFERRO, Rob^. WYNNE, Peter James BAILEY
Rec: 28 Mar 1771   John BUTLER L.S.

DB 2, p.93 - FEE from WALTON   DEED, 23 Dec 1770
George WALTON of County of Prince Edward of one part and Thomas FEE of County
of Pittsylvania of other part...just and full sum of £4 Current Money of Virginia...35 acres on North side South fork Mayo River being the place where
said Thomas FEE now Lives.
Note also this Deed ought to have been passed many years ago for which Reason
said George WALTON only intends hereby to Convey all his right and Interest
in said Land.
Wit: James ROBERTS, Joseph COOK, Andrew GIBSON, John SALMON(Memo: Richard MARR)
Rec: 29 Mar 1771   George WALTON L.S.

DB 2, p.95 - GORDON BOND FOR SHERIFALTY   28 Mar 1771
Archebald GORDON, John BLAGGE, John ROWLAND, Arthur HOPKINS and William
TUNSTALL of County of Pittsylvania are bound to Sovereign Lord king George
the third in sum of £1000 Current Money...Condition of above obligation is
such the above bound Archibald GORDON is Constituted and appointed Sherriff
of the County, during pleasure by Commission from his honour the president
under seal of the Colony dated 15 Mar. GORDON shall Collect all quitrents,
fines, forfietures.
                                              Arch^d. GORDON   L.S.
                                                 John BLAGGE   L.S.
                                                 John ROWLAND L.S.
                                               Arthur HOPKINS L.S.
Rec: 28 Mar 1771   Will. TUNSTALL   L.S.

DB 2, p.96 - GORDON BOND FOR SHERIFALTY   28 Mar 1771
Archebald GORDON, John ROWLAND, William TUNSTALL, John BLAGG and Arthur
HOPKINS of County of Pittsylvania are bound to Sovereign Lord king george...
in sum of £1000 Current money...Condition of above obligation is such that
above bound Archebald GORDON is constituted and appointed Sherrif of the County...to collect all officers fees and dues put into his hands, account for
and pay same to officers to whom such fees are due...pay and satisfy all sums
of Money and Tobacco by him received.
                                              Arch^d. GORDON   L.S.
                                                 John ROWLAND L.S.
                                               Arthur HOPKINS L.S.
                                                 Will TUNSTALL L.S.
Rec: 28 Mar 1771   John BLAGGE   L.S.

DB 2, p.98 - COKER from BURKS   BILL SALE, 7 Mar 1771

I, John BURKS of Pittsylvania County for sum of £04·03·09 Current money of
Virginia by me Justly due and owing William COKER have granted and sold to
William COKER two feather Beds and furniture.   his

Wit: Edmund LYNE, Julius SCRUGGS   John _/_/_/_BURKS ·L.S

Rec: 28 Mar 1771   mark

DB 2, p.98 - SMITH from BLACKLEY   DEED, 8 Jan 1771

James BLACKLEY and Rebeca his wife of Pittsylvaney County of one part and
John SMITH of same County of other part...for £10 Current Money of Virginia...
100 acres more or less lying on Middle fork of Strabery Creek...Beginning on
a chesnutt in the 400 acres of Land formly surveyed for Thomas HARGETT but
now persest by John COOK runing a North Corse to mouth of a small Dreen
Called the Miry branch, up the branch to the former line then Bound by
LOGINGS line the same Granted to said BLACKLEY by patents dated 1762.

Rebecca relinquishes her Dower right   his

                            James / BLACKLEY L.S.
                            mark

                                her
Wit: John COOK, James DEVIN, William DEVIN   Rebeaca P BLEACKLEY
Rec: 28 Mar 1771   mark

DB 2, p.100 - STAMPS from WYNNE   DEED, 28 Mar 1771

Thomas WYNE of County of Pittsylvania of one part and John STAMPS of aforesd.
county of other part...for £42·02·00 Current Money of Virginia...194 acres
on Sandy Creek of Dan River being part of a Tract of Land containing 435
acres that I,Thomas WYNNE bought of John BUTLER...Crossing the Creek.

               his   his
Wit: Robert WYNNE, John / WALLER, Edward / BURGES
                 mark   mark
Rec: 28 Mar 1771   Thomas WYNNE L.S

DB 2, p.101 - COOK from BLACKLEY   DEED,(no date)

James BLEAKLEY and Rebaker his wife of Pittsylvania County of one part and
John COOK of same County of other part...for £30 Current Money of Virginia...
Land containing by Estimation 200 acres...Beginning in ROBORDS Line on the
Middle fork of Straberry Creek, along ROBARDS line, crossing Hickeys Rod to
a branch thence up Crossing Joseph AUSTINS Rode...in HILLS line...to SMITHS
Line...Granted to same James BLEACKLEY by patent 12 Jul 1762.

No witnesses   James BLAKELY L.S.

Rec: 28 Mar 1771 & Rebecea relinq. Dower right   Rebeca BLAKELY L.S.

DB 2, p.103 - HILL from BLACKLEY   DEED, 28 Feb 1771

James BLEACKLY and Rebecca his wife of Pittsylvania County of one part and
Thomas HILL of same County of other part...for £10 Current Money of Virginia...
100 acres in fork of HICKEYS and Joseph AUSTINS Rods...on the Branches of
Middle fork of Straberry Creek the same being Granted to same James BLACKLEY
by patent.

No witnesses   James BLAKELY L.S.

Rec: 28 Mar 1771   Rebecca BLAKELY L.S.

Rebecca, wife of said James, being privily Examined as Law directs Relinquished her right of Dower

DB 2, p.104 - WALLER from HARDY   DEED, 19 Sep 1770
John HARDY of Pittsylvania County of one part and Zachariah WALLER of County
aforesd. of other part...for £47 Current Money...314 acres Beginning at
Frances LUCKS corner...crossing Polleys Branch to pointers in LUCKS line,
along his line.

Wit: John WALTERS, Robt. WALTERS, John ⤬ WALLER   John 🖊 HARDY L.S.
                                      mark   mark

                                                    Martha ⋀⋀ HARDY L.S.
                                                      her
Rec: 28 Mar 1771   mark

DB 2, p.106 - WARD FROM SIMMONS   DEED, 13 Oct 1770
John SIMMONS of County of Prince Edward of one part and Jeremiah WARD of
County of Pittsylvania of other part...for £30 Current Money of Virginia...
150 acres More of Less part of the 300 acres which Frances BUCKNALL obtained
a patent for Lying on both sides of Reddis Creek...William ATKINSONS line,
up both sides said Creek to dividing line betwixt David POLLEY and John
SUMMONS including half of the 300 acres which Frances BUCKNALL had a patent for.
Wit: Samuel BOLLING, Robert SANDERS, Richard BENNETT
Rec: 29 Nov 1770
Further proved: 28 Mar 1771   John SIMMONS L.S.

DB 2, p.109 - HALL from CHOICE   DEED, 27 Mar 1771
Tully CHOICE of Pittsylvania County of one part and William HALL of same
County of other part...for Natural love and affection which he hath and bear-
eth unto said William HALL hath given granted enfeoffed and doth give one
certain Tract of Land on Snow Creek containing by Estimation 222 acres...
Pointers in old line...crossing Glady fork...crossing Snow Creek.
No witnesses
Rec: 28 Mar 1771   Tully CHOICE L.S.

DB 2, p.111 - BOLLING from CHOICE   DEED, 28 Mar 1771
Tully CHOICE OF Pittsylvania County of one part and Saml. BOLLING of same
County of other part...for natural love and affection which he hath and bear-
eth unto said Samuel BOLLING...207 acres on Snow Creek...Begining at William
HALLS corner in old line...on a step hill side on the Creek, down the creek
as it Meanders to the old line.
No witnesses
Rec: 28 Mar 1771   Tully CHOICE L.S.

DB 2, p.113 - TREDWAY from JEFFERSON   DEED, 28 Mar 1771
George JEFFERSON of Pittsylvania County of one part and William TREDWAY of
same County of other part...for £40 Current Money of Virginia...162 acres
more or less on turkey Cock Creek...Begining at Arther HOPKINS corner in old
line.
No witnesses
Rec: 28 Mar 1771   G. JEFFERSON L.S.

DB 2, p.114 - FOWLER from MACKAM   DEED, 6 Dec 1770
James MACKAM of County of middlesex of one part and John FOWLER of County of
Bedford of other part...for £18 Current Money of Virginia...Land in County
of Pittsylvania containing by Estimation 240 acres...oak in Clay Branch, up
the Remanders of said Branch.

Wit: Lewis MOUNTAGUE, James $\overset{his}{\underset{mark}{+}}$ FLANAGIN, Ralph SMITH

Rec: 28 Mar 1771   James MACKAM L.S.

DB 2, p. 117 - WIER from WILSON   DEED, 28 Mar 1771
John WILSON of Parish of Camden in County of Pittsylvania of one part and
Thomas WIER of Parish and County aforesd. of other part...for £233·06·08
Current Money of Virginia...All that Tract of Land containing 400 acres lying
on Both sides Fall Creek...crossing both forks of the Creek...crossing a
branch...crossing the Creek below the fork.
No witnesses
REc: 28 Mar 1771   John WILSON L.S.

DB 2, p.119 - DALTON from MACKAN   DEED, 6 Dec 1770
James MACKAN of County of Middlesex of one part and John DALTON of County of
Pittsylvania of other part...for £25 Current money of Virginia...270 acres
more or less...along a branch.
                    his
Wit: James $\overset{his}{\underset{mark}{\times}}$ FLANAGIN, Ralph SMITH, John FOWLER
Rec: 28 Mar 1771   James MACKAN L.S.

DB 2, p.122 - DUDLEY from WYNNE   DEED, 29 Dec 1770
Thos. WYNNE Junr. of County of Pittsylvania of one part and Thomas DUDLEY of
same County of other part...for £250 Current money...400 acres more or less
on South Side Dan River being part of a patent of a larger quantity Granted
to William WYNNE Senr. bearing date as by Record may appear...Beginning at
mouth of Jacksons Branch, up said Branch to back line...on that Line to John
DIXES line, down the River as it meanders to the Begining at mouth of said
Jacksons branch.
Wit: John DIX, Henry DIXON, Junr., William WYNNE Junior, Robert PAYNE
Rec: 28 Mar 1771   Thomas WYNNE L.S.

DB 2, p.124 - COCKE from BOWMER   DEED, 28 Mar 1771
John BOWMER of Pittsylv^a. of one part and John COCKE of same County of other
part...for £15 Current money of Virginia...200 acres more or less according
to the Bounds being part of a patent of 400 acres Granted first to Charles
BOSTICK baring date 10 Aug 1759 in County above said and on the frying Pan
Creek being the upper part of said Tract.
No witnesses
Rec: 28 Mar 1771   John BOWMER L.S.

DB 2, p.126 - LUMKIN from TAYLOR   DEED, 22 Dec 1770
Edmund TAYLOR of County of Macklenburg and Colony of Virginia of one part
and George LUMPKIN of County of Pittsylvania and Colony aforesd. of other
part...for £525 Current money of Virginia...4,750 acres on both sides Marrowbone Creek...Begining at RANDOLPH & companys corner at the wart mountain...
the same Land being Granted to said Edmund TAYLOR 3 May 1763.
Wit: John WILSON, Robert CHANDLER, Robert LUMKIN
Rec: 28 Mar 1771   Edmund TAYLOR L.S.

DB 2, p.128 - MURPHEY from TERRY   DEED, 22 Mar 1769
Nathaniel TERRY Gen^t. of Halifix County of one part and James MURPHEY of
Pittsylvania County of other part...for £20 Current money of Virginia...173
acres it being part of a Larger quantity Granted to said Nathaniel TERRY by

patent...in LEAKS line thence by new dividing lines...crossing the fork Branch
of Elkhorn Creek...in GLASSCOCKS line...Along LEEKS line...crossing aforesd.
fork Branch of Elkhorn Creek to the Begining it being the Land and Plantation
whereon said James MURPHEY now Lives be the same more of less.
Wit: Isaac READ, Benj. TERRY, Haynes MORGAN, John SALMON
Rec: 28 Mar 1771   Nathaniel TERRY L.S.

DB 2, p.131 - SMITH & C$^{\circ}$. from ROWLAND   DEED, 14 Mar 1771
John ROWLAND of Pittsylvania County of one part and James SMITH and Company
of other part...for £100 Current Money of Virginia...272 acres more or Less
on Branches of Wet Sleave Creek and branches of Sandy River...in John COOKS
which is William ROBERTS's line thence new lines North...in James ROBERTS
line...corner in James ROBERTS line...crossing a Branch of Sandy River Near
the Courthouse thence new lines...crossing Wet Sleave Creek...in William
ROBERT's line...crossing a Branch...Crossing wet Sleave Creek and a branch.
Wit: John SALMON
Rec: 28 Mar 1771   John ROWLAND L.S.

DB 2, p.133 - SARTAIN from SARTAIN   DEED, 28 Mar 1771
Josiah SARTAIN and his wife (no name mentioned) of Pittsylvania County of one
part and Jacob SARTAIN of same County of other Part...for £20 Current Money
of Virginia...95 acres more of less on frying pan Creek it being Part of the
tract said Josiah SARTAIN now lives on...north side said Creek on old line,
crossing said Creek on John GOADS line along his line to old line...Crossing
Two Creeks.
No witnesses   Josiah CERTAIN L.S.
Rec: 28 Mar 1771
Wife of said Josiah CERTAIN privily Examined as law directs Relinquished her
right of Dower

DB 2, p.135 - CAMPBELL from SIMPSON   DEED, 28 Mar 1771
William SIMPSON of County of Botetourt of one part and Archebald CAMPBELL of
County aforesaid of other part...for £50 Current money of Virginia...168
acres in Pittsylvania Co. on Tomahawk Creek which Land was Conveyed to said
William SIMPSON by Archebald GRAYHAM by Deed recorded in County Court of Pitt-
sylvania...oak of Isaac CLOUNDS...Crossing two branches and the Creek.
No witnesses
Rec: 28 Mar 1771   William SIMPSON L.S.

DB 2, p.137 - OWEN from DUNCAN   DEED, 22 Nov 1770
James DUNKIN of County of Pittsylvania of one part and Thomas OWEN of same
County of other Part...for £150 Current money of Virignia...103 acres on
north side Dan River...on River bank in Henry STONES line by a Branch...in
William MC DANIELS line.

Wit: Elizabeth X YATES, Thos. X SHELTON, Marthe X YATES,
                her   his   her
              mark   mark   mark

                 his   his
William W SHELTON, Benjamin B GWILLAMS
        mark   mark

                              her
Memorandum signed by: Hannah X SHELTON   his
                             mark   James 4 DUNKIN L.S.
Rec: 28 Mar 1771   mark

DB 2, p.139 - ROWLAND to the Court   30 Aug X[th] year of Reign
We Michael ROWLAND, John ROWLAND and John BLAGGE are firmly bound to Justices
of Pittsylvania County in sum of £150 Current Money of Virginia...Condition
of above obligation is such that if above bound Michael ROWLAND shall Truly
build a prison in said County of Pittsylvania Convenient to said Court House
of following plan...a prison Twenty four feet by sixteen Seven feet between
floors the body to be Built of Good Saw.d or hew.d plank twelve Inches thick
the floors of said Size and Sort of Timber Cover.d with Good nail.d Shingles
three good doors in Convenient Parts of said prison the inside of said
prison to be Seal.d with oak plank Inch and ahalf Thick naild on with half
Crown nails the doors of said prison to have Sufficent Locks to Each of them
all so three Windows in said Prison well bard with Iron Grates Sufficent to
keep out assistance to Risque either Debter or folon also a Good Chimney in
Convenient part of said Prison well Iron Grated above and below all and
every part of said prison to be done and finish.d in the term of Six Months
from the date here of to the Satisfaction of said Court of Pittsylvania.
BOND FOR BUILDING A PRISON   Michael ROWLAND L.S.
Wit: John SALMON   John BLEAGG L.S.
Rec: none   John ROWLAND L.S.

DB 2, p.141 - WALTERS from WALLER   DEED,19 Sep 1770
Zachariah WALLER of Pittsylvania County of one part and Thomas WALTERS of
County aforesaid of other part...for £80...284 acres more of less being part
of a Greater Quantity and being within said Thomas WALTERS old pattern.

                                    his
Wit: John WALTERS, Robert WALTERS, John ⟍✗ WALLER
                                    mark   his
Rec: 28 Mar 1771   Zachariah ⟋ WALLER L.S.
                                                          mark

                                                          her
Acts and Deed of above named Zachariah   Dianah ✗ WALLER
WALLER and Dianah his wife   mark

DB 2, p.142 - COLLINS from VAUGHAN   DEED, 26 Mar 1771
John VAUGHAN and Sarah his wife of County of Pittsylvania of one part and
William COLLINS of same County of other part...for £15 Current money...all
that tract of Land Containing by Estimation 25 acres...where said John
VAUGHAN's lyne Crosses Straitstone Creek near the mouth of Camp branch, down
said Creek as it meanders to the mouth of said William COLLINS Spring branch
on south side said Straitstone Creek, up said Spring branch as it meanders
to the head...near to Dicks Cabbin in said COLLINS pasture.
No witnesses
Rec: 28 Mar 1771   John VAUGHAN L.S.

DB 2, p.145 - IRBY from SHORT   DEED, 22 Feb 1770
John SHORT of Pittsylvania County of one part and Peter IRBY of Halifix
County of other part...for £10 Current money of Virginia...10 acres begining
on flyblow Creek at mouth of Thomas FARIS's spring branch Runing up said
Creek to John SHORTS line, along another new line to aforesd. Spring Branch
down the branch.
No witnesses   his
Rec: 28 Mar 1771   John ⟋ SHORT L.S.
                                                      mark

DB 2, p.146 - GOAD from FOWLER   DEED, 28 Mar 1771
John FOWLER of County of Bedford of one part and Abraham GOAD of Bedford
County of other part...for £30...240 acres in Clay branch, up remainders of
said branch.
No witnesses
Rec: 28 Mar 1771   John FOWLER L.S.

DB 2, p.149 - JONES from JONES   DEED, 26 Mar 1771
Robert JONES of Pittsylvania County and Colony of Virginia of one part and
Thomas JONES, Junr. of County and Colony aforesaid of other part...for £60
Curant money of Virginia...all that parcel of Land on both sides south fork
of Pig River...on south side of the Creek of Pig River thence new lines
north...Crossing one branch...93 akers part of 230 akers the Paton baring
date 10 Sep 1767.
No witnesses
Rec: 28 Mar 1771   Robert JONES L.S.

DB 2, p.151 - JONES from JONES   DEED, 26 Mar 1771
Robert JONES of Pittsylvania County and Colony of Virginia of one part and
Henry JONES of other part County and Coloney aforesaid...for £50 Curent money
of Virginia...Land on both sides of north fork of Pige River...Crossing a
Branch...Crossing three branches...south side of the Creek...160 acres the
patent bearing date 10 Sep 1767.
Wit: Thomas JONES Junior
Rec: 28 Mar 1771   Robert JONES L.S.

DB 2, p.153 - COPLAND from COPLAND   DEED, 26 Feb 1771
Peter COPLAND of County of Pittsylvania of one part and Richard COPLAND of
same County of other part...for £55·10   Current money of Virginia...100
acres more or less on bever Creek and its branches...on west bank of Beaver
Creek, running north.
No witnesses
REc: 29 Mar 1771   Peter COPLAND L.S.

DB 2, p.156 - BLEVINS from LUMPKIN   DEED, 20 May 1771
George LUMPKINS and Mary his wife of Colony of Virginia in County of Pittsyl-
vania of one part and William BLEVINS younger son to William BLEVINS the
Elder of said Colony of other part...for £160 Current Money of Virginia...
Land on north side Marrowbone Creek...on the Creek at the mouth of the branch...
west up the Branch...in PRICES line...300 acres.
Wit: Walters DUNN, Burditt ESKRIDGE, Joseph FARGUSON
Rec: 30 May 1771   George LUMKIN L.S.
Mary, wife of said George, being privily   her
Examined as Law directs Relinquished   Mary _C_ LUMPKINS L.S.
her right of Dower   mark

DB 2, p.158 - TAYLOR from LUMKIN   DEED, 30 May 1771
George LUMPKIN of County of Pittsylv^a. of one part and James TAYLOR of same
County of other part...for £90 Current money of Virginia...319 acres more or
less being part of Lands of said George LUMKINS Tract...on Marrowbone Creek...
to old order line.
Wit: Waters DUNN, Burditt ESKRIDGE
Rec: 30 May 1771   George LUMKIN L.S.

DB 2, p.161 - ESKRIDGE from LUMKIN   DEED, 20 May 1771
George LUMKIN and Mary his wife of County of Pittsylvania in Colony of Vir-
ginia of one part and Burditt ESKRIDGE of aforesaid Colony of other part...
for £100 Current Money of Virginia...Land on east side Marrowbone Creek...
Mouth of a Branch, down said Creek...345 acres.
Wit: Waters DUNN, Joseph FARGESON, Enoch GRIGSBY
Rec: 30 May 1771   George LUMKIN L.S.
Mary, wife of said George, privily   her
Exam^d. as Law directs Relinquished   Mary ⌒ LUMKIN L.S.
her right of Dower   mark

DB 2, p.163 - SMITH & Co. from CHRYST   DEED OF TRUST, 5 Mar 1771
Henry CHRYST of County of Pittsylvania on one Part and James SMITH & Company
of said County of other part...whereas said Henry CHRYST stands Justly indebted to said James SMITH & Co. in sum of £08·11·03 Current money of Virginia now this Indenture...and for sum of 5s to Henry CHRYST by James SMITH
& Co...hath sold one Waggon & Geears, 3 Horses one I had in swap with Arch^d.
GRAHAM, one I purchased of George DILLINGHAM and other a white Horse I Bought
of James TALBOT, 3 mares one of which I Purchased of William HALE branded
thus IXI on her near buttock, the other two I brought from Pennsylvania, 6
head of Catle, 3 Beds and furniture and every article of my personall Estate...
lawful Interest from date of these Presents to 5 Mar 1772 and all Costs that
shall become due in this mortgage within space of one year after date.

Wit: Elish ⨏ ESTES, Arch^d. SMITH   his
                                                   Henry ⊢ CHRYST L.S.
Rec: 30 May 1771   mark

DB 2, p.166 - MANN from LACEY   DEED, 30 May 1771
Theop^s. LACEY of County of Pittsylvania of one Part and Robert MANN of County
of Halifix of other part...for £100 Current Money...all that Tract of Land
containing 300 acres more of less...in Mrs. Roger ADKINSON line formerly
WHITEBREADS...it being the same Land said Theop^s. Purchased of Francis NEW
who purchased same from William WRIGHT.
No witnesses
Rec: 30 May 1771   Theop^s. LACY L.S.

DB 2, p.169 - PRICE from LUMKIN   DEED, 30 May 1771
George LUMKIN of County of Pittsylvania of one Part and Joseph Shores PRICE
of amherst County of other part...for £265 Current money of Virginia...530
acres, it being part of Lands said George LUMKIN's Tract...on a small branch,
down said branch as it meanders to Marrowbone Creek, down said Creek as it
meanders to RANDOLPH & Companys order line.
Wit: Waters DUNN, Burditt ESKRIDGE
Rec: 30 May 1771   George LUMKIN L.S.
Mary, wife of said George, being privily Exam^d. as Law directs Relinquished
her right of Dower

DB 2, p.171 - MOSS from CHAMBERLAIN   DEED, 17 Dec 1770
Richard CHAMBERLAIN of New Kent County of one part and Moses MOSS of Prince
William County of other Part...for £150 Current money of Virginia...Land on
Banister River, containing 400 acres...Beginning at ELKINSES, now Capt.
John PIGGS

Wit: John PIGG, Willm. $\times$ OWEN, Betsy PIGG

Rec: 30 May 1771   R. CHAMBERLAYNE L.S.

DB 2, p.173 - OZBURN from GRAYHAM   DEED, 30 May 1771

William GRAHAM of Pittsylvania County and Colony of Virginia of one part and
David OZBURN Senr. of County of Frederick and Colony aforesaid of other part...
for £55 Current money of Virginia...all that Tract of Land on both sides Tomehawk Creek...Crossing the Creek aforesaid...as may more fully appear by Patent Granted to John CHESWEL bearing date 10 Sep 1755, also a Deed Convey^d.
out of said Patent by said John CHESWEL unto above named William GRAYHAM as
may appear by Record Containing by Estimation 198 acres.
No witnesses
Rec: 30 May 1771   William GRAHAM

DB 2, p.176 - GREENWOOD to PERRY   DEED, 17 Apr 1771

Thomas GREENWOOD and Jeane his wife of Parish of (none given) in County of
Maclingburg of one part and William PERRY of Parish of Cambden in County of
Pittsylvania of other part...for £100 Current money of Virginia...250 acres
more of less by patent bearing date 15 Mar 1747...on Panther Creek.

Wit: Crispin SHELTON, Abr^a. SHELTON, Beverley SHELTON, Peter $\times$ BROOKS,

Charles SIMMONS
Rec: 30 May 1771   Thomas GREENWOOD L.S.

DB 2, p.179 - SANDFORD from LUMKIN   DEED, 20 May 1771

George LUMKIN and Mary his wife of Colony and dominion of Virginia in County
of Pittsylvania of one part and George SANDFORD of said Colony of other part...
for £50 Current money of Virginia...Land on east side Marrowbone Creek...
east down the Creek...mouth of a branch, up the branch as it meanders...in
old line...247 acres.
Wit: Waters DUNN, Burditt ESKRIDGE, Joseph FARGESON
Rec: 30 May 1771   George LUMKIN L.S.
Mary, wife of said George, Exam^d. and   her
Relinquished her right of Dower   Mary $\curvearrowleft$ LUMKIN L.S.
                                                         mark

DB 2, p.182 - GRIGSBY from LUMKIN   DEED, 20 May 1771

George LUMKIN and mary his wife of Pittsylvania County in Colony of Virginia
of one part and Enoch GRIGSBY of Colony and County aforesaid of other part...
for £160 Current money of Virginia...land on both sides Marrowbone Creek...
Beginning on east side of said Creek at mouth of a branch, up the branch north.
520 acres.
Wit: Waters DUNN, Burditt ESKRIDGE, Jo^s. FARGESON
Rec: 30 May 1771   George LUMKIN L.S.
Mary, wife of George, privily Exam^d. and   her
Relinquished her right of Dower   Mary $\curvearrowleft$ LUMKIN L.S.
                                                         mark

DB 2, p.184 - CHANDLER from LUMPKIN   DEED, 30 May 1771

George LUMKIN of County of Pittsylvania of one part and Robert CHANDLER of
same County of other part...for £100 Current money of Virginia...530 acres
more of less, it being part of the lands of said George LUMKINS Tract...on

Marrowbone Creek...in old line.
Wit: Waters DUNN, Burditt ESKRIDGE
Rec: 30 May 1771   George LUMKIN L.S.

DB 2, p.187 - BURGESS from CARTER   INDENTURE OF APPREN[S]., May 1771
I, Marget CARTER in County of Pittsylvania, for love and Good will and affection which I have and do bear unto my Eldest son Lewis CARTER in County of
Pittsylvania and for futer support and well being of said Lewis, I do bind
said Lewis unto Mr. Thomas BURGESS in County of Pittsylvania...do grant give
and Confirm to said BURGESS said LEWIS untill he is the years of twenty one
and said BURGESS do oblize his Self...such diat and apperal as he makes use
of him self and if said boy behaves him self as a Servent...ought to do
oblige him Self to give "afreedum sule" to value of £03.

                              his
Wit: Jn[o]. KEARBY, Sam[1]. X KEARBY   her
                             mark   Marget // CARTER L.S.
Rec: 30 May 1771   mark

DB 2, p.188 - WIMBISH from HAMILTON   DEED TO LOTTS, 13 Apr 1771
John HAMILTON of Orange County in Province of North Carolina of one part and
John WIMBISH of Pittsylvania County of other part...for £26·05   Current
Money of Virginia...all those four Lotts or half acres of Land in Town of
Peytonsburg that is to say one Corner Lott on Main Street where Thomas
SPRAGIN formerly lived Number ninety eight, one Lott or half acre on South
west side Mountain Street number 107 and other two Lotts or half acres of
Land on south side of Forest Street Number 206 and 193 and all the Lotts
that are now my property in said Town of Peytonsburg as well those inumerated
as those not inumerated.
Wit; Abraham SHELTON, Thomas HUTCHINGS, H. CHALLES, Theop[s]. LACY
Rec: no date   John HAMILTON L.S.

DB 2, p.191 - LAYNE from LAYNE   DEED, 25 Jun 1771
Dutton LAIN of Pittsylvania County of one part and John Fuller LAIN of said
County of other part...for £100 Current money...137 1/2 acres on both sides
mountain Creek...Beginning on east side line of Tract of Land said Dutton
LAIN lives on...to large high Clay bank along olde lines as they are mentioned
in the patton of said land.
No witnesses
Rec: 27 Jun 1771   Dutton LAIN L.S.

DB 2, p.193 - HOPKINS from JEFFERSON   BILL SALE, 26 Mar 1771
I, George JEFFERSON, of Pittsylvania County for sum of £68·16 Current money
of Virginia have Sold to Arthur HOPKINS of same County one negro man Slave
named Chance...and keep harmless said Arther HOPKINS on account of his being
Security to Bennet GOODE of Mecklenburge County for Purchase of said negro
Chance...above bill of Sale to be void if above sum not paid or other wise
said Arther HOPKINS when he shall be obliged to pay said money, is to Sell
said negro at publick auction for best price that he can git in order to discharge same and ballance if any to pay to said George JEFFERSON.

           her
Wit: Mary // SWANSON   David WILLIS, Edmund BOAZ
         mark
Rec: 27 Jun 1771   G. JEFFERSON L.S.

DB 2, p.195 - DUNN from FARGESON   POWER OF ATTORNEY, 14 Jun 1771
I, Joseph FARGASON of County of Esex and South Farnham Parrish appoint my
trusty friend Waters DUNN of County of Pittsylvania and Parrish of Camdens
my true and Lawfull attorney for me in my name...receive from such Person and
Persons the several debts that may appear to be Justly due to me, also to
finish all my Business at Law within Dominion of Virginia with every person...
Granting my said attorney my Soul full power and authority to take such Legal
Courses...could do were I Personaly present.
Wit: Robert CHANDLER, Richard COPLAND, Joshua BROWN
Rec: 27 Jun 1771   Joseph FARGESON L.S.

DB 2, p.196 - ROBERTS from PAYNE   BILL SALE, 28 Jun 1771
I, William PAYNE, hath this day sold unto James ROBERTS of said County one
Certain Stoned Horse branded CT on the near Buttock his Colour of a blue
Roan paces. Ten years old for the Consideration of £06.
Wit: John SALMON, Theop[s]. LACY   his
Rec: 28 Jun 1771   W[m]. PAYNE L.S.
                                                  mark

DB 2, p.197 - MC DANIEL from TERRY & LEWIS   DEED, 29 Nov 1770
Champness TERRY of County of Pittsylvania and John LEWIS Jun[r]. of County of
Halifax Gentlemen of one part and William MC DANIEL of County of Halifax of
other part...for £50 Current money of Virginia...two Lotts or half acres of
Land in Town of Peytonsburg and County of Pittsylvania, which according to
the plan of said Town are known by Numbers 98 and 99 and which said Champness
TERRY purchased of William MC DANIEL and were by said William MC DANIEL by
Indenture bearing date 21 Jun 1764 conveyed by said Champness TERRY as by
said Indenture recorded in Court of County of Halifax.
Wit: William THOMAS, William OWEN, Sen[r]., Johnson MC DANIEL
Rec: 29 Nov 1770   Champ[s]. TERRY L.S.
Sarah, wife of said Champness, being privily   John LEWIS Jun[r]. L.S.
Examined, relinquished her right of Dower
Again proved: 28 Mar 1771 and 27 Jun 1771

DB 2, p.200 - THOMAS from WATKINS   DEED, 28 Jun 1771
Isaiah WATKINS of county of Pittsylvania of one part and William THOMAS of
said County of other part...for £300 Current money...Land on Caskaid Creek
together with 23 Head of Cattle, 10 Horses and 100 head of Hoggs.
Wit: Haynes MORGAIN, G. MARR
Rec: 28 Jun 1771   Isaiah WATKINS L.S.
Alice, wife of said Isaiah, being privily Exam[d]. as Law directs Relinquished
her right of Dower

DB 2, p.201 - WIMBISH & HUGHES from WALTON   DEED, 18 Jun 1771
George WALTON of Prince Edward County of one Part and John WIMBISH and
Archelius HUGHES of Pittsylvania County of other part...for £42·10 Current
money of Virginia...Land on South Mayo River Containing 497 acres...on
ROBERTS line...on FONTAINES line.
Wit: Is. READ, Haynes MORGAN, Ep[m]. DUNLAP, John AYLETT
Rec: 27 Jun 1771   George WALTON L.S.

DB 2, p.204 - BALLENGER from AUSTIN   DEED, 22 Apr 1771
John AUSTIN of Province of North Carolina and County of Roan of one part and
Joseph BALLENGER of Colony of Virginia and County of Pittsylvania of other
part...for £200 Current Money...all that tract of Land on North fork of Sandy
River containing by extimation 200 acres being part of a Greater tract of 400

Joining Lands of Josiah MANN, Jehu MORTON and Joseph AUSTIN.
Wit: Jn°. GLASS, Jehu MORTON, Joseph MORTON, Joseph AUSTIN

his
John A AUSTIN L.S.
mark

Rec: 27 Jun 1771

DB 2, p.207 - LOGAN from HARGET DEED, 27 Jun 1771

Thomas HARGET of County of Pittsylvania and Colony of Virginia of one part and Samuel LOGAN of County aforesaid of other part...for £15 Current money of Virginia...all that tract of Land on both sides Strawberry Creek containing by Estimation 279 acres being part of a tract which was granted to said Thomas HARGET by Letters patent under Seal of Colony bearing date at Williamsburg 12 Jul 1762...south side of Creek thence Crossing the Creek.
No witnesses
Rec: 27 Jun 1771 Thomas HARGET L.S.

DB 2, p.210 - EDWARDS from EDWARDS DEED, 17 Jan 1771

William EDWARDS of County of Pittsylvania of one part and Thomas EDWARDS of same County of other part...for £400...all that parcel of Land on west side of Irvin River...containing by estimation 91 acres...down the River as it meanders.
Wit: James STRONG, Allen DODD, Edmund EDWARDS
Rec: 27 Jun 1771 William EDWARDS L.S.

DB 2, p.213 - EDWARDS from EDWARDS DEED, 17 Jan 1771

William EDWARDS of County of Pittsylvania of one part and James EDWARDS of same County of other part...for £400...Land on west side Irvin River, containing by Estimation 91 acres...Beginning at Thomas EDWARDS on the River thence on Thomas EDWARDS line as it meanders...at the indian grave ridge thence as the indian grave ridge mainders to the ould back line.
Wit: Allen DODD, Jo[s]. STRONG, Edmund EDWARDS
Rec: 27 Jun 1771 William EDWARDS L.S.

DB 2, p.215 - HOPKINS from JEFFERSON DEED, 18 Mar 1771

George JEFFERSON of Pittsylvania County of one part and Arthur HOPKINS of same County of other part...for and in Consideration of the Friendship and esteem which George JEFFERSON hath and beareth unto said Arthur HOPKINS Hath granted and confirmed to said Arther HOPKINS a tract of Land containing by Estimation 200 acres on Turkey Cock Creek being part of Land said JEFFERSON purchased of Clement READ...in old line.

her
Wit: Mary M SWANSON, David WILLIS, Edmund BOAZ
mark

Rec: 27 Jun 1771 G. JEFFERSON L.S.

DB 2, p.217 - HOPKINS from JEFFERSON DEED, 20 Mar 1771

George JEFFERSON of Pittsylvania County of one part and Arther HOPKINS of same County of other part...for £48 Current money of Virginia...300 acres on Turkey Cock Creek being part of Land said JEFFERSON purchased of Clement READ...at said HOPKIN's corner in old line.

her
Wit: Mary M SWANSON, David WILLIS, Edmund BOAZ
mark

Rec: 27 Jun 1771 George JEFFERSON L.S.

DB 2, p.219 - HANKINS from GRAYHAM   DEED, 22 Oct 1770
William GRAYHAM of County of Pittsylvania in Colony of Virginia of one part
and Daniel HANKINS of said County and Colony of other part...for £70 Current
money of Virginia...all that devided remainder parcel of Land containing by
estimation 100 acres being part of a Greater Tract of 150 acres which said
William GRAYHAM bought of Nathaniel TERRY which said TERRY purchased of one
John AUSTIN and was by said AUSTIN by Indenture bearing date 18 Sep 1754 Con-
veyed to Nathaniel TERRY...50 acres part of said 150 acres said Nathaniel
TERRY sold to William SATTERWHITE by Indenture.
            his   his
Wit: Benjamin X WHEAT, James   DEAR, Bennet BALLEW
            mark   mark
Rec: 28 Mar 1771   William GRAHAM L.S.
Proved again: 27 Jun 1771

DB 2,p.223 - JENNINGS from RICE   DEED, 1770
John RICE of Pittsylvania County of one part and Miles JINNINGS of said County
of other part...for £25 Current money of Virginia...80 acres more or less, on
south side Mayo River...mouth of branch.
                                    her
Wit: Peter PERKINS, Isaiah WATKINS, Alice A WATKINS
                                    mark
Proved 29 Nov 1770, again 27 Jun 1771   John RICE L.S.

DB 2, p.225 - HILL from HALL   DEED, 27 Jun 1771
William HILL of County of Pittsylvania of one part and Isham HALL of same
County of other part...for £17 Current Money...all that Track of Land Con-
taining by estimation 100 acres...on south side Pig River...fork of a branch,
down said branch, up the River.
No witnesses. Memorandum wit: Lewis MORGAN   his
Memorandum: 27 Jun 1771, Isham HALL and his   Isham X HALL L.S.
wife Mary delivered to William HALL said land   mark
Rec: 27 Jun 1771

DB 2, p.228 - HOFF from STINNET   DEED, 27 Jun 1771
Benjamin STINNET planter of one part and Thomas HOOF planter both of County
of Pittsylvania and Colony of Virginia of other part...for £03·10 Lawfull
money of Colony of Virginia...4 acres on Irvin River...Small branch...in old
Line being between them both.   his
Wit: Samuel PACKWOOD, Mark FOSTER   Benjamin X STINNETT L.S.
Rec: 27 Jun 1771   mark
Ussley, wife of s^d. Benj^a., privily Exam^d. as Law directs Relinquished her
right of Dower

DB 2, p.230 - HOFF from STINNETT   DEED, 27 Jun 1771
Benjamin STINNETT planter of one part and Samuel HOFF planter of other part
both of County of Pittsylvania...for £30 lawfull money of Colony of Virginia...
Land on Iriven River, being part of Land said STENNETT now lives containing
76 acres more or less...up River to a bent of River then Crossing said River,
along old line...Crossing the river at the mouth of flaat Creek.
Wit: Samuel PACKWOOD, Mark FOSTER   his
Rec: 27 Jun 1771   Benjamin X STINNETT L.S.
Ussley, wife of said Benjamin, privily Examined   mark
as Law directs Relinquished her right of Dower

DB 2, p.232 - ORDER OF COURT TO VALUE THE IMPROVEMENTS OF JOHN SMITHS LAND
May Court 1771 Ordered that Robert HILL, Swinfield HILL, Thomas HILL and
William TREDWAY or any three of them do value the Improvements of 58 acres
of Land in this County belonging to John SMITH and make Report to Court.
Test.   John COX
4 Jun 1771 Robert HILL, Thomas HILL and William TREDWAY Sworn to value Improvements Certified under my hand - Hugh INNES
5 Jun Land viewed and Land could not be done under £30
Rec: 27 Jun 1771

DB 2, p.233 - HUTCHINGS from WELLS & WIFE   DEED, 29 Aug 1771
John WELLS and Judith his wife of one part Parrish of Camden in County of
Pittsylv^a. and Thomas HUTCHINGS of parrish and County aforesaid of other
part...for £70 Current money of Virginia...all that tract of Land on both
sides Shoko Creek containing by estimation 400 acres.
Wit: Thomas HILL, John EAST, Joseph COOK
Rec: 29 Aug 1771   John WELLS L.S.

DB 2, p.236 - CLARKSON from HILL   DEED, 23 Mar 1771
William HILL of Pittsylvania County of one part and David CLARKSON of Bedford
County of other part...for £35 Current Money of Virginia...120 acres more or
less being part of Tract of Land containing 223 acres the Pattern bearing
date 22 Sep 1766 lying on both sides of bull Run...towards black Water and
Crossing bull run.
Wit; Nathan SWANSON, John ROYSTON, William SWANSON
Rec: 29 Aug 1771   William HILL L.S.

DB 2, p.239 - LUMKIN from BLEVINS   DEED, 29 Aug 1771
William BLEVINS Son of William BLEVINS and Ann his wife of County of Pitt-
sylvania in Colony of Virginia of one part and George LUMKIN of County and
Colony aforesaid of other part...for £100 Current money of said Colony...
Land on north side Marrowbone Creek...mouth of a branch...in PRICES line...
300 acres.
Wit: Robt. LUMKIN, W^m. FARRIS, John WELLS   William BLEVINS Junr. L.S.
                                                         her
                                                  Ann ─┼─ BLEVINS L.S.
Rec: 29 Aug 1771   mark

DB 2, p.241 - BRUCE from EAST   DEED, 29 Aug 1771
John EAST of County of Pittsylvania of one part and James BRUCE of County of
Halifax of other part...for £120 Current money of Virginia...all that Tract
of Land lying on Stinking River...on line of Thomas TUNSTALL on said River,
along his line to Elisha FARRIS line, thence to Hickeys road, Down the road
to flyblow Creek, down the Creek to Charles FARRIS's line on Stinking River,
containing 190 acres more or less being the Land whereon said John EAST formly lived and by him Sold to Joseph ROBARDS who hath agreed to transfare all
his Right and Interest to said James BRUCE.
Wit: Jno.CLEVER Jo^s. ROBERTS, Robt. X BRUCE
                                           mark
Rec: 29 Aug 1771   John EAST L.S.

DB 2, p.244 - TALBOTT from LUCAS   POWER OF ATTORNEY, 22 Aug 1771
I, John LUCAS, of Charlotte County planter appoint my Trusty friend James
TALBOTT of Pittsylvania County my true and Lawfull attorney to Receive from
all my part of the Pursial Estate of John LUCAS Deceased and whereas I have
one Track of Land Containing 100 acres being the Land where said John LOOKAS

deceased formly lived...impower said James TALBOT to sell said Land as he
may think Proper as well as if I my self was Persinal Present.
Wit: Peyton SMITH, John MC KINNEY, David NOWLING, John LONG, John KERBY

his

John ⊢─⌐LUCAS L.S.

Rec: 29 Aug 1771   mark

DB 2, p.246 - BARRET from LANKFORD   DEED, 27 Jun 1771
Benjamin LANKFORD of County of Pittsylvania of one part and John BARRETT Sen[r].
of County of Louden of other part...for £20 Current money of Virginia...Land
on both sides magotty Creek containing by estimation 220 acres...crossing the
Creek.
No witnesses
Rec: 29 Aug 1771   Benjamin LANKFORD L.S.

DB 2, p.249 - WIMBISH from MC DANIEL   DEED, 27 May 1771
William MC DANIEL of County of Halifax of one part and John WIMBISH of County
of Pittsylvania of other part...for £91 Current money of Virginia...all that
Tract of Land containing 606 acres which said Tract is part of 3,620 acres
Granted said William MC DANIEL by patent bearing date 10 Jul 1766...on a bank
of yellow arth...in TERRYS branch at the County line, along the County line.
Wit: John WHITE, Thomas BALDWIN, Rubin TERRY, Johnson MC DANIEL
Rec: 29 Aug 1771
Ann, wife of said William, privily Examined
Relinquishes her right of Dower   William MC DANIEL L.S.

DB 2, p.253 - LYLE from SMITH   MORTGAGE, 27 Jan 1768
Samuel SMITH of County of Pittsylvania on one part and James LYLE of County
of Chesterfield of other part...for £276·17·09 Current Money of Virginia...
38 acres Land in fork Stantion and black Water being part of a Larger tract
purchased by said Samuel SMITH of William MEAD, the other part being sold by
said Samuel SMITH to Walter MAXEY, also a tract of Land supposed to contain
150 acres on both sides of black water purchased by said Samuel SMITH of
Henry HAINS of record in Bedford Court, also a Survey of Land runing to black
Water and Joining above mentioned tract, Purchased of HAINS as Lastly survey'd
by Surveyer of Pittsylvania County and also five Negroe Slaves Viz. Humphrey,
Tom, Hannah, Bess and Lucy and their Increase...if said Samuel SMITH shall
pay to said James LYLE the above sum with Lawful Interest from date hereof -
in and up the first day of January ensuing...everything herein contained be
void.
Wit: Cha[s]. IRVING, Robert GORDON, Alexander BAILLIE, James BUCKANAN,
James DEWALL
Rec: 24 Jun 1768   Sam[1]. SMITH L.S.

DB 2, p.257 - HOLLAGUN from HOLLAGUN   DEED, 29 Aug 1771
Patrick HOLLAGUN of Bedford County of one part and James HOLLAGUN of other
part of County aforesd...for £20 Current Money of Virginia...170 acres on
both sides Peeping Creek...new lines...Crossing the Creek.
No witnesses   his
Rec: 29 Aug 1771   Patrick ⌐D⌐ HOLLAGUN L.S.
                                                          mark

---

DB 2, p.258 - MITCHELL from CLEMENTS   DEED, 1 Aug 1771
James CLEMENTS and Martha his wife of County of Bedford of one part and James
MITCHELL of County of Pittsylvania of other part...for £60 Current Money of

Virginia...136 acres on both sides Potters Creek...pointers in BEARDINGS
line...Crossing the Creek...Crossing two Branches.
Wit: James DALTON, Jno. HENSLEE, John FOWLER
Rec: 29 Aug 1771
Martha, wife of James CLEMENT, privily Examined
as Law directs Relinquished her right of dower   James CLEMENT L.S.

DB 2, p.262 - LEEKE from LEEKE   DEED, 20 Mar 1771
James LEEKE Senr. of parrish of Camden in County of Pittsylvania on one part
and James LEEKE Junior of parrish and County aforesaid of other part...James
LEEKE Senr. and Rebeckah his wife for sum of £40 Current Money of Virginia...
all that Tract of Land whereon said James LEEKE Junr. and Joseph LEEKE
now lives Containing 200 acres being part of Tract whereon said James LEEKE
Senior Lives on both sides Elkhorn Creek...in John STEWART line...up the
creek as it meanders...in old line.
Memorandum that above James LEEKE before assignment of these presents did
oblige himself to make Good Sufficent deed in law to Jo^{s}. LEEKE 50 acres
of Land where said Joseph LEEK now lives.
Wit: John DONELSON, Thomas HUTCHINGS, Henry MC DANIEL, Thomas LEAK
Rec: 29 Aug 1771   James LEEK L.S.

DB 2, p.265 - LUMKIN from SANDFORD   DEED, 5 Jun 1771
George SANDFORD and Sarah his wife of County of Pittsylvania in Colony of
Virginia of one part and George LUMKIN of aforesaid Colony of other part...
for £100 Current money of Virginia...Sartain piece of Land on east side
Marrowbone Creek...mouth of a branch thence up the branch as it Meanders
and containing 247 acres.
                              his   his
Wit: Dan^{1}. FORD, Hezekiah X SALMON, Will FARIS, David X FORD
                             mark   mark
Rec: 29 Aug 1771   Geo. SANFORD L.S.

DB 2, p.267 - TOSH FROM SIMPSON   MORTGAGE, 15 Mar 1771
William SIMPSON and Elizabeth his wife on one part and Thomas TOSH of other
part both of Botetourt County in Colony of Virginia...for £30 more or less
Good and Lawfull money of Virginia...168 acres more or less lying on Tomehack
Creek Joyning lines with Robert NEILLY on lower side said Creek...for and
during the Terms of five hundred years next and Immideately Ensuing...to pay
full Sum of £30 Like money upon 15 Sep 1773 next Coming.

                                      his
Wit: Jno. NEELEY, Dan^{1}. MC NEEL, Phillip O BROGAN, Jno. BOWMAN, John MC NEEL
                                     mark   William SIMPSON L.S.
Rec: 29 Aug 1771   Elizabeth SIMPSON L.S.

DB 2, p.270 - HARNESS from MORGAN   DEED, 20 May 1771
Daniel MORGAN of County of Pittsylvania of one part and John HARNESS of same
County of other part...for £100 Current Money of Virginia...256 acres more
or less being part of greater Tract Granted to said MORGAN by Patent bearing
date 14 Jul 1769 and lying on Branches of Allens Creek...Joining lines of
Benjamin LANKFORD, John PEMBERTON and Joseph FARRIS...along Joseph FARRIS's
line.
Wit: Thomas DILLARD Jr., Elisha FARRIS, W^{m}. SHORT, James LEAK
Rec: 27 Jun 1771, further prv: 29 Aug 1771   Daniel MORGAN L.S.

DB 2, p.273 - MC KAIN from LUMKIN   DEED, 29 Aug 1771
George LUMKIN and Mary his wife of county of Pittsylvania in Colony of Vir-
ginia of one part and Hugh MC KAIN of County and Colony afores^d. of other
part...for £20 Current Money of said Colony...Land on west or South side
Marrowbone Creek...in old line...111 acres.
Wit: Robt. LUMKIN, Edward BRANDLEY, William FARRIS, Frederick FULKERSON
                                                    George LUMKIN L.S.
                                                       her
                                               Mary ⬯ LUMKIN L.S.
Rec: 29 Aug 1771   mark

DB 2, p.275 - MITCHELL from CLEMENTS   DEED, 1 Aug 1771
James CLEMENTS and Martha his wife of County of Bedford of one part and
James MITCHELL of County of Pittsylvania of other part...for £40 Current
Money of Virginia...116 acres more or Less Lying on potters Creek...in Ben-
jamin LANKFORDS line...Crossing fox Branch..in ROBERSONS line...Crossing
Potters Creek...new lines.
Wit: James DALTON John HENSLEE, John FOWLER
Rec: 29 Aug 1771
Martha, wife of James, privily Exam^d. as Law directs
Relinquished her right of Dower   James CLEMENT L.S.

DB 2, p.278 - KEEZIE from JONES   DEED, 25 Jul 1771
Jonathan JONES and Anne his wife of County of Pittsylvania of one part and
George KEESEE of same County of other part...for £45 Current Money of Vir-
ginia...300 acres more or less...on Abraham PAYNES line...on Jacob FARRIS's
line, along his line...Crossing a small Creek...to Abraham PAYNES...north
side above Creek, along PAYNES line.
No witnesses
Rec: 29 Aug 1771
Anne, wife of Jonathan, being privily Exam^d.   Jonathan JONES L.S.
Relinquished her right of Dower   Anne JONES L.S.

DB 2, p.280 - HOFF from WARD   DEED, 29 Aug 1771
John WARD of Bedford County and Colony of Virginia of one part and Thos. HOFF
of County of Pittsylvania and Colony aforesaid...for £25 lawful money of Virginia...all that parcel of Land on both Sides flat Creek, containing 210
acres...south side said Creek, New lines...up the Creek as it meanders.
Wit: John TODD, Junr., James CALLAWAY, Abra^m. SHELTON
Rec: 30 Aug 1771   John WARD L.S.

DB 2, p.282 - WIMBISH from MC DANIEL   DEED, 27 May 1771
William MC DANIEL of County of Halifax of one part and John WIMBISH of County
of Pittsylvania of other part...for £150 Current Money of Virginia...all
those five Lotts, each Containing half an acre of Land in Town of Peytonsburg, to wit, one lott, or half acre of Land on north side of Mountain Street
where Thomas DUNCAN formerly lived opposet the dwelling House of said John
WIMBISH and adjoining a Corner Lott formerly the Property of ALFREIND and
HAMILTON but now belongs to said John WIMBISH, one other lott or half acre of
Land on North side of Main Street adjoining said Corner lott and known in plan
of said town by Number Eighty five, one other lott or half acre on South side
of Main Street opposet to the last mentioned lott Adjoining a Corner lott on
which the Ordinary House Stands and known in the Plan by Number Eighty Six,
one other Corner lott or half acre of Land on which the said ordinary house

Stands where said William MC DANIEL formerly lived and known in said Plan by
Number Ninety nine, and one other Corner Lott or half acre of Land on which
the Store House formerly occupied by said William MC DANIEL Stands opposet
to said Ordinary house and known in the Plan by Number one hundred Twelve.
Wit: John WHITE, Thos. BALDWIN, Robin TERRY, Johnson MC DANIEL
Rec: 29 Aug 1771
Ann, wife of said William MC DANIEL, Relinquished
her right of Dower   W^m. MC DANIEL

DB 2, p.285 - SMITH & CO. from COX JUNR.   DEED OF TRUST, 27 Feb 1771
James COX Junr. of Pittsylvania County Virginia of one part and James SMITH
& Co. of other part...James COX jun^r. stands justly indebted to said James
SMITH & Co. in sum of £26·10·03 farthings Current money of Virginia...also
sum of 5s paid by said James SMITH & Co....130 acres more or less adjoining
Absaloman BOSTICK and Edward ?KEEHAL...shall after 1 Aug 1772 or as soon
after said James SMITH & Co. think Proper...sell for best price after 10
days Publick notice...out of Money arising from Sale discharge them selves
above Sum with Interest from 1 Apr ensuing the date...James SMITH & Co. to
pay over pluss if any.

Wit: Henry CONWAY, Arch^d. SMITH, John X BENTLY
                                        his   mark
Rec: 30 May 1771, further prv.: 30 Aug 1771   James COX L.S.

DB 2, p.287 - SMITH & CO. from CHOICE   DEED OF TRUST, 17 Aug 1771
Tully CHOICE of Pittsylvania County on one Part and James SMITH & company on
other Part...for £71 Current money of Virginia which said Tully CHOICE is
Justly Indebted to them and honestly desires to pay them...in Consideration
of sum of 5s like money paid by them...Tully CHOICE hath Sold to said James
SMITH & Co. a Tract of Land Containing 400 acres on Snow Creek whereon said
Tully CHOICE lives and also all and every article of personall Estate...after
1 Sep 1773 or as soon as he shall think Proper or said Tully CHOICE shall
request, whichever shall first happen Sell for best price that can be gotten
after Ten Days Publick notice said Land and out of Money arising pay and
Satisfy themselves above sum with Interest from date of these Presents till
same be fully Discharged.
Wit: James BREWER, Christopher OWEN
Rec: 30 Aug 1771   Tully CHOICE L.S.

DB 2, p.289 - SMITH & CO. from BISWELL   DEED OF TRUST, 24 Jul 1771
John BISWELL of Pittsylvania County on one part and James SMITH and Company
on other part...for £100 Current Money of Virginia which said John BISWELL is
Justly indebted to them and honestly desires to pay and in Consideration of
5s like money...hath sold Two Tracts of Land that said John BISWELL purchased
of Thomas WATKINS, Deed Recorded in Pittsylvania Court Sepr. 1769 also all
Stock of Cattle which is 17 head, 2 Horses, 2 Mares and Colts, 30 head of
hogs mark'd with a Crop and underKeel in each ear, all his Pewter Tools, a
Riffle and Smooth Boad Gun with every article of Beding and household furniture
Belonging to him...James SMITH & CO. shall after 1 Sep 1772 or as soon as
they shall think Proper or said John BISWELL Shall Request them, sell for
Best price that can be gotten after Ten days Publick notice...out of money
arising pay themselves above sum with Interest from date of these Presents
till fully Discharged...pay overplus if any.
Wit: John SHORT, Arch^d. SMITH, Henry CONWAY
Rec: 30 Aug 1771   John BISWELL L.S.

DB 2. p.292 - WEBB from WEBB   DEED OF GIFT, 29 Aug 1771
I, Thomas WEBB of County of Pittsylvania and Parrish of Camden doe give grant
and makeover unto my Daughter Susanna WEBB one feather Bed and furniture...
unto my Daughter Bettey WEBB a feather Bed and furniture, a Cow and Calf...
to Son Larkin WEBB one feather Bed and furniture also 1 Cow and Calf and for
further Consideration of £5 paid by my two Daughters and Son have Give and
grant to my Two Daughters and Son before mentioned the said feather Beds and
furniture and Cattle above mentioned.
Wit: John SALMON, Robt. CHANDLER
Rec: 29 Aug 1771   Thomas WEBB L.S.

DB 2, p.293 - TURNER from TURNER   DEED, 29 Aug 1771
Shadrack TURNER of Pittsylvania County of one part and John TURNER of same
County of other part...for £30 Current Money of Virginia...30 acres more or
less, it being part of Land I live on and on north side Butterham Town
Creek...along the old lines to said Creek, thence down the Creek as it meanders.
Wit: Robert PERRYMAN, Jeremiah ⊹ WORSHAM, William WATSON
                       his / mark
Rec: 29 Aug 1771   Shadrack TURNER L.S.

DB 2, p.295 - COCKERHAM from CANTERBURY   DEED, 10 Aug 1771
Samuel CANTEBERRY of County of Pittsylvania of one Part and Abner COCKERHAM
of said County of other Part...for £200 Current Money of Virginia...50 acres
more of less on ?Ilante Creek...at head of a branch...to olde order line, up
olde line to Methias ?CRONESTORS line.
Wit: John ⊹ LAW Senr., John LAW Junior, William HAYNES
      his / mark   Samuel CANTERBURY L.S.
Rec: 29 Aug 1771   her
Elizabeth, wife of s^d. Samuel,   Elizabeth ⊹ CANTERBURY L.S.
privily Examined Relinquished her Dower   mark

DB 2, p.297 - DAVIS from LUCAS   DEED, 20 Aug 1771
John LUCAS of Charlotte County and John DAVIS of Pittsylvania County in other
part...for £50 Current Money of Virginia...50 acres more or less on north
side Pigg River...new chop line to River then up River.
Wit. John CERTAIN, John LUCAS, John KEARBY, John LONG
                              his
                              John ⊹ LUCAS Senr. L.S.
Rec: 29 Aug 1771   mark

DB 2, p.300 - CLAY from CLAY   DEED, 21 Aug 1771
William CLAY of Pittsylvania County and Colony of Virginia do give unto
Michael CLAY 100 acres more or less...on River, up the Stream as it meanders...
of old line on north side.
Wit: James DILLON, Jesse ⊹ DILLON, Danl. ✗ WARD, Jesse HEARD
                his / mark   his / mark
Rec: 29 Aug 1771   William CLAY L.S.

DB 2, p.301 - MCKAIN from LUMKIN   DEED, 29 Aug 1771
George LUMKIN and Mary his wife of County of Pittsylvania in Collony of Virginia of one Part and Alexander MC KAIN of same County and Collony of other
part...for £35 Current money of said Colony...Land on East side Marrowbone

Creek...in Robert CHANDLERS line...in old line...to a branch, down said branch...Containing 147 acres.
Wit: Robert LUMKIN, Edward BRADLEY, William FARRIS, Fredrick FULKERSON

George LUMKIN L.S.

her

Mary Ⴔ LUMKIN L.S.

mark

Rec: 29 Aug 1771

DB 2, p.302 - SMITH & C°. from COOK   DEED OF TRUST, 16 Apr 1771

Harmon COOKE of County of Pittsylvania on one part and James SMITH & C°. of said County on other Part...Harmon COOKE Stands Justly indebted to said James SMITH & C°. in sum of £72 Current money of Virginia...in Consideration of Securing payment of said Sum and in Consideration of 5s to him in hand paid by said James SMITH & C°....Tract of Land on Turkey Cock Creek, which I Purchased of Elisha ESTES recorded in Pittsylvania County Court...after 1 Apr 1774 Sell for best price after Ten days publick notice and out of Money discharge themselfs above sum with Interest from date of the Presents till same be fully discharged...James SMITH & C°ᵈ to pay over plus if any remain.
Wit: Abraham ARON, Henry CONWAY, Archᵈ. SMITH
Rec: 30 Aug 1771   Harmon COOK L.S.

DB 2, p.305 - SHELTON from BOWMAN   DEED, 29 Aug 1771

John BOWMAN and Elizabeth his wife of County of Botetourt on one part and Pelatiah SHELTON of County of Pittsylvania of other part...for £50 in hand paid by said SHELTON...all that Tract of Land granted to Robᵗ. PEWSEY by patent dated 29 May 1760 and from him conveyed to said John BOWMAN by Deed bearing date 15 Jan 1767 Containing 165 acres in County of Pittsylvania formerly Halifax on both sides Irvin River...at Robert WALTON & Companys...west side Irvin River...Crossing a branch...crossing Irvin River up same as it meanders.
Wit: Edmund WINSTON, Wᵐ. FLEMING, John AYLETT

John BOWMAN L.S.

Rec: 29 Aug 1771   Elizabeth BOWMAN L.S.

DB 2, p.307 - ROWLAND from COPLAND   DEED, 1 Jul 1771

Peter COPLAND of County of Pittsylvania on one part and John ROWLAND of same County on other part...for £28·10 Current Money of Virginia...Land on Irvin River and waters thereof Containing by Estimation 153 acres...South side Irvin River thence new lines...on Sycamore Creek, down same to Irvin River, down the River to PEWSEYS lines.
No witnesses
Rec: 29 Aug 1771   Peter COPLAND L.S.

DB 2, p.309 - SHELTON from LEAKE   DEED, 6 May 1771

Josiah LEAKE and Anne his wife of County of Goochland of one part and Ralph SHELTON of County of Pittsylvania of other part...for £25 Current money of Virginia...Land on South fork of Mayo River Containing 400 acres more or less...South side of the River.
Wit: Thoˢ. HODGES, John JACKSON, Moses HODGES

Josiah LEAK L.S.

Ann LEAK L.S.

Rec: 26 Sep 1771

DB 2, p.311 - HENDERSON from HENDERSON   DEED, 27 Sep 1771

Thomas HENDERSON Senʳ. of county of Pittsylvania on one part and Thomas HENDERSON Junʳ. on other part...sum of £40 current money of Virginia...150 acres on both sides Irvin River...on Thomas HENDERSON Senior corner...south side the river thence new lines...on side of a hill...crossing the river by a branch...crossing the river.
Rec: 27 Sep 1771   No witnesses   Thomas HENDERSON L.S.

DB 2, p.313 - CHRISTAIN from SIMPSON   DEED, 27 Sep 1771

William SIMPSON, other wise called William SIMPSON of County of augusta and
Colony of Virginia of one part and Israel CHRISTIAN of Botetourt County of
other part, a power of attorney dated 25th day of March 1769 and proved same
day in Court of Augusta County, William SIMPSON did appoint Archebald GRAYHAM
of County of Pittsylvania his Lawful attorney in his name to acknowledge and
make a deed of Conveyance of a Tract of Land to Israel CHRISTIAN, which was
formerly conveyed by GRAYHAM to SIMPSON and to CHRISTIAN to Convey in fee simple.
GRAYHAM in name of SIMPSON for £40 hath Sold to Israel CHRISTIAN all that Tract
of Land of 166 acres on Tomahack Run...reference made to former patent granted
to Colonel John CHESWELL and by him Conveyed to Archebald GRAYHAM and from
GRAYMES to William SIMSON the Present bargainds by power of attorney from SIMP-
SON to Archd. GRAYHAM recorded in Augusta County to Convey Deed to CHRISTIAN.
Wit: John TODD, junr., Will. TUNSTALL   for William SIMPSON
Rec: 27 Sep 1771   Archebald GRAHAM L.S.

DB 2, p.314 - LUMKIN Junr. from LUMKIN Senr.   DEED, 25 Sep 1771

George LUMKIN Senr. of Parrish of Camden in County of Pittsylvania of one
part and George LUMKIN Junr. of parrish and County aforesaid or other part...
for £200 Current Money of Virginia...all that Tract of Land on South side
Dan River Containing 150 acres and Joining William WYNNES upper line on South
side dan River, Beginning at WYNNES corner...along his line west...on a branch.
No witnesses
Rec: 26 Sep 1773   George LUMKIN L.S.

DB 2, p.317 - RENTFROW from BLEVINS   POWER OF ATTORNEY, 1 Jul 1771

We Daniel BLEVINS Senr. of Pittsylvania County in Virginia and Daniel BLEVINS
son of said Daniel BLEVINS Junr. in Botetourt County in Virginia do appoint
our Trusty friend James RENTFROW Senr. of Pittsylvania County in Virginia our
true and lawfull attorney for us in our name and to our use to ask Demand
Recover or Receive of and from Joseph STANTONE in Westerly formaly Narragency
in new ingland one peice of Land Containing 100 acres more or less in Westerly new ingland...our Sole and full Power and authority to follow such
Legal Courses...as we our Self might or Could do were we Personally present...
all things which may be necessary Concerning the Premises.
Wit: Thos. FLOWERS, Geo. LUMKIN, Robt. LUMKIN, Robt. PEWSEY

                                         his
Rec: 27 Sep 1771   Daniel X BLEVINS Senr. L.S.
Power of attorney from Danl. BLEVINS   mark
Senr. and Sarah his wife and Daniel   her
BLEVINS Junr. to Jas. RENTFROW proved   Sarah / BLEVINS L.S.
                                  mark
                       Daniel X BLEVINS jr. L.S.

DB 2, p.318 - OWEN from WILLIAMSON   DEED, 27 Apr 1771

Thomas WILLIAMSON of Pittsylvania County of one part and John OWEN of aforesd.
County of other part...for £25 Current money of Virginia...Tract of Land containing 100 acres more of less on South Side Dan River...down the River.

                                his   his
Wit: Archelius YANCEY, Richd. BYRD, John ⨏ OWEN, Junr., David X OWEN,
                               mark   mark
Thomas EARLES, James DENTON, Charles DUNKIN
Rec: 26 Sep 1771   Thomas WILLIAMSON L.S.

DB 2, p.321- GRIFFETH from TAYLOR   DEED, 25 Sep 1771
James TAYLOR and Liddia his wife of one part and William GRIFFETH of other
part...for £25 Current money...Tract of Land Containing 400 acres more or
less...obtained in a patent bearing date 12 May 1770.
No witnesses   his
Rec: 26 Sep 1771   James X TAYLOR L.S.
                                                  mark

DB 2, p.323 - FARIS Junr. from INNES   DEED, 29 Aug 1771
Hugh INNES of parrish of Cambden in County of Pittsylvania of one part and
James FARRIS Junr. of parrish and County aforesaid of other part...for £10
Current Money of Virginia...200 acres more of less being part of a patent
bearing date 16 Feb 1771 in County of pittsylvania and Lying on panther
Creek...at Lower line of said patent...Crossing above mentioned Creek up a
ridge...upper line of patent.
No witnesses
Rec: 26 Sep 1771   Hugh INNES L.S.

DB 2, p.325 - LANE from SWEETING   POWER OF ATTORNEY, 26 Sep 1771
I, Robert SWEETING of Colony of Virginia do appoint Dutton LANE of same
Colony to go to Province of Maryland and there to act as my attorney in fact...
give him full power to demand and Recover possession of all Lands and other
Estate that I have any Right to Claim...to Commence and process Suits for me
against any person holding out possession of any such Lands...full power to
sell and Dispose of all such Estate to any persons for such price as he shall
think fit...to receive the Consideration Money...same force as if I had
Princippally and personally acted myself.
Wit: G. MARR, James DENTON, John MARR
Rec: 26 Sep 1771   Robert SWEETIN   L.S.

DB 2, p.327 - FARRIS from INNES   DEED, 29 Aug 1771
Hugh INNES of parrish of Cambden in County of Pittsylvania of one part and
John FARRIS of parrish and County aforesaid of other part...for £10 Current
Money of Virginia...200 acres more of less and being part of a patent of
Land Granted to said Hugh INNES bearing date 16 Feb 1771 and lying on Pan-
ther Creek...on Lower line of said Patent...up a ridge.
No witnesses
Rec: 26 Sep 1771   Hugh INNES L.S.

DB 2, p.328 - KOGER from ECHOLS   DEED, 25 Sep 1771
Jacob ECHOLS of one part and John KOGER of other part...for £30...Tract of
Land formerly belonging to Isham BARRETT, on north fork of Gobling Town
Creek...containing 113 acres.
Wit: Edmund WINSTON, James CALLAWAY, John AYLETT
Rec: 26 Sep 1771   Jacob ECKOLS L.S.

DB 2, p.330 - LANE from MOBERLY   DEED, 23 Feb 1771
Eleaz^r. MOBERLY of Provice of South Carolinia in County of Craven of one
part and Dutton LANE of County of Pittsylvania and parrish of Cambden of
other part...for £20 Current Money of Virginia...all that Tract of Land Con-
taining 150 acres more of less on uper double Creek which was granted to
William MOBLEY by pattent...by a branch thence new lines.
Wit: John HARDIMAN, Jno. LANGFORD, Chas. D. BRADFORD
Rec: 27 Jun 1771 and Haynes MORGAN attorney for Isaiah WATKINS came into
Court and entered a Contest to said Indenture.
Prv: 26 Sep 1771   Eleazar MOBLEY L.S.

DB 2, p.332 - COOK from GIBSON   BILL SALE, 20 Mar 1771
I, Andrew GIBSON of Pittsylvania County, have sold to Joseph COOK of said
County one Gold Watch marked In Le Roy Parris for sum of £16.
Wit: Shem COOK Junr.
Rec: 26 Sep 1771   Andrew GIBSON L.S.

DB 2, p.332 - GRAYHAM from SIMPSON   POWER OF ATTORNEY, 25 Mar 1769
I, William SIMPSON of County of augusta and Colony of Virginia, do appoint
Archebald GRAHAM of County of Pittsylvania in Colony aforesaid my true and
Lawfull attorney for me and in my name to acknowledge and make a Deed for a
Certain Tract of land in Pittsylvania County to Israel CHRISTIAN formerly
conveyed and Sold by said GRAHAM to said William SIMPSON by Deed recorded in
County Court of Pittsylvania...as if I myself were Personally present.
Wit: Thos. MADISON, William FLEMING, Mich^l. BOSRYER
Rec: 27 Sep 1771   William SIMPSON L.S.

DB 2, p.334 - MARR from LANE   POWER OF ATTORNEY, 26 Sep 1771
We, John fuller LANE and Elizabeth his wife of Pittsylvania County in Colony
of Virginia, have appointed Gidion MARR Gen^t. of Colony and County aforesaid
to go to Pencylvania and act as our attorney both at Law in fact...recover
all Estate Real and Personal that may Lawfully descend to said Elizabeth
LANE one of the Daughters Coheirs of Isaac CLOUD dece^d. in the Province of
Pencylvania...Impower him to Commence and prosecute Suits against any Person
as Shall or may hold out or withold any such Estate from him...full Power to
Sell and dispose of all or any part of such Estate for such prices as he
shall think fitt to Convey said Estate to Purchaser by Lawfull Conveyance.
Wit: Dutton LANE, James DENTON, Henry STONE   his
                                          John fuller I LANE L.S.
                                                      mark
                                                       her
                                          Elizabeth   I   LANE L.S.
Rec: 26 Sep 1771   mark

DB 2, p.335 - GORDON from VESTRYMEN OF ANTRIM PARISH   DEED, 18 Jul 1771
George BOYD, Evan RAGLEAND, James BATES, Thomas TUNSTALL, William THOMPSON,
Moses TERRY, Walter COLES, William STOKES and Edward WADE and Thos. YUILLE
Vestrymen of parrish of antrim in County of Hailfax of one part and Reverend
Alexander GORDON of parrish and County aforesaid of other part...for £300...
Tract of Land in Parrish of Cambden in County of Pittsylvania Containing by
Estimation 800 more of less being the same Land which said Vestrymen Purchased
of James TERRY for use of a Glebe for said parish of Antrim and was by said
James by two Deeds one of which bearing date 15 Mar 1764 and other 15 Jul 1771
Conveyed to said vestrymen by Deed of record in Courts of said Counties of
Halifax and Pittsylvania...on lower side of Hay Stack branch...Crossing the
long branch and a fork thereof to Theophilus LACYS corner...Crossing Echols
fork...Crossing Sandy Creek...Crossing a small branch...up the Creek as it
meanders to mouth of said hay stack branch, up as it meanders.
Wit: Thos. DILLARD, Junr., R. WILLIAMS, Haynes MORGAN, Benjamin LANKFORD
George BOYD, Junr. L.S.   Moses TERRY L.S.
James BATES L.S.   William STOKES L.S.
Thos. TUNSTALL L.S.   Edward WADE L.S.
William THOMPSON L.S.   Thos. YUILLE L.S.
Rec: 26 Sep 1771

DB 2, p. 338 - COX from POLLEY   DEED, 29 Nov 1771
Edward POLLEY of parrish of Cambden in County of Pittsylvania of one part and
James COX of Parrish and County aforesaid of other part...for £60 Current
Money of Virginia...all that Tract of Land Containing 125 acres lying on
sides Mill Creek being the Land Conveyed by Anthony STREET and William   .
HAWKINS to said Edward POLLEY by Deed bearing date 10 Dec 1767 and recorded
in Court of said County.   his
No witnesses   Edward A POLLEY L.S.
Rec: 28 Nov 1771   mark

DB 2, p.340 - DOSS from HODGES   DEED, 24 Oct 1771
Welcom William HODGES and Mary his wife of province of North Carolinia of
one part and William DOSS of County of Pittsylvania and Colony of Virginia
of other part...for £50 Current money of Virginia...300 acres on branches of
allens Creek...at BAKERS upper corner...Crossing a branch...in William
FARRIS's line.
          his   his
Wit: John Ø FARREL, Benjamin HENDRICK, Francis F SHORT
          mark   mark
                                     Welcom W. HODGES L.S.
Rec: 28 Nov 1771   Mary HODGES L.S.

DB 2, p.342 - WEATHERFORD from HARDY   DEED, 25 Nov 1771
Thomas HARDY of Parrish of Cambden and County of Pittsylvania of one part
and John WEATHERFORD of same Parrish and County of other part...for £10 Current money of Virginia and for Love and affection said Thomas HARDY doth beare
to his Daughter Elizabeth the wife of above John WEATHERFORD hath granted
one certain Tract of Land Containing 200 acres more or less lying on Branches
of great CheryStone it being part of a patent of Land granted to Thomas
HARDY bearing date 14 Jul 1769...in PHINNEYS order line.
Wit: Crispin SHELTON, Abraham MOTTLEY, John PAYNE, Junior, David
               his
WEATHERFORD, David X WADE
               mark
Rec: 28 Nov 1771   Thomas HARDY L.S.

DB 2, p.344 - LAWRANCE from INNES   DEED, 27 Nov 1771
Hugh INNES of County of Pittsylvania of one part and Thomas LAWRENCE of said
County of other part...for £10 Current Money of Virginia...doth Sell to sd.
Thos. LAWRENCE in his actual possession...tract of Land Containing by Esti-
mation 100 acres...on mountain fork of Snow Creek being the Land where said
LAWRENCE formerly lived and being also part of 800 acres granted said INNES
by patent bearing date 27 Aug 1770...in line that devides LAWRENCES Land
from William HALES Land thence along patent line south.
Wit: Robt. PERRYMAN, Robt. JONES, William COOK
Rec: 28 Nov 1771   Hugh INNES L.S.

DB 2, p.347 - SHORT from SHORT   DEED, 28 Nov 1771
William SHORT of County of Pittsylvania of one part and Joell SHORT of same
County of other part...for £50 Current Money of Virginia...Tract of Land on
north side of Banister River, Joining lines of William Welcome HODGES and
Benjamin HENDRICK Containing by Estimation 100 acres...Begining at Mouth of
William Welcome HODGES Spring Branch of said River thence up the branch where
old line Crosses, along old line to Benjamin HENDRICKS line, along his line
to the River, up the River as it meanders.
Wit: Philip BREWER, Josiah MANN, Francis HENRY
Rec: 28 Nov 1771   William SHORT L.S.

DB 2, p.349 - HENDERSON from LANKFORD   DEED, 28 Nov 1771
Benjamin LANKFORD and Henerico his wife of Pittsylvania County of one part
and James HENDERSON of County of Louden of other part...for £45 Current money
of Virginia...Land on both sides Allens Creek Containing 232 acres...in the
mountain line...in HARRISES line...Crossing Allens Creek and runing along
south side thence a new line Crossing the Creek.
Wit: James WILSON, Thos. HENDERSON, James HENDERSON Junr.
                                           Benjamin LANKFORD L.S.
Rec: 28 Nov 1771   Heanrica LANKFORD L.S.

DB 2, p.352 - WADE from HARDY   DEED, 25 Nov 1771
Thomas HARDY of parrish of Cambden in Pittsylvania County of one part and
David WADE of same Parrish and County of other part...for £5 Current money
of Virginia...for Love and affection said Thomas HARDY doth bear to his Dau-
ghter Agness the wife of above said David WADE Hath granted and sold to David
WADE one Certain Tract of Land Containing 100 acres more or less being on
branches of Banister River it being part of a patent of Land granted to said
Thomas HARDY bearing date 14 Jul 1769...in said HARDYS line, along his line...
along new marked line to PHINEYS order line.
Wit: Crispin SHELTON, Abraham MOTTLEY, John WEATHERFORD, David WEATHERFORD,
Greenwood PAYNE
Rec: 28 Nov 1771   Thomas HARDY L.S.

DB 2, p.354 - MORGAN from MORGAN   DEED
Lewis MORGAN of County of Pittsylvania of one part and Thomas MORGAN of County
aforesaid of other part...for £50 Current Money of Virginia...Land on East
side Chesnut Creek Containing 50 acres more or less...Begining at mouth of
the branch below the Chalk hill then runing south to back line next the
mounting thence along said old Line to the Creek, down the Creek as it Meanders.
No witnesses
Rec: 28 Nov 1771   Lewis MORGAN L.S.

DB 2, p.355 - CHILES from PEAK   DEED, 31 Oct 1771
John PEAK of County of Prince Edward and John CHILES of County of Bedford of
other part...for £100 Good and Lawfull money of Virginia...Land on north side
Pigg River, containing 195 acres more or Less it being part of 585 acres said
PEAK purchased of Jeremiah WARD with a patent bearing date 7 Aug 1761...at
mouth of Rockey branch, up the branch...Crossing a branch...up the River as
it Meanders.
Wit: Ja^s. TALBOT, Ja^s. DILLARD, George PEAK   his
                                           Jno. ⨍ PEAK L.S.
Rec: 28 Nov 1771   mark

DB 2, p.357 - ADAM from OWEN   DEED, 14 Nov 1771
Thomas OWEN of County of Pittsylvania of one part and Silvester ADAM of
County of Fairfax of other part...for £100 Current Money of Virginia...Land
on north side Dan River Contain___ 103 acres...on River bank in Henry STONES
line thence along his line...in William MC DANIELS line...up the River as it
meanders.
Wit: George ROSS, Jno. ANDERSON, Thomas WILLIAMS, Thomas HOPER, Ann OWEN,
Charles DUNKIN
Rec: 28 Nov 1771   Thomas OWEN L.S.

DB 2, p.359 - HARRISS from HARRISS   DEED, 10 Jun 1769

Jn°. HARRISS Sen*. of County of Pittsylvania and Colony of Virginia of one
part and David HARRISS of County and Colony aforesaid of other part...for
£15 Current Money of Virginia...100 acres part of a Sertain Tract of Land
containing 300 acres more or less and being on both sides of a large fork of
Cascade Creek, Beginning at David STEPHENS Corner, thence down the old South
line for 100 acres thence a Cross to the old line on north side of said fork
of Cascade, along old line to SAID STEPHENS'ES line...being heretofore Granted to Jn°. HARRIS by Letters patent Bearing Date under Seal of our Collony
5 Jun 1765.

Wit: Henry ⟋ LANSFORD, W^m. ⟋ STEPHENS Senr., W^m. ⟋ STEPHENS Junr.
           his   his   his
          Mark   mark   Mark

Rec: 28 Nov 1771   John HARRISS L.S.

DB 2, p.361 - POPE from BUTLER   DEED, 23 Nov 1771

John BUTLER of County of Pittsylvania of one part and Nathaniel POPE of
County of Louisa of other part...for £100 Current Money of Virginia...Tract
of Land on north side Banister River Containing 150 acres...Beginning at
the Mountain...to John DONELSON Corner at the Mountain, along said Mountain.
Wit: Benjamin LANKFORD, Joseph ROBERTS, James WILSON
Rec: 28 Nov 1771
Mary, wife of said John privily Exam^d. as Law   John ⊢ BUTLER L.S.
directs Relinquished her right of Dower   mark
                                                         his

DB 2, p.363 - ADAMS from OWEN   DEED, 14 Nov 1771

Thomas OWEN of County of Pittsylv^a. of one part and Sylvester ADAMS of County
and Parrish of Fairfax of other part...for £200 Current Money of Virginia...
240 acres being the Land which said OWEN Purchased of William MC DANIEL and
by him by Indenture bearing date 29 Aug 1771, which Land was purchased by
said William MC DANIEL of Robert WADE, Junr. and which said Robert WADE Purchased of Joseph PARRISH and was by said Joseph PARRISH by Indenture bearing
date 18 Jan in year aforesaid Conveyed to said Robert WADE of Record in Court
of County of Halifax.
Wit: George ROSS, James REDMON, Jn°. ANDERSON, Thomas WILLIAMS, Charles
DUNKIN, Thomas HOPER, Ann OWEN
Rec: 28 Nov 1771   Thomas OWEN L.S.

DB 2, p.365 - JONES from JONES   DEED, 27 Nov 1771

Robert JONES of Pittsylvania County and Colony of Virginia of one part and
Abraham JONES of County and Colony aforesaid of other part...for and in Consideration of sum of £50 lawfull money of Virginia...156 acres on Both sides
north fork of pigg River...in old Line...by a branch...Crossing north fork
of Pig River...Crossing Two forks of a branch...on Joseph ELLISES line.
Wit: Hugh INNES, W^m. COOK, Robert PERRYMAN
Rec: 28 Nov 1771   Robert JONES L.S.

DB 2, p.367 - FEARIS from INNES   DEED, 15 Apr 1771

Hugh INNES of County of Pittsylv^a. of one part and James FARIS Senior of
said County of other part...for £25 Current money of Virginia...Sell and confirm unto said James FARIS in his actual Possession now being by a Virtue of
a bargain and Sale...Tract of Land Containing 400 acres on north fork of
Panther Creek...on Lower side the Cattail fork...crossing the Creek...on a
branch, crossing said branch Several times and a large meadow...Crossing two
Branches.

Wit: Abraham SHELTON, Gabriel SHELTON, James LEAK
Rec: 28 Nov 1771   Hugh INNES L.S.

DB 2, p.369 - HAILE from INNES   DEED, 27 Nov 1771
Hugh INNES of County of Pittsylvania of one part and William HALE of said
County of other part...for £10 Current Money of Virginia...Hugh INNES Doth
Sell unto William HALE in his actual possession now being by virtue of a
bargain to him made...Land on Mountain fork of Snow Creek...on line of the
Patent, along said line...dividing HALES Land from Thomas LAWRENCES land...
in Abraham ARDINS field...100 acres more or less being part of 800 acres
Granted to INNES by patent bearing date 27 Aug 1770 and being the land where-
of said HALE now lives.
Wit: Robt. PERRYMAN, Robt. JONES, William COOK
Rec: 28 Nov 1771   Hugh INNES L.S.

DB 2, p.372 - HEARD from FARLEY   BILL SALE, 17 May 1771
I, Francis FARLEY, hath Sold unto Stephen HEARD Junior one Sartain black
mare with a blase in her face about fore feet fore Inches high Branded but I
cant tell what.   his
Wit: John HEARD   Francis C FARLAY
Rec: 28 Nov 1771   mark

DB 2, p.372 - PEAKE from SHOCKLIE   DEED, 28 Nov 1771
James SHOCKLEY of Pittsylvania County of one part and William PEAKE of said
County of other part...for £50 Current Money of Virginia...200 acres more or
less...branch of Pey Creek...Crossing Pye Creek and two Branches...Crossing
the Creek.
No witnesses   his
Rec: 28 Nov 1771   James /—/ SHOCKLEY L.S.
Margaret, wife of James SHOCKLEY, privily Examined   mark
Relinquished her right of Dower

DB 2, p.374 - POLLEY from PROSIZE   BILL SALE, 20 Apr 1771
I, William PROSIZE of Pittsylvania County, hath Sold to Edward POLLEY of said
County one black horse with a Stare in his forehead and a Snip on his nose
one hind foot white Branded on near Buttock thus ⟑ also one white Gray Mare
no Brand perceiveable for Consideration Sum of £03·16·07 Current Money, the
said Edward POLLEY became my Security to the Sherrif for which said Horse and
Mare...untill said PROSIZE shall Discharge said sum and all Costs that accrue.
Wit: Abra^m. SHELTON
Rec: 28 Nov 1771   William PROSIZE L.S.

DB 2, p.375 - TURNER from BOLTON   DEED, 28 Nov 1771
Robert BOLTON of County of Pittsylvania and Mary his wife of one part and
Meshack TURNER of County of Halifax of other part...for £100 Current money...
Land on Banister River Containing 354 acres...north side the River thence new
lines...down the River as it Meanders and Crossing it...to CANNONS corner, on
his line...to Stinking River, down Stinking River to Banister River and down
said river as it meanders and Crossing it.
No witnesses
Rec: 28 Nov 1771   Robert BOULTON L.S.

DB 2, p.377 - SHOCKLEY from SHOCKLEY   DEED, 28 Nov 1771
James SHOCKLEY of Pittsylvania County of one part and Levi SHOCKLIE of said
County of other part...for £50 Current Money of Virginia...200 acres more or

less on Both Sides Little Pye Creek...Crossing a branch...Crossing a Small
Branch...in William PEAKS line by a branch.
No witnesses

Rec: 28 Nov 1771

Margeret, wife of above named James SHOCKLEY,
privily Examined Relinquished her right of Dower

James ⎯⎯ SHOCKLEY L.S.
Mark
(his)

DB 2, p.378 - OWEN from DUNCAN   DED^s., 26 Sep XI year of our Reign
George the third by the grace of god of great Brittain France and Ireland
king Defender of the faith &c to John WILSON and Jno. OWEN or any two his
Majestys Justices of the County...whereas James DUNCAN by his Certain Indent-
ure of Feoffment hath Conveyed unto Thomas OWEN of Pittsylvania Co. one Certain Tract of Land containing 103 acres and whereas Elizabeth wife of said
James DUNCAN Cannot Conventantly Travel to County Court of Pittsylvania...
Examined Elizabeth, the wife of James DUNCAN, from and apart from her said
husband whether she does freely Relinquish her Right of Dower...when you
have it done you Certifie to our Justices.
By virtue of above Dedimus we have Examined Elizabeth, the wife of James
DUNCAN, apart from her husband...Relinquished her Right of Dower to Land
25 Oct 1771.

John WILSON L.S.
John OWEN L.S.

DB 2, p.380 - COX from SLONE & WIFE   DEED, 11 Jan 1772
James SLONE and alice his wife of Parish of Cambden in County of Pittsylvania
of one part and John COX of Parish and County aforesaid of other part...for
£75 Current Money of Virginia...all that Tract of Land on both sides Mill
Creek Containing 100 acres more or less which land was Conveyed to said James
SLONE by John SLONE and Elenor his wife by Indenture duly Recorded in County
Court of Halifax...Land whereon said John COX now lives.
Wit: Abraham MOTTLEY, Thos. WATKINS, Caty TUNSTALL

James X SLONE L.S.
mark
(his)

Rec: 27 Feb 1772

DB. 2, p.382 - SLOANE from MC DANIEL   DEED, 1772
Henry MC DANIEL of County of Pittsylvania of one part and James SLONE of
County aforesaid of other part...for £75 Current money of Virginia...all
that Tract of Land on South side Banister River Containing 181 acres more
or less...in old line...down the River as it Meanders.
No witnesses
Rec: 27 Feb 1772   Henry MC DANIEL L.S.

DB 2, p.384 - ROBERTS from AUSTIN   DEED, 30 Jan 1772
Hannah AUSTIN of parish of Raleigh and County of Amelia of one part and
James ROBERTS of Cambden parish and County of Pittsylvania of other part...
for £45 Current money of Virginia...all that Tract of Land Containing by
Estimation 303 acres...Begining at AIRS corner thence a new line...to REEDS
line, along his line..to AIRS line, on his line...Crossing the north fork of
Sandy River and is the same Land granted to said Hannah AUSTIN by Letters
patent bearing date XXVth Day of March 1762.

Wit: William COMPTON, Gregory DURHAM, David ⎯ WEATHERBY, Jean OAKES,
(his) mark

George PEAYO, Joseph AUSTIN, Syrus ROBERTS   Hannah ⎯ AUSTIN L.S.
(her) Mark
Rec: 27 Feb 1772

DB 2, p.386 - CLEMENTS from ABSTON   DEED, 4 Nov 1771
John ABSTON of province of South Carolina of one part and Stephen CLEMENT of
Bedford County in Virginia of other part...for £45 Current money of Virginia...
300 acres more or less lying on both Sides Strait Stone Creek formily pattent
for Francis POLLARD...Beginning at WILLOCKS Corner in the Low Grounds of said
Creek, up and Down both sides of said Creek Concluding the wide Low Grounds
being part of above mentioned Land their being part Sold off.

                                              his
Wit: Benjamin CLEMENT, Joshua ABSTON, Thos. T ROBERTSON,
          his   mark
Benjamin BH HOLLAND
          mark

Rec: 27 Feb 1772   John ABSTON L.S.

DB 2, p.387 - EASELEY from FINNEY   DEED, 22 Feb 1772
William FINNEY of Parish of Raleigh and County of Amelia of one part and
Pyrant EASELEY of Parrish of Cambden and County of Pittsylvania of other
part...for £70 Lawfull money of Virginia...Tract of land Containing 200 acres
on both sides Banister River...on S^o. Side Banister.
                    his   his
Wit: Thomas $Thornay$ HARDIE, Thos. X WATTSON, William PIGG
               mark   mark
Rec: 27 Feb 1772   William FINNEY L.S.

DB 2, p.389 - FIELD & CALL from HICKEY   BILL OF SALE
I, John HICKEY of County of Pittsylvania have Sold unto FIELD & CALL of
county of Prince George merchants, 3 feather beds and furniture, 11 head of
Cattle with their Increase Viz. 5 Cows and three Calves and 3 Earling heifers
marked with a Smooth Crop in Each Ear and under keel in Right for Sum of
£20·16·10 half Penny...HICKEY at present time Stands Justly in debt to said
FIELD & CALL and being Desirous to pay with Interest doth Impower them to
Sell said items for best price giving 10 days publick notice...discharge debt
and Interest...if not sold for money Sufficent to Satisfie Debt then said John
HICKEY doth oblige himself to pay on Demand Ballance Remaining with Interest
from date hereof untill time of Payment...5 Jul 1771...FIELD & CALL agree to
give 12 months Credit for above Sale unless they find themselves in any Dan-
ger by Delaying it.
Wit: Jno. WILSON, Merry HALL, Jacob DAINS, William WIDBY
Rec: 27 Feb 1772   John HICKEY L.S.

DB 2, p.391 - BURCH from BURCH   BILL SALE
I, Henry BURCH of Pittsylvania County in Colony of Virginia have in Consideration of £12 Current money of Virginia Sold unto John BURCH of same place 2
Two year old heafers both of a red pyde, 1 black mare branded on near Buttock,
M , 1 black horse Colt Branded on near Shoulder with the Check of a Curl
Bridle, 1 Black mare and a Dark bay Colt by her Side no white nor any other
mark about them, 15 barrels of Corn, 1 Bed and furniture and the bed Stock
and Cord there with, 1 Loom and Geers, 1 dish, 2 Basons, 6 plates.
30 Sep 1771
Wit: John BRISCOE, Jarob BURCH
Rec: 26 Mar 1772   Henry BURCH L.S.

DB 2, p.391 - TERRY from READ   DEED, 1 Jul 1771
Thomas READ one of the Executors of Clement READ Junr. Gent. dec^d. of County
of Charlotte of one part and Joseph TERRY of County of Pittsylvania of other

part...Whereas said Clement READ Junr. by his Last Will gave all his Lands
to said Thomas READ to make Conveyances to such that he in his lifetime had
sold and other of his land to Dispose of as is Directed by the Will and
whereas said Clement READ Junr. in his life time had Sold to said Joseph
TERRY a Certain Tract of 353 acres more or less and is same Land that Clément
READ Senr. in his lifetime purchased of Robert WEAKLEY by Deed recorded
in County Court of Halifax bearing date 1 Aug 1753...for £50 Current money
of Virginia to Mary READ Senr. have sold to Joseph TERRY 353 acres.
Wit: R. WILLIAMS, Haynes MORGAN, Jo. READ
Rec: 28 Nov 1771
Further proved: 26 Mar 1772   Thomas READ Ex^r. L.S.

DB 2, p.393 - WIMBISH from MC DANIEL   DEED, 4 Mar 1772
Henry MC DANIEL of County of Pittsylvania of one part and John WIMBISH of
same County of other part...for £60 Current Money of Virginia...Land in Pittsylvania County on both sides Rackoon run a branch of Elkhorn Creek Containing 188 acres...in Robert WEAKLEYS line thence new lines...Crossing a branch...
in WEAKLEY's line, along his line...Crossing a Branch to his corner, Still
along said WEAKLEY's line...Crossing the Rackoon run.
Wit: James PIGG, Thos. LOVELACE, Jno. WHITE
Rec: 26 Mar 1772   Henry MC DANIEL L.S.

DB 2, p.395 - WIMBISH from ROBERTS   DEED 2 LOTTS, 26 Mar 1772
James ROBERTS of Pittsylvania County of one part and John WIMBISH of same
County of other part...for £10 Current Money of Virginia...Two Lotts or half
acres of Land in Town of Peytonsburg on East side of Randolph Street one of
them on the Main Street and by the Plan of said Town known by Number 103, the
other adjoining on the back of the same and known in said plan by number 90.
No witnesses
Rec: 26 Mar 1772   James ROBERTS L.S.

DB 2, p.397 - COOK from JUSTICE   DEED, 12 Mar 1772
Ezra JUSTICE of County of Pittsylvania of one part and Harmon COOK of said
County of other part...for £100 Current Money...354 acres on both sides
harping Creek...at WALTONS corner thence new lines...Crossing harping Creek...
in WALTONS line, along his line, up said Creek as it meanders to his Corner,
Crossing said Creek, along his line south.
Wit: John HENSLEE, Eusebus HUBBARD, John GOODE
Rec: 26 Mar 1772   Ezra JUSTICE L.S.

DB 2, p.400 - BOAZ from BOAZ   DEED, 30 Dec 1771
Thomas BOAZ of County of Pittsylvania of one part and Edmund BOAZ of said
County of Pittsylvania of other part...for £40 Current money of Virginia...
404 acres more or less, on both sides Stewards Creek...at Thomas BOAZS lower
corner...Crossing the Creek, thence new Lines...Crossing a branch, on a
marked Ridge.
Wit: Arch^d. SMITH, John SMITH, James GARNER
Rec: 26 Mar 1772   Thomas BOAZ L.S.

DB 2, p.402 - WOMACK from HENRY   DEED 26 Mar 1772
Hugh HENRY and Mary his wife in Cambden parrish in Pittsylvania County of
one part and William WOMACK of County of amherst of other part...for £250
Current Money of Virginia...all that Tract of Land on both sides Banister
River...up said River...Land granted to Isaac CLOUD by Letters patent Bear-

date 25 Jul 1746 Containing 304 acres more or less.
No witnesses
Rec: 26 Mar 1772   Hugh HENRY L.S.
Mary, wife of said Hugh, privily Examined as Law directs Relinquished her
right of Dower

DB 2, p.404 - GEORGE from FARRIS   D. TRUST, 8 Jul 1771
William FARRIS of County of Pittsylvania of one part and David GEORGE of Province of South Carolina of other part...for £47·02·03 Current Money of Virginia...One dark bay horse Branded on near Buttock *60* and has a Slit in his
Right Ear, one Dark bay horse five Years old not Branded, one old bay horse
his brand is unknown, Ten head of Black Cattle marked with two Slits in Each
Ear, with all and every other part of my Estate too Tedious to mention...if
said William FARRIS shall pay above amount on or before 24 Dec 1772 with
Lawfull Interest from 11 Dec last pass'd together with Costs of Recording
this Indenture and Contengent Charges of the sales and other necessary Expences.
Wit: Thos. MUSTAIN, Richard KEEZEE, Abra^m. SHELTON

                                                            his
                                           William $\times$ FARRIS L.S.
Rec: 26 Mar 1772   mark

DB 2, p.405 - WILSON from WEBB   DEED, 12 Mar 1772
Merry WEBB of Parrish of in County of Pittsylvania of one part and James
WILSON of County and parish afores^d. of other part...for £50 Current Money
of Virginia...all that Tract of Land Containing 70 acres, it being part of
252 acres granted to said Merry WEBB by Letters patent Bearing date 16 Aug
1756...on Leatherwood Creek...in a bottom...on Smiths River, up the same as
it Meanders to mouth of Leatherwood Creek, up it as it meanders.
Wit: Thomas NELSON, Samuel BURNS   Merry WEBB L.S.
Rec: 26 Mar 1772   her
Elizabeth, wife of s^d. Merry WEBB, privily   Eliz^a. $\times$ WEBB L.S.
Exam^d. Relinq^d. her right of Dower   mark

DB 2, p.408 - CANTEBERRY from REAVES   DEED, 26 Mar 1772
Fredrick REEVES of parrish of Cambden in County of Pittsylvania of one part
and Samuel CANTERBURY of Parrish County aforesaid planter of other part...for
£35 Current Money of Virginia...all that Tract of Land on Mountain Creek a
branch of Pigg River...on order line on East side of said Creek, down said
Creek partly a north course...branch of said Creek, down said branch to the
Creek Crossing the Creek Runing up a branch partly south west...on David
KERBYS line, along his line to the order line...Containing 100 acres more or
less.
No witnesses   Fredrick RIVES L.S.
Rec: 26 Mar 1772   Mary magdalene RIVES L.S.
Mary magdalene, wife of said RIVES, Privily Exam^d. as law directs Relinq^d.
her right of Dower.

DB 2, p.410 - AUSTIN from AUSTIN   25 Mar 1772
I, John AUSTIN of province of North Carrolina and County of Surrey appoint
Joseph AUSTIN of Colony of Virginia and County of Pittsylvania my Lawful
attorney to act for me in making a Good Sufficent Deed for a Tract of Land
in County of Pittsylvania and said John AUSTIN do agree to abide by and make
good all Conveyances that Joseph AUSTIN Should make for me in my name Concerning the Premises.

Wit: Jehu MORTON, Joseph MORTON, Matthew $\overset{his}{\underset{mark}{M}}$ PIGGS, James $\overset{his}{\underset{mark}{X}}$ GRAVELEY

John $\overset{his}{\underset{mark}{/}}$ AUSTIN L.S.

Rec: 27 Mar 1772

DB 2, p.411 - YOUNG from DANIEL   DEED, 24 Sep 1772
James DANIEL of Halifax County of one part and William YOUNG of Pittsylv^a.
County of other part...for £150 Current money of Virginia...1,250 acres on
south side Pigg River, being part of an order of Councell formerly Surveyed
for Ashford HUGHS and William GRAY...on Jno. ELLISE line, thence new line
west Course to said River...on Benjamin POTTERS line...to William HAYNE's
line, along his line to William STEEGALS line, to old order line to Pigg
River, along said River.
No witnesses
Rec: 24 Sep 1772   James DANIEL L.S.

DB 2, p.413 - MC DANIEL from CALDWELL   DEED, 28 Feb 1772
Alexander CALDWELL of County of Pittsylvania of one part and William MC DANIEL
of County of Halifax planter of other part...for £200 Current money of Virginia...all that Tract of Land on South side Banister River Containing 300
acres, being the Plantation where Alexander CALDWELL now lives...on River,
runing new lines...Down a Branch...Containing 200 acres which Alexander CALD-
WELL purchased of George WATKINS as per Indenture Duly recorded in Court of
Halifax 20 Sep 1759, a small segment of above 200 acres being Cutt off by
runing the County line which is in County of Halifax, also 100 acres which
Alexander CALDWELL purchased of Reverend James TOWLES p^r. Indenture Recorded
and bearing date 16 Sep 1762, it being part of Larger Tract granted to James
FOWLES p^r. Letters patent Recorded in Secretary office of this Colony, Joyn-
ing above said 200 acres of Land which Alexander CALDWELL Purchased of above
George WATKINS...in CALDWELL line.

Wit: John WIMBISH, Johnson MC DANIEL, Eliz^a.$\overset{her}{\underset{mark}{/}}$ YATES, Stephen YATES,

Thos. BALDWIN   Alexander $\overset{his}{\underset{mark}{(l}}$ CALDWELL L.S.

Hanah $\overset{her}{\underset{mark}{V}}$ CALDWELL L.S.

No recording date

DB 2, p.416 - MC DANIEL from CALDWELL   DED^s., 29 Feb 12 year of our Reign
George the third by grace of god of great Brittain France and Ireland King
Defender of the faith &c to Thomas DILLARD Junr. and Benjamin LANKFORD or
any two his majestys Justices of County of Pittsylvania...whereas Alexander
CALDWELL by Indenture of Feoffment hath conveyed to William MC DANIEL of
County of Halifax one Certain Tract of Land in Pittsylvania Containing 300
acres and Hannah, wife of Alexander CALDWELL Cannot Conveniantly Travel to
our County Court of Pittsylvania...Relinquishes her Right of Dower to Land
Conveyed by her Husband...4 Mar 1772.

Thos. DILLARD, Junr. L.S.
Ben. LANKFORD L.S.

Rec: 26 Mar 1772

DB 2, p.417 - AUSTIN from GRAVELY   DEED, 20 Mar 1772

James GRAVELY Senr. of parrish of Camden and County of Pittsylvania of one
part and Joseph AUSTIN of County and parrish aforesaid of other part...for
£45 Current Money of Virginia...all that Tract of Land Containing by Estimation 172 acres lying on a fork of Sandy River...Beginning at Daniel HANKINS
corner...in William PAYNES line...in James MORTONS line...Crossing the fork...
along TWITTEYS and Companys line...along Daniel HANKINS line.

                                        his

No witnesses   James_____GRAVELY L.S.
Rec: 27 Mar 1772   mark

DB 2, p.419 - MC CAUL and LYLE from BYNUMS   DEED OF TRUST, 31 Jan 1772

Jn^r. BYNUM, Senr. and Arther BYNUM of County of Pittsylvania of one part and
Alex^r. MC CAUL, James LYLE & Co. of other part...Jno. and Arther BYNUM Justly
indebted to them in sum of £246·10·06 Current money of Virginia and is Willing to Secure said Sum...for further Sum of £5 Current money of Virginia...
hath sold Tract of Land in County of Pittsylvania Containing 200 acres...on
Hugh MAHOONS line, Saml. BYNUMS line and Jacob ?SETTWEELS line Excepting the
Mill and two acres of land on both sides Rutleges Creek that is to say one
acre on each side of the Creek more or less which is the Remainder of a larger
Tract that BYNUM bought of Col^o. William WYNNNE...MC CAUL & LYLE at end of
three years after date sell for most that can be got...out of money arising
Satisfy themselves Sum above with Lawfull Interest...pay overplus to BYNUM.

                               his

Wit: Thomas DUNCAN, Peter PERKINS, Jno. CHADWELL
                               mark   Jno. BYNUM L.S.
Rec: 26 Mar 1772   Arther BYNUM L.S.

DB 2, p.421 - STONE from FARRIS   DEED, 28 Aug 1771

James FARRIS Senr. of County of Pittsylvania of one part and Joshua STONE of
same County of other part...for £160 Current money of Virginia...Tract of
Land on Both Sides Allen's Creek, Containing 200 acres more or less...on old
line, along said line north...along the Rockey Hill...north fork of said Creek
Down the fork as it meanders...Just above the plantation...to Joseph FARRIS's
corner pine Just by his Tob^o. Ground, along FARRIS's line South...Joins the
lines of Joseph FARRIS, William VAUGHAN, Junr. and James DEJARNET.

                     his   his

Wit: Benjamin LANKFORD, Jno. FERRELL, Francis SHORT
                     mark   mark   his
                                   James FARRIS L.S.
Rec: 28 Aug 1771   mark

DB 2, p.423 - STONE from FARRIS   DED^s., 5th Jany. in 13th Year of our Reign

Jno. DONELSON, Thos. DILLARD, Ben^j. LANKFORD and Crispen SHELTON Gen^r. of
any two his majestys Justices of County of Pittsylvania...whereas James
FARRIS Senr. by his Indenture of Feoffment hath Conveyed unto Joshua STONE
of County of Pittsylvania a Tract of Land Containing 200 acres more or less
and Susannah the wife of said FARRIES Cannot Conveniantly Travel to said
County Court of Pittsylvania...Susannah apart from her Husband did freely
Relinquish her Right of Dower to said Land. 2 Feb 1773.
Rec: 29 Aug 1771   Benj^a. LANKFORD L.S.
Further prv: 29 Jul 1773   Crispen SHELTON L.S.

DB 2, p.424 - DONALD & Co. from TALIAFERRO   DEED TRUST, 27 Mar 1772
John TALIAFERRO of County of Pittsylvania of one part and James and Robert
DONALD & Company merchants in Glasgow of other part...for £114·11·03·03 which
Jno. TALIAFERRO is indebted to James & Robert DONALD & Co. and desires to
pay them...further Consideration of Sum of 5s like money paid by DONALD & .C^o.
Sell to James & Robert DONALD & Co. Tract of Land containing 532 acres more
or less on a branch of Banister Called white oak Creek adjoining Lands of
Ambrose PORTER and Robert ADAMS, whereon said TALIAFERRO now lives and three
Enteres of Land adjoining said Land...DONALD & Co. after 10 Dec. next ensuing or when they shall think proper or TALIAFERRO shall request them...
best price that can be gotten...money arising from Sale Satisfy them the
above sum with Lawfull Interest from 19 Jun 1771 until fully discharged...
pay overplus to TALIAFERRO.
Wit: Jn^b. MENRIES , Jo^s. BALLENGER, Isaace READ, Edmund WINSTON, John AYLETT
Rec: 27 Mar 1772   John TALIAFERRO L.S.

DB 2, p.426 - BULLOCK from BARNETT   BILL SALE, 26 Mar 1772
I, Isaace BARNETT of Colony of Virginia and County of Pittsylvania and Parrish
of Camden for £50 good and Lawfull money of Virginia to me in hand by Thomas
BULLOCK Senr. of above Colony and County...Sell 10 head of Cattle marked Thus
two Crops and two under kiels in each ear, two feather beds and furniture,
3 turned Bedsteads, 7 turned Chairs, 3 axes, 1 barr Share and Coulter, 6 hoes,
1 Smooth bore Gun, 5 pewter plats, 1 small pewter dish, 1 Stone pitcher, 2
Stone Quart Mugs, 2 Earthen dishes, 2 Iron potts, 1 Dutch oven, 1 black Horse
aged 13 years old Branded thus with   on near Buttock, 1 black mare with
a yearling Colt the mare Branded thus   on the near Shoulder and thus
near Buttock...only Excepted Sufficent to pay my yearly thyes or County and
Parrish charges if need requires...full Sum with Lawfull Interest on 1 Jan
1784...if paid then above to be void.
Wit: Thos. WILLINGHAM Senr., Danl. HANKINS, Thos. NELSON

                                                   his
                                        Isaace   BARNETT
Rec: 26 Mar 1772   mark

DB 2, p.428 - TALBOT from GAMBLE   POWER OF ATTORNEY, 8 Jan 1772
I, Samuel GAMBLE of Rowan County N^o. Carrolinia and Ginnet my wife, appoint
John TALBOTT of Pittsylvania County in Virginia my Lawfull attorney for us
to Demand Recover from John MILLER of County of Bedford in Colony and Dominion aforesaid one Certain Tract of Land in County of Bedford on Maggetty
Creek in County aforesaid Containing a parcel of Land which was purchased of
a Certain RANDOLPH Gen^t. by aforesaid John MILLER and Land being vested in
heirs of John MILLER in County of Bedford John TALBOTT now of County of Bedford who purchased the adjoining or Remainder part of said RANDOLPHS Land in
Bedford...caused a Deed in Law to be made to Ginnet MILLER the only heir of
John MILLER which Gennet MILLER has sence Come of full age and married to
Samuel GAMBLE late of province North Carrolinia Rowan County...gave TALBOT
of Pittsylvania full Power to follow all legal for Recovery of same Lands
Conveyed to us.

                                         his
Wit: John SALMAN, Burditt ESKRIDGE, Rich^d.   BARNETT
                                        mark

                                          his
                              Saml. X GAMBLE L.S.
                                         mark
                                          hir
                              Ginnet X GAMBLE L.S.
Rec: 26 Mar 1772   mark

DB 2, p.430 - SMITH & C°. from SMITH   DEED TRUST, 10 Aug 1771
Peyton SMITH of Pittsylvania County on one part and James SMITH & C°. of
said County on other part...for £200 Current Money of Virginia which said
Peyton SMITH is Justly indebted and desires to pay them and for further Consideration of 5s Like money paid by James SMITH & C°....Tract of Land where
on said Peyton SMITH now lives, which he Purchased of Henry KEARBY Containing
135 acres more or less, also Two Wenches and three Negro Boys, Named Betty,
Letty, mercer, Tom and Isaac, with every other Articls of my personall Estate...
James SMITH & C°. after 1 Nov 1773 or when they think proper or Peyton SMITH
shall request...Sell for best price, pay themselves above Sum with Interest...
pay overplus to Peyton SMITH.

Wit: John THOMPSON, Arch^d. SMITH, Henry ⊢ KEARBY
                                         his
                                         mark

Rec: 26 Mar 1772   Peyton SMITH L.S.

DB 2, p.432 - TERRY from DAUGHARTY   DEED, 21 Nov 1771
Thos. DAUGHIRTY Late of Charlotte of one part and David TERRY of Halifax
County of other part...for £40 Current Money of Virginia...Tract of Land Con-
taining by Patent 176 acres more or less lying on both sides Sandy Creek...
Down the Creek...being the Land granted to Thomas DAUGHERTY by patent Bearing
date 6 Apr 1769.
Wit: Isaac READ, H. MORGAN, R. WILLIAMS
Rec: 28 Nov 1771
Further prv: 26 Mar 1772   Thomas DAUGHERTY L.S.

DB 2, p.434 - LANKFORD from GORDON   LEASE OF REDEEMP., 31 Jan 1772
I do throw up all my Right and Title of redeeming of Two negroes Names
Kildare and Sally and their Increase unto Benjamin LANKFORD who hath a bill
of Sale or Morquage in Halifix County Court Dated 8 Apr 1767.
Wit: Abraham SHELTON, Crispin SHELTON
Rec: 26 Mar 1772   Arch^d. GORDON

DB 2, p.435 - GEORGE from WATKINS   DEED OF TRUST, 27 Aug 1771
David GEORGE of County of Charlotte of one part and Jno. WATKINS of County of
Pittsylvania of other part...for £20·02·08 Lawfull money of Virginia which
said John WATKINS is Justly Indebted to said David GEORGE and desires to pay...
further Consideration of 5s like money to Jno. WATKINS paid by David GEORGE...
Sell Tract of Land in County of Pittsylvania Containing 100 acres more or
less being the Land and plantation said John WATKINS now lives on, Bounded by
James CALDWELLS land and is part of Tract of Land CALDWELL owns...Bounded by
William GLASCOCKS Land...after 1 Sep. next sell Land for best price Giving 10
Days Publick notice...money arising pay above sum with Interest...pay overplus
from Sale if any to John WATKINS.

Wit: John ✗ BAYES, Jeane ⊘ CALDWELL, W^m. HARDWICK, RWILLIAMS,
          his   mark   hir mark
Saml. WIMBISH, WBARKSDILL
Rec: 26 Mar 1772   John WATKINS L.S.

DB 2, p.437 - PETTY from WATKINS   DEED, 1 Jan 1772
John WATKINS of Parrish of and County of Pittsylvania of one part and William
PETTY of Parrish of Cornwall and County of Charlotte of other part...for £40
Current Money of Virginia...all that Tract of Land on Both sides north fork

of Double Creek Containing 150 acres more or less.
Wit: John MADING, Junr., Jno. CREEL, Lazarus DODSON, Joseph PETTY
Rec: 28 May 1772   John WATKINS L.S.

DB 2, p.439 - EAST from PERRY   DEED, 28 May 1772
William PERRY of parrish of Camden and County of Pittsylvania of one part
and John EAST of Parish and County aforesaid...for £100 Current Money of Virginia...Tract of Land on both sides Panther Creek...up the Creek as it meanders...250 acres more or less, it being the Land Thomas GREENWOOD Conveyed to
said William PERRY by Indenture bearing date 17 Apr 1771 and Recorded in
County Court of Pittsylvania.
No witnesses
Rec: 28 May 1772   William PERRY L.S.
Mary, wife of William PERRY, privily Exam^d. as Law directs Relinquished
her right of Dower.

DB 2, p.441 - BIRD from BIRD   DEED, 28 May 1772
Joseph BIRD of Pittsylvania County of one part and Francis BIRD of same
County of other part...for £45 Current money of Virginia...Tract of Land
Containing 200 acres more or less on Pig River...in old line thence a new
line...on a branch, up same as it Meanders to old line...on a branch, down
same as it meanders to the River, down the River as it meanders.
No witnesses
Rec: 28 May 1772   Joseph BIRD L.S.
Hannah, wife of Joseph, being privily Exam^d. as Law directs Relinquished
her right of Dower.

DB 2, p.443 - ATKINSON from ATKINSON   DEED, 19 May 1772
William ATKINSON Senr. of Pittsylvania County planter of one part and parker
ATKINSON of other part...for £5 Current Money of Virginia...Tract of Land
Containing 50 acres more or less on Pigg River...south side the River...
Crossing a branch...on south side thence up said River as it meanders.

                                              his
Wit: William WITCHER, Harmon COOK, William /\ ATKINSON
                                              mark

                                            his
                               William /\ ATKINSON Senr. L.S.
Rec: 28 May 1772   mark

DB 2, p.445 - WEATHERFORD from HARDY   DEED, 26 May 1772
Thos. HARDY and An his wife of Parrish in County of Pittsylvania of one part
and John WEATHERFORD of same Parrish and County of other part...for £55 Curr-
ent money of Virginia...Tract of Land Containing 248 acres in order line...
Runing up south side Chery Stone Creek...on Thomas HARDY line...along order
line...on David WAID line...along order line.
No witnesses
                                               his
                                   Thomas   HARDY L.S.
Rec: 28 May 1772   mark

DB 2, p.447 - ASTIN from DUDLEY   DEED, 21 Apr 1772
Thomas DUDLEY of county of Pittsylvania of one part and William ASTIN of said
County of other Part...for £300 Current Money of Virginia...Tract of Land of
400 acres more or Less on South Side Dann River begining at Mouth of Jacksons
Creek, thence up the Creek to the Back line, on that line to Thomas WYNNES

line, on his Line to William BOYD's line, on his line to the River, down the
River as it Meanders to Begining at mouth of Jacksons Creek.
Wit: Robt. RAKESTRAW, Robt. PAYNE, Henry CLAY, John DIX, Larkin DIX
Rec: 28 May 1772   Thomas DUDLEY L.S.

DB 2, p.448 - ATKINSON from ATKINSON   DEED, 18 May 1772
William ATKINSON Senr. of Pittsylvania County planter of one part and Henry
ATKINSON Planter of other part...for £15 Current Money of Virginia...Tract
of Land Containing 50 acres more or Less on north side Pigg River...north
side River...up River as it Meanders.

Wit: William WITCHER, William [his mark] ATKINSON Junr., Danl. [his mark] WITCHER

                                    William [his mark] ATKINSON Senr. L.S.
Rec: 28 May 1772

DB 2, p.450 - RICHEY from COOK   DEED, 29 Oct 1771
John COOK of County of Pittsylvania of one part and William RICHEY of said
County of other part...for £20 Good and Lawful money of Virginia...Tract of
Land on waters of Strawberry Creek...joining John SMITHS line...joining John
BISWELLS line...joining Thomas HILLS line...Containing 240 acres more or less
which being part of 400 acres that was Granted to Thomas HARGET by patent
bearing date at Williamsburg 12 Jul 1762 it being the Land said John COOK is
now in Possession of also the same that I had of Andrew POLSON all the same
Land.
Wit: William SHIELDS, Thomas ROBERSON, James FULTON

                                             John COOK L.S.
                                             her
Rec: 28 Nov 1771   Mary [mark] COOK L.S.
Further prv: 28 May 1772   mark

DB 2, p.452 - LYNES from BURCH   BILL SALE, 11 Apr 1772
I, John BURCH of Pittsylvania County, are Justly indebted to Henry and Edmund
LYNE merchants of said County the Just sum of £13·16·03 Current Money of Virginia and being desirous to do LYNE justice...Sold 1 pide Cow, 2 yearlings
markt with a Crop and Hole in Each ear, 1 white mare, 1 bay horse Colt no
brand perceiviable, 2 Beds and furniture, 20 Head of Hogs and all the Rest of
my Estate of whatkindsoever and their future Increase including my Tob^o. not
carried Down...said Henry and Edm. LYNE at any time from 1 Aug. next may dispose for best Price to discharge sum with legal Interest.

                     her
Wit: Jacob BURCH, Clara [mark] BURCH
                    mark
Rec: 28 May 1772   John BURCH L.S.

DB 2, p.453 - JACKSON from GORMAN   DEED, 21 Dec 1771
John GORMAN of county of Pittsylvania and John JACKSON of said County...for
£80 Current money of Virginia...200 acres of Land Bounded by Land of CHAMBERLAND
and PIGGS abounded by new line that said John GORMAN and his Father made to
devide said Land.

                                his
Wit: Thomas HODGES, Moses HODGES, Christopher [mark] GORMAN
                                mark

Rec: 28 May 1772
Hannah, Wife of Jn°. GORMAN, privily Examined
and Relinquished her right of Dower.

John his GORMAN L.S.
mark

DB 2, p.455 - DUDLEY from ASTIN   DEED, 21 Apr 1772

William ASTIN of County of Pittsylvania of one part and Thomas DUDLEY of
said County of other part...for £600 Current Money of Virginia...Tract of
Land Containing 203 acres more or less on South Side Dann River, Beginning
at a Corner between ASTIN and John DIX...up the River as it meanders.
Wit: Robt. PAYNE, Henry CLAY, Robt. RAKESTRAW, Larkin DIX, Jn°. DIX

William X ASTIN L.S.
his mark

Rec: none

DB 2, p.457 - HARDY from FINNEY   DEED, 24 Apr 1772

William FINNEY of Parrish of Railagh and County of amelia of one part and
Thomas HARDIE Senr. of Parrish of Cambden and County of Pittsylvania of other
part...for £20 Lawfull money of Virginia...all that Messuage or Tenement of
Land on Cherry Stone Creek Bounded by Lands of said William FINNEY, William
PIGG and Thomas WATTSON...600 acres.
Wit: Richard PIGG, Jn°. NUCKELS, William PIGG , John WEATHERFORD

Rec: 28 May 1772   William FINNEY L.S.

DB 2, p.458 - PARBERY from CENTER   DEED, 28 May 1772

Stephen CENTER of County of Bedford of one part and James PARBERY of County
of Pittsylvania of other part...for £60 Current Money of Virginia...Tract of
Land on Waters of Frying pan Creek...on a branch thence new lines...Crossing
a branch.
Wit: Hugh INNES

Stephen O CENTER L.S.
his mark

Rec: 28 May 1772

DB 2, p.460 - NICHOLES from HARDY   DEED, 27 May 1772

Thomas HARDIE Senr. of Parrish of Cambden and County of Pittsylvania of one
part and John NICHOLES of above Parrish and County of other part...for £25
Good and Lawfull Current money of Virginia...100 acres more or less with the
Plantation...on Cherry Stone Creek...tree of Thomas HARDIES...Land along the
order line.
No witnesses

Thomas HARDY L.S.
his mark

Rec: 28 May 1772

DB 2, p.461 - HARBOUR from WITT   DEED, 22 May 1772

David WITT of Pittsylvania County in Virginia of one part and David HARBOUR
son of Elijah HARBOUR Deceased of said County and Collony aforesaid of other
part...for £40 Good and Lawfull Current Money of Virginia...Tract of Land
Containing 313 acres more or less on both sides south fork of Goblin Town
Creek...Crossing a branch...Crossing a Creek...Pointers in the old line.
No witnesses
Rec: 28 May 1772   David WITT L.S.

DB 2, p.464 - BYNUM from STILWELL   DEED, 27 May 1772
Jacob STILWELL and Nancy his wife of County of Pittsylv^a. of one part and
Arther BYNUM of said County of other part...for £100 Current Money of Virginia...
all that Tract of Land on both sides Rutlages Creek, Beginning on South side
the Creek on BYNUMS line Runing North on said line Crossing the Creek...on
WYNNES old line thence South Crossing the Creek to WYNNES back line...as
STILWELLS Deed from William WYNNE Senr. Specifies in all Containing 200 acres
more or less being part of a Larger Tract belonging to William WYNNE Senr.
and being the whole of the tract STILWELL bought of W^m. WYNNE Senr. in year
17__, Recorded in Halifax office.
Wit: Thomas DUNCAN, William WYNNE, Junr., Henry DIXON Junr.

                                            Jacob STILWELL L.S.
                                            her
                                     Nancy ⟋ STILWELL L.S.
Rec: 28 May 1772   mark

DB 2, p.466 - BRILLIMAN from TITLE   DEED, 28 May 1772
Anthony TITLE of Pittsylv^a. County and Colony of Virginia of one part and
Jacob BRILLIMAN of County and Colony aforesaid of other part...for £180 Law-
full money of Virginia Tract of Land on Mill Run a branch of Black Water
River. [no acreage listed]
No witnesses
Rec: 28 May 1772   Anthony TITLE L.S.
Ann, wife of Anthony, being privily Examined as Law Directs Relinquished
her right of Dower.

DB 2, p.468 - PIGG from FINNEY   DEED, 24 Apr 1772
William FINNEY of Parrish of Railagh and County of Amelia of one part and
William PIGG of Parrish of Camden and County of Pittsylv^a. of other part...
for £20 Lawful money of Virginia...all that Tenement of Land on Banister
River Bounded by lines of Thomas HARDIE, William FINNEY...Containing 1,200 acres.
                                                 his
Wit: Thomas HARDIE, Jno. WEATHERFORD, Jno. X NUCKELS
                                                 mark
Rec: 28 May 1772   William FINNEY L.S.

DB 2, p.470 - LANIER from LUMKIN   DEED, 8 Apr 1772
George LUMKIN and Mary his wife of county of Pittsylvania of one part and
Lemuell LANIER late of County of Brunswick of other part...for £100 Current
Money of Virginia...Tract of Land Containing 168 acres or there^d about which
being part of a Larger Tract Granted by Letters Patton to Edm^d. TAYLOR bear-
ing date 3 May 1763 and then Conveyed by said Edmund TAYLOR to said George
LUMKINS in County of Pittsylvania...on John HARDIMAN line...in ALEXANDERS
line...to William ALEXANDER...to the old Station line.
Wit: Benj^a. HICKS, David LANIER, Robt. LUMKIN, Geo. ROWLAND, James HICKS
Junr., Burdith ESKRIDGE, James CRUTCHFIELD, William KENNER
                                            George LUMKIN L.S.
                                            her
                                     Mary ⫰ LUMKIN L.S.
Rec: 28 May 1772   mark

DB 2, p.472 - ESTES from HALL   DEED, 28 May 1772
William HALL of one part and Elisha ESTES of other part...Sum of £150 Current
Money of Virginia...Tract of Land in County of Pittsylvania lying on Snow and
Grassey Creeks Containing 222 1/2 acres.
No witnesses
Rec: 28 May 1772   William HALL L.S.

DB 2, p.473 - COX from THOMAS   DED^s., 2 May 1772
To John DIX and Robt. PAYNE Gen^t. or any two his majestys Justices of County
of Pittsylvania whereas William THOMAS by his Certain Indenture of Feoffment
hath Conveyed unto John COX of County of Pittsylvania Tract of Land Containing 240 acres and whereas Joyce wife of said W^m. THOMAS, cannot Conveniantly
Travel to County Court of Pittsylvania...Joyce THOMAS apart from her Husband
did freely Relinquish her right of Dower.

                                             John DIX
Rec: 28 May 1772   Robt. PAYNE

DB 2, p.475 - SNEED from THOMAS   DED^s., 2 May 1772
To John DIX and Robert PAYNE Gent. or any two his majestys Justices of County
of Pittsylvania, whereas William THOMAS by his Certain Indenture of Feoffment
hath Conveyed unto Zachariah SNEED of County of Pittsylvania Tract of Land
Containing 160 acres and whereas Joyce, wife of said William THOMAS, Cannot
Travel to County Court of Pittsylvania...Joyce, wife of William THOMAS,apart
from her Husband relinquished her right of Dower.

                                             John DIX
Rec: 28 May 1772   Robt. PAYNE

DB 2, p.476 - HARDIE from HARDIE   DEED, 15 May 1772
Thomas HARDIE Senr. of one part and Thomas HARDIE Junr. of other part both of
Pittsylvania and in Colony of Virginia...Tract of Land Contain. 200 acres
more or less on both sides Chery Stone Creek...Beginning at John NICCKLES
on North side the Creek, Runing south Crossing the Creek and Runing up the
Little meddow branch to the corner on FINEYS order line, along FINIES line,
runing along Thos. WATSONS line North Crossing the Creek.
No witnesses
Rec: 28 May 1772   Thomas HARDY L.S.

DB 2, p.478 - WITCHER from ATKINSON   DEED, 28 May 1772
William ATKINSON Junr. of Pittsylvania County planter of one part and John
WITCHER Planter of other part...for £16 Current money of Virginia...Tract of
Land Containing 50 acres more or Less on north side Pigg River...Beginning
at mouth of a branch, up the Branch to the Line, along the line.
Wit: William WITCHER, Charles PARTIN, Rich^d. ATKINSON

                                 his
                         William |/ ATKINSON Junr. L.S.
Rec: 28 May 1772   mark

DB 2, p.480 - FARTHING from HIX   DEED, 28 May 1772
John HICKS of County of Hanover of one part and Richard FARTHING of Parrish
of Camden and County of Pittsylvania of other part...for £20 Current Money
of Virginia...all that Tract of Land Containing 400 acres more or Less and
adjoining the Lands of Richard PARSONS and Christopher GORMANS old Survey
and on both Sides Little Cherystone Creek and whereon said Richard FARTHING
now lives and on both sides Hickeys old Road it being the Land that was
granted unto said John HIX by Letters Patent bearing date in the Secretarys
Office...from the Day before the date hereof for and during the full Term and
time of one whole Year from thence next ensuing, fully to be Complete and
ended yielding and paying therefore the Rent of one Pepper Corn on Lady Day
next if be Lawfull.   his
No witnesses   John X HIX L.S.
Rec: 28 May 1772   mark

DB 2, p.482 - LANIER from LUMKINS   DEED, 27 Apr 1772
George LUMPKIN and Mary his wife of County of Pittsylvania in Colony of Virginia of one part and David LANIER of County of Brunswick and Colony aforesaid of other part...for £160 Current money of Virginia...Parcel of Land on
North side Marrowbone Creek...Benj[a]. HICKS corner...in old line...on a branch
and down said branch as it meanders...272 acres.
Wit: George ROWLAND, Burdith ESKRIDGE, William KINNER, Benj[a]. HICKS

                                              George LUMKIN L.S.
                                              her
                                        Mary   LUMKIN L.S.
Rec: 28 May 1772   mark

DB 2, p.483 - WATTSON from FINNEY   DEED, 24 Apr 1772
William FINNEY of Parrish of Raileigh, County of Amelia of one part and Thomas
WATTSON of Parish of Camden and County of Pittsylvania of other part...for
£45 Lawfull Money of Virginia...Land on Cherystone Creek Bounded by Lands of
Shadrick TURNER, Thomas HARDIE Jun[r]....Containing 166 acres.

                            his
Wit: Thomas HARDEY, Jn[o]. X NUCKELS, David WEATHERFORD
                           mark
Rec: 28 May 1772   William FINNEY L.S.

DB 2, p.485 - ERNN from JEFFERSON   DEED, 27 May 1772
George JEFFERSON of County of Pittsylvania of one part and Abraham ERNN of
said County of other part...for £50 Current Money of Virginia...Tract of Land
Containing 210 acres which was granted to George JEFFERSON by patent Bearing
date 6 Apr 1769 lying on Aarons Creek a branch of Turkey Cock Creek...Crossing
North fork of Sandy River.
Wit: James SMITH, Arch[d]. SMITH, John THOMPSON
Rec: 28 May 1772   G. JEFFERSON L.S.

DB 2, p.487 - BALLINGER from AUSTIN   DEED, 27 May 1772
Joseph AUSTIN of Pittsylvania County Lawful attorney for John AUSTIN of North
Carolinia of one part and Joseph BALLINGER of said County of Pittsylvania of
other part...for £150 Current money of Virginia...Tract of Land Containing
390 acres more or less on Sandy River...Beginning at Sandy River in Jehu
MORTONS line...to AUSTIN's great branch, down same as it meanders to the Riv-
er and down same as it Meanders...200 acres of said Land being Conveyed to
said Joseph BALLINGER by AUSTIN by a former deed Recorded in Pittsylvania
Court and the Residue of 190 acres was Granted to said Jn[o]. AUSTIN by Patent
dated 16 Feb 1771.
Wit: G. JEFFERSON   Joseph AUSTIN L.S.
Rec: 28 May 1772
Susannah, wife of John AUSTIN, privily Examined as law directs Relinquished
her right of Dower.

DB 2, p.489 - POLLEY from GORMAN   DEED, 28 May 1772
John GORMAN of Parrish of Camden and County of Pittsylvania of one part and
Edward POLLY of Parrish and County aforesaid of other part...for £15 Current
money of Virginia...Tract of Land on branches of Mill Creek it being part of
a greater Tract which was Granted to Christopher GORMAN by patent bearing
date at Williamsburgh 25 Sep 1762 and Conveyed by said Christopher GORMAN to
said John GORMAN by Deed Recorded in County Court of Halifax Containing 100
acres more or less...Beginning at a branch on ADAMS line, up the branch...on

HIX's line and so Concluding the up part of said Tract of 294 for
compliment.

Rec: 28 May 1772   No witnesses   John ✗ GORMAN L.S.
                                                  his
                                                  mark

Hannah, wife of said Jno., privily Exam^d. as law directs Relinquished her ·
right of Dower.

DB 2, p.490 - GARRAT from SMITH   DEED, 25 Sep 1771

Peyton SMITH and Judith SMITH of Pittsylvania County and Parrish of one part
and Robert GARRET of St. Marys Parrish and County of Caroline of other part...
for Sum of £200...Tract of Land Containing 100 acres more of less and lying
on south side Pigg River...Top of a hill from Runing a strait line to Snow
Kreek then down the Kreek to the River, down the River to said Creek.
Wit: Rich^d. HAMMACK, John LONG, Nathan SWANSON   Peyton SMITH L.S.
Rec: 28 May 1772   Judith SMITH L.S.
Judith, wife of said Peyton, privily Examined as Law directs Relinquished
her right of Dower.

DB 2, p.492 - DODSON from DODSON   DEED, 27 May 1772

Thomas DODSON of County of Pittsylvania in Colony of Virginia of one part
and Jesse DODSON Son of said Thomas DODSON of County aforesaid of other part...
in Consideration of Natural love and affection he hath and beareth unto said
Jesse DODSON and is more especialy for better maintainance of said Jesse
DODSON...Tract of Land in his actual Possession, part of Tract Purchased by
Thomas DODSON of Joseph TERRY Senr. in County aforesaid...Beginning at Joseph
TERRYS Lower line where it Crosses Burches Creek...in the mill yard...Down
the Creek as it Meanders...100 acres more or less.
Wit: John CREEL, Lazarus DODSON, Charles CHILTON
Rec: 28 May 1772   Thomas DODSON Senr. L.S.

DB 2, p.494 - HICKS from LUMKINS   DEED, 21 Feb 1772

George LUMKIN and Mary his wife of County of Pittsylvania in Colony of Virginia of one part and James HICKS Junr. of County of Brunswick and Colony
aforesaid...for £500 Current money of Virginia...Land on both sides Marrowbone Creek...mouth of a branch, up said Branch...on David LANIERS corner,
south on LANIERS line...mouth of a branch on west side of said Creek...in
CHANDLERS Line...Containing 512 acres.
Wit: Lemuel LANIER, Josiah SMITH, Dav^d. LANIER   George LUMKIN L.S.
                                                            her
                                                  Mary ╱ LUMKIN L.S.
Rec: 28 May 1772   mark

DB 2, p.496 - HICKS from LUMKIN   DEED, 24 Feb 1772

George LUMKIN and Mary his wife of County of Pittsylvania in Colony of Virginia of one part and Benjaman HICKS of Brunswick County and Colony aforesaid of other part...for £240 Current Money of Virginia...Land on north
side Marrowbone Creek...beginning at mouth of a branch on the Creek, up the
Branch...Containing 312 acres.
Wit: Lemuel LANIER, Josiah SMITH, Dav^d. LANIER   George LUMKIN L.S.
                                                            her
                                                  Mary ╱╲ LUMKIN L.S.
Rec: 28 May 1772   mark

DB 2, p.497 - SMITH & Co. from DEVIN   DEED OF TRUST, 25 Apr 1772
William DEVIN of Pittsylvania County Virginia on one part and James SMITH &
Company on other part...Sum of £03·18·03 3/4 Current money of Virginia which
said William DEVIN is Justly Indebted to them and Desires to pay and for farther Sum of 5s paid by James SMITH & Co....Sell to James SMITH & Co. 6 Milk
Cows and Calves, 4 yearlings, 1 Bay horse, 1 Bay mare, 2 feather Beds and
furniture with every other part of his Personal Estate...SMITH & Co. shall
after 1 Mar. next sell for best price after Ten days Publick notice...pay
themselves above sum with Interest from date of these Presents...pay overplus to said DEVIN.
Wit: Jno. THOMPSON, Arch^d. SMITH
Rec: 29 May 1772   William DEVIN L.S.

DB 2, p.499 - ROSS from WALTON   DED^s., 15 Aug 1767
To James SCOTT and Henry WATKINS two of his majestys Justices for County of
Prince Edward Gent...whereas John WALTON, Robert WALTON and Fanney Wife of
said Robert of one part have agreed to Convey to David ROSS of other part
the fee Simple Estate of and in a Certain parcel of Land in County of Halifax
on South side Stanton River Containing by Estimation 665 acres...said Fanney
lives so Remote that she cannot conveniently Travel to our said County Court
of Pittsylvania...Examined Privately apart from her Husband...freely Relinquished her Right of Dower 4 Apr 1772.
                                                    James SCOTT L.S.
Rec: 28 May 1772   Hen. WATKINS L.S.

DB 2, p.501 - BALLINGER from AUSTIN   DEED, 28th Day 1772
Joseph AUSTIN of County of Pittsylvania of one part and Joseph BALLINGER of
same County of other part...for £50 Current Money of Virginia...Tract of Land
Containing 110 acres more or Less on Sandy River being part of a Larger Tract
on which said AUSTIN now lives...on a branch...in said BALLINGERS plantation...
to AUSTINS great Branch.
No witnesses
Rec: none   Memorandum: 28 May 1772   Joseph AUSTIN L.S.

DB 2, p.502 - HOLLIDAY from BIRD   DEED, 28 May 1772
Joseph BIRD of Pittsylvania County of one part and Robert HOLLIDAY of same
County of other part...for £25 Current money of Virginia...Tract of Land Con-
taining 200 acres more or less on Waters of Pig River.
No witnesses   his
Rec: 28 May 1772   Joseph   BIRD L.S.
                                                     mark
Hannah, wife of said Jo^s. privily Examined as Law directs Relinquished her
right of Dower.

DB 2, p.504 - SMITH & Co. from JEFFERSON   DEED, 13 Jan 1772
George JEFFERSON of Pittsylvania County of one part and James SMITH & Company
of same County of other part...for £130 Current money of Virginia...Tract of
Land Containing 500 acres more or less on Sailors Creek a branch of Turkey
Cock Creek being part of Windsor Forrest...in H. HOBARTS line.
                                        his
Wit: James BREWER, George PEAY, William   PEAY, Arch^d. SMITH
                                        mark
Rec: 28 May 1772   G. JEFFERSON L.S.

DB 2, p.506 - HUNT from HUNTS   DEED, 21 May 1772

James HUNT Senr. and Charles HUNT of County of Charlotte of one part and Nathaniel HUNT of Halifax County of other part...for £28 Current money of Virginia...Tract of Land Containing 400 acres more or less...on both sides middle fork of Straight Stone Creek it being part of 820 acres Granted to said James HUNT and Charles HUNT by patent bearing date 15 Aug 1764...on James HUNTS line...Crossing Straitstone Creek...to David HUNTS corner. Wit: Edm^d. TUNER, Dav^r. HUNT, Gilbert HUNT, Jno. WIMBISH, RWILLIAMS, Thomas DILLARD j^r., Isaac READ, H. MORGAN

                                          James HUNT L.S.

Rec: 28 May 1772   Charles HUNT L.S.

DB 2, p.508 - HUNT from HUNTS   DEED, 21 May 1772

James HUNT and Charles HUNT of County of Charlotte of one part and David HUNT of aforesaid County of other part...for 5s Current Money of Virginia... Tract of Land on Both sides middle fork of StraightStone Creek Containing 604 acres, 404 acres of which was Granted to James HUNT by Pattant bearing date 16 Aug 1756 and the other 200 being part of 820 acres Granted to said James HUNT and Charles HUNT by pattant baring date 15 Aug 1764...Crossing a branch. Wit: Nathniel HUNT, Gilbert HUNT, Edm^d. TUNER, Jno. WIMBISH, RWILLIAMS, Thomas DILLARD Junr., Isaac READ, H. MORGAN

                                          James HUNT L.S.

Rec: 28 May 1772   Charles HUNT L.S.

DB 2, p.511 - SMITH & Co. from TOUNSAND   DEED, 28 May 1772

Thomas TOUNSAND of Pittsylvania County on one part and James SMITH and Company on other part...for £169·18...Tract of Land on both sides Bare Skin... up the Creek as it meanders...Containing 360 acres more or less.
No witnesses

                                   his
                          Thos. TOUNSAND L.S.

Rec: 28 May 1772   mark

DB 2, p.513 - SMITH & Co. from ERNN   DEED OF TRUST, 28 May 1772

Abraham ERNN in Pittsylvania County of one part and James SMITH & Company of other part...for £94 Current Money of Virginia which said Abraham ERNN is Justly indebted to said James SMITH & Co. and Honestly desire to Secure and pay, for further Consideration of Sum of 5s Like money paid by SMITH & Co... Tract of Land which said Abraham ERNN now lives on lying and being on Aarons Creek a branch of Turkey Cock Creek which ERNN Purchased of George JEFFERSON Deed dated 27 May of this Present year, with all his smiths Tools, Household furniture, horses, Cows, Sheep and hoggs and everything of my Personal Estate. SMITH & Co. after 1 May 1775 or ERNN shall Request them, Sell for best price Given Ten Days Publick notice...to pay above sum with Lawfull Interest from date of these presents.
No witnesses
Rec: 29 May 1772   Abraham ERNN L.S.

DB 2, p.515 - BULLOCK from CARROLL   BILL SALE, 26 May 1772

I, John CARROLL of Colony of Virginia and County Pittsylvania for Consideration of Sum of £30 Good and Lawfull money of Virginia paid by Thomas BULLOCK of above said Colony and County...have Sold and Delivered in plain and open market according to Due form of Law...Deliver unto Thomas BULLOCK 17 Head of Cattle marked thus a Swallow fork on Left ear and a Crop a Slit and under

keel in right ear...pay above Sum with Lawfull Interest by 1 Jun 1784...shall
be void if payment made.

Wit: Joseph BAKER, Joseph $\overset{his}{\underset{mark}{\times}}$ CAMERON

Rec: 28 May 1772   John CARROLL L.S.

DB 2, p.516 - MC DANIEL from ROBERTS   DEED, 28 May 1772
James ROBERTS of County of Pittsylvania of one part and James MC DANIEL of
County aforesaid of other part...for £35 Current Money of Virginia...Land on
upper Sandy Creek of Dan River...Containing by Estimation 100 acres, being
part of a greater Tract of 1,040 acres granted unto Redman FALLON by Pattent.
No witnesses
Rec: 29 May 1772   James ROBERTS L.S.
Elizabeth, wife of said James, being privily Examined as law directs Relinquish-
ed her right of Dower.

DB 2, p.518 - BUCKLEY from PEMBERTON   DEED, 28 May 1772
John PEMBERTON of County of Halifax of one part and James BUCKLEY of County
of Pittsylvania of other part...for £95 Current money of Virginia...Tract of
Land on both Sides allins Creek Joining lines of Joseph FARRIS, John HARNESS
&c. Containing by Estimation 200 acres...on Joseph FARRIS's line...at East
fork of allins Creek thence up the Creek as it meanders...head of the branch
thence down the branch as it meanders to ALLENS, up the Creek to old line,
along old line.
No witnesses
Rec: 28 May 1772   John PEMBERTON L.S.
Ann, wife of said Jno., privily Examined as Law directs Relinquished her
right of Dower.

DB 2, p.520 - EAST from HUDSON   DEED, 28 May 1772
Hall HUDSON and Frances his wife of Pittsylvania County of one part and John
EAST of County aforesaid of other part...for £13 Current money of Virginia...
Tract of Land Containing 35 acres more or Less...being part of a Tract said
Hall HUDSON Purchased of Henry BUFORD of amelia County...Beginning at Crispin
SHELTONS Corner...along AMEYS Crossing a Small Branch, on Hickeys Road...on
PERRYS line.
Wit: Jno. PAYNE, Armistead SHELTON, Newsom PACE, Abra^{m}. SHELTON,
Spencer SHELTON

                                                    Hall HUDSON L.S.

                                            Frances $\overset{her}{\underset{mark}{\times}}$ HUDSON L.S.
Rec: 28 May 1772

DB 2, p.522   DEED, 13 Dec 1770
Richard CHAMBERLAYN of New Kent County of one part and Thomas TOWSEN of Pittsylvania of other part...for £110 Current money...tract of Land Containing
360 acres more or less...Bareskin Creek...up said Creek as it meanders.

Wit: John PIGG, Archelaus YANCEY, William $\overset{his}{\underset{mark}{\times}}$ OWEN

Rec: 30 May 1771   R. CHAMBERLAYNE (Seal)

                            END OF DEED BOOK II

PITTSYLVANIA COUNTY, VIRGINIA
DEED BOOK 3, 1772 - 1774

DB 3, p.1 - COOK from TREDWAY   DEED, 18 Feb 1772
William TREDWAY of County of Pittsylvania of one part and Harmon COOK of
parrish and County aforesaid of other part...for £60 Current Money of Virginia...162 acres on both Sides Turkey Cocke Creek which said Tract was Conveyed by George JEFFERSON to said William TREDWAY by Indenture bearing date
28 Mar 1771 and recorded in County Court of Pittsylvania...at Arthur HOPKINS
corner...new line east.
Wit: William HALL, William POTEET, John HOLLOWAY   William TREDWAY L.S.
Rec: 25 Jun 1772

DB 3, p.2 - DENTON from LAYNE   DEED, 15 Apr 1772
Dutton LAIN of Pittsylvania County of one part and Abraham DENTON of said
County of other part...for £25 Current Money of Virginia...106 acres on both
sides Shugar tree Creek...crossing the Creek.
                       his
Wit: John MACK, John ╱ COX, James COX   Dutton LANE L.S.
                      mark
Cert: 28 May 1772, Rec: 25 Jun 1772

DB 3, p.4 - OAKES from LAYNE   DEED, 15 Apr 1772
Dutton LAIN of Pittsylvania County of one part and James OAKES of said County
of other part...for £25 Current Money of Virginia...112 acres both sides
Shugar Tree Creek...crossing the creek...crossing a branch...on a Little
branch thence up the branch to olde line.
                       his
Wit: John MACK, John ╱ COX, James COX   Dutton LANE L.S.
                      mark
Cert: 28 May 1772, Rec: 25 Jun 1772

DB 3, p.5 - COX from LAIN   DEED, 17 Apr 1772
Dutton LAIN of Pittsylvania County of one part and John COX of other part...
for £25 Current Money of Virginia...42 acres on both sides Shugar tree Creek...
on a Branch...in THOMAS's line...Crossing the Creek.
Wit: James BURNETT, John MACK, James COX   Dutton LANE L.S.
Cert: 28 May 1772, Rec: 25 Jun 1772

DB 3, p.6 - MACK from LAYNE   DEED, 17 Apr 1772
Dutton LAIN of Pittsylvania County of one part and John MACK of said county
of other part...for £25 Current money of Virginia...140 acres on Both sides
Shugar tree Creek...Crossing the Creek above the fork...down the old line...
West along the old line to a Little branch, down the branch.
                          his
Wit: Ja^s. BURNETT, Jno.╱ COX, Ja^s. COX   Dutton LAIN L.S.
                         mark
Cert: 28 May 1772, Rec: 25 Jun 1772

DB 3, p.8 - HUGHES from LOVING   BILL SALE - 16 May 1772
Adam LOVING of County of Pittsylvania of the Colony of Virginia for Sum of
£13·18 Current Money of Virginia to me paid by Arch^s. HUGHES...sell to said
Arch^s. HUGHES one Chesnut Sorrel Mare branded on the Near Shoulder thus Ʌ Ļ ,
Two Cows and Calves Mark.d with two Crops two Under Keeles ·and two over D ·,

1 Black Horse Branded with _L_ on the Near Buttock and Two feather Beds and furniture.

Wit: George TAYLOR, Edward YOUNG, John X ALSOP   Adam /-| LOVING L.S.
                                  his   his
                                  mark   mark

Rec: 25 Jun 1772

DB 3, p.9 - LAW from FULKERSON   DEED, 25 Jun 1772

Frederick FULKERSON of Parrish of Camden in County of Pittsylvania Planter of one part and Thomas LAW of Parrish and County aforesaid Planter of other part... for £90 Current Money of Virginia...134 acres on Mayo River being part of 370 acres Granted to said Frederick FULKERSON by Indenture baring date 18 Nov 1762 as by Records of County Court of Halifax...on Mayo River Runing down as it Meanders, near the mouth of Green Creek...Crossing the Creek.

No witnesses   Frederick FULKERSON L.S.

Rec: 25 Jun 1772

DB 3, p.11 - ROWLAND & LAMB from TATE   BILL SALE, 25 Jun 1772

Henry TATE of Pittsylvania County for £80 Goods and Lawfull Money of Virginia paid by John ROWLAND of said County and Rich^d. LAMB of Dinwidia County...the said Henry TATE in order to Secure to said ROWLAND & Richard LAMB the above Sum...Sell to them Two feather Beds and furniture, ten Head of Cattle Marked in both Ears with a hollow Crop and under Keel, Twenty head of young and old hogs marked as above, Two Horses a bright bay Branded on the near Sholder and joy _F_ a Dark Bay Branded on the Near Shoulder _T_ and all the Rest of my household furniture not above mentioned, Crop of Corn & Tob°. now in hand and Growing...agree to allow said Henry TATE untill 1 Mar 1773 to Discharge above Sum of Money, then may sell for most that Can be got and if any overplus to Return to said Henry TATE.

Wit: George ELLIOT, John FLEMING, Michael ROWLAND

Rec: 25 Jun 1772   Henry TATE L.S.

DB 3, p.12 - KIRBY from KIRBY   DEED, 25 Jun 1772

David KIRBY of County of Pittsylvania of one part and Henry KIRBY of said County of other Part...for £57·10 Current Money of Virginia...160 acres being the same more or Less, on North side Pigg River.   his

No Witnesses   David X KIRBY L.S.

Rec: 25 Jun 1772 & Elizabeth, wife of David   mark

KIRBY privily Examined and Relinquished her right of Dower

DB 3, p.13 - WIMBISH from MEDKIFF   DEED, 26 Jun 1772

James MEDKIFF of County of Halifax of one part and John WIMBISH of Pittsyl- vania County of other part...for £125 Current money of Virginia...on both Sides Elkhorn Creek Containing by Estimation 321 acres it being part of Two Tracts of Land Granted to Joseph MEDKIFF by Patents and by said Joseph MEDKIFF conveyed to said James MEDKIFF by a Deed Recorded in Pittsylvania Court...at John MEDKIFF's corner Pointers in the Patent line, along patent line to Joseph MEDKIFF junior...crossing Elkhorn Creek...along John MEDKIFF's line crossing Elkhorn Creek.   his

No witnesses   James -/ MIDKIFF L.S.

Rec: 26 Jun 1772   mark

DB 3, p.15 - WILLIAMS from ASTIN   DEED, 21 Dec 1771

William ASTIN of County of Pittsylvania of one part and Robert WILLIAMS of same County of other part...£120 Current money of Virginia...177 acres, all

the Lands he is now in possession or claims on Sandy Creek, on both sides...
part was Granted to David HAILEY by patent under Seal of our Colony Contain-
ing 137 acres Bearing date 22 Aug 1745 also forty acres granted to Frederick
FULKERSON by Patent Bearing date 7 Jul 1763...since has been Conveyed to said
William ASTIN by Deeds from said David HAILY and Frederick FULKERSON Record-
ed in County Court Halifax with following Bounds, Kennons order and Theophel-
ous LACEYS Entery.
Wit: Theop^s. LACY, HCHALLES, Richard GWYN,   Will. /\ ASTIN L.S.
Hugh HENRY, Thos. TERRY   mark his
Cert: 27 Mar 1772, Rec: 25 Jun 1772

DB 3, p.16 - SMITH & CO. from SHOCKLIE   DEED TRUST, 14 May 1772
Levi SHOCKLIE of Pittsylvania County on one part & James SMITH & Company on
other part...for £43·04·06 Current money of Virginia which said Levi SHOCKLIE
is Justly Indebted to them and honestly desires to pay...further Consideration
of 5s Like money...200 acres, said Land made over to me by my Father James
SHOCKLIE by Deed Recorded in Pittsylvania Court also all my horses, Cows,
Stock of hoggs and all Remainder of my household furniture or Personal Estate.
After 1 May 1773 or as Soon after as said James SMITH & Co. think proper or
said Levi SHOCKLIE shall Request...sell for best price after Ten Days Publick
notice...pay themselves above Sum.
Wit: Arch^d. SMITH, William ROBERTS, Charles OAKES   Levi SHOCKLIE L.S.
Cert: 29 May 1772, Rec: 25 Jun in year aforesaid

DB 3, p.18 - OAR & TRIMBLE from NEELIE   MORTGAGE, 21 Dec 1771
Robert NEELIE of Pittsylvania County Virginia on one part and Robert OAR and
George TRIMBLE on other part...Robert NEELIE stands Justly Indebted to said
Robert OAR and George TRIMBLE in Sum of £110 Current money of Virginia...
also for Sum of 5s paid by said Robt. OAR & George TRIMBLE...Tract of Land
said Robert NEELIE now lives upon with every other part of his Personal Estate.
Provided Robert NEELIE make a Good & Sufficent Right in fee Simple of 3
Entries of Land Lying and being in County of Pittsylvania on south fork of
Tomahawk Creek to Include all Vacant Lands Beginning on George JEFFERSON's...
John LAVORYS line to Col^o. CHEZZELS line, along Col^o. CHIZZELS line to John
BALLS line, along BALLS line to ELLIOTS line, to said ELLIOTS line to George
JEFFERSON line...800 acres...all Costs due on this mortgage within Space of
one month after Date hereof...be utterly Void.
Wit: Arch^d. SMITH, Patrick MC KAIN, John THOMPSON
Cert: 28 May 1772, Rec: 26 Jun 1772   Robert NEELIE L.S.

DB 3, p.20 - ADAMS from OWEN   DED^s., 30 Apr in XII Year of our Reign
George the third by the grace of god of great Brittain France and Ireland
King Defender of the Faith &c. To John WILSON and John OWEN or any two of
his majestys Justices of County of Pittsylvania...Thomas OWEN by Certain
Indenture of Feofment hath Conveyed to Sylvester ADAMS of County of Fairfax
Two Certain Tracts of land Containing 343 acres on Dan River and whereas
Jane OWEN the wife of said Thomas OWEN cant Conveniently Travel to and from
our County Court of Pittsylvania...we Trusting to your Faithfull and Provident
Care and circumspection in Examining the wife of Thomas OWEN from and apart
from her Husband whether She does freely and Volinteryly Relinquish her Right
of Dower to the Land.
By Virtue of above Dedimus to us Directed we have Examined Jane OWEN the wife
of Thomas OWEN...relinquished her right of Dower to said Land 31 Mar 1772.
                                                   John WILSON L.S.
Rec: 25 Jun 1772   John OWEN L.S.

DB 3, p.21 - WARE from GREEN   DED^s., 23 Jul in Eleventh year of our Reign

George the third by the grace of god of great Brittain France and Ireland
King Defender of the Faith &c To David GREENHILL and Benjamin WARD or any two
his majestys Justices of the County of Amelia Greeting whereas Henry GREEN
by his Indenture of Feofment hath Conveyed unto John WARE of County of Goochland Tract of Land in County of Pittsylvania Containing 350 acres and Whereas
Lucy GREEN the wife of said Henry GREEN cannot Conveniantly Travel to and from
our County Court...apart from her Husband examine if she does freely relinquish
her right of Dower.   Amelia   Sc^b.
By virtue of above Dedimus we have Examined lucy GREEN the wife of Henry GREEN
apart from her Husband...touching her Relinquishment of her Dower to 350 acres
of land conveyed to John WARE 23 Jan 1772.

                                            David GREENHILL L.S.
Rec: 25 Jun 1772   Benj^a. WARD L.S.

DB 3, p.22 - GOODE from COOLEY   DEED, 25 Jun 1772

James COOLEY of Parrish of Cambden in County of Pittsylvania of one Part and
John GOODE of parrish and County aforesaid Planter of other part...for £30
Current money of Virginia...Land on Keeton Creek...100 acres.
Wit: Gideon RUCKER, John HENSLE, William FROGG   his
Rec: 25 Jun 1772 and Ann wife of   James ⟨mark⟩ COOLEY L.S.
said James privily Exam^d. Relinq^d. right of Dower   mark

DB 3, p.24 - BASNETT from LANSFORD and COCKRAM   DEED, 13 Apr 1772

Henry LANSFORD and Nathan COCKRAM of Colony of Virginia and County of Pitt-
sylvania of one part and Isaac BASNETT of same place of other part...for £50
Current money of Virginia...77 acres on North side Smiths River...North side
of the River...on the Country line to said River as it meanders.
Wit: William EDWARDS, John HARRIS, Thomas BULLOCK   his
                                            Henry | LANSFORD L.S.
                                                  mark
Rec: 25 Jun 1772   Nathan COCKRAM L.S.

DB 3, p.27 - FARRIS from INNES   DEED, 10 Jun MDCCLXXII

Hugh INNES of County of Pittsylvania of one Part and James FARISH Junr. of
County of Halifax of other Part...for £30 Current money...Land in Counties of
Pittsylvania and Halifax on branches of North side Banister and head of
Brush Creek...line of Thomas SMITH's thence new lines...crossing a branch of
Brush Creek...Crossing two Branches..Containing by Patent 330 acres.
No witnesses   Hugh INNES L.S.
Rec: 23 Jul 1772

DB 3, p.28 - JETT & others from SHORT   DEED TRUST, 23 Jul 1772

John SHORT of County of Pittsylvania on one Part and Thomas JETT and William
ROBERSON of King George County also Stephen HERD junior and Mary SHORT of
Pittsylvania County being all of the other part...John SHORT being Indebted
to them in sum of £120 Current money and being desirous to Secure Payment of
it...further sum of 5s paid to said John SHORT...the following Slaves:
Abraham, Jack, Sarah, four feather Beds and furniture, four dozen pewter
plates, six Pewter Dishes, four Iron Potts, one Womans Sadle, two mens
Saddles, dark bay Stallion known by Names of the Dutch man, one other bald
eagle colour.d Gilding branded *O* on the near Shoulder, black Horse branded
I S on near Buttock, 14 head Cattle marked with a Swallow fork in right ear

and a Crop and two Slits in left, also 40 Hogs in same mark, also 15 Sheep
of same mark, two walnut Tables...if John SHORT shall not within Twelve
months after date pay said Sum of £170...sell slaves, Household Goods, and
Stock for best Price that can be got, giving 30 days notice to SHORT.
Wit: Edmund WINSTON   John SHORT L.S.
Rec: 24 Jul 1772

DB 3, p.30 - WIMBISH from SPRAGIN   DEED, 10 Nov 1770
Thomas SPRAGIN of Saluda in Province of South Carolina of one Part and John
WIMBISH of Pittsylvania County of other part...£5 Current money of Virginia...
all those two pieces of Land adjacent to the Lotts of Town of Peytonsburg at
the Lower end of said Town one piece Containing 3 1/2 acres and other 3 1/10
acres it being same Lands conveyed to William WRIGHT by James ROBERTS and by
said William WRIGHT conveyed to said Thomas SPRAGIN by Indenture recorded in
Halifax Court
Wit: John WHITE, John MARTIN, John POWELL
Cert: 28 May 1772, Rec: 23 Jul 1772   Thomas SPRAGINS L.S.

DB 3, p.32 - COX from HAYLE   DEED, 29 May 1772
Joseph HAYLE and Rachel his Wife of Parish of Cambden in County of Pittsylvania of one part and John COX of Parish and County aforesaid of other part...
for £50 Current money of Virginia...100 acres both sides Mill Creek...Land
was Conveyed from John SLONE and Elenar his wife to said Jo^s. HAYLE by Indenture recorded in County court of Halifax...adjoins lands whereon said John
COX now lives, and Edward POLLEY.
Wit: Arch^d. SMITH, Ja^s. SMITH, John THOMPSON
Rec: 24 Jul 1772   Joseph HALE L.S.

DB 3, p.34 - BUCKNALLS from BUCKNALL   BILL SALE, 7 Jul 1772
I Francis BUCKNALL of Pittsylvania County in Colony of Virginia...for love
and Goodwill that I ?a_ my Grand Children Ruth BUCKNALL and William BUCKNALL
a Daughter and Son to Thomas BUCKNALL...give my Grand Daughter Ruth BUCKNALL
one black and white pid Cow with her in Crease and likewise to my Grand Son
William BUCKNALL one Red and white Cow with her increase...have Put said
Ruth and William BUCKNALL in full Possession by delivery 7 Jul 1772.
            his   her
Wit: James   TAILER, Mary   FOARD
           mark   mark
Rec: 23 Jul 1772   Francis BUCKNALL L.S.

DB 3, p.35 - THRIFT from FARRIS   DEED, 9 Dec 1771
John FARRIS of County of Halifax of one Part and John THRIFT of County of
Pittsylvania of other part...for £75 Current money of Virginia...Land on
Panther Creek Adjoining the Lands of John PAYNE Senior...Crossing the Creek
thence taking the Ridge to the upper line...200 acres, thence the old line
Round the beginning taking the Plantation whereon he is now Settled.
Wit: George MURDOCK, Abra^m. SHELTON, W^m. SHORT
      Cert: 28 May 1772, Rec: 23 Jul 1772   John FARRIS L.S.

DB 3, p.36 - THOMPSON from COX   DEED, 25 Jun 1772
John COX of Parish of Cambden and County of Pittsylvania of one Part and John
THOMPSON of Parrish and County aforesaid of other Part...for £18 Current
money of Virginia 100 acres on South fork of Strawberry Creek...in SULLIVENTS
line thence new lines...Crossing said Creek...Crossing a Branch...from the

118.

Day hereof for and During the Term and time of one whole year from thence
next ensuing fully to be complete and ended yielding and Paying therefore the
Rent of one pepper Corn on Lady Day next if Demanded.
No witnesses
Rec: 23 Jul 1772

John COX L.S.

DB 3, p.37 - SHELTON from HOLLAND   DEED OF TRUST, 3 Mar 1772
George HOLLAND of County of Pittsylvania of one part and Lewis SHELTON of
said County of Pittsylvania of other part...for £9 Current money of Virginia...
Lewis SHELTON's Security for Payment to Gabriel SHELTON...said George HOLLAND
Honestly desires to pay...further Sum of 5s like Current Money paid by Lewis
SHELTON...Sell to Lewis SHELTON one negro Boy Slave named Sam...pay before 25
Dec next Ensuing with Lawfull Interest.
Wit: Dan¹. SHELTON, Spencer SHELTON, Abraham SHELTON   his
Rec: 23 Jul 1772   George 〇 HOLLAND L.S.
                                                                mark

DB 3, p.39 - MORTON from HODGES   DEDˢ., 6 Apr 12th year of our Reign
George the third by the grace of god of great Brittain France and Ireland
King Defender of the faith &c To Gidion WRIGHT, Malcom CURRY and William HALL
or any two his majistys Justices of County of Surry...whereas Welcom William
HODGES by Indenture of feoffment hath Conveyed to Jehu MORTON of County of
Pittsylvania two Tracts of land in County of Pittsylvania Containing 332 acres
and whereas Mary HODGES the wife of Welcom William HODGES cannot Conveniantly
Travel to and from our County Court...examine Mary HODGES apart from her Hus-
band whether she freely Relinquishes her right of Dower.
North Carolina, Surry County, Scᵇ...We have Examined Mary HODGES wife of Wel-
com Wᵐ. HODGES...freely Relinquishes her right of Dower 4 Jul 1772.
                                                   Gidion WRIGHT L.S.
Rec: 23 Jul 1772   Malcom CURRY   L.S.

DB 3, p.40 - JONES from COPLAND   DEED, 21 Jul 1772
Peter COPLAND of County of Pittsylvania on one part and Ambrose JONES of
same County on other part...for £40 Current money of Virginia...120 acres on
Beaver Creek...down the Creek as it meanders.
Wit: Richard COPLAND, Charles COPLAND, Sally COPLAND
Rec: 23 Jul 1772   Peter COPLAND L.S.

DB 3, p.41 - SYMS from LOGAN   DEED, 6 Jul 1771
David LOGAN of Charlotte County of one part and James SYMS of the County of
other part...for £40 Current money of Virginia...275 acres on North side of
middle fork of mayo River...Crossing a branch....Crossing a Branch...up the
River as it meanders.
Wit: John COX, Philip BREWER, Josiah MANN, Isaac READ, RWILLIAMS, Haynes MORGAN
Rec: 23 Jul 1772   David LOGANS L.S.

DB 3, p.43 - SHELTON from INNES   DEED, 25 Jun 1772
Hugh INNES and Hannah his wife of Pittsylvania County of one part and Benjamin
SHELTON of amelia County of other part...for £20 Current money of Virginia...
317 acres, it being part of a patent of Land granted to said Hugh INNES Bearing date 3 Aug 1771...north fork of Panther Creek...in CHANDLERS line...Cross-
ing the Creek...Crossing a branch...in JOHNSONS line...new lines...Crossing
a fork and Buck branch to pointers in CHANDLERS line.
No witnesses   Hugh INNES   L.S.
Rec: 23 Jul 1772   Hannah INNES L.S.

DB 3, p.45 - SHORT from CADLE   DEED, 22 Aug 1772
Benjamin CADLE of County of Pittsylvania of one part and William SHORT of
same County of other part...Benjamin CADLE and Sephfire his wife for £40
Current money of Virginia...100 acres...on John ABSTONE line...Crossing
Straitstone Creek...on a hill at the head of the Faull Branch.
No witnesses
Rec: 27 Aug 1772 and Sefiah wife of Benjamin   Benjamin CADLE L.S.
privily Examined Relinquished her right of Dower   Sephfire CADLE L.S.

DB 3, p.46 - DEATHERAGE from GOING   DEED, 30 Dec 1771
David GOING of County of Pittsylv^a. and Colony of Virginia and George
DEATHRAGE of County of Surry and province of North Carrolina...for £50 Current
money of Virginia...270 acres on both sides Russels Creek a branch of Mayo...
John HUNTERS line...Crossing the Creek...crossing two Branches.
                          his   his
Wit: John DEATHERADGE, David /| MOSLEY, Thomas / ROGERS
                          mark   mark
Rec: 29 May 1773   David GOING L.S.

DB 3, p.48 - LYNES from TATE   DEED TRUST, 1 Jun 1772
I Henry TATE of Pittsylvania County am indebted to Henry and Edmund LYNE of
said County full sum of £37·06·06 Current money of Virginia and being Truly
desirous to do them Justice, secure to them payment...with Legal Interest
from 18 Mar...sell Two Feather Beds and furniture, six head Cattle marked with
hollow Crop and under keel in both Ears, 12 hogs of same mark, 2 Horses and
my other Estate being of what kind soever, Together with my Crop Corn now
Growing...Henry and Edm^d. LYNE after 1 Apr 1773 after Giving ten Days notice
dispose for best price that can be got...to dischage sum.
Wit: Brice MARTIN   Henry TATE L.S.
Rec: 27 Aug 1772

DB 3, p.49 - LYNE'S from ACUFF   DEED TRUST, 1 Apr 1772
I John ACUFF of Pittsylvania County are Justly Indebted to Henry & Edmund LYNE
merchants of said County the Sum of £35·18·10 Current money of Virginia and
being Truly desirous to Secure to them the Payment with legal Interest...sell
my stock of Cattle being in Number nine, four head Sheep, my stock Hogs, One
Spotted Horse, all my household furniture of whatsoever kind and plantation
Tools of all Sorts with the Increase of the Stock...after ten Days Notice may
dispose for best Price...pay to John ACUFF overpluse money.
Wit: Brice MARTIN
Rec: 27 Aug 1772   John ACUFF L.S.

DB 3, p.51 - SHELTON from WADE   DEED TRUST, 24 Apr 1772
James WADE of County of Pittsylvania and Parrish of Cambden of one part and
Abraham SHELTON of other part...for £10 Current money of Virginia said James
WADE Justly Indebted to said Abraham SHELTON and further Abraham SHELTON is
Security for James WADE to James CALLAWAY of Bedford County for sum of £5
money and Cost of a Suit...James WADE honestly Desires to Secure and pay...
further sum of 5s Like Current money paid by said Abraham SHELTON...174 acres
on Both sides Frying pan Creek it being part of Tract of Land Granted to
Timothy DOLTON by Patent bearing Date 4 Jul 1759...crossing frying Pan Creek...
Crossing buck branch...after 1 Sep next on giving Ten Days Lawfull notice sell
at auction for most that can be got for same.
Wit: John PAYNE, Thomas PAYNE, Spencer SHELTON
Rec: 27 Aug 1772   James WADE L.S.

DB 3, p.53 - JUSTICE from JUSTICE   BILL OF SALE, 12 Jun 1771
I Ezra JUSTICE of Pittsylvania County for sum of £62·10 Current money of
Virginia paid by Mary JUSTICE of said County...sell to Mary JUSTICE one negro
Woman Named Cato.
Wit: Thos. JUSTICE, W^m. JUSTICE, Simeon JUSTICE, William SHELTON, William PROSISE
Rec: 27 Aug 1772   Ezra JUSTICE L.S.

DB 3, p.53 - CHANEY from WALLER   DEED, 22 Aug 1772
John WALLER of Pittsylvania County of one part and Jacob CHAINEY Senr. of the
other part...for £30 Current money of Virginia...350 acres on Burchess Creek...
North side said Creek...Crossing two branch...in TERRYS line...Crossing the
Creek, down the Creek.
Wit: Thomas RICHARDS, James CHANEY, Isaiah CHANEY   his

                                         John ✝ WALLER L.S.
Rec: 27 Aug 1772   mark

DB 3, p.55 - WORSHAM from DIXON   DEED, 19 Mar 1771
Henry DIXON of County of Orange North Carolina of one part and John WOSHAM of
County of Pittsylvania Virginia of other part...for £45 Current money of Vir-
ginia...north side Dan River...Edmund FLOYDS corner...Joshua WORSHAM's line...
down the River as it meanders...60 acres...Excepting about three or four
acres at the Lower end Bounded by a Dry Branch.
Wit: Robt. PAYNE, Larkin DIX, Redmond FALLON
Rec: 27 Aug 1772   Henry DIXON junior L.S.

DB 3, p.57 - SMALL from ROWLAND   DEED, 28 Aug 1772
John ROWLAND of County of Pittsylv^a. of one part and Matthew SMALL of County
aforesaid of other Part...for £30 Current money of Virginia...153 acres on
Irvin River...on south side...on Sycamore Creek along same to Irvin River,
down same as it meanders to PUSEYS line.
No witnesses
Rec: 28 Aug 1772   John ROWLAND L.S.

DB 3, p.59 - DUNCAN from NEALLEY   DEED, 28 Aug 1772
William NEALLEY of County of Pittsylvania in Colony of Virginia of one part
and Benjamin DUNCAN late of said place of other part...for £100 Current money
of Virginia...Tract of Land it being part of Land where said William NEALLEY
now lives...on Pye Creek or Tomachawk Creek so Called and Bounded a Crop from
said Creek and from Robert NEALLEY's Dividing line...NEALLEY's Out side line
which it is the Lower part of his Tract...which from that said Crop line
Downwards which is part of the 200 acres Pattent in a greater Tract to Col^o.
John CHISWELL and Conveyed by Deeds as by Record...to hold the said Lower
part by Compotation 100 acres.
Rec: 28 Aug 1772   No witnesses   William NEALLEY L.S.

DB 3, p.61 - SPRAGINS from DEJARNETT   DEED, 22 Aug 1772
James DEJARNET of County of Halifax of one part and William SPRAGINS of Pitt-
sylvania County of other part...for £51 Current money of Virginia...Land lying
on East fork of Allins Creek joining lines of Joshua STONE, James GEORGE and
John BUTLER Containing 137 acres....near a Spring.
Wit: Thos. DILLARD j^r., Benj^a. LANKFORD, Benj^a. JOHNSON
                                       James DEJARNETT L.S.
Rec: 28 Aug 1772 and also the Dedimus thereto   Edna DEJARNETT L.S.
Annexed was Ordered to be Recorded

DB 3, p.63 - SPRAGINS from DEJARNET   DED[s]. 7 Aug XII year of our Reign
George the third by the grace of god of great Brittain France and Ireland
King Defender of the Faith &c to Thomas DILLARD j[r]. and Benjamin LANKFORD or
any two his majestys Justices of County of Pittsylvania...James DEJARNETT by
his Indenture of feofment Conveyed to William SPRAGINS of County of Pittsylvania Tract of Land...130 acres...Edda the wife of said DEJARNETT cannot conveniently Travel to our County Court...whether she does freely and Volentarily Relinquish her right of Dower..when you have it done that you Certifie to
our Justices of Court of Pittsylvania.   Will TUNSTALL
By virtue of above Dedimus we have Examined Edda the wife of James DEJARNETT
apart from her Husband...did freely relinquish her right of Dower 22 Aug 1772.
                                          Tho[s]. DILLARD j[r]. L.S.
Rec: 27 Aug 1772   Benj[a]. LANKFORD L.S.

DB 3, p.64 - STOCKDONE from ALLEY   DEED, 27 Aug 1772
Nicholas ALLEY of Pittsylvania County of one part and Robert STOCKTON of
same County of other Part...£130 to him in hand...325 acres on Both sides of
Nicholas's Creek a Branch of Irvin River...Crossing the Creek...Crossing a
branch...Crossing a Great branch and a small branch...Crossing two branches.
Rec: 27 Aug 1772 and Ann wife of said Nicholas   No witnesses
privily Examined Relinquished her right of Dower   Nicholas ALLEE L.S.

DB 3, p.66 - HUCHENSON from PATTERSON   DEED, 27 Aug 1772
Samuel PATTERSON of County of Pittsylvania of one part and Sarah HUTCHERSON
of same county of other part...for £90 Current money of Virginia...320 acres
on a fork of Snow Creek...Crossing the said fork.
No witnesses
Rec: 27 Aug 1772   Samuel PATTERSON L.S.

DB 3, p.68 - CALLAWAY from JUSTICE'S   DEED TRUST, 27 Aug 1772
Ezra JUSTICE and Mary JUSTICE of Pittsylvania County of one part and James
CALLAWAY of Bedford County of other part...for £17·17·10 which they are indebted to James CALLAWAY and honestly desire to pay him and in farther consideration of sum of 5s Like money...300 acres on both sides Harping Creek
being the Land whereon said Ezra JUSTICE and Mary JUSTICE now lives also a
bright bay Horse with a Star and Snip in his Face Branded with 𝑈 on near
Shoulder about four years old Last Spring...after 25 Dec 1772 Sell for best
price giving ten Days Publick Notice...money arising from such Sale discharge
sum with Lawfull Interest from 29 Aug 1772 until fully discharged..CALLAWAY
to pay any overplus.
No witnesses   Ezra JUSTICE L.S.
                                                     her
                                           Mary X JUSTICE L.S.
Rec: 27 Aug 1772   mark

DB 3, p.70 - HEWSTON from HEWSTON   DEED OF GIFT, 27 Aug 1772
I Peter HEWSTON of Pittsylv[a]. County send Greeting &c...for Divers good
causes...more Especialy for Love and duty I am bound unto my children James
HEWSTON & Sarah HEWSTON of said County...absolutly give grant make over...be
equally Devided between them...Two Cows and Calves, four two year old heifers
five year old hifers, two Sows and Eighteen Shoats, one Roan horse, one Bay
mare, one bed and furniture, two Iron pots, one frying pan, a parcel of
Earthen ware, one Large plow, one fluek plow, three Broad hoes, one pole ax,
one washing Tub, Two Water pales, one half bushel, one Iron Tea Kittle, one
Riffle Gun, Two mans Saddle and Bridle, two pair horse Collers hams and
Traces, one Cotton wheel and Cards, one hand Mill, one Sorrell mare and a

Sorrell Colt, one pair of Iron Wages, one Grubbing hoe, two Smooth bore Guns,
half a dozen ˉpewther plats, three Basons, two Dishes, one box Iron, one
Large Trunk and all my Crop of Corn fodder and my Crop of pottaos....have put
the said James & Sarah in full Possession of all aforesaid Premises by Delivery of one bason in the Name of all the said Goods and Chattles.
Wit: Thomas DUNCAN, John LIN
Rec: 28 Aug 1772

                                     his
                          Peter HEWSTON L.S.
                                 mark

DB 3, p.71 - LOVEN from HILL   **DEED, 3 Feb 1772**
William HILL of Pitsilvany County of one part and James LOVEN of same County
of other part...for £20 Good and Lawful money...Tract of Land Containing one
100 acres...on south side Pigg River...on Robert BOULTON line on Pigg River...
to John ELLISES corner...a Small branch and on the branch to pigg River, up
the River.
Wit: Robᵗ. BOULTON, Joseph ✝ KIRBY, James ✗ BOULTON
                          mark

Cert: 28 May 1772, Rec: 27 Aug 1772   William HILL L.S.

DB 3, p.72 - COPLAND from MORRIS   **DEED, 4 Feb 1771**
Thomas MORRIS of County of Botetort on one part and Peter COPLAND of County
of Pittsylvania on other part...for £93 Current money of Virginia...Land on
Beaver Creek...120 acres...nigh a branch...up the Creek as it meanders...
being the Tract of Land conveyed by said Peter COPLAND to said Thomas MORRIS
by a Deed bearing date 13 Apr 1765.

                       his   his
Wit: Richard COPLAND, Samˡ. ✗ MERREDITH, John ʀ MC GILL, Joseph AKIN,
       his   mark   mark
Jnᵒ. ✝ BLEVINS jʳ.
  mark
Cert: 27 Jun 177?, Rec: 27 Aug 1772   Thomas MORRIS L.S.

DB 3, p.74 - FIELD & CALL from STEPHENS'S   **DEED TRUST, 15 Aug 1772**
David STEPHENS and William STEPHENS of County of Pittsylvania of one part and
FIELD & CALL Merchants in Prince George County of other part...for £75·06·01
Current money of Virginia which David and William STEPHENS is Justly Indebted
to FIELD & CALL and honestly desire to secure and pay...farther Consideration
of sum of 5s like money...Two Tracts of Land on Kaskade Creek Containing 200
acres it being that Tract whereon said David STEPHENS now lives, the other
Tract lying on home Creek Containing 175 acres it being that Tract whereon
said William STEPHENS now lives, Nineteen head of Cattle, Twelve Head Marked
with a Crop and Slit in right Ear and Crop and a hole in Left, Seven head
marked with a Crop and hole in Right Ear and Crop and Slit in left, six head
of Horses, three horses and three mares, Seven head Sheep marked Crop and hole
in Right ear and Crop and Slit in left...forever defend to said Theophilus
FIELD & William CALL...shall after 25 Dec 1772 sell for best price after Ten
Days publick Notice...Lawful Interest from 15 Aug 1772 untill fully discharged.
Wit: Drury BIRCHETTE, John OWEN, Thoˢ. OWEN,   his
John WILSON   David ✗ STEPHENS L.S.
                                  mark
                                  his
                          William ✗ STEPHENS L.S.
Rec: 27 Aug 1772   mark

DB 3, p.77 - FIELD & CALL from BEEN   DEED OF TRUST, 27 Jun 1772
William BEEN on Holston River of one part and FIELD & CALL Merchants in
Prince George County of other part...for £48·12·06 Current money of Virginia
which William BEEN is Justly indebted to FEILD & CALL and honestly desire to
pay them...farther Consideration of sum of 5s Like money...five Negroes Bob,
Senior, Grace, lucy and James and their Increase, one Roan mare Branded
on near Buttock about Six years old...after 30 Oct 1772 sell for best price
Giving Ten Days Publick Notice and pay said sum with Lawful Interest from
27 Jun 1772 until fully Discharged.
Wit: Drury BIRCHETT, Littleberry BOSTICK, John WILSON
Rec: 27 Aug 1772   William BEEN L.S.

DB 3, p.79 - TUNSTALL from ROBERTS   DEED TRUST, 4 Jul 1772
James ROBERTS Pittsylvania County of one part and William TUNSTALL on his
part...Sum of £690 12/2 and all Costs Current Money of Virginia which James
ROBERTS is Justly Indebted unto William TUNSTALL and honestly desires to pay
him...further Consideration of Sum of 5s like money paid by William TUNSTALL...
Negroes Pritchet, Docter, Dinah, Jinny, Isbell, Rachell, Annia, Hany, Ben
and Beckey, 6 Tables, 5 Trunks, 1 Desk, 1 Chest of Drawers, 4 Waggons old &c,
12 Tubs and pails, 13 Iron potts, 32 horses mares and Guildings mostly Branded thus£ £ R 47   Cattle with Sundrey markes mostly marked with upper half
Crops, 3 Copper Stills with Sundrey Casks Barrells &c, 137 hoggs marked most
part 2 half Crops upper side Ear, 14 Goats unmarked, 8 feather Beds and furniture, 2 Casses and Bottles, 9 Chests and Boxes, Two Silver Watches, 8 Pewter Dishes, 7 D°. Basons, 5 1/2 dozen D°. plates, 3 Setts Tea Wear, 4 Sugar
Boxes, 5 Mens Saddles and 2 Womans D°., 4 1/2 dozen Earthen Bowles Together
with all the househould furniture I do now Possess and Injoy with part of
hh°. Rum, one Barrell D°., 1 D°. Vinigar, one Quarter Cask of Wine, 1 hh°.
Bowles and hh°. Rum now at Warwick, some Spiritts and 303 acres Land I now
live on and Courthouse of Pittsylvania Stands...William TUNSTALL after 1 Sep
1772 sell for best price after Ten days publick Notice...Discharge above sum
with Lawful Interest...pay overplus if any to James ROBERTS.
                              his
Wit: Francis COX, John   J OLDHAM, Jo^s. COOK
                             mark
Rec: 27 Nov 1772   James ROBERTS L.S.

DB 3, p.82 - LYNE'S & ROWLAND from LUMKIN   DEED OF TRUST, 18 Sep 1772
I George LUMKIN of Pittsylvania County am justly indebted to Henry & Edm^d.
LYNE in sum of £34.08.08 with Interest from 9 Jul Last past & to John ROWLAND
Sum of £69·17 with Interest from this date and being Truly desirous to secure
Payment to them...Tract of Land lying upon Marrabone about 1100 acres being
the residue of the Tract I purchased of Col°. Edmund TAYLOR and being the
place I now live Together with a Grist mill...after 1 Oct 1773 after Giving
Ten Days Notice...Dispose for best Price...pay overplus if any.
Wit: John SALMON, John BLEVIN, Mordicai HORD
Rec: 24 Sep 1772   George LUMKIN L.S.

DB 3, p.83 - CLEVER from FARRIS   DEED, 16 Sep 1771
Elisha FARRIS of County of Pittsylvania of one part and John CLEVER of the
County aforesaid of other part...for £300 Current money of Virginia...365
acres on Flyblow Creek which was granted to Elisha FARRIS by Letters patent
dated 16 Feb last past...at Echolls's line...in Andersons line..
Wit: William SHORT, Geo. MURDOCK, Joseph ROBARDS
Rec: 24 Sep 1772   Elisha FARRIS L.S.

DB 3, p.85 - BALLINGER from HARGET   DEED, 25 Sep 1772

Thomas HARGET and Elizabeth his wife of Pittsylvania County of one part and
Joseph BALLENGER of same County of other part...for £5 Current Money of Vir-
ginia...45 acres...stump in BALLENGER's cornfield.
No witnesses
Rec: 25 Sep 1772   Thomas HARGET L.S.

DB 3, p.86 - WILSON from LUMKIN   DEED TRUST, 20 Jul 1772

George LUMKIN of Pittsylvania County of one part and John WILSON of County
afores^d. of other part...for £493·04·09 which said George LUMKIN justly Indebted to said John WILSON and honestly desire to Secure and pay to WILSON
and in farther Consideration of Sum of 5s Like money...Eight Negroes: Jack,
James, Joe, Luke, Nays, Jinney, Dinah and her Child Sauny and there Increase,
one Sorrel Gilding Branded on each Quarter, also Twenty two head of
Cattle with Crop and Slit in Right ear and under Keel in Left ear, four feather Beds and furniture, one Desk, one dozen Leather Cheers, Twenty five Head
of hogs marked as above Cattle and all rest of household furniture and Work-
ing Tools...after 25 Dec 1773 sell for best price after Giving Ten Days publick...Money arising from Sale Discharge above Sum...with Lawfull Interest
from 21 Sept 1772...pay overplus to George LUMKIN.
No witnesses
Rec: 25 Sep 1772   George LUMKIN L.S.

DB 3, p.87 - CROWLEY from POTEET j^r.   DEED, 24 Sep 1772

James POTEET Junr. of Bedford County of one part and Benjamin CROWLEY of
Pittsylvania County of other part...for £140 Current money of Virginia...Land
on Both Sides Elk Creek a Branch of Irevin River Containing 380 acres as by
patent granted to said Ja^s. POTEET j^r. Dated 27 Aug 1770...by the branch.
Rec: 24 Sep 1772 and ?Jeun wife of said James
privily Examined and Relinquished right of Dower
No witnesses   James POTEET L.S.

DB 3, p.89 - COPLAND from COOPER j^r.   DEED, 21 Sep 1772

Thomas COOPER j^r. of County of Pittsylvania on one part and Peter COPLAND of
same County on other part...for Sum of £75 Current Money of Virginia...100
acres on Waters of Beaver Creek...to Stake in a Littlefieldnigh COOPERS Creek.
Wit: John WELLS, John BARNETT, Charles FINCH, Charles COPLAND
Rec: 25 Sep 1772   Thomas COOPER j^r. L.S.

DB 3, p.90 - THOMSON from NOWLING   DEED, 25 Sep 1772

Bryanward NOWLIN and Lucy his wife of County of Pittsylvania of one part and
William TOMSON of County afores^d. of other part...for £18 Current money of
Virginia...100 acres.
No witnesses
Rec: 25 Sep 1772   Bryanward NOWLIN L.S.

DB 3, p.92 - WALLER from MOSS   DEED, 25 Sep 1772

Moses MOSS and Mary his wife of County of Pittsylvania of one part and John
WALLER of said County of other part...for £210 Current money of Virginia...
sell to said John WALLER that Land whereon I now live situating and being on
Banister River it being all the Land I bought of Rich^d. CHAMBERLAYNE and con-
taining 400 acres...at Richard ELKINS...runing According to Courses of Deed
made by Richard CHAMBERLAYNE.
No witnesses
Rec: 25 Sep 1772 & Mary wife of said Moses MOSS   Moses MOSS L.S.
Exam^d. as Law directs Relinquished her right of Dower

DB 3, p.94 - HIX from SHELTON   DEED, 14 Sep 1772
James SHELTON of Parish of Cambden and County of Pittsylvania of one part
and James HIX of County of Brunswick of other part...for £500 Current money
of Virginia...400 acres on Both sides Beaver Creek...on a branch of Leatherwood Creek...Crossing Beaver Creek.
Wit: Will. MACCRAW, Mary MACCRAW, James M^{C}CRAW
Rec: 24 Sep 1772   James SHELTON L.S.

DB 3, p.96 - HIX FROM SHELTON   DEED, 14 Sep 1772
James SHELTON of Parrish of Cambden in County of Pittsylvania of one Part
and James HIX of County of Brunswick of other part...Sum of £500 Current mon-
ey of Virginia...400 acres on South side South fork of Leatherwood Creek.
Wit: Will MACCRAW, Mary MACCRAW, Ja^S. M^{C}CRAW
Rec: 24 Sep 1772   James SHELTON L.S.

DB 3, p.98 - COOK from BALLEW   BILL OF SALE,7 Mar 1772
I Charles BALLEW of Pittsylvania County doth this Day Sell unto Harmon COOCK
of same County my Waggon and four Horse Beasts, two of which is Horses one
is awhite horse and the other a Bay the other Two is mares both black their
Brands I know not...for £40 Current money.

Wit: Bennett BALLEW, Sarah $\overset{\text{her}}{\underset{\text{mark}}{\text{X}}}$ RIPLY   Charles BALLEW L.S.

This shall oblige me to pay unto Harmon KOOCK Sum of £16 Current money of
Virginia £09·02·10 at May Court and the Remainder on 15 Nov next it being
for value received 7 Mar 1772.
Rec: 25 Sep 1772

DB 3, p.99 - CLEMENT from CALLAWAY   DEED, 4 Sep 1772
Thomas CALLAWAY Senr. of County of Pittsylvania of one part and James CLEMENT
of aforesd. County of other part...for £100 Current Money of Virginia...100
acres on South fork of Sandy river...it being the place where said Thomas
CALLAWAY now lives on two or three acres Excepted for the use of the Mill.

Wit: Peter MANING, George Fuller HARRIS, John $\overset{\text{his}}{\underset{\text{mark}}{\text{O}}}$ HARRIS j^r.

Rec: 24 Sep 1772   Thomas CALLAWAY L.S.

DB 3, p.101 - COOPER from COPLAND   DEED, 21 Sep 1772
Peter COPLAND of County of Pittsylvania on one part and Joseph COOPER of
same County on other part...for £233 Current money of Virginia...248 acres
on Beaver Creek....Crossing Beaver Creek.
No witnesses
Rec: 25 Sep 1772   Peter COPLAND L.S.

DB 3, p.102 - COOPER j^r. from COPLAND   DEED, 21 Sep 1772
Peter COPLAND of County of Pittsylvania on one part and Thomas COOPER j^r. of
same County on other part...for £105 Current money of Virginia...250 acres
on Beaver Creek...in Joseph COOPERS line....down the Creek as it meanders to
mouth of COOPERS Creek...Thomas COOPERS corner.
Wit: John WELLS, John BARNETT, Charles FINCH, Charles COPLAND
Rec: 25 Sep 1772   Peter COPLAND L.S.

DB 3, p.104 - MORTON from HODGES   DEED, 25 Oct 1771
Welcom William HODGES of Carolina province of one part and Jehu MORTON of
Pittsylvania County of other part...for £150 Current money of Virginia...292
acres on a large Branch of ALLENS CREEK that makes out on the West side...
pointers of Joseph ECKHOLS's thence along FARRIS's line...Crossing a Branch
and said Large Branch to pine in BAKERS line, along BAKERS line.
Wit: William SHORT, Robt. BOWMER, Joseph ROBARDS
Cert: 26 Mar 1772, Rec: 24 Sep 1772   Welcom W. HODGES L.S.

DB 3, p.106 - MORTON from HODGES   DEED, 25 Oct 1771
Welcom William HODGES of Carolina Province of one part and Jehu MORTON of
Pittsylvania County of other part...for £50 Current money of Virginia...40
acres on North side Banister River...Beginning at mouth of the Spring branch
on William SHORTS line, up the branch to MURPHEYS line, along his line to the
River, down the River.
Wit: William SHORT, Jo^s. ROBARDS, Robin BOWMER
Cert: 26 Mar 1772, Rec: 24 Sep 1772   Welcom W. HODGES L.S.

DB 3, p.108 - RICHARDS from COLLINSWORTH   DEED, 24 Nov 1772
James COLLINSWORTH of Parish of Cambden in County of Pittsylvania of one part
and Edward RICHARDS of Parish and County aforesaid Planter of other part...
for £80 Current money of Virginia...Land on Both sides North fork of Chesnut
Creek...Crossing a branch...Crossing the Creek...250 acres.
Wit: Ja^s. STEWART, Saml. PATTERSON, Jacob STOBER
Rec: 27 Nov 1772 and Deborah wife of James COLLINS
privily Examined and Relinquished her Dower   James COLLINSWORTH L.S.

DB 3, p.110 - JONES from COX   DEED, 26 Nov 1772
James COX of Parish of Cambden in County of Pittsylvania of one part and
Thomas JONES of Parish and County aforesaid of other part...for Sum of £60
Current money of Virginia...125 acres on Both sides Mill Creek it being the
Land whereon said James COX now lives and Conveyed to him by Edward POLLEY
by Indenture dated Nov last past and recorded in the County Court aforesaid.
No witnesses   James COX L.S.
Rec: 26 Nov 1772 and Margaret wife of said   her
James privily Exam^d. as Law directs Relin-   Margaret/   COX L.S.
quished her right of Dower   mark

DB 3, p.112 - HUNTER from ROACH   BILL SALE, 24 Nov 1772
I John REACH of Pittsylvania County hath Sold unto William HUNTER of same
County one Wagin and Gear, one Beay horse markt in the left ear, one black
horse and Two beay horses and two mares one black and one white their Brands
unknown which I now Possesith.
Wit: John HOOKER, John GOODE, Thomas MURRELL   his
Rec: 26 Nov 1772   John F REACH L.S.
                                                           mark

DB 3, p.113 - QUINN from CLAY   DEED, 21 Oct 1772
Henry CLAY of Pittsylvania County of one part and William QUIN of other part...
for £35·06 good and Lawfull money of Virginia...153 acres on Draugh of Little
Sandy Creek...in Thomas BILLINGS's line where CLERKS line Intersects...Cross-
ing the Road...Cross.g the Road again...in BILLINGS's line.
Wit: Geo. CARTER, James BURTON, Edmond FALLON
Rec: 26 Nov 1772   Henry CLAY L.S.

DB 3, p.114 - BURTON from CLAY   DEED, 21 Oct 1772
Henry CLAY of Pittsylvania County and James BURTON of County aforesaid...for
£100 Good and lawful money of Virginia...Land on Little fork of the upper
Sandy Creek of Dann...near the Road in Old Order line...Crossing a bent of
a Branch and Little Sandy Creek...pointers in the Deviding line Between said
CLAY and his father M^r. Charles CLAY....500 acres.

                                            his
Wit: George CARTER, Edmond FALLON, William, QUIN
                                            mark

Rec: 26 Nov 1772   Henry CLAY L.S.

DB 3, p.116 - DILLARD to PITTSY^1. COURT   CORONER BOND, 27 Nov 1772
Know all men by these presents that we Thomas DILLARD, Benj^a. LANKFORD and
Robert WILLIAMS are held and firmly bound unto our Sovereign Lord the King
in Sum of £500 Current Money of Virginia...Condition of above obligation is
such that whereas above Bounden Thomas DILLARD hath entered into Bond...for
due Execution of his office as Coronor for this County of Pittsylvania and
that he Serve all Such process that comes to his hands and make Legal re-
turns to Clerk of Court of Pittsylvania County.
                                          Thos DILLARD j^r. L.S.
                                          Benj^a. LANKFORD L.S.
Rec: 27 Nov 1772   RWILLIAMS L.S.

DB 3, p.117 - ROWLAND & LAMB from BLAGGE   DEED TRUST, 13 Jun 1772
I John BLAGGE of County of Pittsylvania am this Day Justly Indebted unto
John ROWLAND and Richard LAMB of aforesaid County the Sum of £150 Current
Money of Virginia and being Truly desirious to do Justice...said Sum of Mon-
ey with Lawful Interest...further Consideration of 5s...Sell Slaves: Abraham,
Frank, Jack, Nann, Jacob, Prue, Joe, Bob and Sall, 12 Head Cattle, 20 Head
Hoggs including young and old, one Waggon and Nine Horses and Mares, all my
Household furniture....at any time after this Day and date, after Giving one
Months due Notice...Sell for best price...discharge Sum.
Wit: Will TUNSTALL, Mountague PACE
Rec: 27 Nov 1772   John BLAGGE L.S.

DB 3, p.119 - LAW from COCKERHAM   BILL SALE, 22 Oct 1772
I Abner COCKERHAM of Pittsylvania County hath Sold unto John LAW jun^r. of
said County - foor Cows and Cavs two Black and 2 white pided one of the Cows
marked with a Crop in Right year and the Two Cows Likewise the other Cow
marked with a Crop in the Left year a Swallow fork in Right the other Two are
Red and with Pided ther Caves also one of the Cows is marked with a Crop in
Right year and the Two Caves also and the other Cow Two Crops and Likewise
one Red awhite Pided heffer marked in Right year with Crop Likewise Two Beds
with their furniture...Likewise hath Delivered unto said LAW 15 Head of hogs
there Coler is black and white and their mark is a Crop in Right year...Like-
wise Twenty Weight of New feathers and a Spinning Weel, 3 Basons, 6 plats,
2 Dishes, a pot, a pan, 3 Cheers, 1 bay horse Branded with a Sturrup Iron,
2 axes, 3 hoes, a plow hoe, 2 hillinghoes, all my Crop of Corn and Tobaco as
it Stands and Tops and Blads and Shocks the said COCKERHAM is to be at Ex-
pence of geting Tob^o. prized and Corn Shuckt and I said COCKERHAM do Deliver
up everything that I am Pursest with in this World all for Value Received of
him.   his
Wit: John LAW j^r., William COCKERHAM, Wm. LAW
                                          mark
Rec: 26 Nov 1772   Abner COCKERHAM L.S.

DB 3, p.120 - LYNE from FROGG   DEED TRUST, 27 May 1772
I William FROGG of Pittsylvania County am justly indebted to Henry & Edm^d.
LYNE of said County the Sum of £33·15·02 Current money of Virginia and being
Truly desirous to pay them with Legal Interest from date hereof...Sell one
Waggon made by Saml. JOHNSON with the Geers, 6 Horses belonging thereto, one
hh^d. Tob^o. Sent down, one of the Horses is a bay horse branded/ /—/one other
horse a Sorrel Branded/\(on near Buttock the Brands of the other Horses for-
got...after 1 Apr 1773 after Giving Ten Days notice may dispose of for best
price that can be got in Cash...secure said Debt.
Wit: Will. TUNSTALL   William FROGG L.S.
27 May 1772 Trust Deed taken for..........................£33·15·10
C^r By bringing a Load Corn from Sarrow Town................ 1·10·0
                                                            £32· 5·10

DB 3, p.121 - TALBOT from HARNESS   DEED TRUST, 14 Aug 1772
John HARNESS of County of Pittsylvania of one part and Charles TALBOTT of
County of Bedford of other part...£62·18·02 lawfull money of Virginia which
John HARNESS is Justly Indebted to Charles TALBOTT and honestly desires to
pay him...farther Consideration of 1s like money...Two Tracts of Land Con-
taining in bouth Tracts 260 acres on Waters of ALLENS Creek, one Tract of
150 Laid of by Joshua STONE for said HARNESS adjoining Land of Danl. MORGAN
across from the Mountain line to line of Jo^s. FARIS the other Tract of 110
acres by Pattent Dated 16 Feb 1771...after 1 Oct 1772 Sell for best price...
Ten Days publick notice...pay above Charles TALBOT with Interest from 14
Aug 1772 til same paid.   his
Wit: Ben. LANKFORD, Heanrica LANKFORD, John// FERRELL
                                            mark
Rec: 26 Nov 1772   John HARNESS L.S.

DB 3, p.124 - GAFFORD from TERRY   DEED, 17 Feb 1773
Joseph TERRY of Camden Parish in Pittsylvania County on one part and Charles
GAFFORD of said parish and County on other part...for £50 Good and Lawful
money of Virginia to his Son Joseph TERRY j^r. paid in hand...150 acres on
north side Birches Creek...Mouth of the great Branch of said Creek runing
with Several meanders of Birches Creek to Large Rock where Thomas TERRYS
line Crosses said Creek...where line Intersects with Branch Called the Sloop
branch, down several meanders of said Branch to where it emptys in the said
Great branch.
No witnesses
Rec: 25 Feb 1773   Joseph TERRY L.S.

DB 3, p.125 - RAMSEY from GORDON   DEED TRUST, Sep 1771
Patrick RAMSEY merchant of Prince George County of one part and Archibald
GORDON of County of Pittsylvania of other part...Arch^d. GORDON being indebted
to the partnership of Arch^d. GORDON now Dece^d. and said Patrick RAMSEY the
Surviving Partner in Sum of £267·12·04 and desirous to Secure to Patrick
RAMSEY Surviveing partner of said Sum with Legal Interest from Date of these
presents...Land on Snow Creek Containing 850 acres being Land whereon said
GORDON now Lives which was pattent to a Certain Obediah WOODSON 5 Jul 1751
and since Conveyed to said GORDON by two Deeds, one from James ROBERTS, the
other from Jno. HICKEY, also Slaves: Dick, Celum, Lucy, Sally, Nancy, Patty...
...before 1 Oct 1773 (if paid) Indenture be Discharged.   d
Wit: Is. READ   Arch. GORDON L.S.
Rec: 25 Feb 1773

DB 3, p.127 - STANDLEY from COOK   DEED,14 Oct 1772

Shem COOK of Pittsylvania County of one part and William STANDLEY of same
County of other part...Sum of £12·10 Current money of Virginia...103 acres
on Butterum Town Creek of Smith's River...west side Creek...Crossing a fork
of said Creek...being part of a Tract of Land granted to Shem COOK by Patent
dated 16 Feb 1771.
Wit: Gideon RUCKER, John HEARD, Amos RICHARDSON
Rec: 25 Feb 1773   Shem COOK L.S.

DB 3, p.129 - MC DANIEL from PIGGS   DEED OF TRUST, 22 Dec 1772

William PIGG, James PIGG, Richard PIGG, Allen ADAMS, Sarah PIGG, Mary PIGG
and Ann PIGG all of Parish of Camden and County of Pittsylvania of one part
and Henry MC DANIEL Executor of Paul PIGG dece. of other part...Henry
MC DANIEL hath this day agreed to deliver unto William PIGG, James PIGG, Richard PIGG, Allen ADAMS Sarah PIGG, mary PIGG and Ann PIGG all the Estate of
said Paul PIGG deceased and they being desirous to Secure the Executor from
all Costs and Damages...for Sum of 5s Current money of Virginia...Land on
both sides Banister River and great Cherry Stone Creek Containing 600 acres,
also Eight Slaves: James, Harry, Peter, Lucy, Hannah, Phill, Abram, Winney...
Sell for best Price after ten Days notice...satisfy Expences then be void.
Wit:John WEATHERFORD, Isaac BRIGGS, David WEATHERFORD
Signed: his   his
William PIGG L.S., James PIGG L.S., Rich^d. X PIGG L.S., Allen X ADAMS,
                                            mark   mark

      her   her   her
Sarah X PIGG L.S., Mary X PIGG L.S., Ann X PIGG L.S.
     mark   mark   mark
Rec: 25 Feb 1773

DB 3, p.131 - YOUNG from CROWLEY   DEED, 25 Feb 1772

Samuel CROWLEY and Elizabeth his wife of Parish of Cambden and County of
Pittsylvania of one part and George YOUNG of Parish and County aforesaid of
other part...Sum of £60 Current money of Virginia...all that Tract of Land
on Both sides South fork Sandy River which was formerly Granted to said
George YOUNG by Letters Patant bearing Date at Williamsburg 15 Jul 1760 and
afterwards Conveyed to said Samuel CROWLEY by Deed recorded in County Court
of Pittsylvania...210 acres...at LANSFORD Corner...Crossing the Creek...in
GRAYS line.   his
No witnesses   Samuel V CROWLEY L.S.
Rec: 25 Feb 1773 and Elizabeth being privily   mark
Examined as Law directs Relinquished her   her
right of dower.   Eliza V CROWLEY L.S.
                                              mark

DB 3, p.133 - MURDOCK & C°. from LEAK   DEED OF TRUST, 1 Jul 1772

James LEAK of County of Pittsylvania of one part and James MURDOCK and Company of said County on other part...for £300 Current money of Virginia which
James LEAK is Justly Indebted to James MURDOCK & Company and Honestly de-
sires to pay...further Consideration of Sum of 5s like...One Sorrell mare
Branded on the off Buttock / , one White mare branded on near Buttock /
Two Cows and Calves, two Stears, two Heiffers and all my Stock of Cattle
whatsoever, Ten Head of Hoggs marked with a Crop and Two Slits and a Swallow
fork in right and a Crop and Two Slits in Left, Two Gunns, a mans Sadle &
Sadle baggs, also all my household furniture whatsoever and plantation
Utencells...after 25 Dec 1773 Sell for best Price...with Lawfull Interest.

Wit: Don^d. MC NICOLL, John EAST, R. FARGUSON
Memorandum: After Sealing and Delivery of Deed James LEAK Hath Sold to James
MURDOCK & Co. all Quantity of Corn and Tob^o. now upon James LEAKS plantation.
Wit: John VAUGHAN, Francis HENRY, Don^d. MC NICOLE
Rec: 25 Feb 1773   James LEAK L.S.

DB 3, p.135 - KERBY from KERBY   DEED, 24 Sep 1772
Henry KERBY and David KERBY his wife of County of Pittsylvania of one part and
David KERBY of said County of other part...said Henry KERBY and Ann KERBY his
wife for Sum of £77·10 Current Money of Virginia...Land on north side Pigg
River...on River Bank in David KERBYS line, down the River to first Island
at mouth of a Branch in REAVES line, on his line to a Corner between REVES
and David KERBYS line on a ridge near Glade Creek...160 acres.
Wit: John KERBY, John KERBY, Peyton SMITH   his
Rec: 25 Feb 1773   Henry   KERBY L.S.
                                                            mark

---

DB 3, p.137 - CLAY from CLAY   BILL SALE, 23 Sep 1772
I William CLAY Senr. of County of Pittsylvania for Consideration of Sum of
£150 Current Money of Virginia hath Sold unto Jesse CLAY of Pittsylvania Coun-
ty the piece of Land on Blackwater River whereon I now live Containing 45
acres as there abouts, all my Beds and furniture, all and everything I am now
Possess.d of, all my Stock of Cattle Hogs and Horses and their Increase.
Wit: John WILKINSON, Reubin WILKINSON
Rec: 25 Feb 1773   William CLAY L.S.

DB 3, p.137 - LAW from STEGALL   6 Feb 1773
William STEGALL of one part and Nathaniel LAW of other part Both of County
of Pittsylvania of the other part...for £20...100 acres on iland Creek...on
WALTONS old order line, on order line...on Iland Creek...line of ?Edanan
CANTLEY?...on the Ridge path Called Reaves's Path, by an olde line run by
Samuel CANTERBERY a Cross the Road...100 acres.
                                  his
Wit: James STEWART, John   LAW, Arch^d. SMITH   his
                         mark   William X STEGALL L.S.
Rec: 25 Feb 1773   mark

DB 3, p.139 - PAINTER from COOK   POWER OF ATTORNEY, 20 Feb 1773
I Harmon COOK of County of Pittsylvania for divers Good Causes...Appoint
Daniel PAINTER of County of Bedford my Lawfull attorney...demand sums of
money owing unto me...for me in my name...all other Lawfull acts whatsoever
as I my self might as Could doe if I were Personally present.
Rec: 26 Feb 1773   Harmon COOK L.S.

DB 3, p.139 - KERBY from KERBY   DEED, 19 Nov 1772
John KERBY Senr. of County of Pittsylvania of one part and Jo^s. KERBY of s^d.
County of other part...for £50 Current money of Virginia...100 acres on Owens
Creek...in patent line and Jesse KERBYS new line runing with patent line...on
THOMPSONS line then on THOMPSONS line to where it Strikes Patent Line...in
Jesse KERBYS line and new line.   his
Wit: William DABNEY, John DAVIS, Peyton SMITH   John   KERBY L.S.
Rec: 25 Feb 1773   mark

DB 3, p.141 - WILLIAMS from PARR   BILL SALE, 21 Aug 1772
I William PARR of Pittsylvania County for Consideration of £50 Current money
of Virginia paid by Robert WILLIAMS hath Sold two feather Beds and furniture,
two flock d°. and furniture and all my house and Kitchen furniture, one mare
Branded _TD_ , three Cows and Calves and all other things that I do Possess...
I have Received full Satisfaction for the same.
Wit: Jo^s. FARGUSON, James CONWAY
Rec: 25 Feb 1773   William PARR L.S.

DB 3, p.142 - BALLINGER from AUSTIN   DEED OF TRUST, 20 Jan 1773
Joseph AUSTIN of Pittsylvania County on one part and Joseph BALLENGER on
other part...for £100 Current money of Virginia which Joseph AUSTIN is Justly
Indebted to Joseph BALLENGER and honestly desires to pay him and further Sum
of 5s Like money paid by Joseph BALLENGER...Tract of Land that Joseph AUSTIN
now lives upon and one negro Boy named Tom, 15 head Horses that AUSTIN is now
Possesd of Likewise his Stock of Cattle and hoggs...after 25 Dec 1773 may
Sell for best price Ten Days Publick notice...pay and Satisfy himself.
Wit: Will TUNSTALL, Jn°. THOMPSON, Arch^d. SMITH
No recording date   Joseph AUSTIN L.S.

DB 3, p.143 - KERBY from KERBY   DEED, 19 Nov 1772
John KERBY of County of Pittsylvania of one part and Jesse KERBY of said
County of other part...for Sum of £50 Current money of Virginia...200 acres
on Owens Creek...oak Both the Patent and new Lines, on Patent line bearing
Towards the North and Continuing on Patent line.   his
Wit: William DABNEY, Jn°. DAVIS, Peyton SMITH   John -|- KERBY L.S.
Rec: 25 Feb 1773   mark

DB 3, p.145 - MC KINSEY from DUNN   DEED, 28 Dec 1772
Waters DUNN and Sarah his wife of County of Pittsylvania of one part and
Kinney MC KINSEY of same County of other part...for £40 Current money of
Virginia...Land on south side Smith's River...south side said River thence
new lines...80 acres.   her
Wit: Waters DUNN j^r., James MAY, Eliz^a. X DUNN
                                           mark   Waters DUNN L.S.
Rec: 25 Feb 1773   Sarah DUNN L.S.

DB 3, p.146 - BOLLING MUNFORD from HUTCHERSON   DEED OF TRUST, 10 Sep 1772
Sarah HUTCHERSON of County of Pittsylvania of one part and Thomas Bolling
MUNFORD of Parish of Nottoway and County of Amelia of other part...for £75
Current Money of Virginia which said Sarah HUTCHERSON is now justly Indebted
to Thomas Bolling MUNFORD and honestly desire to pay...farther Sum of 5s
Like money paid by Thomas Bolling MUNFORD...sell 320 acres, the Land whereon
Sarah HUTCHERSON now Lives and which She Purchased of Samuel PATTERSON...
Thos. Bolling MUNFORD Shall after the Death of Sarah HUTCHERSON , as soon as
proper or Sarah HUTCHERSON shall Request...Sell for best price giving Ten
Days Publick notice...pay above Sum with Lawfull Interest from 1 Mar 1773
until fully discharged.   her
No witnesses   Sarah -|- HUTCHERSON L.S.
Rec: 25 Feb 1773   mark

DB 3, p.148 - HARRISON to THOMAS   RELEASE, 8 Feb 1773
I Sarah HARRISON do hereby Release disclaim and Surrender all Claims. Titles
intries or Right, or entry to William THOMAS in and for a Certain Tract of
Land in Pittsylvania County containing 400 acres on a Creek.
Wit: Isaac READ, Francis BARNES, Charles SWILLEVANT, RWILLIAMS
No recording date .   Sarah HARRISON L.S.

DB 3, p.148 - COPLAND from COOPER   DEED, 7 Mar 1771

Thomas COOPER of County of Roan in province of North Carolina on one part
and Peter COPLAND of County of Pittsylvania on other part...for £244·18·03
Current money of Virginia...Two Tracts of Land Containing 367 Acres...One
Tract...in order line...containing 177 acres...Last Tract Containing 190
acres they being same Two Tract Conveyed by Peter COPLAND to Thomas COOPER
by two Deeds bearing date 30 Apr 1765

Wit: Thos. COOPER j^r., Danl. $\subset$ MC BRIDE, Andrew KNOX, Howell LEWIS, John

SMITH, James SIMPLS, Jno. WELLS, Chas. COPLAND, Ambrose JONES, Joseph COOPER,
Edmund LYNE, Rich^d. COPLAND

This Deed was executed at Salisbury Court in north Carolina before the first
four Witnesses and afterwards Re acknowledged in Pittsylvania on 17 Oct 1772
before next four witnesses.

DB 3, p.150 - GEORGE from TERRY   DEED TRUST, 19 Jun 1771

William TERRY of County of Pittsylvania of one part and David GEORGE of County
of Charlotte of other part...for £23·12·02 Current money of Virginia which
William TERRY is Justly indebted to David GEORGE and honestly desires to pay
and for further Consideration of £23·12·02 Like money...200 acres it being
part of Land my father wild to me in his Last will and Testament and being
part of Larger Tract which my father bought of James TERRY and Bounded by
Peter POLLYES Land and by an Entere that John DONOLDSON made on Waters of
Shocko Creek...after 1 Jul next Sell after Giving ten Days Publick notice...
pay overplus.
Wit: Jo^s. FARGASON, Ja^s. CONWAY, RWILLIAMS, James DAUGHERTY, Saml. LOESON,
William SOBLET
Pres: 27 Jun 1771, Rec: 25 Feb 1773   William X TERRY L.S.
                                                    mark

DB 3, p.152 - SMITH from EAST   DEED TRUST, 1 Aug 1772

John EAST, Senr. of Pittsylvania County of one part and John SMITH of Halifax
County of other part...for £48 Current money of Virginia which John EAST is
Justly indebted to John SMITH and honestly desires to pay him, farther Sum of
5s like money paid by John SMITH...100 acres Including the Plantation whereon
said John EAST now Lives being part of Tract which said John EAST purchased
of George THOMAS and Conveyed to him by Deed from William THOMAS Recorded in
Pittsylvania Court, also one Copper Still and worm, one Black mare Branded
on near Shoulder and Buttock $\int$, Two Cows and Calfs, a hiffer, Two feather
Beds and furniture, Two Iron potts and all Remainder of his house hold furniture...after 1 Aug 1774 Sell for best price after Ten Days Publick notice.
Wit: Joel HURTT, W^m. GIELIANTIL, Thomas EAST
Rec: 25 Mar 1773   John EAST L.S.

DB 3, p.154 - FINCH from COX   DEED, 25 Mar 1773

John COX of Fincastle County of one part and Charles FINCH of Pittsylvania
County of other part...for £73·10 Current money of Virginia...180 acres on
north side Irvin River...mouth of Rugg Creek Randolph HARMER and KINGS corner, new lines...Crossing two Branches and Rugg Creek...Crossing three Branches...crossing the Little Creek...down the River as it meanders.
Wit: Edmund LYNE, Will TUNSTALL, Arch^s. HUGHES, Jo^s. AKIN   his
                                              John / COX L.S.
Rec: 26 Mar 1773   mark

DB 3, p.155 - ALFORD from OWEN   DEED, 22 Mar 1773
John OWEN of County of Pittsylvania of one part and William ALFORD of County
of Bedford of other part...for £20 Current Money of Virginia...62 acres on
South Side Stanton River...Beginning at mouth of Valantines Creek, up the
same as it meanders to back Line of James DOSS's Land...keeping a Straight
line to the River, Down the River...being the Plantation whereon John OWEN
formerly Lived.
No witnesses
Rec: 25 Mar 1773 and Mary wife of John privily
Examined as Law directs Relinquished her
right of dower

           John OWEN   L.S.
           her
Mary   OWEN   L.S.
     mark

DB 3, p.157 - FRANCE from SMITH   DEED, 8 Oct 1772
Phillip SMITH of County of Pittsylvania Planter of one part and Henry FRANCE
of County aforesaid black Smith of other part...for £40 Current money of Vir-
ginia...Land which Phillip SMITH purchased of Samuel COX...on South side
South fork of Mayo River Containing 150 acres...Beginning where the lower
part of a Tract Containing 2,200 acres Granted by patent to George WALTON,
Leaves FOUNTAIN line downwards along Patent Bounderies to where it Strikes
the River, up the River to Bounds of land where Henry SHORT lived, along
Bounderys of that Land...a line to Strike ROBERTS or FOUNTANES.
Wit: Arch^s. HUGHES, Jno. HUGHES, Mary HUGHES, Frederick FULKERSON, Anthony
SMITH, John SIMS

           his
     Phillip   SMITH   L.S.
Cert: 25 Feb 1773, Rec: 25 Mar 1773   mark

DB 3, p.159 - MORTON from HILL   DEED TRUST, 1773
Thomas HILL (Breeches maker) of Parrish of Camden and County of Pittsylvania
of one part and Jehu MORTON of same Parrish and County of other Part...for
£13 Current money of Virginia...100 acres on waters of Strawberry known by
the Place whereon Thomas HILL now lives...Jehu MORTON became Security with
Thomas HILL to Richard DUDGEON for £11·08·03 with Interest from the date
hereof Payable within ninety Days now if Thomas HILL shall pay Richard DUGJEON
according to a Replevea Bond...and keep Jehu MORTON safe from Costs...Indent-
ure to be void otherwise Lawfull.
Wit: John SALMON, James SMITH, Arch^d. SMITH
Rec: 26 Mar 1773

           his
    Thomas   HILL   L.S.
     mark

DB 3, p.160 - ADAMS from PIGG   DEED, 23 Mar 1773
William PIGG of Pittsylvania and Coloney of Virginia of one part and Robert
ADAMS of County and Coloney aforesaid...for £31·10 to him in hand paid...
300 acres, being part of FINES order...on both sides Banister River Supossing
two hundred acres on South side and one hundred acres on north....South side
Banister...upon James PIGG line...in order line...Crossing the River.
No witnesses
Rec: 25 Mar 1773   William PIGG   L.S.

DB 3, p.162 - SHELTON from TERRY   DEED TRUST,30 Oct 1772
William TERRY of County of Pittsylvania of one part and Abraham SHELTON of
said County of other part...for £50 Current money of Virginia which William
TERRY is Justly Indebted to Abraham SHELTON and honestly desire to Secure
and pay to him...further Consideration of 5s Like money paid by Abraham
SHELTON...200 acres on Branches of Elk horn and Joining Lands of Joseph TERRY
and George WATKINS being the Plantation whereon William TERRY now Lives...

...Abraham SHELTON shall after 25 Dec 1773 Sell for best price Giving Ten
Days Publick Notice...out of Money arrising Discharge pay above Sum with Law-
full Interest from 30 Oct 1772.
Wit: Don^d, MC NICOLL, RFARGUSON, Spencer SHELTON   William X TERRY L.S.
                                                            his
                                                            mark
Rec: 25 Mar 1773

DB 3, p.164 - TUNSTALL &c from JEFFERSON   POWER OF ATTORNEY, 26 Mar 1773
I George JEFFERSON of Lunenburg County...appoint my Trusty friends William
TUNSTALL, Hugh INNES, Robert WILLIAMS and Arther HOPKINS Gentlemen my true
and Lawfull attornies jointly for me...to Contract Sell and Dispose of the
whole or any part of my Lands on Turkey Cock Creek in Pittsylvania County as
I shall Direct them, as it is Laid off into Seperate Surveys at such Prices
or on Such Terms as I shall from time to time appoint and instruct them...as
I George JEFFERSON in my own person might or could do.
No witnesses
Rec: 26 Mar 1773   G. JEFFERSON L.S.

DB 3, p.165 - BOSTICK from RUSELL   DEED, 15 Jan 1773
George RUSELL of North Carolinia in Surry County of one part and Absalum
BOSTICK of Pittsylvania County in Virginia of other part...for £60 to him in
hand paid...164 acres on Both sides Cascade Creek...WATKINS corner...to old
back Line...along old Line...Crossing a fork of the Creek...Crossing a
branch...fork of a branch Down same to the Creek, Crossing Creek up the hill.
                        his   his   his
Wit: David HARRIS, Jo^s. M HARRIS, Moliam X STEPHENS, John + BROWN
                        mark   mark   mark
Rec: 25 Mar 1773   George RUSSELL L.S.

DB 3, p.167 - PREWET from LUCK   DEED, 25 Mar 1773
Francis LUCK of Pittsylvania County of one part and Byrd PREWET of same county of other Part...for £200 Current money of Virginia...Land in County above
being first Granted by Patent to Benjamin MOSBY 10 Jan 1748 which for non payment of Quitrents &c was again granted to Pendexter MOSBY which assigned same
to Francis LUCK which new Grant bearing date 23 May 1763 One Tract Containing
400 acres...on his own line...Crossing white Oak Creek...the other Tract containing 337 acres...at Nowel BURTONS...on a branch.
No witnesses
Rec: 25 Mar 1773   Francis LUCK L.S.

DB 3, p.168 - SMITH from TALBOT   DEED, 26 Nov 1772
Charles TALBOT of Bedford County of one part and Peyton SMITH of Pittsylvania
County of other part...for £90 to him in hand paid...Land on North side Pigg
River...in John KERBYS Line...100 acres.
Wit: Haynes MORGAN, Arden EVENS, RWILLIAMS
Rec: 25 Mar 1773   Charles TALBOT L.S.

DB 3, p.169 - CLAY from CLAY   DEED, 25 Mar 1773
Charles CLAY and Martha his wife of parrish of Southham and County of Cumber-
land of one part and Elezar CLAY of Parrish of Manchester of County of Chest-
erfield of other part...for £140 Current money of Virginia...two Tracts of
Lands Containing by Estimation 1,200 acres...400 acres on Cain Creek Survey-
ed by Charles CLAY and paterned in his name...also 800 acres on Dry fork of
Sandy Creek lying up the Creek on both sides as well more fully appear by plat
of Land it being part of Charles CLAYS order for 9,000 and odd acres of Land.
No witnesses
Rec: 25 Mar 1773   Charles CLAY L.S.

DB 3, p.171 - GILBERT from PREWET   DEED, 25 Mar 1773
Bird PREWET of Pittsylvania County and Michael GILBERT of Bedford County...
for £60 Current of Virginia...150 acres on Little Straitston part of old
patent of Isaac ECHELS being the South side of the Land with new made lines
mark.d...thence the Road According to agreement and Bounded as by Patent
dated 20 Sep 1750.
No witnesses
Rec: 25 Mar 1773   Byrd PREWET L.S.

DB 3, p.172 - EAST from PREWET   DEED, 1 Feb 1773
Bird PREWET of Pittsylvania County of one part and Joseph EAST of same County
of other part...£50 Current Money of Virginia...215 acres on Both sides Straitstone Creek being part of a patent of a Greater Quantity granted first to
Isaac ECKHOLS bearing Date 20 Sep 1751 being the North side of said Land...
now Joyned with Land of Joseph COLLINS, Stephen COLLINS and others and Devided from Remainder of patent with new made line and Road.

Wit: Thomas EAST, Jn°. EAST, Elizabeth her ∤ mark COCKERHAM

Rec: 25 Mar 1773   Byrd PREWET L.S.

DB 3, p.173 - LUCK from DYER   DEED, 6 Feb 1773
John DYER and Dinah his wife of County of Halifax on one part and Francis
LUCK of County of Pittsylvania of other part...50 acres on South side Stantaun
River in the fork of the River and Straitstone...for sum of £30 Current...at
mouth of Straitstone Creek then up the Creek as it meanders to CALLAWAYS
line...a new line.
Wit: Byrd PREWET, Manoah DYER, Peter TRIBLE, George LANDDOWN, John MARTEN,
John EAST, Thoˢ. EAST

                                         John DYER L.S.
                                     her
Rec; 25 Mar 1773   Dinah D DYER L.S.
                                      mark

DB 3, p.175 - LACKY from WITCHER   DEED, 25 Mar 1773
Daniel WITCHER of Pittsylvania County and Colony of Virginia of one part and
Alexander LACKY of said County and Colony of other part...for 5s Lawfull
money of Virginia...191 acres it being part, or the one half of a greater
Tract of Land...on Harping Creek and made over to William WITCHER by our Receiver General and Governor of the Kings Revenues in this his Colony and Dominion of Virginia by way of Patent bearing dąte 27 Jun 1764 and by bargain
and Sale made over by William WITCHER to Danˡ. WITCHER...Crossing a branch...
crossing two Branches...in line of original patent...on Harping Creek, up it
as it Meanders...from the Day before date hereof for and During Term of whole
year...yearly Rent of one pepper Corn on Lady Day next.
Wit: W. WITCHER, Thoˢ. LACKY   his
Rec: 25 Mar 1773 and Susannah wife of Daniel   Daniel X WITCHER L.S.
privily Examined, Relinquished right of dower   mark

DB 3, p.177 - PATTY from HENRY   DEED, 30 Sep 1772
Jessey PATEY of County of Pittsylvania of one part and John HENRY and Mary
his wife of same County of other part...for £30 Current money of Virginia...
130 acres on both sides Nixes Creek...it is to be all the Surplous Land contained in a pattent Granted to Jaˢ. PATTEY Decᵈ. for 340 acres on Nixe Creek

after Surveying out to Thomas MUSTEEN 170 acres part of pattented Land on
Lower side being same Land Granted to John HENRY by Charles PATTEY.
Wit: Jno. DONELSON, Thomas HUTCHINGS, Jno. DONELSON j^r., Rachel DONELSON

John HENRY   L.S.

Rec: none

Molley HENRY   L.S.

DB 3, p.179 - PATEY from HENRY   DED^s., 14 Aug in 13th year of our Reign
George the third by grace of god of great Brittain France and Ireland King
Defender of the Faith &c Thomas DILLARD, John DONELSON and Crispen SHELTON
Gent. or any two his Majestys Justices of County of Pittsylvania...John HENRY
by Indenture of feoffment hath Conveyed unto Jesse PATTEY of County of Pitt-
sylvania 190 acres and Molley the wife of John HENRY cannot Conveniantly
Travel to and from County Court...examine Molley apart from her Husband
whether she freely Relinquishes her Right of Dower.
By virtue of above Dedimus...Molley wife of John HENRY apart from her Husband
Relinquished her Right of Dower.

Jno. DONELSON   L.S.

Rec: 26 Mar 1773

Crispin SHELTON   L.S.

DB 3, p.180 - COPLAND &c from BLAND &c   RELEASE,11 May 1772
To Ambrose JONES, Thomas COOPER j^r., Jno. WELLS, Joseph COOPER, Jno. ACUFF,
David MATLOCK, Joseph KING, Samuel KING & Saml. BIRD of County of Pittsylvania
Gent...We are informed by Peter COPLAND that he hath Contracted Severally with
you for Certain Pieces of Land which are part of 7,500 acres on Smiths River
and on Beaver and Ready Creeks...Lands Subject to Mortgages...oblige ourselves
to make Proper & Legal Conveyances of Land...that is to say---To

To Ambrose JONES	120 Acres whereon he Lives price	£ 40..0..0
To Thomas COOPER j^r.	136 Acres on Coopers Creek price	30..0..0
To Jno. WELLS	290 acres part of which he lives on	62..10..0
To Joseph COOPER	188 acres part of Lott call.d Jno. CHANDLERS	113..0..0
To Jno. ACUFF	120 acres whereon he lives	60..0- 0
To David MATLOCK	50 acres part of Lott call.d Danl. MC BRIDES	25..0- 0
To Joseph KING	190 acres a Lott on Ready Creek	50..--
To Saml. KING	172 acres one D^o. on D^o.	50 --
To Saml. BIRD	190 acres one D^o. on D^o.	80

£510..10

The times of Payment to be the 25 Apr 1774 with Interest from this Day...im-
power Peter COPLAND to take each of your Bonds.
Wit: Thos. JETT, Rich^d. HANSON, Edmund LYNE

Peter Randolph BLAND
William BLACK

Rec: 26 Mar 1773

Patrick COUTTS

DB 3, p.181 - MULLINGS from OWEN   29 Sep 1772
William OWEN of County of Pittsylvania planter of own part and Henry MULLINGS
of County aforesaid of other part...Sum of £25 Current Money...Land on the
River...on Edward NIX..Crossing a branch...Down the River according to its
Meanders...100 acres   her   her
Wit: William ALLFORD, Elezeabeth X ALLFORD, Betty X VEST, William DUDLEY
                                   mark   mark   his
Rec: 25 Mar 1773   William | OWEN L.S.
                                                       mark

DB 3, p.183 - COOK from JEFFERSON   DEED, 3 Aug 1772
George JEFFERSON of Lunenburg County of one part and Harmon COOK of Pittsylvania of other part...for £215 Current Money of Virginia...250 acres on
Turkey Cock Creek including said JEFFERSON's upper Mill...Beginning at a
place on the Creek where there was a Bridge about three or four hundred yards
below the mill...runing west to old Patent line, up the Creek on old line...
Except Harmon COOK debared the Liberty of having a mill Dam ever to be higher
than Ten feet from Low water mark at the Mill.

Wit: James PRUNTY, Mich[l]. M COATS, Rob[t]. PRUNTY, David PREWITT Jun[r].
                              mark   mark   mark
Rec: 26 Mar 1773   G. JEFFERSON L.S.

DB 3, p.185 - JEFFERSON from COOK   DEED OF TRUST, 3 Aug 1772
Harmon COOK of Pittsylvania County of one part and George JEFFERSON of Lunenburg County of other part...Harmon COOK is Justly indebted to George JEFFERSON
the Sum of £215 Current money of Virginia payable 1 Apr 1775..250 acres on
Turkey Cock Creek including the Mill known by name of Jefferson's upper Mill
being the same Land purchased by COOK of George JEFFERSON by Deed...after
1 Apr 1775 Sell for best price...out of Money arising pay himself.

Wit: James PRUNTY, Michael M COATS, Robert PRUNTY, Dav[d] PREWETT j[r].
                             mark   mark   mark
Rec: 26 Mar 1773   Harmon COOK   L.S.

DB 3, p.186 - BOLTON from LOVING   DEED, 31 Dec 1772
James LOVIN of County of Gilford in Province of North Carolinia of one part
and Robert BOLTON of Pittsylvania County and of the Colling of Virginia of
other part...for £12·03 Current Money of Virginia...100 acres South side Pigg
River...Beginning at BOULTON's corner...sough side Pig River thence Rob[t].
BOULTON's line to William YOUNGS lines, along his line to John ELLENIS...
to said River, up it as it meanders.

Wit: David NOWLIN, Eusebus HUBBARD, James X BOULTON, Ann O BOULTON
                                           mark   mark
Cert: 25 Feb 1773, Rec: 25 Mar 1773   James X LOVIN L.S.
                                                    mark

DB 3, p.187 - LACKY from WITCHER   DEED, 25 Mar 1773
Daniel WITCHER and Susannah his wife of Pittsylvania County and Colony of
Virginia of one part and Alexander LACKY of said County and Colony of other
part...for £40 Current money of Virginia...191 acres it being part (or the
one half) of a greater piece of Land on Harping Creek and made over to Will-
iam WITCHER by our Receiver General and Governor of the Kings Revenues in
this his Colony and Dominion of Virginia by way of Patent bearing Date 27
Jun 1764 and by Bargain and Sale made over by William WITCHER to Daniel
WITCHER...Crossing two Branches...in line of Original patent...up Harping
Creek as it Meanders,..now in actual Possession of Alexander LACKY
Wit: W. WITCHER, Tho[s]. LACKY, John WIMBISH   Dan[l]. X WITCHER L.S.
Rec: 25 Mar 1773 and Susanah wife of Daniel   mark
privily Exam[d]. as Law directs Relinquished
her right of dower   Susanah WITCHER L.S.

DB 3, p.190 - STOUT from RENTFROW   DEED, 13 Oct 1772
Joseph RENTFROW and Ollive his wife of Pittsylvania County and Colony of
Virginia of one part and Joseph STOUT of County and Colony aforesaid of other
part...for £250 Current Money of Virginia...Land on Both sides South fork of
Black Water River....on a branch then Down the Branch....285 acres it being
first Conveyed from Joseph RENTFRO Sen[r]. Gent. of Bedford County to the Patent
Bearing date 10 Sep 1755.   his
Wit: James RENTFRO, Nicholas ALLEE, Joseph X ELLES
                                      mark   Jo[s]. RENTFRO Jun[r]. L.S.
Cert: 25 Feb 1773, Rec: 25 Mar 1773   Ollive RENTFRO L.S.

DB 3, p.192 - LUCK from CALLAWAY   DEED, 1 Feb 1773
Francis CALLAWAY and Jean his wife of County of Bedford on one part and
Francis LUCK of County of Pittsylvania of other part...13 acres below the
Mouth of StraitStone and part lying in Halifax County...for Sum of £35 Current
money...Beginning as the Patent Begins on the River below the mouth of Strait-
stone Creek...down Stantion River.
Wit: Jemima CALLAWAY, Jn[o]. EAST, Thomas EAST, Jo[s]. EAST, William JONES,
Byrd PREWETT
                                              Francis CALLAWAY L.S.
Rec: 25 Mar 1773   Jane CALLAWAY L.S.

DB 3, p.194 - DILLARD from HARNESS   BILL SALE, 23 Dec 1772
I John HARNESS of Pittsylvania County hath Sold unto Thomas DILLARD j[r]. of
said County of Pittsylvania one Gray mare Branded on near buttock X , one
white Mare Branded & now in my possession, Two Cows & yearlings and a Heffer
Marked with a Crop and Slit and over Keel in Each Ear, Two feather Beds and
furniture and every other my Household furniture for value Received of him.
Wit: Don[d]. MC NICOLL, Abraham SHELTON, Edm[d]. KING, RWILLIAMS, H. MORGAN,
Nath[l]. WILLIAMS
Rec: 26 Mar 1773   John HARNESS L.S.

DB 3, p.194 - MURPHY from ELLIS   DEED, 29 Sep 1772
Joseph ELLES of Pittsylvania County and Colony of Virginia of one part and
William MURPHY of County and Colony aforesaid of other part...for £60 Current
Money of Virginia...Land on both sides north fork of Pigg River...on side of
a Stoney Hill...164 acres being part of Survey of 320 the Patent dated 26
Sep 1760.   his
No witnesses   Jo[s]. X ELLIS L.S.
Rec: 25 Mar 1773   mark

DB 3, p.195 - FOLEY from COPLAND   DEED, 3 Nov 1772
Peter COPLAND of County of Pittsylvania on one part and Bartholomew FOLEY of
said County on other part...£20 Current Money of Virginia...143 acres on
Sycamore Creek....on a Branch...Crossing a Branch...Crossing a small Branch.
                                       his
Wit: Richard WHITE, Tarpley WHITE, John / ROBERTS
                                      mark
Rec: 25 Mar 1773   Peter COPLAND L.S.

DB 3, p.197 - CHRISTAIN from DONALDS & C[o].   RELEASE
I hereby promise to furnish N. CHRISTIEN with a Copy of his Account ?pi_a to the
?backing of his bond. I also give up all DONALDS & C[o]. right to a mortgage
Granted by said CHRISTAIN to D. ROSS and assigned to said Company by Deed or
otherways.
Wit: James CALLAWAY   Patrick HUNTER
Rec: 26 Mar 1773   Bedford 23 March 1773

DB 3, p.197 - PIGG from CHAMBERLAYNE   DEED, 27 May 1773
Richard CHAMBERLAYNE of one part and John PIGG of other part...for £160 Curr-
ent money of Virginia...404 acres on Both sides Bareskine Creek...Between
Ralf ELKINS and Richard EKOLES...along ELKINS line...to Moses EKOLS...
No witnesses
Rec: 27 May 1773   Rich^d. CHAMBERLAYNE L.S.

DB 3, p.199 - HODGE from KIRBY   DEED, 27 May 1773
Dav^d. CIRBBY of County of Pittsylvania of one part and Josiah HODGE of said
County of other part...for £8 to him in hand paid...Land on Pigg River being
part of Robert WEAKLYS order Containing 200 acres...upon old order line on
South side said River...crossing the River.
No witnesses
Rec: 27 May 1773 and Elizabeth wife of David   David KIRBY L.S.
KERBY privily Examined and Relinquished Right of dower

DB 3, p.200 - DAVIS from COLE   DEED, 26 May 1773
James COLE of Pittsylvania County and Colony of Virginia of one part and
William DAVIS of County and colony aforesaid of other part...for £25 Lawfull
money of Virginia...49 acres on both sides Story Creek...new Lines...Crossing
the Creek...Crossing a branch...in his old line.
Wit: Jessee BOUNDS, Elenor COLE, Susanah COLE
Rec: 27 May 1773   James COLE L.S.

DB 3, p.202 - HENRY FROM HALEY   DEED, XXVI Oct 1772
Ambrose HALEY of County of Pittsylvania in Colony of Virginia planter and
Temperance his wife of other part and James HENRY of Accomack County in said
Colony of Virginia Gent of other part...for £45 Current money of Virginia...
Land on a water Course of Sandy Creek call.d John's run being part of Tract
granted by Patent to HALEY bearing date 16 Sep 1765 which said granted Premises hereby intended to be granted...Runing Course to leave out all HALEY's
cleared ground Down the East ward side of the side John's Run till line shall
come opposite to mouth of first Branch falling into John's Run below the Mill
in a Small clearing...runing cross Johns Run to mouth of said Small Water
Course...till it Intersect the line of HALEY's Patent...40 acres Including
the Water mill which HALEY now holds...said Ambrose will not build or Suffer
to be built on any Pretence whatsoever any water Grist mill of any kind or
under any names whatever on HALEY's land on Johns Run...said HALEY may be at
liberty to take away the mill House Stones plank and Iron work off the premises.
Wit: John WIMBISH, Luke WILLIAMS, Lewis HALEY, Charles WORMACK
Rec: 27 May 1773 and Temparance wife of   Ambrose HALEY L.S.
Ambrose privily Examined Relinquished her dower

DB 3, p.203 - SPEIRS & Co. from DUNN   TRUST DEED, 25 Mar 1773
I Waters DUNN of Pittsylvania County being Justly indebted unto Archebald
BUCHANAN merchant at the Rocky Ridge for Alexander SPEIRS & Co. Merchants in
Glasgow in Sum of £200 Current money and being Desirous to pay said Debt with
Costs of a Suit in Halifax County Court...sell to Archebald BUCHANAN negro
Slaves: one negroe Woman Lilley, one negroe Boy Isaace, one negro boy Addam,
one negroe man Tom, one negroe boy Will, negroe boy named Jacob...in case
Waters DUNN Shall not pay before 1 Aug 1768 one half of Debt and Interest to
SPEIRS & Co. for dealings with John ESDALE...sell for best price to dis-
charge whole Debt...pay half by 1 Aug shall forbear selling until 1 Aug 1770.
Wit: Armstead WATLINGTON, P. CARRINGTON   Waters DUNN L.S.
Shall opperate for no more then Just Ballance due said SPEIRS & Co. ·28 Jul1767
Rec: 25 Mar 1773   P. CARRINGTON

DB 3, p.205 - CLEMENT from SERTAINS   DEED, 9 Nov 1771
Josiah SERTAIN and Jacob SERTAIN of Pittsylvania County of one part and James
CLEMENTS of Bedford County of other part...Sum £55 Current money of Virginia...
190 acres on both sides frying Pan Creek being Land where Josiah and Jacob
SERTAIN now live and being part of Tract of Land of 400 granted to John GOADE,
Bounded by Deviding line but west from GOODE and SERTAINS.
Wit: James MITCHELL, Ja^s. DALTON, Robt. DALTON Junr.   his

                                               Josiah   SERTAIN L.S.
                                               mark

No recording date   Jacob SERTAIN L.S.

DB 3, p.206 - WATSON from JUSTICE   DEED OF TRUST, 4 Mar 1773
Ezra JUSTICE of Pittsylvania County on one part and John WATSON Senr. of said
County on other part...for £18·03·10 Current money of Virginia which JUSTICE
is Justly Indebted to WATSON and honestly desires to pay him..further sum of
5s like money paid by John WATSON...Land on harping Creek whereon Izra
JUSTICE now lives...after 1 Mar 1774 Sell for best price after Ten Days Pub-
lick notiçe...discharge and pay above Sum.
Wit: Arch^d. SMITH, Ja^s. SMITH, H. MORGAN
Rec: 27 May 1773   Ezra JUSTICE L.S.

DB 3, p.208 - ARMISTEAD & Co. from SERTAIN   DEED, 27 May 1773
Isaac CERTAIN of County of Pittsylvania in Virginia of one part and Moss
ARMSTEAD & Co. of County and provice aforesaid of other part...for £30 to him
in hand paid...Land on fork of white oak Creek...100 acres.
Wit: Robt. PAYNE, Charles BURTON, John TALIAFERRO   his
Rec: 27 May 1773   Isaac Ɉ CERTAIN L.S.
                                                     mark

DB 3, p.209 - MC LAUGHAN from HENRY   DEED, XXXI Oct 1772
James HENRY of Accomack County in Virginia Gen^t. of one part and Charles
MC LAUGHAN of County of Pittsylvania planter of other part...for Consider-
ation of the Good will and affection he hath unto Charles for his further
Advancement as also for further Consideration of £6 Current money of Virginia...
line of HENRY's order of Council Land to East ward of Bear Branch...Crossing
Bear Branch, with a line westerly to Intersect the line of said HENRY's order
of Council Land, along order line northerly and Easterly.
Wit: William RYBURN, William RUSSELL, Barnet MC LAUGHAN, Thomas LOVELACE
Rec: 27 May 1773   James HENRY L.S.

DB 3, p.211 - BUCKNALL from MC GEEHEE   BILL SALE, Apr 1773
I Samuel MC GEEHEE of County of Pittsylvania for Natural love and affection
which I have and bare unto Martha BUCKNALL of County of Pittsylvania and for
sum of 5s to me paid...five head of Cattle, to Witt, three Cows, one yearling
and one Calf.
            her   his
Wit: Ann C WHERLEE, Thomas BUCKNALL   Samuel X MC GEEHEE L.S.
            mark   mark
Rec: 28 May 1773

DB 3, p.211 - PHILLIPS from DODSON   DEED GIFT, 14 Dec 1772
Hannah DODSON of County of Pittsylvania of one part and Tobias PHILLIPS of
same County of other part...Sum of 5s Current money of Virginia...five negroe
Slaves: Robin, Betty, Rachel, Peter and will and their future ofspring, two
feather Beds and thir furniture, one red Cow and Heifer with a white Tail, a
black white heifer and a red & white Heifer all marked with a Slit in each

ear, two potts, two pair pott Hooks, two Iron Racks, one Bell metal Skillett, one Pewter Bason, two Dishes and two plates, one large Trunk.

Wit: Ja^s. MITCHELL, William $\cancel{M}$ LAWSON, Thos. $\diagdown$ BENNET
mark   mark   her
                                                    Hannah $\diagup$ DODSON L.S.
Rec: 27 May 1773   mark

DB 3, p.212 - TERRY from TERRY   DEED, 19 Mar 1773
Nathaniel TERRY of Halifax County of one part and David TERRY, Son of Champness TERRY, of Louisa County of other part...for £25 Current money of Virginia...179 acres on Branches of Elkhorn Creek it being the fifth and Lower
Survey part of 979 acres granted to Champness TERRY in Halifax County after
his Death which was part of a greater Quantity granted to John ROBERTSON Esqr.
by patent under Seal of our Colony dated 13 Aug 1763 and since Conveyed to
Nathaniel TERRY by deed or deeds the Last Day of General Court began and held
in October 1764...by Stephen COLEMAN's, WATKINS, John WIMBISH's & FARMERS's
Lines.
Wit: Is. READ, John SMITH, H. MORGAN
Rec: 27 May 1773   Nat. TERRY L.S.

DB 3, p.215 - TERRY from TERRY   DEED, 19 Mar 1773
Nathaniel TERRY of Halifax County and William TERRY Son of Champness of Pittsylvania of other part...for £30 Current money of Virginia...200 acres on
waters of Elkhorn Creek it being upper Survey part of 979 acres acknowledged
to Champness TERRY Senr. in Halifax Court after his Death which was part of
greater Quantity granted to John ROBERTSON Esqr. by Patents under Seal of
our Colony bearing date 13 Aug 1763 and Conveyed to Nathl. TERRY by Deed or
Deeds the Last Day of General Court began and held in Oct 1764...by Thomas
HUTCHINGS, William WILLIAMS and George WATKINS lines.
Wit: Is. READ, John SMITH, Haynes MORGAN, RWILLIAMS
Rec: 27 May 1773   Nat. TERRY L.S.

DB 3, p.216 - TERRY from TERRY   DEED, 19 Mar 1773
Nathaniel TERRY of County of Halifax of one part and Thomas TERRY, Son of
Champness, of Pittsylvania County of other part...for £30 Current money of
Virginia...200 acres on Branches of Elkhorn Creek it being the fourth Survey
and part of 979 acres Acknowledged to Champness TERRY Senr. in Halifax Court
1773 after his Death which was part of greater Quantity Granted to John
ROBERTSON Esqr. by patents under Seal of our Colony bearing date 13 Aug 1763
and since Conveyed to Nathaniel TERRY by Deed or Deeds on Last Day of General
Court that began and held in Oct 1764...by Joseph TERRY's, George WATKINS's
and Stephen COLEMAN's Lines.
Wit: Is. READ, John SMITH, H. MORGAN, RWILLIAMS
Rec: 27 May 1773   Nat. TERRY L.S.

DB 3, p.217 - TERRY from TERRY   DEED, 19 Mar 1773
Nathaniel TERRY of County of Halifax of one part and Joseph TERRY, Son of
Champness TERRY, of other part...for £30 Current money of Virginia...200
acres on Branches of Elkhorn Creek it being the third Survey and part of 979
acres acknowledged to Champness TERRY Senr. in Halifax Court after his death
which was part of greater Quantity Granted to John ROBERTSON Esqr. by patent
bearing date 13 Aug 1763. Since Conveyed to Nathaniel TERRY by Deed or Deeds
the last day of General Court that began and held in Oct 1764...by William
DICKERSON, Stephen COLEMAN and George WATKINS Lines.
Wit: Isaac READ, John SMITH, H. MORGAN, RWILLIAMS
Rec: 27 May 1773   Nat TERRY L.S.

DB 3, p.219 - DICKERSON from TERRY   DEED, 19 Mar 1773
Nathaniel TERRY OF Halifax County of one part and William DICKERSON of Charlotte County of other part...for £90 Current money of Virginia...200 acres
on Branches of Elkhorn Creek it being the Second Survey and part of 979 acres
acknowledged to Champness TERRY Sen[r]. in Halifax Court after his death which
was part of greater Quantity granted to John ROBERTSON Esq[r]. by Patent dated
13 Aug 1763 and since Conveyed to Nathaniel TERRY by Deed or Deeds bearing
date Last Day of General Court that began and held in Oct 1764...by William
TERRY, Stephen COLEMANS and George WATKINS line.
Wit: Is. READ, Haynes MORGAN, RWILLIAMS, John SMITH
Rec: 27 May 1773   Nat. TERRY L.S.

DB 3, p.220 - MEDKIFF from CHINA   DEED, 27 May 1773
Jacob China of County of Pittsylvania of one part and John MEDKIFF of Pitt-
sylvania County of other part...for £50 Current money of Virginia...Land on
Elkhorn Creek whereon John MEDKIFF now lives Containing 200 acres...Crossing
Elkhorn Creek...Crossing a branch.
No witnesses   his
Rec: 27 May 1773   Jacob X CHINA L.S.
                                                     mark

DB 3, p.222 - CALLAWAY & TRENTS from DILLARD   DEED OF TRUST, 18 Jan 1773
James DILLARD of Pittsylvania County of one part and James CALLAWAY of Bedford
County, Alexander TRENT of Cumberland County and Peterfield TRENT of Henrico
County of other part...for £60 Current money of Virginia which James DILLARD
is Justly indebted to CALLAWAY and TRENTS and Honestly desires to pay them or
their Attorneys...further Consideration of 5s like money paid by James CALLAWAY
and Alex[r]. & Peterfield TRENTS...100 acres whereon he now Dwells, on North
side Pigg River...after 5 Feb 1773 Sell for best price Giving one Months
notice...pay and Satisfy all Necessary Expences.
Wit: Justinian WILLS, Ja[s]. TALBOT, Joshua ABSTON
Rec: 28 May 1773   James DILLARD L.S.

DB 3, p.223 - STOVER from KERBY   DEED, 24 May 1773
Dav[d]. CURBY of County of Pittsylvania of one part, Obediah STOVER of said
County of other part...for £10 Current money of Virginia...150 acres being
upper the North side Pig River...following the old order...Between Obediah
STOVER and William HALL.
No witnesses   his
Rec: 27 May 1773 and Elizabeth wife of said   David X KIRBY L.S.
David privily Examined, Relinquished her Dower   mark

DB 3, p.225 - HUDSON from HUDSON   DEED, 27 May 1773
Hall HUDSON and Frances his wife of Pittsylvania County and parish of Camben
of one part & Joshua HUDSON of County and Parish aforesaid of other part...
for £50 Current money of Virginia...225 acres being part of Tract Hall HUDSON
now lives on and purchased of Henry BUFORD in Amelia County...on LIGHTFOOTS
line...on John EAST line...on Daniel SHELTON's line...near a branch...on a
hill side near White thorn Creek, down the Creek...back of the Creek at LIGHT-
FOOTS line.   Hall HUDSON L.S.
No witnesses   her
Rec: 27 May 1773   Frances ʃ HUDSON L.S
                                                     mark

DB 3, p.226 - HARBOUR from WITT   DEED, 22 May 1773
John WITT of Pittsylvania County in Virginia of one part & Elisha HARBOUR of
same County and Colony of other part...for £120 Good and Lawfull Current
money of Virginia...243 acres on waters of Marrowbone Creek...fork of said
Creek thence new lines....in TALIAFARRO's Line...up Creek as it meanders.
                              his
Wit: Robt. CHANDLER, Abner _/ HARBOUR, Archebald ROBERTSON
                            mark

Rec: 27 May 1773   John WITT L.S.

DB 3, p.228 - WALLER from CERTAIN   DEED, 27 May 1773
Isaac CERTAIN of County of Pittsylvania of one part and Zacharias WALLER of
aforesaid County of other part...for £25 to him in hand paid...100 acres...
on Isaac CERTAIN's Line...on John Geas Line...on a new line.
Wit: James SMITH   his
Rec: 27 May 1773   Isaac _/_ CERTAIN L.S.
                                                       mark

DB 3, p.230 - LEAK from LEAK   DEED, 10 Mar 1773
James LEAK and Elizabeth his wife of County of Pittsylvania of one part and
Joseph LEAK of same County of other part...for £20 Current money of Virginia...
100 acres on Elkhorn Creek...Corner of STEWARTS....down the Creek as it mean-
ders...in the old line.   James LEAK L.S.
Wit: John WIMBISH, Theop^s. LACY,   her
Luke WILLIAMS, James CONWAY   Elizabeth X LEAK L.S.
Rec: 27 May 1773   mark

DB 3, p.231 - RYON from HALE   DEED, 27 May 1773
John HALE AND Marget his wife of one part and William RYON of other part Each
of Pittsylvania County...for £80 Current money of Virginia...192 acres on a
Large branch of Snow Creek...in Randolph's line...Crossing a branch.
No witnesses   John HALE L.S.
Rec: 27 May 1773 and Margaret wife of John   Margret HALE L.S.
privily Examined Relinquished her right of dower

DB 3, p.233 - SHELTON from SHELTON   DEED, 23 May 1773
Gabriel SHELTON and Elizabeth his wife of Cambden Parrish in Pittsylvania
County of one part and Crispin SHELTON of Parish and County aforesaid of
other part...Sum of £13·04 Current money of Virginia...49 acres...part of
Tract Crispin SHELTON gave to Gabriel SHELTON in the year and adjoining Crisp-
en SHELTON's Land whereon Chrispen SHELTON now lives...on Abraham SHELTON's
line, along Crispen SHELTON's old line...along Crispin SHELTONS old Line...
on South fork of Buck Branch...up Steep bottom along new marked Line.
No witnesses   Gabriel SHELTON L.S.
Rec: 27 May 1773   Elizabeth SHELTON L.S.

DB 3, p.235 - WIMBISH from BAYES Junr.   DEED TRUST, 19 May 1773
I John BAYES jun^r. of County of Pittsylvania for Sum of £13·10 Current money
of Virginia which I am Indebted unto John WIMBISH of s^d. County and being
desires to pay him with legal Interest from this date...5 s like money...one
Red Cow and Calf unmarked the Cow has a white Spot on her rump and a white
Spot on her Shoulder, one Red and white Cow marked a Crop and underkeele in
right and two Slitts in left ear, one two year old Red Stear of same mark,
Ten head of Hogs of same mark, one red Stear yearling unmarked, one bay Horse
with a Star in his forehead, one feather Bed and furniture, all my house fur-

niture & Plantation Tools of every kind, all my Crop of Corn foder & tob[o].
now Growing...if John BAYES Jun[r]. not pay by 1 Jul next with Interest...Sell
for most he can Git in ready money.
Wit: John WHITE, Rich[d]. YEATS   John ⅃ BAYES Jun[r]. L.S.
                                                         his
Provided John BAYES Continues to live where he   mark
now lives and does not imbezle, Sell or Dispose of any part of his Estate
the Sale will not Proceed Till Christmas next.
Rec: 27 May 1773

DB 3, p.236 - WIMBISH from KING   DEED OF TRUST, 24 May 1773
I Elijah KING for Sum of £56·09·04½ Current money of Virginia which I am
Justly Indebted to John WIMBISH and for further consideration of a Bond which
I executed to Hugh CHALLES wherein John WIMBISH is my Security...further Sum
of 5s like money paid by John WIMBISH...Sell following Slaves and personal
Estate, one negro wench named Abby, one negro wench named Phillis and one
negro Boy named Jerry, 15 head of Cattle and future Increase of female Slaves
and Cattle, one Bay Horse...Sell after Ten days Publick notice....pay overplus.
Wit: John WHITE, James LEAK
Rec: 27 May 1773   Elijah KING L.S.

DB 3, p.238 - WIMBISH from MOTLEY   DEED OF TRUST, 12 Mar 1773
I Abraham MOTLEY of Pittsylvania County for Sum of £58·13·02 Current money
of Virginia which I am Justly indebted to John WIMBISH of said County and
being desires to pay with Legal Interest from this date...further Consideration of £00·05·09 like money paid by John WIMBISH...Sell Slaves, one negro
wench named Jude about 15 or 16 years of age, one negro fellow Named Abram
about 18 or 19 years of age which are now in Possession of John COX of this
County and are hired to him til 25 Dec next Together the future increase of
female Slave...one other negro Boy named Daniel about 13 years of age and now
in my own Possession...give Ten days Publick notice...Abraham MOTLEY Shall
not Secrit or Remove the three Slaves out of this County...till Debt paid.
Wit: Abra[m]. SHELTON, Beverley SHELTON
Rec: 27 May 1773   Abraham MOTLEY L.S.

DB 3, p.240 - WIMBISH from BAYES   DEED OF TRUST, 24 May 1773
I John BAYES of Pittsylvania County for Sum of £38·07 Current money of Virginia which I am Justly indebted to John WIMBISH of said County and being
desirous to Secure and pay him...5s like money...Sell one Black Horse Branded on near Buttock thus ⌐, two feather Beds and furniture and all Rest of
my Household furniture and Plantation utinsels of evey kind, 14 head of hogs
marked a Crop in right and flower Deleius in left ear, two Cows and four
yearlings of same mark of hogs, one white Cow with a little red about her face
which Cow I bought of John BUTLER her ear mark not remembered, future increase
of Stocks of hogs and Cattle, also all my Crop of Corn fodder and Tob[o]. now
Growing on my Plantation...if I fail to pay John WIMBISH above Sum with Interest by 1 Jul next...Sell for most he can get in ready money...pay overplus.
Wit: John WHITE, Dav[d]. MOSS   his
                                                John ┼ BAYES Sen[r]. L.S.
Rec: 27 May 1773   mark

DB 3, p.241 - WIMBISH from CHINA   DEED, 27 May 1773
Jacob CHINA of County of Pittsylvania of one part and John WIMBISH of Pittsylvania County of other part...for £50 Current money of Virginia...200 acres
on Elkhorn Creek...Cross a branch...in WOODSONS line...CHINA's lines...Cross
a branch and Elkhorn Creek.
No witnesses   his
                                                Jacob ✗ CHINA L.S.
Rec: 27 May 1773   mark

DB 3, p.243 - THOMAS from HARRISON's   DEED, 19 Oct 1772
James HARRISON and John HARRISON of County of Surry in province of north Car-
olina of one part and William THOMAS, administrator and heir at Law to George
THOMAS Dec^d. of Pittsylvania County in Colony of Virginia of other part...
for £105 Current money of Virignia...400 acres...at COLLINGS corner...Cross
a branch...Crossing said Creek.
Wit: Anthony HAMPTON, Jo^s. SPEARPOINT, Wade HAMPTON   James HARRISON L.S.
Cert: 26 Nov 1773, Rec: 27 May 1773   John HARRISON L.S.

DB 3, p.244 - MAYES from CHANDLER   DEED, 27 May 1773
Robert CHANDLER and Parthenia his wife of County of Pittsylvania in Colony
and Dominion of Virginia of one part and Henry MAYES of aforesaid County and
Colony of other part...for £75 Virginia Currency...Land on west side of
Marrowbone Creek...mouth of a branch on said Creek, up said Branch...in old
line...on a branch nigh the head..110 acres.
No witnesses
Rec: 27 May 1773   Robert CHANDLER L.S.

DB 3, p.245 - LANKFORD from GOING   DEED, 26 May 1773
David GOING and Martha his wife of County of Pittsylvania in Colony of Vir-
ginia of one part and Henry LANKFORD of County and Colony aforesaid of other
part...Sum of £10 Current money of said Collony...Land on west Side Russells
Creek...near said Creek on a hill Side...in old line...27 acres.
                    the mark of   his
Wit: James LYON, Robert /M\ HINTON, Obediah X HUTSON
                                             mark
Rec: 27 May 1773   David GOING L.S.

DB 3, p.247 - GRAVES from STEGALL   DEED, 4 Jan 1773
William STEGALL of Pittsylvania County and William GRAVES of Caroline County
on other part...for and in Consideration of the Rents and Services herein
after mentioned hath demised Granted Lett and to farm Lett and Grant...500
acres on South side Pigg River joyning William HAINS and Abner COCKRAM,
Lewis JINKINS and John LAW Senr. it being the Land I purchased from James
DANIEL and Hew INNES....for and during ye Term of Ten years from and after
ye date aforesaid...for Sum of £118 Current money of Virginia.
Wit: Peyton SMITH, Susannah DANIEL, Thomas POTTER   his
                                            William X STEGALL L.S.
Rec: 27 May 1773   mark

DB 3, p.247 - GRAVES from STEGALL   DEED, 9 Feb 1773
William GRAVES of County of Pittsylvania of one part and William STEGALL of
County of other part...for £25 Current money of Virginia...100 acres on ILand
Creek Beginning at Abner COCKERAMS line...to old order line...to John LAWS
line...Warrant and Defend forever in Penalty of £100 Currency.
Wit: William DANIEL j^r., William GRAVES,   his
Ja^s. DANIEL   William X STEGALL L.S.
                                                    mark
                                                    her
                                            Betsy (P STEGALL L.S.
Rec: 27 May 1773   mark

DB 3, p.249 - FIELD & CALL from DUNCAN   DEED TRUST, 8 Dec 1772
Charles DUNCAN of Pittsylvania County of one part and FIELD & CALL merchants
in Prince George County of other part...for £21·10·10 Current money of Virginia which Charles DUNCAN Stands Justly indebted to FIELD & CALL and honestly desire to pay them...5 s like money...Sell Ten head of Cattle marked with

a Carpenders Square in Each ear, eight head of hoggs of same as Cattle and three Dack bay mares, one branded with $\mathcal{S}$ on near Shoulder and off Buttock $\mathcal{S}$ and near Buttock $\backslash\!\!\backslash\!\!/$ and one with thus $\varnothing\!\!/$ on near Buttock and a Small nick in her ear the other with χ on near Buttock, a young Two year old Colt nither Docked nor Branded with their Increase, also Two Beds and Furniture, Seven pewter plates and Six Basons and all the Corn and household furniture and everything belonging to Charles DUNCAN of his Property...after 25 Day of this Instant Oct 1772...Sell for best price after Ten days Publick notice...Interest from 25 Dec 1772 until fully discharged.
Wit: John WILSON, John DICKINSON

Rec: 27 May 1773

his
Charles   X   DUNCAN L.S.
mark

DB 3, p.251 - ROBERTS from SHORT   DEED TRUST, 4 Jan 1773
Joell SHORT of County of Pittsylvania of one part and Joseph ROBARTS of said County on other part...for £20 which Joell SHORT is Justly Indebted to Joseph ROBERTS and honestly desires to pay...further Sum of 5s Like money...Sell 100 acres Joining Lands of Jehu MORTON and Elisha DYER being the Plantation where on Joell SHORT now lives...after 25 Dec Sell for best price after Ten Days Publick notice...with Interest.   Joell SHORT L.S.
Wit: Don^d. MC NICOLE, Abra^m. SHELTON, Elisha FARRIS
I Joseph ROBERTS for within mentioned consideration...have received of George MURDOCK do assign over to said George MURDOCK all my Claim right property and interest to within expressed Deed of trust for the Land...26 May 1773
Wit: Is. READ, Ben LANKFORD, Don^d. MC NICOLE
Rec: 27 May 1773   Joseph ROBORTS

DB 3, p.253 - VESTRYMEN from CHAMBERLAYNE   DEED, 28 May 1773
Richard CHAMBERLAYNE of parish of St. Peters in County of New Kent of one part and John DONELSON, John PIGG, Crispin SHELTON, John WILSON, Peter PERKINS, Thomas DILLARD j^r., Hugh INNES, Theop^s. LACY, Abraham SHELTON, George ROWLAND, Robert CHANDLER and William WITCHER Gent. Vesterymen of Parish of cambden in Pittsylvania of other part...for £160 Current money of Virginia...for the use of a Glebe Settlement...588 acres it being of a Greater Tract Granted to Richard CHAMBERLAYNE by pattent bearing date 15 Aug 1770...Pointers in old line.
Wit: John SALMON, Peter PERKINS, Abraham SHELTON
Rec: 28 May 1773   Rich^d. CHAMBERLAYNE L.S.

DB 3, p.254 - HAMILTON from LUMKIN   DEED, 4 May 1773
George LUMKIN and Mary his wife of County of Pittsylv^a. in Colony of Virginia of one part and Thomas HAMILTON of same County and Colony of other part...for £20 Current money of Virginia...Land on Branches of Marrowbone Creek...in small Branch on HAMILTON line, up said Branch a Small peace to the head...to HICKES or LENEARS back line...along David LINARS line...old order line...to Lemuell LENEARS line...to James TAYLORS line...100 acres.
Wit: Gregory DURHAM, Dan^1. FORD, Mich^r. ROWLAND, Alex^r. MC KEEN
Rec: 27 May 1773   George LUMKIN L.S.

DB 3, p.256 - HALL from KERBY   DEED, 24 May 1773
David KERBY of County of Pittsylvania of one part, William HALL of County of other part...for £11 Current money of Virginia...150 acres North side Pigg River...an order of old line, following old line.
No witnesses
Rec: 27 May 1773 and Elizabeth wife of said David   David X KIRBY L.S.
privily Exam^d. and Relinquished her right of dower   mark

DB3, p.257 - MEIRS from CHANDLER   DEED, 26 May 1773
Robert CHANDLER of County of Pittsylvania of one part and Stephen MEIRS of
same County of other part...Sum of £75 Current money of Virginia...220 acres
being part of Lands of said Robt. CHANDLERS Tract, Beginning at fork of a
Branch North of the plantation that John MAJOR Settled on the Land...North
fork of the Branch to old order line...to MAYES Branch, Down the Branch to
marrowbone Creek, down the Creek to first branch.
No witnesses
Rec: 27 May 1773   Robert CHANDLER L.S.

DB 3, p.259 - MACKAIN from LUMKIN   DEED, 27 Mar 1773
George LUMKIN and Mary his wife of County of Pittsylvania on Colony of Virginia of one part and Hugh MC CAIN of County aforesaid and Colony of Virginia of other part...for £50 Current money of Virginia...Land on main long
Branch of marrowbone Creek the harycain Branch...at above Branch is the LANES
line Showed to his own Land bought of George LUMKIN Containing 100 acres...
Runing to main Creek from mouth of said Branch up the Creek to MC CAINS line.

Wit: Thomas his mark WILLINGHAM, Robt. CHANDLER, John his mark HARDIMAN, Lem^l. LENEAR
Rec: 27 May 1773   George LUMKIN L.S.

DB 3, p.260 - TALBOT from BURNETT   BILL SALE, 27 May 1773
I Charles BURNETT of Pittsylv^a. County for Sum of £21·02·08 Current money of
Virginia paid by John TALBOT of same County I do Sell Nine head of Cattle,
Two Cows and Calfs, one Cow and Earling and three two year old heiffers of
Different marks which Cattle and their Increase.
Test: James TALBOT   Charles his mark BURNET L.S.
Rec: 27 May 1773

DB 3, p.261 - MATLOCK from WITT   BILL SALE, 11 May 1773
I John WITT of County of Pittsylvania and Colony of Virginia for divers Good
Causes and Considerations...more Especially for Good will and natural affect-
ion I bear to John MATLOCK of aforesaid County do give and bequeath to him
50 acres, being part of tract of Land I now live on...beginning at Thomas
HARBOURS corner Crossing the Creek...Crossing a Branch.
Rec: 27 May 1773   John WITT L.S.

DB 3, p.261 - HENRY from PERRYMAN   DEED, 11 Apr 1773
Richard PERRYMAN of County of Bedford and Parrish of Russell of one part and
Thomas HENRY of County of Pittsylvania and Parrish of Cambden of other part...
for £50 Current money of Virginia...125 acres on both sides Mill Creek, bound-
ed as by a Deed Conveyed by Anthony STREET and William HAWKINS to Richard
PERRYMAN and Recorded in County Court of Pittsylvania...paying Rent of one
pepper Corn on Lady Day next if same Shall be Lawfull Demanded to the intent
and purpose...of the Statute for Transferring uses into Possession.
Wit: Jno. HENRY, Molly HENRY, Mary PURNALL
Rec: 27 May 1773   Rich^d. PERRYMAN L.S.

DB 3, p.263 - ABSTON from DILLARD & CLEMENTS   DEED, 1 Jan 1773
Jesse ABSTON of County of Bedford of one part and Thomas DILLARD j^r. and
Martha his wife and Isaac CLEMENTS and Anne his wife of County of Pittsylvania of other part...for £50 Current money of Virginia in hand paid...Land
on Both sides ready Creek Containing 214 acres...reference being had to the

Pattent bareing date 20 Jun 1772.
Wit: George MURDOCK, William TODD, Spencer SHELTON, Crispen SHELTON,
Abraham SHELTON
Rec: 27 May 1773 and Ann wife of said Isaac   Thomas DILLARDj^r. L.S.
privily Examined Relinquished her right of Dower   Isaac CLEMENT L.S.

DB 3, p.264 - WITT from HARBOUR   DEED, 22 May 1773
Adonijah HARBOUR of Pittsylvania County in Virginia of one part and John WITT
Senr. of same County and Colony of other part...for £40 Good and Lawfull Cur-
rent money of Virginia...200 acres on both sides fall Creek of Mayo River
being the Lower part of the Tract that Thomas HARBOUR Senr. gave to David WITT
and Palatiah SHELTON.   his
Wit: Robert CHANDLER, Abner ⅃ HARBOUR, Archibald ROBERTSON
No rec. date   mark

                                                  Adonijah HARBOUR L.S.

DB 3, p.266 - HUDSON from HINTEN   DEED, 27 May 1773
William HINTEN of County of Pittsylvania of one part and Obediah HUTSON of
same County of other part...for £100 Current money of Virginia...175 acres
on both sides Russels Creek.   his
No witnesses   William Robert ⋈ HINTEN L.S.
Rec: 27 May 1773 and Mary wife of William Robert   mark
Privily Exam^d. Relinquished her right of Dower   her
to above Granted Land and premises   Mary ⟲ HINTEN L.S.
                                                  mark

DB 3, p.267 - MC DONALD from CARTER   DEED, 27 Apr 1773
George CARTER of Pittsylvania County Planter and Isaac MC DONALD of Bedford
County Joiner...for £100 Good and Lawfull money of Virginia...Land on both
the forks of Rock castle Creek otherwise Call.d peeping Creek Containing 300
acres...N^o. fork of said Creek...Crossing two Branches...Crossing South fork
of said Creek...South fork of Rock castle, down said fork to mouth north fork.
Wit: Timothy STAMPS, Thos. LOVELACE
Rec: 27 May 1773 and Mary wife of George privily
Exam^d. Relinq^d. her right of dower   George CARTER L.S.

DB 3, p.269 - ROBERSON from PIGG   DEED, 23 Mar 1773
John PIGG of Pittsylvania County and Jesse ROBINSON of County and Colony
aforesaid...200 acres being part of that Tract that Capt. John PIGGS mill
Stands on...on both sides Banister River...Beginning on South side of mill
pond...in WALLERS line...Crossing the River...Crossing the mill pond.
No witnesses
Rec: 27 May 1773   John PIGG L.S.

DB 3, p.270 - SMITH from SINGLETON   DEED, 27 May 1770
Robert SINGLETON of Pittsylvania County of one part and James SMITH of said
County of other part...for £70 Current money of Virginia...618 acres on Waters
of Tomahawk Creek and Buckhorn Branch...in JEFFERSONS line...in CHESWELLS line.
Wit: Arch^d. SMITH, Jo^s. MORTON, Jo^s. CUNNINGHAM
Rec: 27 May 1773 and Susannah wife of said Robert
privily Exam^d. Relinquished her right of dower   Robert SINGLETON L.S.

DB 3, p.272 - MEDCALF from PARSONS   DEED, 26 May 1773
Joseph PARSONS of Pittsylvania of one part and James MEDCALF of same County
and Colloney aforesaid of other part...Sum of £36·10 Good and Lawfull money

part of a Tract of Land in said County Containing 50 acres, part of 386 acres
Survey for Richard PARSONS on both sides Little Cherrystone Creek...CURRYS
order...to MARTINS order.

Joseph PARSONS L.S. (his mark)

Wit: Richard PERRYMAN, William MOORE,
Stephen YATES
Rec: 27 May 1773 and Peggey wife of said Joseph
privily Examined Relinquished her right of Dower

Peggy PARSONS L.S. (her mark)

DB 3, p.273 - NOWLAND from MEAD   DEED, 23 Feb 1773
William MEAD of Bedford County of one part and John NOWLAND of Pittsylvania
County of other part...for £40 to him in hand paid...420 acres on South side
Black Water River...Down the same as it meanders.
Wit: JWALKER, RWILLIAMS, John AYLETT
Rec: 28 May 1773   W^m. MEAD L.S.

DB 3, p.274 - BROWN from RUSSELL   DEED, 15 Jan 1773
George RUSSELL of North Carolina in Surrey County of one part and John BROWN
of Pittsylvania County in Virginia of other part...for £20 to him in hand
paid...16 acres on both sides Cascade Creek...Beginning at WATKINS corner
Runing up old line...fork of a gut Absolums BOSTICKS corner...a Cross the
Creek to BOSTICKS and WATKINS corner along WATKINS lines...it being the 16
acres that Richard BROWN bought of George RUSSELL.

Wit: Dav^d. HARRIS, Joseph HARRIS (his mark), William STEPHENS (his mark), Absalum BOSTICK
Rec: 27 May 1773   George RUSSELL L.S.

DB 3, p.276 - ROSS from SUTTON   DEED, 30 Apr 1773
Christopher SUTTON of Parish of Antrim in County of Pittsylvania of one part
and David ROSS of County of Dinwidie of other part...Sum of £35 to him in
hand paid...150 acres...north side frying pann Creek thence along BOTOBETTS
line...Crossing the Creek...Crossing a branch...up the Creek as it meanders.
Wit: Ansel GEORGE, Jno. CAMPBELL, George HERNDON
Rec: 27 May 1773   Christopher SUTTON L.S.

DB 3, p.278 - KEEN from KERBY   DEED, 24 May 1773
David KERBY of County of Pittsylv^a. of one part and Currell KEEN of said
County of other part...£8 Current money of Virginia...100 acres upon North
side Pigg River...following a old line...oak Joynin of KERBYS line.
No witnesses
Rec: 27 May 1773 and Elizabeth wife of said   David X KERBY L.S. (his mark)
David privily Exam^d. Relinquished her right of dower

DB 3, p.279 - LYON from HENTON   DEED, 21 Feb 1773
William HENTON and Mary his wife of County of Pittsylvania in Colony of Vir-
ginia of one part and James LYON of same County and Collony of other part...
Sum of £5 Current money of said Colony...Both sides Russells Creek...in
HENTONS line on South side of Creek...Crossing said Creek...a new Devision
line between LYON and HENTON...54 acres.
Wit: Arch^s. HUGHES, Jonathan HANBY,   W^m. Robert HINTON L.S. (his mark)
Hamon CRITZ Junr.
Rec: 27 May 1773 and Mary wife of said HINTON   Mary HINTON L.S. (her mark)
privily Exam^d. as Law directs Relinquished
her right of dower

DB 3, p.280 - FISHER from LEAK j^r.   DEED, 24 May 1773
James LEAK Junr. of County of Pittsylvania of one part and John FISHER of
Chesterfield County of other part...for £100 Current money of Virginia...Land
on Elkhorn Creek where said James LEAK formerly lived Containing 100 acres...
Beginning on South side said Creek in James LEAKE Senr. his old line...to a
Bent opposet to Joseph LEAKES Plantation where it Crosses the Creek...Cross-
ing a Branch...it being part of 200 acres Conveyed to said Ja^s. LEAK Junr.
by James LEAK the Elder by Deed Bearing date 20 Mar 1771 and Recorded in
Pittsylvania Court.
Wit: Elijah KING, John WHITE, John WIMBISH
Cert: 25 Mar 1773, rec: 24 Jun 1773   James LEAK Junr. L.S.

DB 3, p.282 - WILLIAMS from GOODMAN   BILL OF SALE, 6 Jun 1773
I William GOODMAN of Pittsylvania for Consideration of £20 Current money of
Virginia paid by RoWILLIAMS of said County hath Sold to Robt. WILLIAMS one
bed and furniture, one Horse Bridle and Sadle, Six plates, one Dish, one
Bason, one pott, one Blankit, one Case of Knives and forks, one Gunn and all
my Joiners tools.
Wit: Matthew MILLS, Thos. HODGES, Edm^d. TAYLOR
Rec: 24 Jun 1773   W^m. GOODMAN L.S.

DB 3, p.283 - BELCHER from HEARD   DEED, 24 Jun 1771
Stephen HEARD and Isum BELCHER of Pittsylvania County...Sum of £20 paid...93
acres on the Timber Ridge, in Pittsylvania County...Crossing a branch of
Simmons Creek.   his
No witnesses   Stephen   HEARD Senr. L.S.
Rec: 24 Jun 1773   mark

DB 3, p.284 - ROBERSON from SAUNDERS   BILL OF SALE, 4 Jun 1773
I Charles SAUNDERS of Amhurst County Bargain and Sell unto Jesse ROBINSON of
Pittsylvania County one Sorrel mare with a white face Branded on near Should-
er O and on near Buttock O , also one Black mare about Twelve years old
with a not on one of her fore legg...£18 Current Money of Virginia.
Wit: John PIGG, Edey OWEN
Rec: 24 Jun 1773   Charles SAUNDERS L.S.

DB 3, p.285 - BOOKER from HOPKINS   DEED OF TRUST, 24 Jun 1773
Richard BOOKER of one part and Arthur HOPKINS of County of Pittsylvania of
other part...Sum of £42·02·04 due to Richard BOOKER by Bond payable 24 June
also for Consideration of Sum of 5s..Sold a negro Wench named Silvey, negro
fellow named George, negro fellow named Bowson, negro Wench named Moll...
before 25 Dec next ensuing Sell to highest Bidder for ready money having first
advertised the Sale in the Virginia Gazette and Likewise at Pittsylvania
Court house...pay overplus if any.
Wit: Rich^d. MOORE, Robt. PAYNE, Moss ARMSTEAD
Rec: 24 Jun 1773   Arther HOPKINS L.S.

DB 3, p.286 - HUNT from HUNT   DED^s., 27 May in 13th year of our Reign
George the third by the grace of god of great Brittain France and Ireland
King Defender of the Faith &c to James HUNT, Thomas CARTER and John BRENT or
any two of his majestys Justices of County of Charlotte Greeting whereas
Charles HUNT by his Indenture of Feoffment hath conveyed unto Nathaniel HUNT
of County of Halifax...402 acres...Tabbitha wife of said Charles HUNT cannot
Conveniantly Travel to and from our County Court of Pittsylvania...apart
from said Husband Relinquish her Right of Dower...that you Certifie to our

Justices of our Court.

Will. TUNSTALL

By Virtue of above Dedimus...have Examined Tabitha HUNT wife of Charles HUNT apart from her Husband...voluntarily Relinqhished her Right of Dower this 28 May 1773.

James HUNT L.S.
Thomas CARTER L.S.

DB 3, p.287 - MURDOCK & C°. from SHELTON   DEED OF TRUST, 19 Jun 1773
Gabriel SHELTON of County of Pittsylvania of one part and Thomas MURDOCK for James MURDOCK & C°. of said County of other part...Sum of £176.15·02 which Gabriel SHELTON is Justly Indebted to Thomas MURDOCK for James MURDOCK & C°. and honestly desire to pay them...Sum of 5s like money...200 acres lying upon whitethorn and Joining Lands of Crispin SHELTON and Daniel SHELTON being part of Tract whereon Gabriel SHELTON now lives, also 400 acres on Stinking River Joining Lands of Thomas MUSTEEN, Lewis SHELTON and the Estate of Col°. William LIGHTFOOT being half of 800 acres belonging to Gabriel SHELTON and John EAST...Shall after 25 Dec 1774 Sell for best price after Giving Ten Days Publick notice...Interest from 19 Jun 1773 untill fully discharged.
Wit: Don^d. MC NICOLE, W^m. LONDON, Armstead SHELTON
Rec: 24 Jun 1773   Gabriel SHELTON L.S.

DB 3, p.289 - FARRIS from EAST   DEED, 24 Jun 1773
John EAST of Parish of Cambden in County of Pittsylvania of one part and Elisha FARRIS of Parrish and County aforesaid of other part...Sum of £50 Current money of Virginia...30 acres...on Hickeys Road thence along John CLEVERS line to William TODDS line, along his line to flyflow Creek, down the Creek to Hickeys Road.
No witnesses
Rec: 24 Jun 1773   John EAST L.S.

DB 3, p.290 - FULTCHER from ROBERTS   DEED, 1762
James ROBERTS of County of Pittsylvania of one part and William FULTCHER of other part...Sum of £50 Current money of Virginia...Land in County of Pitt-sylvania formerly Halifax Containing 325 acres lying on South Branch of Sand Creek...Deviding line which is marked and agreed on as may appear in every point by a Deed from Peter WILSON to David LAY Recorded in County Court of Halifax.   her
Wit: John SALMON, Jo^s. ASHURSTH, Susannah ✗ STOVALL
                                             mark
Rec: 24 Jun 1773   James ROBERTS L.S.

DB 3, p.292 - HENDERSON from TALBOT   DEED, 26 May 1773
Charles TALBOT of County of Bedford of one part and James HENDERSON of County of Pittsylvania of other part...for £70 Current money of Virginia... 260 acres on Drafts of allens Creek...in Benjamin LANKFORDS line...near CLEMENTS Road...Crossing Rocky Creek...Crossing a Branch...in Daniel MORGANS line...in Joseph FARRIS line...Deviding line Between John HARNESS and Charles TALBOTT...in the old line Joining the new Survey.
No witnesses
Rec: 24 Jun 1773   Charles TALBOTT L.S.

DB 3, p.293 - ABSTON from DILLARD   DED^s., 31 May 1773
George the third by the grace of god of great Brittain France and Ireland King Defender of the Faith &c John DONELSON, Crispin SHELTON and Benjamin

LANKFORD or any two of his majestys Justices of the County of Pittsylvania
Greeting whereas Thomas DILLARD j[r]. by his Indenture of Feoffment hath Con-
veyed unto Jesse ABSTON of County of Pittsylvania...214 acres and whereas
Martha DILLARD wife of Thomas DILLARD j[r]. cannot Conveniantly Travel to said
County Court of Pittsylvania...Examine Martha from and apart from her Husband
whether she does freely Relinquish her Right of Dower.

Will. TUNSTALL

By virtue of above Dedimus we have Examined Martha DILLARD...did freely Relinquish her Right of Dower.   Benj[a]. LANKFORD L.S.
Rec: 24 Jun 1773   Crispen SHELTON L.S.

DB 3, p.294 - TALBOT from HARNESS DED[s]., 19th May in 13th year of our Reign
George the third by the grace of god of great Brittain France and Ireland...
To Benjamin LANKFORD, Thomas DILLARD & John DONELSON or any two of his majes-
tys Justices of County of Pittsylvania...whereas John HARNESS by Indenture of
Feoffment hath conveyed unto Charles TALBOT of County of Bedford...260 acres
of Land and whereas Elizabeth wife of John HARNESS cannot Conveniantly Travel
to and from our County Court...Examine whether she freely and voluntarily
Relinquishes her right of Dower in and to Land.   Will. TUNSTALL
By virtue of above Dedimus we have Examined Elizabeth the wife of John HARNESS
apart from her Husband...Certifie that Elizabeth Relinquishes her Right of
Dower 31 May 1773.   Thomas DILLARD j[r]. L.S.
Rec: 24 Jun 1773   Benj[a]. LANKFORD L.S.

DB 3, p.295 - CLEVER from ROGERS   DEED, 20 May 1773
John ROGERS of Bedford County (attorney in fact for Thomas DOUGHERTY of Pen-
sylvania formerly of Virginia Charlotte County) of other part and John CLEVER
of Pittsylvania County of other part...for £18 Current money of Virginia...
Land in Countys of Pittsylvania & Halifax on Buffoloe Creek Containing 400
acres...at MARCHBANK's lower Corner...Crossing two Branches...to Luke SMITH's
line...Crossing the Creek.
Wit: Haynes MORGAN, Is. READ, RWILLIAMS
Rec: 24 Jun 1773   John RODGERS L.S.

DB 3, p.297 - MAGBEE from PERKINS   DEED, 24 Jun 1773
Nicholas PERKINS of Parish of Cambden in County of Pittsylvania of one part
and William MAGBEE of Parish and County aforesaid of other part...Sum of £150
Current money of Virginia...650 acres on both Sides mountain Creek it being
part of a greater Tract Granted to William BEEN by Patent Bearing date 30 Aug
1763...on Jeremiah WALKERS line...Crossing said Creek or a Branch...Crossing
two Branches and the Creek.
No witnesses
Rec: 24 Jun 1773   Nicholas PERKINS L.S.

DB 3, p.299 - SPANGLER from BIRD   DEED, 21 Jun 1773
Francis BIRD of Pittsylvania County and Colony of Virginia of one part and
Daniel SPANGLER of same County & colony of other part...for Sum of £150 to
him in hand paid...Land on both side of South Branch of Black Water River
Containing 250 acres...Crossing a branch...in Daniel DONOHOES line...Cross-
ing three Branches.
No witnesses
Rec: 24 Jun 1773   Francis BIRD L.S.

DB 3, p.300 - FITZ PATRICK from CHISUM's   DEED, 27 Jun 1770

John CHISUM and James CHISUM of Halifax County of one part and John F[erased]
PATRICK of Bedford County of other part...for £220 Current money of Virginia...
400 acres on South side Stanton River opposet RANDOLPHS long Island...on the
River thence by a Deviding line between John CHISUM and John DYER...on old
Patent line...lines of new patent...down the River as it meanders.
Wit: Elijah CHISUM, John ESTIS   John CHISUM L.S.
Rec: 24 Jun 1773   James CHISUM L.S.

DB 3, p.302 - MURDOCK from PAYNE Senr.   DEED TRUST, 23 Jun 1773

John PAYNE Senr. of County of Pittsylvania of one part and Thomas MURDOCK for
James MURDOCK & Co. of s^d. County of other part...for £102·03·07½ Curr^t.
money of Virginia which said John PAYNE Senr. is Justly Indebted to Thomas
MURDOCK for James MURDOCK & Co. and honestly desire to pay...farther Sum of
5s like money...400 acres upon north fork of white thorn and Joining lands
of Hugh INNES and John THRIFT also a copper Still and worm, one Compleat
Sett of Black Smiths Tools...Shall after 25 Dec 1774 Sell for best price...
Lawfull Interest from 23 Jun 1773 until fully discharged.
Wit: Don^d. MC NICOLE
Rec: 24 Jun 1773   John PAYNE Senr. L.S.

DB 3, p.304 - PENN from COPLAND   DEED, 30 Oct 1772

Peter COPLAND of County of Pittsylvania on one part and Abraham PENN of
County of Amhurst on other part...for £65·10 Current money of Virginia...
Land on Bever Creek...125 acres...oak by a path...crossing Beaver Creek.
Wit: John STOKES, Charles COPLAND, Thomas COOPER Junr.
Rec: 24 Jun 1773   Peter COPLAND L.S.

DB 3, p.305 - COOPER from COPLAND   DEED, 1 Apr 1773

Peter COPLAND of County of Pittsylvania on one part and Joseph COOPER of
same County on other part...for £34 Current money...112 acres on Beaver
Creek...corner of Ambrose JONES's land...down the Creek as it meanders.
Wit: Thomas COOPER jun^r., James ANTHONY
Rec: 24 Jun 1773   Peter COPLAND L.S.

DB 3, p.307 - ANTHONY from COPLAND   DEED, 31 Oct 1772

Peter COPLAND of County of Pittsylvania on one part and James ANTHONY of
County of Bedford on other part...Sum of £150 Current money of Virginia...
350 acres on Beaver Creek...on west Bank of Beaver Creek...to Joseph COOPERS
red oak...in Abraham PENN's line...Crossing Beaver Creek...Thomas COOPERS
corner...to mouth of Cooper Creek, thence up Beaver Creek as it meanders.

Wit: John WELLS, Thomas COOPER Junr., Edwd. his
                                      / JONES
                                 mark

Rec: 24 Jun 1773   Peter COPLAND L.S.

DB 3, p.309 - MURDOCK & Co. from MATHEWS   DEED TRUST, 27 Apr 1772

Samuell MATTHEWS of County of Pittsylvania of one part and James MURDOCK & Company of said County on other part...for £50 Current money of Virginia which
Samuell MATHEWS is Justly Indebted to James MURDOCK and Company & Honestly
desires to pay...in farther Consideration of sum of 5s like money...Land in
County of Pittsylvania Joining Lands of Meshack TURNER and Jo^s. BAYES Containing by Estimation 600 acres...Likewise one Sorrell Horse not Branded, one

Bay mare Branded on Left Buttock this $\emptyset$, one Cow & Calf mark with a under
Keille in Right ear and Crop in left...after 1 Dec 1772 Sell for best price
after Ten Days Publick notice...discharge pay and Satisfy themselves.
Wit: John PAYNE, William SHORT, R. FARGUSON
Rec: 22 Jul 1773   Samuell MATHEWS L.S.

DB 3, p.311 - ROBERTS from KEEZEE   DEED, 19 May 1773
Rich^d. KEEZEE and Anne his wife of Parish of Cambden and County of Pittsylvania of one part and Joseph ROBERTS of Parish and County aforesaid of other
part...for £100 Current money of Virginia...87 1/2 acres on both sides Stinking River...Beginning on Stinking River the north side in Ja^s. BREWAS's line
to Charles FARRIS's line...up the River as it meanders to HAWKINS corner...
crossing the River...to Fulker FULKERSON's line...to John EAST new line...on
a Small Branch down same to mouth in Stinking River.
Wit: Crispin SHELTON, Jno. PAYNE, Jno. GRIGGORY, Abra. SHELTON
Cert: 27 May 1773, Rec: 22 Jul 1773   Richard KEEZEE L.S.

DB 3, p.312 - LYONS from CHILDS   DEED, 22 Jul 1773
Francis CHILDS of County of Pittsylvania of one part and James LYONS of s^d.
County of other part...for £40 Current money of Virginia...200 acres on both
sides South fork of Mayo River...Crossing the river and a branch...Crossing
a Creek...South Crossing the River.   her
No witnesses   Frances ⌒ CHILDS L.S.
Rec: 22 Jul 1773   mark

DB 3, p.314 - WIMBISH from FARRIS   DEED OF TRUST, 9 Jun 1773
Know ye that I William FARRIS of Pittsylvania County for £38·14 Current money
of Virginia which I am Justly indebted to John WIMBISH of the s^d. County and
being desirous to pay him the same with legal Interest from this date...for
further Consideration of 5s like money paid by Jno. WIMBISH...Sell one Bay
Horse Branded with a hook on near Buttock and has a Slitt in right ear, one
other Bay horse his right eye out and has some white hairs about his head neck
and tail, 21 head of Cattle, 23 head of Hoggs marked with two Slits in each
ear, all the Cattle and Hoqs I own with future Increase, also three feather
Beds and furniture, one Rifle Gunn, all my Pewter, House furniture and plantation utensils of every kind......Sell for most that can be got.
Wit: Jno. WHITE, Luke WILLIAMS   his
                                                    William W FARRIS L.S.
Rec: 22 Jul 1773   mark

DB 3, p.315 - FARGUSON from FARGUSON   DEED OF TRUST, 15 Jan 1773
Joseph FARGUSON of Parish of Cambden and County of Pittsylvania of one part
and Robert FARGUSON of County and Parish aforesaid of other part...for £20
Current money of Virginia which Joseph FARGUSON is Justly indebted to Robert
FARGUSON and honestly desires to pay...farther Consideration of 5s like money...
Seven Head of Cattle one of which is marked with a Swallow fork in each ear
the other Six are marked with two Crops and a hole in the Left ear Together
with all the future Increase, one feather Bed and furniture, two Iron potts
and Sundry Pewter as also all his other Household and Kitchen furniture...
after 16 Jan 1774 Sell for best price...pay overplus if any.
Wit: William TODD, Milly FARGUSON, Eliz^a. FARGUSON
Rec: 22 Jul 1773   Joseph FARGUSON L.S.

DB 3, p.317 - KING from COLLINS   DEED, 13 Jul 1773

William COLLINS of Pittsylvania County of one part and James KING of same County...Sum of £30 to him in hand pay...300 acres on east Branches of Great Strait Stone and west side of Allens Mountain...Crossing a branch...upon the old line, thence along that line.
Wit: Edm^d. KING, Hermon KING, Joel SHORT
Rec: 22 Jul 1773   William COLLINS L.S.

DB 3, p. 318 - CALLAND & Co. from JUSTICE   DEED, 1 Jun 1773

John JUSTICE of County of Pittsylvania of one part and Samuel CALLAND & Co. of said County of other part...for £40 Current money which Jno. JUSTICE is Justly indebted to Saml. CALLAND & Co. and honestly desire to pay...farther consideration of 5s like money...Tract of Land formerly the property of George WALTON the main Road going through the Land Containing 100 acres, it being the Land whereon Jno. JUSTICE lives at this time...Deed made by Jno. JUSTICE father unto him Recorded in Halifax County...after 25 Dec 1773 Sell for best price after Ten Days Publick notice...Discharge above Sum.

Wit: Jno. GLASS, Harmon COOK, Thos. X LAWRANCE, Paul RAZAR, W^m. YOUNG
                       his / mark
Cert: 24 Jun 1773, Rec: 22 Jul 1773   Jno. JUSTICE L.S.

DB 3, p.320 - CALLAND & Co. from YOUNG   DEED OF TRUST, 20 Jul 1773

William YOUNG of County of Pittsylvania of one part and Samuel CALLAND & Co. of County of Pittsylvania on other...for £100 Current money of Virginia which William YOUNG is truely Indebted to Saml. CALLAND & Co. and desireing to pay him and further Consideration of 5s like money...Land on Pig River it being part of an order of Council Surveyed formerly for Ashford HUGHES and William GRAY...on Jno. ELLIS line...on Benjamin POTTERS line...to William HAYNES line thence along his line to William STEGALLS line...to old order line....1,250 acres...also one Tract on Sycamore Creek...it being the Land Surveyed for Thomas HUFF...after 25 Dec 1774 Sell to highest Bidder after Giving ten days publick notice....pay overplus if any.
Wit: Jo?. CRAWFORD
Rec: 22 Jul 1773   William YOUNG L.S.

DB 3, p.322 - WALTERS from WALTERS   DEED, 21 Jul 1773

Thomas WALTERS of Pittsylvania County on other part planter and John WALTERS of said County planter on other part...for £100 Good and Lawful Money of Virginia...Land on both sides Lower Double Creek of Dann...north side Lower Double Creek...Crossing said Creek...down the Creek...Corner of Jeremiah VIDETOES...near a branch Corner of William CHANDLER...Containing 200 acres.
Wit: George CARTER, Rich^d. CARTER, Robt. WALTERS   his
Rec: 22 Jul 1773   Thomas T WALTERS L.S.
                             mark

DB 3, p.324 - JEFFERSON from YOUNG   DEED, 22 Jul 1773

William YOUNG of Pittsylvania County of one part and George JEFFERSON of Lunenburg County of other part...for £50 Current money...166 acres on Turkey Cock Creek...near Snow Creek in GRAYHAMS line...in old line...by branch.
No witnesses
Rec: 22 Jul 1773   W^m. YOUNG L.S.

DB 3, p.325 - RAGSDALE from MURPHY   DED[s]., 8 May In 13th year of our Reign
George the third by grace of god of great Brittain France and Ireland King
Defender of the Faith &c to Gideon WRIGHT, Charles MC HANALLY and Moses
MARTIN Esq[rs]. or any two of his majestys Justices of the County of Surry...
whereas Richard MURPHY by Indenture of Feoffment hath Conveyed to William
RAGSDALE of County of Pittsylvania one Certain Tract of Land Containing 200
acres and whereas Keziah the wife of Richard Cannot Conveniantly travel to
and from our said County Court of Pittsylvania...Trusting to your faithfull
and provident Circumspection in Examining Keziah apart from her Husband...
whether she freely Relinquishes her Right of Dower.   Will. TUNSTALL
By virtue of above Dedimus we have Examined Keziah the wife of Rich[d]. MURPHY
apart from her husband...hereby Certifie did Relinquish her Right of Dower.
12 Jul 1773   Gideon WRIGHT   L.S.
                                                Charles MC HANALLY L.S.
Rec: 22 Jul 1773   Moses MARTIN   L.S.

DB 3, p.326 - HAILE from CHRISTAIN   DEED, 5 Jan 1773
Nathaniel CHRISTAIN and Jean his wife of County of Pittsylvania and Lewis
HAILE of Bedford of other part...by Indenture Bearing date the day before the
date whereof for Consideration therein mentioned did Grant and Sell to Lewis
HAILE 130 acres it being part Pattent Granted to Thomas HESTIE on 15 Jul 1760
Including the plantation whereon Nathaniel CHRISTAIN now lives...on the River..
for £47·10 Current money.
Wit: Parmenas HAYNES, Jonathan PRATT, Gwyne DUDLY   Nathaniel CHRISTAIN L.S.
Rec: 22 Jul 1773   Jean CHRISTAIN   L.S.

DB 3, p.329 - ADAMS from TAYLOR   DEED, 22 Jul 1773
James TAYLOR of County of Amelia of one part and William ADAMS of County of
Pittsylvania of other part...for £20 Current money to him in hand paid...
Land on South side Gobblin Town Creek...on Smiths River up the same as it
meanders...upper side of Creek...Crossing the Creek. [no acreage given]
No witnesses
Rec: 22 Jul 1773   James TAYLOR   L.S.

DB 3, p.330 - STEGALL from INNES   DEED, 22 Jul 1773
Hugh INNES of parrish of Cambden in County of Pittsylvania of one part and
William STEGALL of Parrish and County aforesaid planter of other part...for
£100 Current Lawfull money of Virginia...Land on Pig River...on the Bank of
the River above the fish Trap...to old line a westerly Course to the line
that Devides Samuel CANTERBURY part of said 550 acres...in William STEGALS
line...Containing 300 acres.
No witnesses
Rec: 22 Jul 1773   Hugh INNES   L.S.

DB 3, p.332 - WATLINGTON FROM PORTAS   DEED TRUST, 23 Jul 1773
John PORTAS OF County of Pitts[a]. of one part and Armistead WATLINGTON of
County of Halifax of other part...for £6 Current money which Jn[o].PORTAS is
Justly indebted to Armistead WATLINGTON and honestly desire to pay to him...
further Consideration of Sum of 5s Like money...two Cows and two Calves mark-
ed with a Swallow fork and under keel on the Right ear and a Crop and two
Slits in left ear and one mare Branded with thus *O.O.O.* on the near Shoulder.
Sell for best price that can be gotten after Giving Ten Days Publick notice...

                           his
Wit: Haynes MORGAN, Rich[d]. ⚘ PIGG
                          mark
Rec: 22 Jul 1773   John PORTARS   L.S.

DB 3, p.333, LUMKIN j^r. from LUMKIN Senr.   BILL SALE, 10 Jun 1773

I George LUMKIN of Pittsylvania County have Bargained and Delivered to George
LUMKIN j^r. One Black mare with a Stare in her forehead Branded on near Butt-
ock thus $\mathcal{FS}$ paces and Trotts and her Colt and one Gray mare abought one
year old for £20 to me in hand paid.
Wit: Jno. WILSON, jn^o. LUMKIN
Rec: 22 Jul 1773   George LUMKIN L.S.

DB 3, p.334 - ADAMS from PIGG   DEED, 22 Jul 1773

William PIGG of Pittsylvania County of one part and John ADAMS of same county
of other part...for £10 Current money of Virginia...14 acres on South side
Banister River...on said ADAMS line on said River, along FINNES line...new
line marked by Reubin PAYNE and James STONE to head of a small Branch.
No witnesses
Rec: 22 Jul 1773   William PIGG L.S.

DB 3, p.335 - JEFFERSON from JEFFERSON   DEED, 19 Jun 1773

George JEFFERSON of Lunenburg County of one part and John JEFFERSON of Cum-
berland County of other part...Sum of £180 Current money...500 acres on
Turkey Cock Creek...being part of a larger Tract purchased by George JEFFER-
SON of Clement READ Dec^d..
Wit: Peter F. JEFFERSON, Sam. GARLAND, Susanah NICHOLS
Rec: 22 Jul 1773   G. JEFFERSON L.S.

DB 3, p.336 - CARTER from CARTER   DEED, 21 Jul 1773

Richard and Frances CARTER wife of said Richard of Halifax County of one part
and George CARTER of Pittsylvania County of other part...for £12·10 Good and
Lawfull money of Virginia...100 acres on Draughts of Lower Double Creek of
Dann...at VADETOES corner now a Corner of Capt. Jno. WILSONS...in WILSONS
line, along his line.
                 his
Wit: Thomas $\mathcal{T}$ WALTERS, Jno. WALTERS, Robt. WALTERS
                mark   Richard CARTER L.S.
Rec: 22 Jul 1773   Frances CARTER L.S.

DB 3, p.338 - WATKINS from CANNADAY   DEED, 23 Apr 1773

William CANNADAY of one part Jno. WATKINS of County of Pittsylvania of other
part...for £25 Current money to him in hand paid...375 acres...Beginning at
Thomas WALTERS corner...Crossing a branch...in WATERS line.
                                          his
Wit: Jno. WALTERS, Robt. WALTERS, Thomas X MADING
Rec: 22 Jul 1773   mark   William CANNADAY L.S.

DB 3, p.340 - BURNS from WEBB   DEED, 20 Jul 1773

Merry WEBB of Pittsylvania County of one part and Samuel BURNS of County
aforesaid of other part...for £20 to him in hand paid...45 acres on South
side Ervin River...Beginning at his own Corner on the River side thence on
his line...Down the River as it meanders.
No witnesses
Rec: 22 Jul 1773   Merry WEBB L.S.

DB 3, p.341 - LEWIS from MC DANIEL   DEED, 23 Sep 1773

William MC DANIEL Gent. of County of Halifax of one part and John LEWIS Gent.
Elder of County of Pittsylv^a. of other part...Sum of £1005 Current money of
Virginia...Two Tracts of Land on North side Dann River One Tract whereon John
LEWIS now lives and Contains 443 acres...Contain the whole of three Different

Purchases of said William MC DANIEL Viz. 275 acres of the Honble William BYRD Esqr. with 16 acres MC DANIEL purchased of Nathaniel TERRY Gen^t. as by their Deeds now in possession of said LEWIS...Together with 152 acres lying Contiguous to aforesaid two Tracts the same being patented for s^d. MC DANIEL 14 Feb 1771...on both sides Sandy Creek and Contains 299 acres being the whole of that patent Granted to said MC DANIEL 15 Aug 1764 Together with a Survey of 404 acres Lying between and adjoyning aforesaid Lands and which Survey makes whole Lands Contiguous and whereas William MC DANIEL Gen^t. did some years ago give to Jno.   DONELSON Gent. Surveyer of Pittsylvania a proper Certificate...to Issue his proper Certificate to our Secretary office to Include a patent to Jno. LEWIS for above patented 742 acres with new Survey of 404 acres ...considering that MC DANIELS Certificate may be Lost or mislaid.
No Witnesses
Rec: 23 Sep 1773 and Ann wife of said William
privily Examined relinquished her Right of Dower   William MC DANIEL L.S.

DB 3, p.343 - CALLAND & Co. from ATKINSON   DEED TRUST,15 Mar 1773
Henry ATKINSON of County of Pittsylvania of one part and Samuel CALLAND & Co. of s^d. County of other...Sum of £20 Current money of Virginia which Henry ATKINSON Senr. is Truly indebted to Samuel CALLAND & Co. & Honestly desireing to pay him...Sum of 5s paid by Samuel CALLAND & Co....Land on Pig River joining William ATKINSON Senr. Bounded by Pig River on south side it being the Land Henry ATKINSON Now lives on which he Bought of his Brother Parker ATKINSON 50 acres...more fully appear by his Deed he had from his Father William ATKINSON Senr. now in office of aforesaid County...after 1 May 1774 Sell to Highest Bidder for Ready money.
                                       his
Wit: W^m. PEEKE, W^m. YOUNG, Morris /M/ ATKINSON, Jno. HUNDLEY, Joseph CALLAND,
                                      mark   his
Thos. MURDOCK, Geo. MURDOCK   Henry /—/ ATKINSON Sen. L.S.
Cert: 27 May 1773, Rec: 23 Sep 1773   mark

DB 3, p.345 - TODD to KING   BOND FOR BUILDG. A BRIDGE, 14 Aug 1773
We William TODD, Daniel SHELTON and John EAST of County of Pittsylvania are bound unto our Sovereign Lord King George the Third in Sum of £100 Current money...Whereas above bound William TODD Hath this day undertaken to build a Bridge across Stinking River near where the Waggon Road Crosses said River... if William TODD doth keep and maintain the Bridge in Good repair for and during Term of Seven years from 1 Nov next...above obligation void.
Wit: Jno. DONELSON, Crispin SHELTON   William TODD L.S.
                                                        Daniel SHELTON L.S.
                                                        Jno. EAST L.S.

DB 3, p.345 - WIMBISH from MEDKIFF   30 Aug 1773
Jno. MEDKIFF of Pittsylvania County of one part and Jno. WIMBISH of said County of other part...for £50 Current money of Virginia...100 acres on both sides Elk horn Creek...along patent line...crossing the Creek.
Wit: Luke WILLIAMS, Rawley WHITE, Richard PASS
Rec: 23 Sep 1773   Jno. MEDKIFF L.S.

DB 3, p.347 - ROBERTSON from ESKRIDGE DED^s.21 Jul in 13th year of our Reign
To Robert CHANDLER & Arch^s. HUGHES or any two his majestys Justices of County of Pittsylvania Greeting whereas Burdit ESKRIDGE by his Indenture of Feoffment conveyed unto Archibald ROBERTSON of County of Pittsylvania Tract of

Land containing 345 acres and whereas Ann ESKRIDGE the wife of Burdit cannot
Conveniantly travel to our County Court of Pittsylvania...Trusting to your
faithfull & provident Circumspection in Examining Ann ESKRIDGE apart from
her Husband whether she does freely Relinquish her Right of Dower.
By virtue of above Dedimus...Certifie Ann did freely Relinquish her right
of Dower 17 Sep 1773.

Robt. CHANDLER L.S.

Rec: 23 Sep 1773   Arch^s. HUGHES L.S.

DB 3, p.348 - ARMISTEAD & Co. from GEE   DEED OF TRUST, 21 Aug 1773
I John GEE of Pittsylvania County for Sum of £35 Current money of Virginia
which I am Justly Indebted unto Moss ARMISTEAD & Co. and being desirous to
pay same...further consideration of 5s like money...Sell a Dark Bay mare
Branded with a Crop on near Buttock, one Cow and Earling mark with a Swallow
fork in left ear and Slit in right Ear, Two Feather Beds and furniture, all
rest of my Household furniture of what kind soever, also my Crop of Corn &
Tobacco that is now Growing, 18 Head of Hoggs mark.d with a Swallow fork in
left ear and a Slit in right ear...after 10 Mar next ensuing...Sell for as
much as they can Get in ready money...Discharge debt.   his
Wit: Thomas OWEN, Henry STONE, Ch. BURTON   John X GEE L.S.
Rec: 23 Sep 1773   mark

DB 3, p.349 - CALLAWAY from DILLINGHAM   DEED, 14 Sep 1773
Vachel DILLINGHAM of County of Pittsylvania of one part and James CALLAWAY
of County of Bedford of other part...for £120 Lawfull money of Virginia...
100 acres on both sides south fork of Black water being the Land Covyed to
him by James RENTFROW...Corner Tree of Capt. Joseph RENTFROW also of Mathew
TALBOTTS...to SPRINGLES corner.
Wit: Gross SCRUGGS, William COOK, James RENTFROW Junr., Peter VARDEMAN
Rec: 23 Sep 1773   Vachel DILLINGHAM L.S.

DB 3, p.350 - CALLAWAY from COOK   DEED, 23 Sep 1773
William COOK of County of Pittsylvania of one part and James CALLAWAY of
County of Bedford of other part...Sum of £62·10 Current Lawfull money of Vir-
ginia...188 acres on both sides fox Run.
No witnesses
Rec: 23 Sep 1773 and Margaret Wife of William   William COOK L.S.
COOK privily Examined Relinquished her Right of Dower

DB 3, p.351 - JONES from FLOWER   DEED, 26 Aug 1773
Thomas FLOWER of Pittsylvania County in Virginia of one part and Jno. JONES
Senr. of same County and Colony afores^d. of other part...for £60 Good and
Lawfull Current money of Virginia...140 acres...on branch of Wighing Creek
thence New Lines...Crossing Wighen Creek...South fork of Creek....to Mouth
of a Branch, up said Branch.
No witnesses   Thomas FLOWER L.S.
Rec: 23 Sep 1773 and Prudence wife of said   Prudence FLOWER L.S.
Thomas Examined Relinquished her Right of Dower

DB 3, p.353 - SOUTHERLAND from LITTLES   DEED, 15 Jun 1773
Anne LITTLE and Charles LITTLE of Pittsylvania County of one part and George
SOUTHERLAND of said county of other part...Sum of £222 Curr^t. money to them
in hand paid...Land on North side Dan River and Joining Down to Mouth of
Sandy River Containin 80 acres...mouth of Sandy River, up the River as it

meanders...to Valentine HATCHERS line, Down his line to Dan River as it meanders.

her
Anne A LITTLE L.S.
mark
his
Charles C LITTLE L.S.
mark

Wit: Peter PERKINS, Jn°. WILSON,
Absolum BOSTICK, John DICKINSON

DB 3, p.354 - RENTFROW from COOK   DEED, 23 Sep 1773

William COOK of County of Pittsylvania of one part and James RENTFRO Junr.
of same County of other part...for £100 Current money of Virginia...220 acres
on both sides fox Run.
No witnesses
Rec: 23 Sep 1773 and Margaret wife of William
Prively Examined Relinquished her Right of dower   William COOK L.S.

DB 3, p.356 - WITCHER from DOSS   DEED, 23 Sep 1773

Zachias DOSS and Elizabeth DOSS of Bedford County planter of one part and
Daniel WITCHER of Pittsylv^a. County planter of other part...for £28 Current
money of Virginia...50 acres on North side Pigg River...Down the River.
Wit: W^m. WITCHER, Henry MC DANIEL, James MITCHELL   his
Rec: 23 Sep 1773 and Elizabeth wife of said   Zachias DOSS L.S.
Zachias privily Examined as Law directs Rel-   mark
inquished her Right of Dower   Elizabeth DOSS L.S.

DB 3, p.357 - POTEET from CRAWLEY   DEED, 23 Sep 1773

Benj^a. CROWLEY of Pittsylvania and James POTEET of Bedford County...for £120
Current money of Virginia...380 acres upon Elk Creek...by a Branch.
No witnesses   his
Rec: 23 Sep 1773 and Sarah wife of s^d.   Benjamin CROWLEY L.S
Benjamin privily Examined Relinquished her Dower   mark

DB 3, p.359 - INNES from DONELSON   DEED TRUST, 22 Jul MDCCLXX??

John DONELSON of County of Pittsylvania of one part and Hugh INNES of said
County of other part...for £1000 Current money for which Sum John DONELSON
stands Justly indebted to Hugh INNES he said John DONELSON having received
the Value thereof from said Hugh INNES...sell 1019 acres being the Tract of
Land whereon said John now lives also the following Slaves: Peter, Cancer,
Toby, James, Somerset, Frank, Jacob, Ben, George, Joe, Sampson, Hannah,
Sarah, agnes, Candus, Lariana, Rodde & Winny...with their Increase...if John
DONELSON shall pay Hugh INNES full Sum before 22 Jul MDCCLXXV in following
manner, Viz, John DONELSON to Deliver to Hugh INNES forty Tuns of Iron at
eight equal payments after date of this Deed on or before 22 Jul MDCCLXXV
Viz. five Tunns of Barr Iron on or before 22 Oct next ensuing and other five
Tunns of Barr Iron on or before 22 Jan MDCCLXXIV and other five Tunns of Barr
Iron on or before 22 Apr in said year and other five Tunns on or before 22
Jul in said last year and other five Tunns of barr Iron on or before 22 Oct
in said Last year and other five Tunns of Barr Iron on or before 22 Jan in
year MDCCLXXV and other five Tunns of Barr Iron at or before 22 Apr in said
last year and other five Tunns of Barr Iron on or before 22 Jul in said Last year.
Hugh INNES doth oblige himself to Discount said £1000 allowing for each Tunn
Sum of £25... pay before 22 Jul MDCCLXXV
Wit: Abra^m. SHELTON, Jn°. TODD j^r., Jn°. PARR
Rec: 23 Sep 1773   Jn°. DONELSON L.S.

DB 3, p.361 - CREEL from DODSON   DEED, 22 Jun 1773
Thomas DODSON of County of Pittsylvania in Colony of Virginia of one part
and John CREEL of County and colony aforesaid of other part...for £50 Current money of Virginia...200 acres on both sides Burch Creek...as it meanders
to a Sharp Corner.d Rock on side of said Creek...Crossing the mill Pond to
oak near the road...in the mill yard.
Wit: Jeffery JOHNSON, Dav^d. DODSON, Caleb DODSON
Rec: 23 Sep 1773   Thomas DODSON Senr. L.S.

DB 3, p.362 - DODSON from CREEL   B^d, 22 Jun 1773
I John CREEL of County of Pittsylv^a. and Colony of Virginia are held and firmly Bound and stand Justly Indebted unto Thomas DODSON or his wife in Sum of
£1000 Current money of Virginia...Condition of above obligation is such that
if the above Bound John CREEL Shall Continue to find Thomas DODSON and his
wife a place to live on during their lives which shall be the place whereon
they now live as the place whereon they formerly lived or such a place as
Shall Content them when this is Complyed with above obligation to be void
otherwise in full force Power and Virtue.
Wit: Jeffery JOHNSON, Dav^d. DODSON, Caleb DODSON
Rec: 23 Sep 1773   John CREEL L.S.

DB 3, p.362 - HENDERSON from CREEL   DEED, 22 Sep 1773
Jno. CREEL of County of Pittsylvania in Colony of Virginia of one part and
John HENDERSON of County and Colony aforesaid of other part...Sum of £40
Current money of Virginia...150 acres on both sides Irvin River or Smiths
River...Beginning at STINETS corner...on an Ivy Hill...Crossing the River...
oak on a Hill...to flat Creek, Down the Creek as it meanders to the mouth.
Wit: Jeffery JOHNSON, Thomas HILL, Caleb DODSON
Rec: 23 Sep 1773   John CREEL L.S.

DB 3, p.364 - WINFARRY from HARDY   DEED, 20 Aug 1773
Thomas HARDY Junr. of Pittsylvania of one part and John WINFARRY of County of
Cumberland of other part...for Consideration of one Tract of Surveyed Land
containing 298 acres on both sides the India Field Branch Transfered to him
before the Ensealing of thes presents...Hath Given Granted Swopt and Confirm-
ed to John WINFERRY Tract of Land on Sweeting fork of Sandy Creek containing
400 acres...south side Sandy Creek...Crossing two Branches...in Pittsylvania
County.   his
No witnesses   Thomas   HARDY L.S.
Rec: 23 Sep 1773 and Mary wife of said Thomas   mark
Privily Examined Relinquished her Right of Dower

DB 3, p.365 - SHORT from CLAY's   DEED, 31 Jul 1773
By and Between William CLAY Senr. & Jesse CLAY and John Randall SHORT of
Pittsylvania...William & Jesse CLAY for sum of £30 to them in hand paid sold
unto John Randall SHORT...Land on Black Water River...south side of River at
a valey that doth Devide s^d. Land from Land of Michael CLAY...to back line...
along old line to the River thence down the River....58 acres.
Wit: Jessee HEARD, W^m. COCKERHAM, Stephen HEARD, Chedle COCKERHAM,
Thomas SHORT   William CLAY L.S.
Rec: 23 Sep 1773   Jessee CLAY L.S.

DB 3, p.367 - PURNELL from INNES   DEED, 23 Sep 1773
Hugh INNES Gent. of parrish of Cambden in County of Pittsylvania of one part
and Mary PURNELL of Parish and County aforesaid of one part...Sum of £70 Current money of Virginia...Land on both sides White Thorn Creek...Crossing a
Branch...Crossing two Brances...Crossing the Creek Several times...Crossing
four Branches..it being the Land Granted to Hugh INNES by Letters Patent bearing date at Williamsburgh 1 Aug 1772. [No acreage given]
No witnesses
Rec: 24 Sep 1773   Hugh INNES L.S.

DB 3, p.368 - MAYBERRY from JONES   DEED, 23 Sep 1773
John JONES of Pittsylvania County of one part and Jo^s. MABRY of aforesaid
County of other part...for £100 of Good and Lawfull Money of Virginia...200
acres part of 400 acres Surveyed for William RICKEL on both sides south
Branch of south fork of Sandy River...in Lower East line and Runing a due
West Course to upper West line.
No witnesses   Jno. F F JONES Senr. L.S.
Rec: 23 Sep 1773   mark

DB 3, p.369 - RENTFRO from COOK   DEED, 23 Sep 1773
William COOK of Pittsylvania County and Colony of Virginia of one part and
James RENTFRO of County & Colony aforesaid...for £10 Current money to him in
hand...60 acres on fox Run a branch of Black Water River...in old line.
No witnesses
Rec: 23 Sep 1773 and Margeret wife of W^m. privily
Examined Relinq^d. her Right of dower   William COOK L.S.

DB 3, p.371 - RUSSELL from KERBY   DEED, 15 Sep 1773
David KIRBY of County of Pittsylvania of one part and Peter RUSSELL of said
County of other part...for £25 Current money of Virginia...100 acres...upon
Pig River joining to HODGES line Runing up a branch to the head...joining
William HALLS line.   his
Wit: Elisha ESTIS, Jno. BROCK, Obed X STOBER   his
                              mark   Dav^d. X KERBY L.S.
Rec: 24 Sep 1773   mark

DB 3, p.371 - CRAUFURD from LANIER   DEED OF TRUST, 21 Sep 1773
David LANIER of County of Pittsylvania of one part and Thomas CRAUFURD of
County of Brunswick of other part..for £220 Current money which David LANIER
is Justly indebted to Thomas CRAUFURD and Honestly desire to pay to him...
farther Consideration of Sum of 5s Like money...Land on waters of Marrowbone
Creek whereon LANIER now lives which he Purchased of George LUMKIN, Bounded
as expressed in a Deed from LUMKIN to LANIER Recorded in County Court and Con-
tains 273 acres, also Negroe man named Plato Purchased by him from said CRAU-
FORD...after 1 Oct 1774...Sell for best price after Ten Days Publick notice...
with Lawfull Interest from 21 Sep 1773 until fully discharged.
Wit: Robert TURNBULL, Edward WALKER, Archebald ROBERTSON
Rec: 23 Sep 1773   David LANIER L.S.

DB 3, p.373 - MURDOCK & Co. from MURPHEY   DEED OF TRUST, 15 Jul 1773
James MURPHEY of County of Pittsylvania of one part and Thomas MURDOCK for
James MURDOCK & Co. of said County of other part...for £59·18·09½ Current
Money which James MURPHEY justly Indebted to Thomas MURDOCK & Co. and Honest-
ly desire to pay...farther consideration of sum of 5s Like money...Sell 200
acres of Land upon a Branch of Elkhorn Creek and Joining the Lands of James

LEAK Senr. and Thomas GLASSCOCK being the Plantation whereon James MURPHEY
now lives...Nevertheless after 25 Dec 1774...Sell for best Price.
Wit: Don^d. MC NICOLE, Francis HENRY, Robt. FARGUSON.
Rec: 23 Sep 1773   James MURPHEY L.S.

DB 3, p.374 - BUCKLEY from STONE   DEED, 18 Aug 1773
Joshua STONE of County of Pittsylvania of one part and James BUCKLEY of same
County of other part...for £150 Current money of Virginia...Land on both
sides Allens Creek including the Plantation where STONE now lives Containing
200 acres...on old line...in another Branch...along the Rockey Hill and oak
on east fork of Allens Creek, down the Creek as it meanders to oak Just above
the Plantation...to Joseph FARRIS's.
Wit: Thos. DILLARD j^r., Ben. LANKFORD, James WILSON

                                                       Joshua STONE L.S.

DB 3, p.376 - BUCKLEY from STONE   DED^s., 12 Aug 13th year of our Reign
George the third by grace of god of great Brittain France & Ireland King
Defender of the Faith &c To Thomas DILLARD, Benjamin LANKFORD and Crispin
SHELTON Gent. or any two his majestys Justices of County of Pittsylvania...
Joshua STONE by his Indenture of Feoffment hath Conveyed unto James BUCKLEY
of County of Pittsylvania...200 acres...whereas Mary wife of Joshua STONE
cannot Conveniently Travel to and from our County Court...Trusting to your
faithfull and Provident Circumspection in Examining Mary...whether she does
freely Relinquish her Right of Dower.
                                                       Will. TUNSTALL
By Virtue of above Dedimus we have Examined Mary wife of Joshua STONE apart
from her Husband...did freely & Volentarily Relinquish her Right of Dower
this 18 Aug 1773.
                                             Thomas DILLARDj^r. L.S.
Rec: 25 Nov 1773   Ben. LANKFORD L.S.

DB 3, p.377 - CUNINGHAM FROM SHIELDS   DEED, 13 Oct 1773
James SHIELDS of Pittsylvania County one the one part and Joseph CUNINGHAM
of said County one the other part...for £3 Current money of Virginia...eleven
acres and Ten poles on South fork of Sandy River...on James SHIELDS line.
Wit: Joseph SHIELDS, W^m. RICHEY, William SHIELDS
Rec: 25 Nov 1773   James SHIELDS L.S.

DB 3, p.378 - HENRY from POLLEY   DEED, 22 Oct 1773
Edward POLLEY of Parish of Cambden and County of Pitsylvania of one part and
John HENRY of Parish and County aforesaid of other part...for £25 Current
Money of Virginia...Land on Branches of Mill Creek it being part of a Greater
Tract which was Granted to Christopher GORMAN by Patent bearing date at Will-
iamsburg 25 Sep 1762 and Conveyed by Christopher GORMAN to Jno. GORMAN by
Deed recorded in County Court of Halifax and by John GORMAN Conveyed to said
Edward POLLEY by Deed recorded in County Court of Pittsylvania Containing 100
acres...Beginning at a Branch on ADAMS line...on HICKS line so Concluding the
upper Part of 294 acres for Compliment.
Wit: John COX, Nottley WHEATE, James COX, Jo^s. AKIN   his
                                             Edward (/) POLLEY L.S.
Rec: 25 Nov 1773   mark

DB 3, p.380 - PERKINS from MAGBEE   DEED OF TRUST, 28 Aug 1773
William MAGBEE of Pittsylvania County of one part and Nicholas PERKINS of
said County of other part...for Sum of £88 Current Money of Virginia which

William MAGBEE is justly Indebted to Nicholas PERKINS and Honestly desire to
pay...in farther Consideration of 5s like Money...Sell to Nicholas PERKINS
one Sorrell mare Branded thus on off buttock K and on Near Buttock thus
A , One Sorrell mare Branded on near Buttock thus θ , one Sorrell mare
Branded on near Buttock thus RP, two year old Colts one a Bay the other
Sorrell both Branded on near Buttock thus 76 , 20 head Cattle marked with
two Swallow forks, two feather Beds Bed Steads & all the furniture, 12 plates,
Six Dishes & ten Basons, four pots Spoons Knives & forks and Remainder of
house hold furniture, four head of Sheep marked with a Swallow fork in each
Ear, two Big bibles and BUCKLEY writings on the New Testament, one Hoghead
of Tob°. Pris.d lying on Burchets Creek and all my crop of Tob°. made this
year on Mountain Creek and Corn that is now on said Plantation...after 10 Oct
1774 Sell for best price...interest from 1 Oct 1773 until fully Discharged...
pay overplus.

Wit: Peter PERKINS, Jn°. $\mathcal{F}$ LAIN, Rach¹. $\times$ MAGBEE, Jn°. P. SMITH
mark   mark

William M MAGBEE L.S.
Rec: 25 Nov 1773   mark

DB 3, p.382 - MURDOCK & C°. from DOSS   DEED OF TRUST, 5 Jun 1773

Thomas DOSS of County of Pittsylvania of one part and James MURDOCK & C°. of
said County of other part...for £31·02·03½ which Thomas DOSS is Justly indebted to James MURDOCK & C°. and honestly desire to pay...farther Consideration of 5s like money...Land on Stinking River and Joining Lands of Thomas
MUSTEIN and Jacob FARRIS being the Plantation whereon Thomas DOSS now lives,
One Sorrell mare and one Bay Horse both Branded on near Buttock this θ ,
one Bay Horse Branded on Near Shoulder and Buttock thus 96, one Bay Colt
not Branded, three Cows, three Heiffers, two yearlings and one Calf marked
with a hole in Right Ear and two smoth Crops, 20 head of hoggs Marked the
same with the Cattle, Two feather Beds & furniture with my household & Kitchen furniture and Plantation Utenciles...after 25 Dec 1774 Sell for best
price...Discharge above sum...Interest from 5 Jun 1773 until Discharge.
Wit: John CLEVER, Will. TODD, Thomas MURDOCK
Cert: 22 Jul 1773, Rec: 25 Nov 1773   Thomas DOSS L.S.

DB 3, p.384 - SIMS from COX   DEED, 27 Jan 1773

Jacob COX of County of Surry and Province of north Carolina of one part and
Jn°. SIMS of County of Pittsyvania and Colony of Virginia of other part...
sum of £45 Current money of Virginia...119 1/2 acres on waters of Green
Creek...on Bank of south Mayo River and on north side...up the River.
Wit: Archˢ. HUGHES, Henry FRANCE, Frederick FULKINSON
Cert: 25 Mar 1773, Rec: 25 Nov 1773   Jacob COX L.S.

DB 3, p.386 - THOMPSON from HILL   DEED, 25 Nov 1773

Thomas HILL of Pittsylvania County on one part and John THOMPSON of said
County on other part...for £30 Current Money of Virginia...100 acres on waters
of Strawberry Creek as by Deed from James BLACKLIE to said Thomas HILL Rec-
orded in Pittsylvania Court
No witnesses   Thomas $\bigvee$ HILL L.S.
Rec: 25 Nov 1773   mark

DB 3, p.387 - LACY's BOND FOR SHERIFALTY   25 Oct 1773

We Theophilus LACY, Joseph MORTON, Jn°. DIX, Thomas DILLARD jʳ., William
TUNSTALL, Henry MC DANIEL, John PIGG, John WILSON, William THOMAS, Benjamin

LANKFORD and John MORTON of County of Pittsylvania are bound to our Sovereign
Lord King George the third...sum of £1000 Current Money...Condition of above
obligation...above Bound Theophilus LACY is Constituted and appointed Sherif
of the County...collect all officers fees and dues put in his hands...pay
same to officers.   Theop^s LACY L.S.   Joseph MORTON L.S.
Rec: 25 Nov 1773   John DIX L.S.   Thomas DILLARD j^r. L.S.
                                Will TUNSTALL L.S.   Henry MC DANIEL L.S.
                                John PIGG L.S.   Jno. WILSON L.S.
                                William THOMAS L.S.   Benj^a. LANKFORD L.S.
                                John MORTON L.S.

DB 3, p.388 - LACY's BOND FOR SHERIFALTY   25 Nov 1773
Theophilus LACY, Jo^s. MORTON, John DIX, John PIGG, W^m. TUNSTALL, Thomas
DILLARD, Henry MC DANIEL, John WILSON, William THOMAS, Benj^a. LANKFORD &
John MORTON of County of Pittsylvania are Bound unto Sovereign Lord King
George the third...£1000 Current Money...Theophilus LACY is Constituted &
appointed Sherif of the County...Commission from his Excellency the Governor
under Seal of Colony dated 25 Oct...Collect all Quitrents fines forfeitures
& amerciaments Accuring or becoming due...Account for & pay to officers of
his Majestys Revenue on or before second Tuesday in June annually.
No witnesses   Theop^s. LACY L.S.   John DIX L.S.
Rec: 25 Nov 1773   Joseph MORTON L.S.   John PIGG L.S.
                                Will. TUNSTALL L.S.   Thos. DILLARD j^r. L.S.
                                Henry MC DANIEL L.S.   Jno. WILSON L.S.
                                W^m. THOMAS L.S.   Benj^a. LANKFORD L.S.
                                Jno. MORTON L.S.

DB 3, p.389 - HANKINS from MORTON   DEED, 25 Nov 1773
James MORTON of Pittsylvania County of one part & Daniel HANKINS of same
County of other part...for £72 Current Money of Virginia...96 acres on Rob-
ert's Creek of Sandy River,including the place where said HANKINS is building
a Mill and also all Damages that may accure to MORTONS other Land by said
Mills being built.
No witnesses
Rec: 25 Nov 1773   James MORTON L.S.

DB 3, p.391 - MC KINSEY from PIGG   DEED, 22 Nov 1773
John PIGG of County of Pittsylvania of one part and Daniel MC KINZEY of
County of other part...£50 Current Money to him in hand paid...100 acres on
both sides Bearskin Creek being part of Tract of 400 acres of said PIGGS &
lying at Lower end...in Original Patent, Runs with s^d. Patent north...across
the whole original Tract...on the great rode side.
No witnesses
Rec: 25 Nov 1773   John PIGG L.S.

DB 3, p.392 - LOVELL from TOWNSEND   DEED, 18 Nov 1773
Thomas TOWNSAND of County of Pittsylvania in Colony of Virginia of one part
and Daniel LOVELL of same place of other part...Sum of £40 Current Money of
Virginia ...Land on both sides Great Cherry Stone Creek...Containing 150
acres it being part of Greater quantity Granted by Patent to John LOVING...
in WATSONS line...Cross the Creek...Cross a Branch...it being the Land and
plantation whereon Charles BELEW did live.   his

Wit: Jno. PORTARS, William LOVELL, George P PARSONS   his
                                       mark   Thomas T TOWNSAND L.S.
Rec: 25 Nov 1773   mark

166.

DB 3, p.395 - HARDMAN from HARDMAN   DEED, 27 Jul 1773
John HARDMAN of County of Pittsylvania of one part and William HARDMAN Son of
said John HARDMAN of other part...for natural Love & affection which he hath
and beareth unto s^d. William HARDMAN and for better maintenance and Livehood
give 100 acres of Land...Corner of Lemuel LANIER on west side Marrowbone
Creek, along LANIERS line...small Brance then Down the meadows of said brance,
on the Creek, down the said.
Wit: Lem^l. LANIER, Jessee WILLINGHAM, Elizabeth LANIER   his
Rec: 25 Nov 1773   John 2 HARDMAN L.S.
                                                    mark

DB. 3, p.396 - YOUNG from YOUNG   BILL SALE, 4 Aug 1773
I Allen Ridley YOUNG of Pittsylv^a. County have this Day Sold unto Archibald
YOUNG of said County one feather Bed & furniture, two Pewter Basons, nine
Pewter plates, one Spining wheel, half dozen Knives & forks, two water pails
and one Washing Tubb, two Small Chests, one Iron Pott & fraying pan and two
flatt Irons for Consideration of one entrey of Land on Leatherwood Creek...
if said Allen Ridley YOUNG shall pay unto said Archibald YOUNG £20 Good and
Lawfull Money of Virginia by 10 Aug 1775 above Bill shall be void.
                                    his
Wit: Shem COOK, Junr., Henry // BOND, William YOUNG
                                  mark
Rec: 25 Nov 1773   Allen Ridley YOUNG L.S.

DB 3, p.397 - YOUNG from YOUNG   DEED, 24 Nov 1773
William YOUNG of Pittsylvania County of one part and Archibald YOUNG of said
County of other part...£50 Current Money of Virginia...100 acres on both
sides Snow Creek...on Arch^d. GRAHAMS line, along said YOUNGS old line...Cross-
ing Snow Creek to George JEFFERSONS line.
No witnesses
Rec: 25 Nov 1773   William YOUNG L.S.

DB 3, p.398 - SMITH from TALBOT   DED^s., 25 Mar in 13th year of our Reign
George the third by the grace of god of great Brittain France & Ireland King
Defender of the Faith &c to [no names inserted here] or any two of his Maj-
estys Justices of County of Bedford Greeting whereas Charles TALBOT by his
Indenture of Feoffment hath conveyed unto Peyton SMITH of County of Pittsylvania Tract of Land Containing 100 acres and whereas Drucilla the wife of
said Chas. TALBOT cannot Conveniantly Travel to and from our County Court...
Trusting your faithfull and Provident Circumspection in Examining Drucilla...
if she freely Relinquishes her Right of Dower.
Bedford Sc^t.   By virtue of above Dedimus we have Examined Drucilla the
wife of Charles TALBOT apart from her husband...certifie she did freely and
volentarily Relinquish her right of Dower. 24 May 1773
Rec: 25 Nov 1773   Francis CALLAWAY L.S.
                                             John TALBOT L.S.

DB 3, p.399 - STEAGALL from LAWRANCE   DEED, 25 Aug 1773
Thomas LAWRANCE of Parish of Cambden in County of Pittsylvania of one part
and William STEGAL of Parish & County aforesaid Planter of other part...for
£25·10 Current Money of Virginia...Land on Dittoes Creek...line that Devides
LAWRANCE's land from William HALES land, along the Patent line...100 acres.
No witnesses   his
                             Thomas ⟋ LAWRANCE L.S.
Rec: 25 Nov 1773   mark

DB 3, p.401 - TALBOURNE from HARDMAN   DEED, 20 Jul 1773
John HARDMAN and Elizabeth his wife of County of Pittsylvania of one part
and Elenor TALBOURN of other part...for £30 Current Money of Virginia...50
acres...which may fully appear by Letters Patent bearing date 16 Feb 1771...
on Marrowbone Creek...in old line...in a small Brance, down the brance to the
Creek, down the Meadows of said Creek.   his
Wit: Lem[1]. LANIER, Jesse WILLINGHAM   John ⟨2⟩ HARDMAN L.S.
William HARDMAN, Eliz[a]. LANIER   mark

                                                        her
                                         Elizabeth /" HARDMAN L.S.
Rec: 25 Nov 1773   mark

DB 3, p.402 - MITCHELL from GOAD   DEED OF TRUST, 16 Nov 1773
I John GOAD of County of Pittsylvania being Indebted to James MITCHELL of
said County in full and Just Sum of £34·07·00 3/4 Current Money of Virginia
and being Desirous to Secure Payment...further Consideration of 5s to me in
hand paid by James MITCHELL...Sell Land on Frying Pan Creek Containing 160
acres being the Land where I now live...by William BENNETS line and John
CLEMENTS (his Heirs) & John COX's..shall not before 25 Dec next pay with
Lawfull Interest...Sell for best price.
Wit: Sam[l]. BOLLING, Benjamin TARRENT, Robt DOLTON Jun[r].
Rec: 25 Nov 1773   John GOAD L.S.

DB 3, p.404 - CLAY from CLAY   DEED, 25 Nov 1773
Eleazar CLAY and Jane his wife of Parish of Manchester of County of Chesterfield of one part and Charles CLAY of Parish of [blank] of County of Cumberland of other part...£32·12·11 Current Money of Virginia...five Sixths of
5,835 acres of Land on Sandy River and Cascaid Creek which Land is to be Devided between said Charles CLAY and his son Charles CLAY j[r]. of Albemarle
the son to have 972 1/2 acre and the Father to have 4,862 half to be Devided
at their Descresion as will more fully appear by their Plats.
No witnesses   Eleazar CLAY L.S.
Rec: 25 Nov 1773   Jane CLAY L.S.

DB 3, p.405 - CLAY from CLAY   DEED, 25 Nov 1773
Eleazar CLAY and Jane his wife of Parish of Manchester of County of Chesterfield of one part and Charles CLAY of Parish of St. Anns of County of Albe-
narle of other part...for £6·10·07 Current Money of Virginia...one Sixth
part of Tract on sandy River and Cascaide Creek and is part of 5,835 Paterned
by Eleazar CLAY, which Land is to be Devided between said Charles CLAY and
his Father, his Father Charles CLAY Sen[r]. to have 4,862 1/2 and Charles CLAY
jun[r]. of Albemarle County of St. Ann Parish to have 972 1/2 to be Devided as
they shall think fit or agree...Bounded by Patern and Plat.
No witnesses   Eleazar CLAY L.S.
Whereas Eleazar CLAY of Chesterfield County   Jane CLAY L.S.
did on 25th of this Instant Execute a Deed in Pittsylvania Court to the Subscribers Charles CLAY Sen[r]. of Cumberland County and Charles CLAY Jun[r]. of
Albemarle for Land on waters of Cascaid and Sandy River this Shall oblige us
the subscribers to abide by the Devision made by Mr. George CARTER......con-
tains the courses of that part allotted to and Excepted by Charles CLAY the
younger marked and known by N[o]. one in the Plott and lying in fork of Cascade.
27 Nov 1773
Teste: Charles BURTON, George CARTER, Eleazer CLAY   Charles CLAY L.S.
                                                  C. CLAY Jun[r]. L.S.
Courses of the proportion of Cascade Patent No. 1 Chosen by Rev[d]. Mr. Charles

CLAY as his part of that Land...long line near the head of Sugartree B^r....
Crossing Cascade Creek several times...Crossing a branch...Crossing middle
fork of said Creek.

George CARTER

Rec: 25 Nov 1773   23 Nov 1773

DB 3, p.408 - JUSTICE from JUSTICE   DEED, 11 Jun 1773

Ezrah JUSTICE planter of County of Pittsylvania and Colony of Virginia of
one part and Thomas JUSTICE Planter of said County and Colony of other part...
for £55 Current Lawfull Money of Virginia...a part of a Tract of Land on both
sides Harping Creek Containing 100 acres being part of a Greater Piece made
over to John JUSTICE by way of Patent from the King office bearing date 14
Feb 1761 it being that part on which Ezarah JUSTICE now lives....Line of the
Oreginal Patent...corner of Simeon JUSTICE's.

            his   her
Wit: James———SHOCKLEY, Margrat ———SHOCKLEY, John CAMPBELL
            mark   mark
Rec: 27 Jan 1774   Ezra JUSTICE L.S.

DB 3, p.410 - BUCHANAN HASTIE & Co.   DEED OF TRUST, 3 Jan 1774

BUCHANAN HASTIE and Company Merchants in Glasgow of one part and Edm^d.
BREWER of County of Charlotte of other part...for £50 Lawfull Money of Virginia which Edm^d. BREWER is Justly indebted to BUCHANAN's HASTIE & CO. and
Honestly desires to pay...5s like money...100 acres being the land and Plantation whereon John WATKINS now lives and Bounded by James CALDWELLS Land and
is part of CALDWELL's Land, also Bounded by William GLASCOCKS land...after
1 Feb 1774 Sell for best price...after Ten Days Publick notice.
Wit: Thomas HOPE, John LINDSAY, Christopher OWEN, Isaac READ
Rec: 27 Jan 1774   Edm^d. BREWER L.S.

DB 3, p.412 - CLEMENT from GOAD   DEED, 26 Jan 1774

John GOAD & Margret his wife of County of Pittsylvania of one part and Benj^a.
CLEMENT of same County of other part...50 acres Beginning on his Patern line
thence up the line to W^m. MACKINGS...being part of Patent Granted to GOAD
7 Jul 1763.
Wit: James CLEMENT, Jonathan FAR, W^m. GOAD   John GOAD   L.S.
Rec: 27 Jan 1774 and Margret wife of said   Margreat GOAD L.S.
GOAD Privily Examined and Relinquished her right of Dower

DB 3, p.413 - BUCHANAN & Co. from TUNSTALL   DEED OF TRUST, 23 Jun 1773

Thomas TUNSTALL of County of Halifax of one part and BUCHANAN HASTIE & Co.
of Glasgow Merchant of other part...for £500 Lawfull Money of Virginia which
Thomas TUNSTALL is Justly Indebted to BUCHANAN HASTIE & Co. and honestly
desires to pay...farther consideration of 5s like Money...350 acres in Parish
of Antrim and County aforesaid whereon William WRIGHT now lives, also one
other Tract containing 430 acres whereon Thomas TUNSTALL now lives likewise
18 Negro Slaves namely Cupid, Will, Bristol, Betty, Fanny, Milinda, Beck,
Joan, nunn, Peter, Titus, amey, John, Flurry, Milley, Phill, Cyres, Bobb with
all future Increase of s^d. Female Slaves, 10 Beds and furniture, 11 Horses,
60 head of Cattle and all other Personal Estate...after 1 Apr 1775 sell for
best price after ten days Publick notice...discharge with Interest.
Wit: Thomas HOPE, RWILLIAMS, James STEVEN, Isaac READ, Thomas BLACKSTOCK,
Hayes MORGAN
Rec: 27 Jan 1774   Thos. TUNSTALL L.S.
Halifax County Court 21 Oct 1773...memorandum signed by John FISHER & rec:
27 Jan 1774   Test: P. CARRINGTON

DB 3, p.415 - OWEN from ANDERSON   POWER OF ATTORNEY, 25 Dec 1773
I John ANDERSON of County of Orrange and province of North Carolinia appoint
Thomas OWEN of County of Guildford and Province aforesaid my True and Lawfull
attorney...to ask Demand Sue for Recover and Receive all the Estate negroes
Sums of Money due and owing me in County of Hanover and Colony of Virginia...
now lying in hands of M^r. Nelson ANDERSON of Hanover County it being in Heir-
ship which falls to me of Estate of John ANDERSON Senr. and Sarah his wife.

                 his
Wit: John OWEN Senr., John THOMPSON, James MITCHELL, Benjamin GWILLIAMS
Rec: 24 Feb 1774   mark

                John ANDERSON L.S.

DB 3, p.416 - OWEN from ANDERSON   RELEASE, 25 Dec 1773
I Jno. ANDERSON of Province of north Carolinia and County of Orrange and Son
and Heir of Alcanah ANDERSON Dec^d, in Virginia...Sum of £150 Current Money
paid by Thomas OWEN of County of Guildford and same Province have released
all Right and Title to that Estate both Real and Personal that is supposed
to be in hands of Nelson ANDERSON and others in Virginia which Estate I
claim under my s^d. Father Alcanah ANDERSON Dec^d. by decent. his
Wit: John THOMPSON, John OWEN Senr., James MITCHELL, Benjamin GWILLIAMS
                  mark

Rec: 24 Feb 1774   John ANDERSON L.S.

DB 3, p.417 - HARDY from TERRY   DEED, 27 Aug 1773
Joseph TERRY Senr. of county of Pittsylvania and Colony of Virginia of one
part and George HARDY of County and Colony aforesaid of other part...Sum of
£16 Current Money of Virginia...181 acres on both sides mine branch of Sandy
Creek...Crossing three branches...in Thomas TERRYs line...to James TERRYS.
    his   his
Wit: Charles SHELTON, George HARDEY j^r., Marke X SHELTON
   mark   mark
Rec: 24 Feb 1774   Joseph TERRY L.S.

DB 3, p.418 - ADAMS from BOSTICK   DEED, 15 Mar 1773
Littleberry BOSTICK of County of Pittsylvania of one part and Sylvester
ADAMS of County aforesaid of other part...for £265 Current Money of Virginia...
134 acres being Part of Tract granted by Patent to Nathaniel TERRY bearing the
12 Jan 1746 and by several Conveyances came in Possession of Littleberry
BOSTICK as by County Court of Halifax....North side Dann River...Devideing
line Between Valentine HATCHER and said Littleberry BOSTICK...to old line.
           his
Wit: George ROSS, Jacob DAINS, Thomas X PERKINS
           mark
Cert: 25 Mar 1773, Rec: 26 Feb 1774   Littleberry BOSTICK L.S.

DB 3, p.420 - HALL from WEBB   DEED OF GIFT, 16 Feb 1774
I Merry WEBB of County of Pittsylvania for love and affection which I have
and do bear towards my Daughter Million HALL wife of Samuel HALL of said
County...one negroe woman called Jude together with the Increase.
Wit: George ELLIOTT, Frank TALIAFERRO
Rec: 24 Feb 1774   Merrey WEBB L.S.

DB 3, p.420 - SMITH & Co. from STEWART j^r. DEED OF TRUST, 24 Feb 1774
James STEWART Junr. of one part and James SMITH & Company of other part...
Sum of £42·19·02 Current Money of Virginia which James STEWART j^r. is Justly
indebted unto them and Honestly desire to pay...5s like Money...100 acres on

both sides Chesnut Creek being the land that was Convey.d to me by my Father
James STEWART Senr. as by Deed Recorded in Pittsylvania County and is the
Plantation whereon I now live being part of Tract my Father Purchased of Tully
CHOICE by Deed Recorded in Pittsylvania...after 1 Jan 1776 Sell for best price
giving Ten days Publick notice...Lawfull Interest untill fully discharged.
Wit: Arch^d. SMITH, James STEWART, L^s. GWILIM,   his
Don^d. MC NICOLE   James Ƒ STEWART Junr. L.S.
No rec. date   mark

DB 3, p.422 - SMITH & Co. from STEWART Sen.   DEED OF TRUST, 24 Feb 1774
James STEWART Senr. of Pittsylvania County on one part & James SMITH & Company
of said County on other part...sum of £76·11·04 Current Money of Virginia
which James STEWART SEN^R. is Justly indebted unto James SMITH & Company and
honestly desires to pay...farther sum of 5s like Money...Land on Both sides
Chesnutt Creek being part of Tract James STEWART Purchased of Tully CHOICE as
per Deed Recorded in Pittsylvania County Containing 120 acres, whereon he now
lives and whereon his Plantation is...after 1 Jan 1776 Sell for best price
after Ten days Publick notice...with Lawfull Interest.

                           his
Wit: Arch^d. SMITH, James Ƒ STEWART, Junr., L^s. GWILLIM, Don^d. MC NICOLE
                          mark

No rec. date   James STEWART L.S.

DB 3, p.424 - SMITH & Co. from WILLINGHAM   DEED OF TRUST, 7 Dec 1773
James SMITH & Company of one part and Thomas WILLINGHAM Senr. of other part...
Sum of £61·16 Current Money which Thomas WILLINGHAM Senr. is Justly Indebted
to James SMITH & Co. and honestly desire to pay...sum of 5s like Money...one
negro man Cald Dick about Twenty years of age Virginia Born, allso 200 acres
being part of Tract or adjacent to Tract whereon John HARDMAN lives on waters
of Grassey Creek a water course of Arvine River..after 1 Mar 1774 sell for
best price that Can begotten after giving Ten Days Publick notice.
Wit: Jno. SALMON, Jno. PURSELL, Arch^d. SMITH, his
Harry INNES   Thomas ⟋ WILLINGHAM, Senr. L.S.
Rec: 25 Feb 1774   mark

DB 3, p.426 - SMITH & Co. from BURCH   DEED OF TRUST, 7 Jan 1774
John BIRCH of Pittsylvania County of one part and James SMITH & Girard BIRCH
of said County of other part...for £20·16 Current Money of Virginia which
John BIRCH is Justly indebted to James SMITH & Co. and honestly desire to pay
them...farther Consideration of 5s like Money...Two feather Beds & furniture,
two Sows, 12 Piggs and four Shoats markt with Crop and a hole each ear, two
Smooth Board Guns, two Plowghs and Geers for Plowgh, four Pewter Dishes, six
plates and two Basons, 1 Cotton and 1 Linen wheel, one saddle with every
article of my Real or Personal Estate...after 1 Jan 1775...Sell for best price
that can be gotten after Giving Ten Days Publick notice...Lawfull Interest.
Wit: Will. TUNSTALL, Arch^d. SMITH, Henry CONWAY.
Rec: 25 Feb 1774   John BURCH L.S.

DB 3, p.428 - SMITH from NEELEY   DEED, 1 Feb 1774
Robert NEELEY of County of Pittsylvania on one part and George SMITH of said
County on other part...for £86 Current Money of Virginia...Land on south side
Tomhawk Creek...corner of William NEELEYS land, up said Creek...189 acres
which is part of tract John NEELEY Purchased of Col^o. Jno. CHISWELL and sold
to Robert NEELEY.
Wit: Arch^d. SMITH, Danl. BAUGH, George HUNDLEY   Robert NEELEY L.S.

Rec: 24 Feb 1774 and Ann wife of Robert NEELEY privily Examined as Law
directs Relinquis^d. her right of Dower

DB 3, p.430 - THOMPSON from CLANDENNING   DEED, 8 Nov 1773
Jeaney CLANDENNING of Parish of Camden in County of Pittsylvania of one part
and Ja^s. THOMPSON of Parish and County aforesaid of other part...for sum of
£11·10 Current Money of Virginia...all that Lott or half acres of Land in
Town of Peytonsburgh and adjoining main Street and according to plann of
said Town is known by number Fifty nine.
Wit: Nathan BOSTICK, Jo^s. AKIN, Jno. BYNUM, Jno. MARTIN
Rec: 24 Feb 1774   Jeney CLANDENNING L.S.

DB 3, p.431 - PIGG from ROBERTSON   DEED, 24 Feb 1774
Jesse ROBERTSON of Pittsylvania County of one part and Hezekiah PIGG of
county aforesaid of other part...for £70 Current Money of Virginia...100
acres on south side Banister River...on said ROBERTSONS line...up said River
as it meanders...to WALLERS line...to John PIGG line.
Wit: H. FORD, Jno. ADAMS, Jno. PIGG
Rec: 24 Feb 1774   Jesse ROBINSON L.S.

DB 3, p.433 - MABRY from PERKINS LEAVINS   DEED, 15 Jan 1774
Nicholas Perkins LEAVINS of one part of County of Pittsylvania and Joseph
MABRY of same County of other part...for sum of one and fifty Pounds Current
Money of Virginia...250 acres on both sides Crabtree fork of Snow Creek and
part of 400 acres formerly Granted to Obadiah WOODSON by patent bearing date
10 Sep 1755...
Wit: Ben COOK, Allen Ridley YOUNG, Gideon RUCKER
Rec: 24 Feb 1774   Nicholas Perkins LEAVINS L.S.

DB 3, p.434 - KEARBY from GWYN   DEED, 21 Feb 1774
Richard GWYN on one part and Henry KEARBY on other part...Sum of £200 Current
Money of Virginia...Land on Branches of Sandy Creek of Banister Containing
335 acres...on Isham KENNONS line...Crossing both Branches...Crossing two
Small Branches.   his
Wit: John KEARBY, Henry X KEARBY j^r.
                          mark
Rec: 24 Feb 1774   Richard GWYN L.S.

DB 3, p.435 - CHADWELL from TURNER   DEED, 16 Sep 1773
Jesefey TURNER of Pittsylvania County of one part and David CHADWELL of said
County of other part...for £50 Current Money of Virginia...57 1/2 acres being
my moiety of certain Tract of land being in County of Pittsylvania contain-
ing by Patent 115 acres...on Irvin River near Buttram Town Creek...west side
of the Town Creek up the Creek,,,crossing mouth of the mill creek.
Wit: Rich^d. WHITE, Abraham PENN, George REAVES   her
Cert: 23 Sep 1773, Rec: 24 Feb 1774   Jesefey (TURNER L.S.
                                                          mark

DB 3, p.437 - LYNES from BLEVINS   DEED TRUST, 5 Oct 1773
Dillion BLEVINS of Pittsylvania County justly indebted to Henry & Edmund
LYNE sum of £33·09·08 Curr^t. Money of Virginia on my own private Account
also Sum of £46·05·04 By Bond with my Bro^r. John BLEVINS jointly due unto
Henry & Edmund LYNE which Debt was contracted by my Father, also sum of
£43·11·08 Current Money being a Debt Contracted by my Bro^r. John BLEVINS

and myself in Partnership for Goods bo^t. of Henry & Edmund LYNE...truly
desirous to pay with legal Interest on first mentioned sum from this day, on
second sum from 8 Mar 1773 and on third Sum from 22 Aug 1773...Sell three
negroes, Mill, Bett and Lewis, 2 Beds and furniture, all my household furniture, 12 head nett Cattle of various marks, 10 head Sheep, 50 head Hogs marked Crop & underkeel in right and underkeel in left ear, a mare dark brown bay
and 2 Colts both Sorrels, a Sorrel blaze face Horse not Branded, all my Corn
& Fodder, my Corn in quantity 150 Barrels...after 1 Apr 1774 after giving
Ten Days notice...dispose for best price.
Test: Jno. BLEVIN
Rec: 24 Feb 1774   Dillion BLEVINS L.S.

DB , p.438 - DILLARD from DILLARD   BILL SALE, Jan 1774
I Thomas DILLARD of County of Pittsylvania do bargain and make over all my
Right and Title of one negro Woman named Rouse to Thomas DILLARD j^r. also to
negroes Anecay, Sarah, Peter, Chloe, Hanah & Robin...with their Increase.
Rec: 25 Feb 1774   Thomas DILLARD

DB 3, p.439 - MURDOCK from CLEVER   DEED TRUST, 3 Dec 1773
John CLEVER of Pittsylvania County of one part and Thomas MURDOCK of said
County of other part...for £152·14·07 which John CLEVER is Justly indebted to
Thomas MURDOCK and honestly desire to pay...farther sum of 5s like Money...
400 acres being the Land where John CLEVER now lives and which he Purchased
of Elisha FARRIS...after 3 Dec 1775 Sell for best Price after Giving Ten Days
Publick...pay and satisfy himself above sum.
Wit: Jno. SMITH, Don^t. MC NICOLE, George MURDOCK, Robt. FARGUSON, Francis
HENRY, William TODD
Rec: 24 Feb 1774   John CLEVER L.S.

DB 3, p.441 - MURDOCK from FREEMAN   DEED TRUST, 23 Feb 1774
William FREEMAN of County of Pittsylvania of one part and Thomas MURDOCK of
said County of other part...for £40 Current Money which William FREEMAN is
justly indebted to Thomas MURDOCK and honestly desire to pay...farther sum
of 5s like Money...Sell one white mare about nine years old not Branded, one
gray Horse Branded on near Buttock thus 3 , Six head of Cattle marked with
different marks being the whole of my Stock, 1 Smooth Board Gun, one hh^d.
Tobb^o. now Prised upon my Plantation, one feather Bed and furniture with the
whole of my household and Kitchen furniture and plantation uttencils with
further Increase of said Cattle and mare...shall after 25 Dec 1774 sell for
best Price...Interest from 23 Feb 1774 until fully discharged.
Wit: Don^t. MC NICOLE, Robt. FARGUSON, George MURDOCK   his
                                          William X FREEMAN L.S.
Rec: 24 Feb 1774   mark

DB 3, p.443 - HARDY from HARDY   DEED, 22 Sep 1773
George HARDY of Pittsylvania County and Colony of Virginia on one part Planter
and George HARDY j^r. of County aforesaid on other part...for £20 Good and Lawfull Money of Virginia...121 acres on both sides mine Branch of Sandy Creek
of Banister River...Beginning at oak on top of a hill on west side mine Branch...Cross said Branch.   mark   mark
Wit: Daniel GARDNER, Charles L CHELTON, Mark X CHELTON
Rec: 24 Feb 1774   George HARDY Senr. L.S.

DB 3, p.444 - PERKINS from MABRY   DEED, 15 Jan 1774
Joseph MABRY of Pittsylvania County of one part and Nicholas Perkins LEAVINS
of aforesaid county of other part···for £150 Good and Lawfull Money of Vir-
ginia...part of Tract of Land Containing 200 acres part of 400 acres Surveyed
for William RICKEL on Both sides south Branch of south fork of Sandy River.
Wit: Ben. COOK, Allen Riddley YOUNG,Gideon RUCKER
Rec: 26 Feb 1774 and Mary wife of said Joseph
Privily Examined Relinquished her right of Dower   Joseph MABRY L.S.

DB 3, p.446 - VAUGHAN from VAUGHAN   DEED, 22 Feb 1774
Thomas VAUGHAN Senr. of Pittsylvania County of one part and John VAUGHAN of
said County of other part...for £25 Current money of Virginia...196 acres
of Land being part of a greater Tract granted to said John VAUGHAN by Patent
dated 15 Jul 1760...North side Straight Stone Creek...by Edward HUBBARDS,
William GRIGORYS and Shadrick TRIBLES lines.
Wit: Don^d. MC NICOLE, Elisha FARRIS, Daniel SHELTON   his
                                                 Thomas X VAUGHAN L.S.
Rec: 24 Feb 1774   mark

DB 3, p.448 - TOWNSEND from BOATMAN   DEED TRUST, 1 Dec 1773
I Richard BOATMAN of Pittsylvania County am Justly indebted to Thos. TOWNSEND
of said County in Just sum of £30·07·04 Current Money of Virginia and being
desirous to pay with Legal Interest...Sell One Waggon and Geers, six Horses
(to wit) one bay Horse branded on near buttock $J\!A$, one flee bitten mare
branded on near buttock Λ , One blk Horse branded on near buttock R and
near Shoulder f , one Sorrel Horse branded on near Shoulder M , one blk
Stallin branded on near Shoulder H , one white Horse branded on near
Buttock $\,J\,H$ ...after 24 Mar next ensuing after giving Ten Days notice dispose
for best price...pay overplus.
Wit: Will TUNSTALL, Jno. PYRTLE, Willm. FROGG   his
                                                 Richard R BOATMAN L.S.
Rec: 24 Feb 1774   mark

DB 3, p.450 - SIRBERT from COOK   DEED OF TRUST, 30 Dec 1773
Harmon COOK of Pittsylvania County & Colony of Virginia of one part and
Christain SIRBERT of above County of other part...for £9 Current Money of
Virginia which Harmon COOK is Justly indebted to Christain SIRBERT and Hon-
estly desires to pay him...farther consideration of 5s like Money...Land
Joining Plantation I now live upon and Richard HAMACKS place and Paul RAZORS,
John JUSTICES and another Survey of my own Benj^a. LEPRAD now lives upon...
400 acres...after 15 Mar 1774 sell for best price after Ten Days Publick notice.
Wit: Willm. WITCHER, James MITCHELL, Saml. CALLAND
Rec: 24 Feb 1774   Harmon COOK

DB 3, p.452 - HARRISON from HARDEMAN   DEED, 2 Oct 1773
John HARDEMAN of County of Pittsylvania of one part and William HARRISON of
County of Goochland of other part...for £500 Current Money of Virginia...
500 acres Joining on north side Dan River bounded by line of Nicholas PERKINS
on upper side from the River...to HARRISS corner...Crossing the creek...to
BEENS line....at William HARRISONS Including all the Lands both high and Low
grounds which John HARDIMAN is Possessed of.
Wit: Moss ARMISTEAD, John DIX, Robt. PAYNE, John ROBERTSON
Ack: 25 Feb 1774, Rec: 28 Apr 1774 and Dorotha wife of said John Relinquished
her right of dower   John HARDIMAN L.S.

DB 3, p.454 - COLLINS from VAUGHAN   DEED, 22 Feb 1774
Jn°. VAUGHAN of Pittsylvania County of one part and William COLLINS of said
County of other part...for £25 Current Money of Virginia...8 acres being part
of greater Tract granted to John VAUGHAN by Patent dated 15 Jul 1760 and
lying on south side Straight Stone Creek.
Wit: Thomas VAUGHAN, William GRIGGORY, William VAUGHAN
Rec: 24 Feb 1774   John VAUGHAN L.S.

DB 3, p.455 - VAUGHAN from VAUGHAN   DEED, 22 Feb 1774
John VAUGHAN of Pittsylvania County of one part and Thomas VAUGHAN Senior of
said County of other part...Sum of £40 Current Money of Virginia...163 acres
being part of greater Tract granted to John VAUGHAN by Patent dated 15 Jul
1760...lying on south side Straight Stone Creek Joining William COLLINS and
Thomas DAVISES lines...Beginning at mouth of Collins old Spring branch from
thence to head of said branch...along old line to HUBBARDS corner.
Wit: Don^d. MC NICOLE, Elisha FARRIS, Daniel SHELTON
Rec: 24 Feb 1774   John VAUGHAN L.S.

DB 3, p.457 - JUSTICE from JUSTICE   DEED, 28 Jul 1773
Ezrah JUSTICE planter of County of Pittsylvania and colony of Virginia of
one part and Simon JUSTICE planter of same County and Colony of other part...
for £20 Current Money of Virginia...a part of Tract of Land on both sides of
Harping Creek that is already lade off by line of marked Trees on uper end of
Tract...containing 100 acres being part of Tract Ezrah JUSTICE lives, 100 acres.
Wit: Jn°. WATSON, Thomas JUSTICE, Thomas WATSON
Cert: 27 Jan 1774, Rec: 24 Feb 1774   Ezra JUSTICE L.S.

DB 3, p.459 - COX from LANSFORD   DEED, 24 Dec 1773
Henry LANSFORD of County of Pittsylvania of one part and Jacob COX of County
of Surry and Province of North Carolinia of other part...for £27·10 Current
Money of Virginia...236 acres on both sides Stewarts Creek of Ararat River...
Crossing a branch...fork of said Creek.

                                            his
Wit: George BRITTAIN, Henry LANSFORD Senr., John \X/ WILLIAMS
Memorandum signed by Thomas FLOWER   mark   his
Rec: 24 Feb 1774 and Catherine wife of said   Henry____|___LANSFORD L.S.
Henry Privily Examined as Law directs   mark
Relinquished her right of Dower to within   her
Granted Land   Catherine his wife( ) L.S.
                                                            mark

DB 3, p.461 - FITZGERRALD from FITZGERRALD   BILL SALE, 21 Dec 1773
I Garrott FITZGERRALD late of County of Halifax have Sold unto John FITZ-
GERRALD of Pittsylvania County for sum of £95 Current Money of Virginia one
negroe Wench Sarah and her two Children Jim and Harrison Together with the
future Increase of said female.
Wit: JWALKER, Jo^s. FARGUSON
Rec: 24 Feb 1774   Garrett FITZGERRALD L.S.

DB 3, p.462 - COLLINS from DAUGHERTY   DEED, 10 Jul 1773
Thomas DOUGHERTY late of County of Charlotte by his attorney John ROGERS of
County of Bedford of one Part and William COLLINS of County of Pittsylvania
of other part...for £20 Current Money of Virginia...400 acres on East Branches of Great Straight Stone and west side of Allens Mountain...in a meadow...
crossing a branch...crossing two Branches.

Wit: William SHORT, Jno. VAUGHAN, Edmund KING, John $\frac{his}{mark}$ SHORT, Jno.BUCKLEY

Cert: 22 Jul 1773, Rec: 24 Feb 1774   Thomas DAUGHERTY L.S.

DB 3, p.464 - PRESTAGE from PRESTAGE   BILL SALE, 20 Sep 1773
I John PRESTIAGE for Sum £50 Current Money of Virginia paid by John PRESTAGE
Senr. have sold him two mares the one Sorrell Branded, the other Grey
Branded with on her Jaw with other Brands and likewise a Corn field, 4
head of Cattle, 6 plates, 2 dishes, 5 Basons, one Smiths bellows, one flax
wheal being now in Possession of Jno. PRESTAGE Senr...Jno. PRESTAGE Junr.
have put said John PRESTAGE Senr. in full Possession.
Wit: Daniel GARDNER, Margreat GARDNER, Nathaniel GARDNER
Rec: 24 Feb 1774   John PRESTAGE j^r.

DB 3, p.465 - WARD from WOODING   DEED, 18 Mar 1774
Robert WOODING of County of Halifax of one part and John WARD of County of
Bedford of other part...for £90 Current Money of Virginia...400 acres on
both sides north fork of Strait Stone...corner of James HUNTS...Crossing the
Creek...Crossing a branch.
Wit: Isaac READ, Haynes MORGAN, RWILLIAMS, Thomas DILLARDj^r
Rec: 25 Mar 1774   RWOODING L.S.

DB 3, p.467 - SMITH & Co. from WALLER   DEED, 15 Nov 1773
Zachariah WALLER of Pittsylvania County on one part and James SMITH and Com-
pany on other part...for £20 Current Money of Virginia...Land in Pittsylvania
County...in Isaac CERTAINS line...along John GEES line...100 acres.

Wit: Arch^d. SMITH, Edgcome GWILLMES, Rich^d. $\frac{his}{mark}$ PREWETT

                                        Zachariah $\frac{his}{mark}$ WALLER L.S.
Cert: 23 Nov 1773, Rec: 24 Mar 1774

DB 3, p.469 - HERNDON from ATKINSON   DEED, 11 Sep 1773
Parker ATKINSON and Mary his wife of County of Fincastle of one part and
George HERNDON of County of Pittsylvania of other part...for £60 Current
Money of Virginia...50 acres...on south side Pig River...to Corner by his
Father the Bounds will more fully appear by a Deed made by said ATKINSONS
Father unto him Recorded in this County Court Pittsylvania.
Wit: Saml. CALLAND, John DAVIS, Samuel EMMERSON
Rec: 24 Mar 1774   Parker ATKINSON L.S.

DB 3, p.471 - ARMISTEAD & Co. from ADAMS   DEED OF TRUST, 1 Mar 1774
Sylvester ADAMS of County of Pittsylvania of one part and Moss ARMISTEAD &
C^o. merch^{ts}. of said County of other part...for £170 Current Money of Virginia which Sylvester ADAMS is Justly indebted to Moss ARMISTEAD & Co. and honestly desire to pay...farther consideration of 5s like Money...200 acres
which Sylvester ADAMS Purchased Valentine HATCHER by Deed bearing date 1 Mar
1774...after 25 Dec 1774 sell for best price after Ten Days Publick notice...
discharge and pay...overplus if any.
Wit: Robt. PAYNE, Thomas DUNCAN, John ROBERTSON
Rec: 24 Mar 1774   Sylvester ADAMS L.S.

DB 3, p.473 - ADAMS from HATCHER   DEED, 1 Mar 1774
Valentine HATCHER of County of Pittsylvania of one part and Sylvester ADDAMS
of s^d. County of other part...for £200 Current Money of Virginia...Land on

North side Dan River adjoining land that Sylvester ADAMS Purchased of Little-
berry BOSTICK and Land formerly the Property of Abram LITTLE at mouth of
Sandy River Containing 200 acres...being the Land said HATCHER Purchased of
Absalem & Nathan BOSTICK and is the land said HATCHER now lives on.
Wit: Robt. PAYNE, Thomas DUNCAN, Levy D. SMITH, Moss ARMISTEAD

                                                    his
                                    Valentine //   HATCHER L.S.
Rec: 24 Mar 1774   mark

DB 3, p.474 - WOODING from PIGG   DEED, 24 Mar 1774
William PIGG of County of Pittsylvania of one part and Robert WOODING of
County of Halifax of other part...for £13 Curr^t. Money of Virginia...26 acres
on north side great Cherry stone Creek...near said PIGGS Mill pond...in WEATH-
ERFORDS line...in PIGGS and WOODINGS old line...Crossing a Slash...Nevertheless
said William PIGG doth Reserve to him self all the land that is at this time
overfloud by said PIGGS Mill or any other mill hereafter Builded at his usual
place on said Great Cherrystone Creek.
Rec: 24 Mar 1774   No witnesses   William PIGG L.S.

DB 3, p.476 - GORDON from WALKER   BILL SALE, 22 Jan 1774
I James WALKER of County of Pittsylvania for sum of £315 Current Money of
Virginia paid to me by Reverend Alexander GORDON of County of Halifax...
fifteen head of Horses, thirty head of Cattle, 200 head of hogs, 15 head of
sheep together with their Increase, five feather beds and all my household
furniture.
Wit: Haynes MORGAN
Rec: 25 Mar 1774   JWALKER L.S.

DB 3, p.477 - WILLIAMS from ADAMS   DEED TRUST, 25 Mar 1774
Sylvester ADAMS of one part and Robert WILLIAMS of other part...for £200 Curr-
ent Money of Virginia which Sylvester ADAMS is Justly indebted to Robert
WILLIAMS and Honestly desire to pay...farther Consideration of 5s like Money
paid...sell five negroes (to Wit) Harry, Bett, Charles, Sal and Jean and their
Increase...after 25 Mar 1775 Sell for best price after Ten Days Publick notice.
Wit: Levy D. SMITH, Jo^s. AKIN, John SALMON   Sylvester ADAMS L.S.
Memorandum...if Sylvester ADAMS discharges Robert WILLIAMS of the Securityship
to FIELD & CAUL on a Suit Bro^t. against said ADAMS by said FIELD & CAUL by Ex-
piration of the term in Trust Deed then Slaves to Revert to ADAMS
No rec. date   RWILLIAMS

DB 3, p.479 - CLEVER from TERRY   DEED, 15 Nov 1773

Moses TERRY of County of Halifax of one part and John CLEVER of county of
Pittsylvania of other part...for £50 Curr^t. Money of Virginia...Tract of Land
on Branches of falls and Sandy Creeks and those of Birches Creek...Crossing
two Branches of Birches Creek...Crossing a branch of Sandy Creek...Crossing
a branch of Falls Creek...400 acres.
Wit: Thomas MURDOCK, Don^d. MC NICOLE, Jo^s. ROBERTS, George MURDOCK
Rec: 24 Mar 1774   Moses TERRY L.S.

DB 3, p.481 - GWILLIAM from HEARD   DEED, 10 Dec 1773
John HEARD and his wife of County of Bedford of one part and Peter GILLAM of
County of Pittsylvania of other part...for £70 Current Money of Virginia...
165 acres on south Branches of black Water River...along Stephen HEARDS.
Wit: W^m. DABNEY, Stephen HEARDj^r, Jesse HEARD
Rec: 24 Mar 1774   John HEARD L.S.

DB 3, p.483 - CALLAWAY from VANBIBBER   DEED, 14 Sep 1773
Peter VANBIBBER of County of Botetourt of one part and James CALLAWAY of
County of Bedford of other part...for £200 Current Lawfull money of Virginia...
200 acres on both sides black Water River...on James RENTFROWES line.
Wit: James RENTFROW j^r., Gross SCRUGGS, Robert JONES
Prv: 23 Sep 1773, Rec: 24 Mar 1774   Peter VANBIBBER L.S.

DB 3, p.484 - FIELD & CAUL from PRICE   DEED TRUST, 21 Sep 1773
John PRICE of one part and FIELD & CAUL merch^{ts}. in Prince George County of
other part...sum of £12·12·07 Current Money of Virginia which I John PRICE
am Justly indebted to FIELD & CAUL and Honestly desire to pay...consideration
of sum of 5s like Money...Sell Two Horses, one Sorrel, Branded on near Shoulder and one Bay, Branded on near Shoulder also Sixty four Drest Bucks
Skins and thirty Raw Ditto, one red Cow with white on her Back marked with
two Crops, one Bed and furniture, one dish & three Plaits, two basons and all
rest of my Household furniture...Nevertheless John PRICE shall after 15 Nov
1772, as soon as John PRICE think proper or FIELD & CAUL Request whichever
of two circumstances shall first happen, Sell for best price that can be
gotten after Given Ten days Publick notice...Money arising from sale discharge
above sum with Lawfull Interest from 21 Sep 1772 until fully Discharged...
pay overplus if any remain from such sale.
Wit: Drury BIRCHETT, L^s. GWILLIM, Jno. WILSON
No recording date   John PRICE L.S.

DB 3, p.490 - HAMILTON from MOORE   DEED, 24 Mar 1774
Mathew MOORE of County of Pittsylvania on one part and Thomas HAMILTON of
County of Pittsylvania of other part...for £165 Current Money of Virginia...
420 acres according to a Survey lately made...on Marrowbone Creek and branch-
es...Begining at a branch which devides Land from Jesse CHANDLERS land...
Down the Creek as it meanders to mouth of the Branch which devides Jesse
CHANDLERS land from above.
Wit: Jno. CHILDRAS, Dav^d. LANIER, Archebald ROBERTSON, Arthur ROBERTSON,
Thomas JAMESON
Rec: 24 Mar 1774   Matthew MOORE L.S.

DB 3, p.493 - HAMILTON from HAMILTON   DEED, 24 Mar 1774
Thomas HAMILTON of County of Pittsylvania on one part and George HAMILTON of
County of Pittsylvania on other part...sum of £70 Current money of Virginia...
250 acres according to a Survey lately made...on Marrowbone Creek and the
Branches...Begining at a branch which devided the after Land from Jesse
CHANDLERS land...up the Creek as it meanders to mouth of the Branch that dev-
ides Jesse CHANDLERS Land from the above.
Wit: Thomas JAMESON, Micajah POOLE, Arthur ROBERTSON
Rec: 24 Mar 1774   Thomas HAMILTON L.S.

DB 3, p.495 - HEARD from HEARD   DEED, 23 Nov 1773
Stephen HEARD Senr. and George HEARD of Pittsylvania County...Stephen HEARD
for Good will and affection I doth owe to my Son Stephen HEARD acknowledge
unto George HEARD 198 acres on Popler Camp Creek being part of same Tract I
now am living upon.
Wit: Jesse HEARD, John HEARD, Stephen HEARD j^r.
No rec. date   Stephen HEARD L.S.

DB 3, p.496 - ADAMS from CLAYBROOKE   DEED, 12 Jan 1774
William CLAYBROOKE of County of Hanover of one part and Nathan ADAMS of
County of Pittsylvania of other part...for £30 Current Money of Virignia...

145 acres on South side Banister River being part of Tract Granted to said
William CLAYBROOKE by patent bearing date 10 Aug 1759.
Wit: H. CHALLES, Benj^a. PORTER, Richard PIGG, John ADAMS Senr., Nathaniel
HYDIN
Rec: 24 Mar 1774   William CLAYBROOK L.S.

DB 3, p.498 - HODNETT from KING   DEED, 27 Jan 1774
William KING of County of Pittsylvania of one part and Ayres HODNETT of County of Buckingham of other part...for £150 Current Money of Virginia...272
acres on both sides Sandy Creek...it being the whole Tract that William KING
and his father Purchased of Joseph ECHOLS...Crossing the Creek.
Wit: RWILLIAMS, HCHALLES, Stephen COLEMAN, Robt. SINGLETON
Rec: 24 Mar 1774   William KING L.S.

DB 3, p.500 - RAMSEY from GORDON   DEED OF TRUST, 28 Jan 1774
Archibald GORDON of County of Pittsylvania of one part and Patrick RAMSEY
Surviving Partner of GORDON & RAMSEY of other part...for £315·06·03 which s^d.
Archebald GORDON is Justly indebted to said Patrick RAMSEY Surviving Partner
and Honestly desire to pay...farther Consideration of sum of 5s Like Money...
Land on Snow Creek Containing 200 acres adjoining Land that Hugh INNES Gent.
now lives on and Conveyed to GORDON by Rich^d. STITH agent & attorney for
Isham RANDOLPH and recorded in Halifax Court...also following Slaves now in
Possession of GORDON: Dick,Celem,negro men, also Lucy, Sally, Nancy and Patty
and their Increase...after 24 Feb 1774 Sell for best price after Ten days
Publick notice...Satisfy above Sum with Lawfull Interest from this day.
Wit: Isaac READ, James ROBERTS, Daniel BAUGH   Arch^d. GORDON L.S.
January 28th 1774
Memorandum. That some time ago Patrick RAMSEY undertook to negotiate a bill
or order drawn by Archibald GORDON on M^r. James CAHOON of Town of Greenock in
Scotland for whatever Sum of Money Should at that time be in hands of said
CAHOON of said Archebalds now whatever Sum be applied to Credit of this Deed
of Trust.
Rec: 24 Mar 1774   Isaac READ

DB 3, p.502 - RAMSEY from GORDON   DEED, 28 Jan 1774
Archebald GORDON of Pittsylvania County of one aprt and Patrick RAMSEY of
Prince George County of other part...for £100 Current money paid by Patrick
RAMSEY...850 acres on Snow Creek being the Land whereon GORDON now lives for-
merly patented to Obediah WOODSON by Patent bearing date 5 Jul 1751 and since
Conveyed to GORDON by two Several Deed, one from James ROBERTS, other from
John HICKEY and recorded in County Court of Halifax.
Wit: Isaac READ, James ROBERTS, Danl. BAUGH
Rec: 24 Mar 1774   Arch^d. GORDON L.S.

DB 3, p.503 - WARD from MEAD   DEED, 16 Sep 1773
William MEAD of Bedford County of one part and Daniel WARD of Pittsylvania
County of other part...for £15 to him in hand paid...150 acres on Simmons
Run...Beginning at WHITTENS and MEADS.
Wit: W. DABNEY, Stephen HOARD j^r., Peter GILLUM
Rec: 24 Mar 1774   W. MEAD L.S.

DB 3, p.504 - FALLON from CLAY   DEED, 19 Nov 1773
Charles CLAY of Cumberland County and Colony of Virginia Planter on one part
and Edmund FALLON of Pittsylvania County and Colony afors^d. Planter on other
part...for £9 Good and Lawfull Money of Virginia...110 acres on upper side

of CLAYS fork of Great Sandy Creek of Dan...in James CLERKS line...Down several menaders of said fork to Redmond FALLINGS order line...south side of the School houses Branch, Crossing said Branch...corner of James BURTONS... in CLERKS line.
Wit: Redmond FALLON, Rich^d. ARDIN, Jasper BILLINGS
Rec: 24 Mar 1774   Charles CLAY L.S.

DB 3, p.506 - TOMBLIN from TOMBLIN   DEED, 23 Mar 1774
John TOMBLINGS of Pittsylvania County of one part and Joseph TOMBLIN of other part...for 5s Current Money of Virginia...100 acres on Sandy Creek... which was Granted to said Joseph TOMBLINGS.
No witnesses
Rec: 24 Mar 1774   John TOMBLINGS L.S.

DB 3, p.508 - WILLCOX from MULLINGS   DEED, 22 Mar 1774
Henry MULLINGS of County of Pittsylvania of one part and George WILLCOX Junr. of same County of other part...Sum of £25 Current Money...on Stanton River and Runing on Edward NIX...Crossing a Branch...100 acres.
Wit: James (his mark) DOSS Senr., Ann CHILES, James (his mark) DOSS j^r.
Rec: 24 Mar 1774   Henry (his mark) MULLINGS L.S.

DB 3, p.509 - ROBERTSON from STEGALL   DEED OF TRUST, 20 Jul 1773
William STEGALL of County of Pittsylvania of one part and Walter ROBERTSON of County of Halifax on the other...for £25 Current Money of Virginia which William STEGALL is Truly indebted to Walter ROBERTSON & honestly desiring to pay him...further consideration of 5s like money...Sell 200 acres...Beginning on Capt. INNES line...Runing on Abraham ARDINS line...it being the Land he now lives on the Bounds will appear by a Deed from William HAILE Recorded in Office of Pittsylvania...shall after 30 Oct 1773 Sell to Highest Bidder after Ten Days Publick notice.
Wit: Saml. CALLAND, Jno. CRAWFORD, Elizabeth (her mark) CHRISTIAN, Isaac READ, John COX
Prv: 24 Feb 1774, Rec: 24 Mar 1774   William (his mark) STEGALL L.S.

DB 3, p.511 - BURTON from CLAY   DEED, 22 Nov 1773
Charles CLAY of Cumberland County and Colony of Virginia Planter on one part and Charles BURTON of Pittsylvania County and Colony aforesaid Planter on other part...for £20 good and Lawfull Money of Virginia...250 acres on Draughts of Clays Little fork of Sandy Creek of Dan...Beginning at Jasper BILLINGS...in CLERKS line...in BACONS line
Wit: Edwd. (his mark) SMITH, Jno. (his mark) LAY Peter (his mark) PERRY
Rec: 24 Mar 1774   Charles CLAY L.S.

DB 3, p.513 - EARLEY from DODSON   15 Jan 1774
Thomas DODSON of County of Pittsylvania and Colony of Virginia of one part and Patrick EARLEY of County and Colony aforesaid of other part...for £10 Current Money of Virginia...30 acres...begining at Birches Creek in said Thomas DODSON upper line...at a Spring Called the meeting House Spring... near the meeting House...oak in the Road.

Wit: Jno. MADING, Thos. HILL, Charles/ his /7/ CHELTON
mark

Prv: 27 May 1773, Rec: 24 Mar 1774   Thomas DODSON L.S.

DB 3, p.515 - CLAY from CLAY   DEED, 24 Mar 1774
Charles CLAY,Martha his wife of County of Cumberland of one part and Thomas
CLAY of County of Pittsylvania of other part...Charles CLAY and Martha his
wife for Natural love and affection which they beare to their Son and for
Consideration of £2...1,000 acres...Beginning on James BURTON...runing to
FAWLINGS...along Charles CLAY jun^r. to old order line...also one other Tract
Containing 1,000 acres...Beginning at HARRISES...along Henry CLAYS to old
order line.
Wit: Samuel CALLAND, Henry CLAY, John COOK
Rec: 24 Mar 1774   Charles CLAY L.S.

DB 3, p.517 - CLAY from CLAY   DEED, 24 Mar 1774
Charles CLAY and Martha his wife of County of Cumberland of one part and
Henry CLAY of County of Pittsylvania of other part...for natural love and
affection which they beare to their Son and for Sum of £2 Current Money...
1,000 acres^l...to old order line.
Wit: Saml. CALLAND, John COOK, Thomas CLAY
Rec: 24 Mar 1774   Charles CLAY L.S.

DB 3, p.518 - CLAY from CLAY   DEED, 24 Mar 1774
Charles CLAY and Martha his wife of County of Cumberland of one part and
Mathew CLAY of County aforesaid of other part...for Natural Love and affect-
ion which they beare to this their Son and for £2 to them in hand paid...
1,000 acres...bounds as followeth James BURTON's line on the Road so to Henry
CLAYS...along Eleazar CLAYS on head of fall Creek then to old order then on
James BURTON again also one other Tract of 1,000 acres...Beginning at
HARRISES...along Henry CLAYS to old order line...to George YOUNGS.
Wit: Charles BURTON, Gideon RUCKER, Thomas CLAY
Rec: 24 Mar 1774   Charles CLAY L.S.

DB 3, p.520 - WALKER from TERRY   DEED, 4 Dec 1773
James TERRY of Orrange County in North Carolinia province of one part and
David WALKER of Pittsylvania County of the Colony of Virginia of other part...
for £140 Current Money of Virginia...709 acres...Corner of John QUARLES...oak
near his gate...in old Pattent line...in a$_t$ branch.
Wit: Jno. DIX, Larkin DIX, Jno. BYNUM, Robt. PAYNE, Nath. DICKERSON,
Theop^s LACY
Rec: Rec: 24 Mar 1774   *Terry*   JTERRY L.S.

DB 3, p.522 - DIX & READ TO THE KING   B^d. f. FERRY, 25 Mar 1774
We John DIX and Isaac READ are bound unto our sovereign Lord the King in sum
of £500 Current Money...Condition of above obligation is such that above
bound John DIX by act of General assembly having a ferry established across
the River Dan, at a place known by DIX's ferry, if DIX shall in all things
discharge the business and duty of a ferry keeper on both sides of the River
by keeping Sufficient boat or boats with necessary hands and assistance to
give all Speedy and Convenient passage to such as apply, and to exact for
ferriage no more then the rate established by Law then above obligation to be
Void, or else to remain in full force.
Rec: 25 Mar 1774   John DIX L.S.
                                              Isaac READ L.S.

DB 3, p.523 - SPANGLE from TALBOT   DEED, 26 Apr 1774
Matthew TALBOT of County of Bedford of one part and Daniel SPANGLE of County
of Pittsylvania of other part...for £273 Current Money of Virginia...Land on
Branches of Black water adjoining Lands of James CALLAWAY and Joseph RENTFROW
Containing 273 acres...Beginning where RENTFROWS line on north fork of Black
water river...Cross the Creek...on fox Creek, up the same as it meanders.
Wit: Harry INNES, RWILLIANS, Jn°. WARD, Robt. COWAN, James CALLAWAY
Rec: 28 Apr 1774   Matthew TALBOT L.S.

DB 3, p.526 - MURDOCK from EAST   DEED OF TRUST, 13 Apr 1774
John EAST of County of Pittsylvania of one part and Thomas MURDOCK of said
County of other part...for £300 Current money which said John EAST justly in-
debted to Thomas MURDOCK and honestly desire to pay...for 5s like money...
Land upon Watters of Stinking River Containing 400 acres...Joining Lands of
William LIGHTFOOT deceased and Thomas MUSTEAN being part of a Tract belong-
ing to John EAST and Gabriel SHELTON, one negro Boy named Will, one Sorrell
Horse, one Gray mare, one black mare two years old not Branded, one year old
Roan Colt, 11 head of Cattle different marks, 40 head of hoggs, two feather
Beds & furniture, one smoth Boad gun, one Riffled gun, with whole of my House-
hold and Kittchen furniture and Plantation Utenciles with future Increase of
mares, Cattle and hoggs...shall after 1 Sep 1775 Sell for best Price after
given Ten Days Publick notice.
Wit: Don^d. MC NICOLE
Rec: 28 Apr 1774   John EAST L.S.

DB 3, p.528 - MURDOCK from BRUAS   DEED OF TRUST, 29 Mar 1774
Robert BRUAS of County of Pittsylvania of one part & Thomas MURDOCK of said
County of other part...for £53.08.05½ Current Money which Robert BRUAS is
justly Indebted to Thomas MURDOCK and honestly desire to pay...in farther
Consideration of 5s like Money...Sell one Horse Branded on near Buttock thus
(, Eight Head of Cattle different marks, 40 head of hoggs marked with
two Cropes and two nicks, three feather Beds & furniture and further In-
creas of said Cattle & hoggs...after 25 Dec 1775 or as soon as Thomas MURDOCK
shall think Proper or Robert BRUAS shall Request him...Sell for best price
after Ten days Publick notice discharge above sum.
Wit: James SPENCER, Don^d. MC NICOLE, Robt. FARGUSON   his
Rec: 28 Apr 1774   Robert X BRUAS L.S.
                                     mark

DB 3, p.530 - DYER from JUSTICE   BILL SALE, 16 Mar 1774
I Thomas JUSTICE of Pittsylvania County have sold unto George DYER of County
of Halifax Namely one Wagin and Gyres and fore Horses for £45.
              his
Wit: John DYER, Ja^s. /X DYER
              mark
Rec: 28 Apr 1774   Thomas JUSTICE L.S.

DB 3, p.531 - SMITH & C°. from HOPKINS   DEED OF TRUST, 27 Apr 1774
Arthur HOPKINS of Pittsylvania County and James SMITH & C°. of said County...
for £46·12 Current Money of Virginia which said Arthur HOPKINS is Justly indebted unto them & Honestly desires to pay...farther Consideration of 5s like
Money...Sell 400 acres on Turkey Cock Creek being same whereon he now Liveth
adjoining Lands of Harman COOK both above and below his Plantation formerly
purchased of George JEFFERSON, Three negroe Slaves (to Wit) Moll, Bowsan &
George, four head of Horses, 30 head of Cattle, 100 head of Hoggs mark.d with

a Crop in left Ear and Swallow fork in right with all his Household furniture.
After 1 Apr 1775 or as soon after as Ja^s. SMITH & Co. Shall think Proper or
Arthur HOPKINS Shall Request which ever shall first happen Sell for best
price after Ten Days Publick notice...pay overplus if any remain.
Wit: Arch^d. SMITH
Rec: 28 Apr 1774   Arthur HOPKINS L.S.

DB 3, p.533 - LACKEY from WITCHER   DEED, 28 Apr 1774
Jno. WITCHER and Anne his wife of Pittsylvania County & Colony of Virginia of
one part and Alexander LACKEY of above County & colony of other part...for
£32·10 Current money of Virginia...191 acres on both sides Harping Creek...in
line of the Patent...Crossing a branch...in James SLONES line...being part of
greater Piece made over to William WITCHER by way of Patent bearing date 27
Jun 1764.   No witnesses.
Rec: 28 Apr 1774 and Ann being privily Examined   John WITCHER L.S.
Relinquished her right of Dower   Anne WITCHER L.S.

DB 3, p.535 - SHELTON & COX from SHELTON   DEED OF TRUST, 4 Mar 1774
Daniel SHELTON of County of Pittsylvania of one part and Abraham SHELTON and
John COX of County aforesaid of other part...for £55·01·04 Current Money of
Virginia which Daniel SHELTON is Justly indebted to Abraham SHELTON & Jno.
COX and Honestly desire to pay...farther Consideration of 5s like Money...
Land on both sides White Thorn Creek it being Land where Daniel SHELTON now
lives Containing 598 acres, 20 head of Cattle marked with a Crop in left &
Swallow forke in right, 30 head of Hoggs of same mark, one Bay Horse, four
mares of different Brands & Colours, five feather Beds & furniture, three
Chests, one Sealskin Trunk and all rest of my Household & Kitchen furniture,
with all my Plantation Utensils which is now in my Possession and head of
Sheep of same mark as Cattle & Hoggs...after 25 Dec 1774 Sell for best price
after Ten Days Publick notice and pay above sum.
Wit: Abraham MOTTLEY, Newsom PACE, Armist^d. SHELTON
Rec: 26 May 1774   Daniel SHELTON L.S.

                         END OF DEED BOOK III

INDEX, DEED BOOKS 1, 2, 3

COUTTS
 Patrick 136
COWAN
 Robert 49,181
COX
 Frances/Francis 7,14,123
 Jacob 29,30,40,164,174
 James 41,91,113,126,163
 James, Jr. 85
 John 12,14,24,25,28,37,39,
  40,41,42,44,48,81,95,113,
  117,118,132,144,163,167,182
 Margaret 126
 Mary 41
 Samuel 20,21,31,32,40,133
 William 37,41
CRAUFURD (see CRAWFORD)
 Thomas 162
CRAVEN Co., SC 89
CRAWFORD
 John 179
 Jo?. 155
CREEK
 Aarons 108,111
 Allen's/Allin's 5,15,16,28,
  47,83,91,92,100,112,120,
  126,128,151,163
 Bearskin 111,139,165
 Beaver 1,7,14,48,54,55,74,
  118,122,124,125,136,153
 Been's 40,43
 Bennett's 55
 Birches/Burches 15,19,33,36,
  62,109,128,176,179
 Black Castle 53
 Bowings 58
 Brush 116
 Buffellow/Buffoloe 53,152
 Burch 161
 Burchess 120
 Burchets 164
 Butterham Town 86
 Butterm Town 20
 Butterum/Buttram Town 129,
  171
 Cain 134
 Camp 18,48
 Cascade/Caskaid 31,60,78,
  93,134,149,167,168
 Cherrystone 4,46103,105,
  107,108
 Cherrystone, Great 10,91,
  129,165,176
 Cherrystone, Little 107,149

CREEK (cont'd)
 Chesnut 16,30,40,47,55,56,
  60,92,126,170
 Coles 56
 Cooper's 124,125,136,153
 Cruddocks 63
 Daniels Mill 36,39,54
 Dillaes 55
 Dinner? 33
 Dittoes 166
 Doe 56
 Double 5,21,67,89,103,157
 Elk 124,160
 Elkhorn 34,48,62,72,83,97,
  114,133,141,142,143,144,
  150,158,162
 Fall 3,71,148
 Falling 19
 Falls 176
 Flat 34,43,53,80,84,161
 Flyblow 66,73,81,123,151
 Fox 58,181
 Frying Pan 8,19,20,22,26,29,
  41,56,65,71,72,105,119,140,
  149,167
 Gills 53
 Glade 49,130
 Goard 8,24
 Gobblin/Gobling Town 37,53,
  54,89,105,156
 Grassey 106,170
 Greasy 53
 Green 40,52,114,164
 Harping 10,97,121,135,137,
  140,168,174,182
 Hogan's 64
 Home 54,122
 Iland 130,145
 Ilante? 86
 Indian 53
 Island 13
 Jacks 45,53,54
 Jackson's 103,104
 Joinerack 53
 Jonekin 31
 Kaskade 122
 Keeton 39,116
 Leatherwood 14,46,54,98,
  125,166
 Little 132
 Lower Double 155
 Lynche's 38
 Maggetty/Magotty 82,101,
 Main 31

CREEK (cont'd)

Marrowbone 44,54,71,74,75,
76,77,81,83,84,86,108,109,
123,143,145,146 147,162,
166,167,177
Mattreymoney 54
Middle 6
Mill 11,14,91,95,108,117,
126,147,163,171
Mountain 30,32,49,62,77,
98,152,164
Mounty 62
Nicholas's 56,121
Nixe's 30,50,58,135
Otter 30,33,46
Owen's 49,50,55,130,131
Panther 16,22,76,89,93,
103,117,118
Peeping 19,59,82,148
Peters 53
Pickings 39
Popler Camp 177
Potter's 7,83,84
Potter's, Lewis 65
Py. 55
Pye 94,120
Pye, Little 95
Read 54
Ready 136,147
Reddis 70
Reedies 2
Reedy 1,8
Roberts 165
Rock Castle 53,148
Rocky/Rockey 49,151
Rugg 132
Runnet Bag 30,55
Russell's 26,39,119,145,
148,149
Rutlages 100,106
Sailors 110
Sand 151
Sandy 3,10,26,36,49,54,68,
69,90,102,112,115,127,134,
139,158,161,169,171,172,
176,178,179
Sandy, Little 61,126,127
Shocko/Shoko 9,81,132
Simmons 150
Snow 6,17,35,38,39,54,55,70,
85,91,94,106,109,121,128,
143,155,166,171,178
Spoon 53
Steabery 17

CREEK (cont'd)

Stewards/Stewarts 2,44,47,
97,174
Stony 2
Story/Storrey 45,56,139
Strabery (see Strawberry) 69
Straightstone 8,9,28,41,67,
73,96,111,119,135,138,155,
173,174,175
Straitstone, Little 47,135
Straitstone, Great 9,11,
12,19
Strawberry 17,18,21,33,79,
104,117,133,164
Sugar Tree 12,25,113
Sycamore 21,53,54,87,120,
138,155
Sycamore, Little 53
Tissle 55
Toby's 9
Toe Clout 54
Tomachawk 120
Tomahawk 49,50,59,72,76,
83,115,148,170
Town 56,171
Turkey Cock 13,25,54,55,59,
70,79,87,108,110,111,113,
134,137,155,157,181
Turkey Cock, Little 25
Turkey Pen 54
Valantine's 133
Vollingtine's 11
Wegion 53,54
Wens 54
Wetsleave 23,32,33,72
White Oak 101,134,140
Whitethorn 142,151,153,162,182
White Walnut 60
Widows 45
Wighen/Wighing 159

CREEL
Agathey 39
John 33,34,36,39,42,103,
109,161
Rhody 33,36
Rosana 43
CRIST
Henry 39
CRITZ
Hamon, Jr. 149
CROLEY (see CROWLEY)
Samuel 4
CRONESTOR?
Methias 86

HUGHES
 Archelius 34,37,78,113,132,
  133,149,158,159,164
 Archs. 11,39,40
 Ashford 33,99,155
 John 133
 Mary 133
HUNDLEY
 George 170
 John 158
HUNGATE
 William 5
HUNT
 Charles 111,150,151
 David 111
 Gilbert 111
 James 9,28,150,151,175
 James, Sr. 111
 Nathaniel 111,150
 Tabitha 150,151
HUNTER
 John 119
 Patrick 138
 William 126
HURTT
 Joel 132
HUTCHERSON
 Sarah 121,131
HUTCHINGS
 Thomas 47,56,77,81,83,
  136,141
HUTSON
 Obediah 145,148
HYDIN
 Nathaniel 178
INNES
 Capt. 179
 Hannah 118
 Harry 170,181
 Hew 145
 Hugh 2,6,8,12,17,19,24,25,
  26,28,37,38,39,41,42,44,
  51,55,81,89,91,93,94,105,
  116,118,134,146,153,156,
  160,162,178
IRBY
 Peter 73
 William, Jr. 45
IRVINE (see IRVING)
 William [Jr.] 63
 William [Sr.] 63
IRVING
 Charles 82

ISBELL
 Henry 13
ISLAND
 Mush 15
 Randolph's Long 153
 Read 53
ISOM
 John 54
JACKSON
 John 87,104
JAMES
 William 54
JAMESON
 David 66
 Thomas 177
JEFFERSON 148
 G. 28,108
 George 13,44,54,55,59,60,65,
  70,77,79,108,110,111,113,
  115,134,137,155,157,166,181
 John 157
 Peter F. 157
JENKINS/JINKINS
 Benjamin 13,16,37,51
 Lewis 16,33,45,50,51,63,145
 Tabitha 51
JENNINGS/JINNINGS
 Jonathan 42,65
 Miles 80
JETT
 Thomas 116,136
JOHNSON 118
 Benjamin 60,120
 Elonar 27
 Jeffery 161
 Saml. 128
JOHNSON Co. 23
JONES
 Abraham 93
 Ambrose 41,48,54,118,132,
  136,153
 Anne 44,84
 Edward 153
 Ellener 57
 Henry 74
 Isaace 23,52
 James 44,57
 John 36
 John, Sr. 159,162
 Jonathan 44,57,84
 Mary 31
 Robert 3,23,30,33,52,74,
  91,93,94,177
 Robert, Jr. 3

MOSS
  David 144
  Mary 124
  Moses 75,124
MOTLEY/MOTTLEY
  Abraham 22,91,92,95,144,182
MOUNTAGUE
  Lewis 71
MOUNTAIN
  Allen's 155,174
  Breiry 60
  Jacks 48
  Little Round 60
  Smiths 50,63
  Wart 71
MULLINS/MULLINGS
  Elizabeth 18,22
  Henry 11,136,179
  William 18,22,26,51,56
MUNFORD
  Thomas Bolling 131
MURDOCK
  George 123,146,148,158,
    172,176,177
  James & Co. 35,40,129,
    130,151,153,162,164
  Thomas 151,153,158,162,
    164,172,176,181
MURPHEY/MURPHY 5,7,34,126
  James 17,71,72,162,163
  John 3
  Keziah 156
  Richard 62,156
  Sarah 3
  William 3,30,37,56,138
MURRELL
  Thomas 126
MURROW
  Dorothy/Dorrity 37,39
  Jeremiah 39
MUSTAIN/MUSTEEN/MUSTEIN
  Thomas 50,58,98,136,151,
    164,181
MUTER
  George 35
NARRAGENCY 88
NEALLEY/NEALLY (see NEELEY)
  John 49,50
  Robert 49,50,120
  William 49,50,120
NEAVILL
  John 53
NEELEY/NEELIE
  Ann 171

NEELEY/NEELIE (cont'd)
  John 83,170
  Robert 115,170,171
  William 170
NEGRO/SLAVE
  Abby 144
  Abraham 116,127
  Abram 13,129,144
  Addam 139
  Agnes 160
  Amey 65,168
  Anecay 172
  Annia 123
  Beck 168
  Beckey 123
  Ben 123,160
  Bess 82
  Bett 172,176
  Betty 102,140,168
  Bob 123,127
  Bobb 7,168
  Bowsan/Bowson 150,181
  Bristol 35,168
  Cancer 160
  Candus 160
  Caroline 25
  Cato 66,120
  Celem 128,178
  Chance 77
  Charles 176
  Chloe 172
  Cloey 58
  Cupid 168
  Cyres 168
  Daniel 43,144
  Darkis 10,13
  Dick 51,128,170,178
  Dinah 43,123,124
  Docter 123
  Euclid 45
  Fanny 168
  Feanny 35
  Filles 65
  Flurry 168
  Frank 127,160
  George 58,150,160,181
  Goliah 45
  Grace 123
  Graw 7
  Hanah/Hannah 13,82,129,
    160,172
  Hany 123
  Harrison 174
  Harry 13,129,176

www.ingramcontent.com/pod-product-compliance
Lightning Source LLC
Chambersburg PA
CBHW021902020426
42334CB00013B/445